OROZCO

OROZCO
THE LIFE AND DEATH OF A
MEXICAN
REVOLUTIONARY

RAYMOND CABALLERO

UNIVERSITY OF OKLAHOMA PRESS : NORMAN

Library of Congress Cataloging-in-Publication Data

Name: Caballero, Raymond, 1942– author.
Title: Orozco : the life and death of a Mexican revolutionary / by Raymond Caballero.
Other titles: Life and death of a Mexican revolutionary
Description: Norman, OK : University of Oklahoma Press, [2017] | Includes bibliographical
    references and index.
Identifiers: LCCN 2017004012 | ISBN 978-0-8061-5755-9 (hardcover : alk. paper)
Subjects: LCSH: Orozco, Pascual, 1882–1915. | Mexico—History—Revolution, 1910–1920. |
    Revolutionaries—Mexico—Biography.
Classification: LCC F1234.O73 C37 2017 | DDC 972.08/1092 [B] —dc23
LC record available at https://lccn.loc.gov/2017004012

Contents

Illustrations

Figures

Maps

OROZCO

Introduction

Van Horn, Culberson County, Texas, August 31, 1915. Curious residents gathered at the courthouse to take in the gruesome sight of five bloody bodies propped up against its cut-stone walls as Sheriff John A. Morine proudly displayed the remains of the Mexican bandits his posse had trapped and killed the preceding day in the nearby High Lonesome Mountains. To everyone's surprise, officials identified one of the dead as Gen. Pascual Orozco Jr.,[1] the famous military hero of the Mexican Revolution.

Desperado, bandit, and horse thief or revered military idol of the Mexican Revolution—those were the conflicting descriptions of Orozco that must have run through the onlookers' minds as they stared at his remains. Faced with that bewildering choice of how to define him, those West Texans joined millions of Mexicans who for years had argued over whether Orozco was indeed a principled military hero and political reformer or was instead a sellout to the oligarchy, a politically ambitious traitor to the revolution and an eager ally of a brutal assassin and dictator.

If Orozco was controversial in death, he was even more notorious in life. How could it be that in the less than five years since the revolution began in 1910, Orozco went from unknown muleteer to become the revolution's most important military leader, national hero, and idol, and then finally to death as a reviled traitor to the revolution? Orozco reached the summit of national prominence but ended his life in West Texas—essentially executed there as a common outlaw. He thus represents Mexican history's most dramatic ascent and shameful fall. That story, of Orozco's meteoric rise and ignominious descent and death, is one of the most important, fascinating, and compelling narratives of the revolution. Apart from his provocative personality, Orozco became the revolution's great paradox. He proclaimed progressive economic and political reforms even after he joined pro–Porfirio Díaz reactionaries—a conflict between his stated beliefs and his deeds. It is a contradiction historians

3

still labor to explain and one leaving a divided legacy, seen alternately as heroic and treacherous.

Orozco's public life began in the year of the revolution, 1910, a time when the nation celebrated its independence centennial and had completed more than thirty years of rule under President Porfirio Díaz. Díaz sought to reach his overarching goals of peace, stability, and prosperity by centralizing power under his arbitrary rule and achieving modernization and economic development through foreign investment and exports. To consolidate and centralize political supremacy, he systematically replaced elected local officials and traditional communal governance with appointed political jefes accountable only to the Díaz hierarchy rather than to the populace. Díaz controlled all offices, even those ostensibly elected. He essentially appointed those offices, because he selected the candidates for elections. His choice was often the only one on the ballot. Across the nation, communities that had previously enjoyed political autonomy and self-governance through their own elected officials now came under the rule of appointed political jefes answerable to governors rather than to the people. One mission of those appointed officials was to foster order and stability and thus make the nation attractive to foreign investors. The appointed jefes had their own regional police and militia, *rurales*, and both jefes and rurales became arbitrary and ruthless. Díaz's structure also controlled the nation's economic system.

Legislation stimulated by liberal economics, in place before Díaz took office, outlawed communal or corporate landownership. Initially, the goal was to market land and foment development and efficiency through private initiative. Liberals sought to convert communal residents into individual farmers. Under Díaz, however, instead of dividing communal lands among residents, the wealthy and powerful used the laws to dispossess villages and the indigenous families of their communal lands, properties many had held from preconquest times. Residents of those communities lost their lands to large haciendas and industrial agricultural operations and their political autonomy to appointed political jefes. The villagers now faced new tax collectors and the dreaded *leva*, impressment into the military. They went from working their communal lands to a serf-like existence on haciendas, with the rurales forcing many to work there. Díaz's legislation of 1883 and 1894 allowed survey companies and others to make claims against and declare vacant any property unless an individual held the title. The survey companies sold most vacant parcels to the already wealthy, the only ones able to bid on the properties, and in the

North, members of the elite assembled enormous haciendas at the expense of small proprietors. Often, political jefes worked in tandem with the oligarchy to dispossess villages of their communal lands. Purposely paid low wages, the political jefes joined other local, state, and federal Díaz officials in using their public offices for private gain. Faced with a hostile political leadership and courts and agencies under the governor's control working together to favor the wealthy, the system left the poor and lower rungs of society powerless.[2]

Chihuahua's tiny oligarchy amassed staggering wealth and political power, but it aggressively reached for more. Combining political monopoly power with legal processes under its control, Chihuahua's landed elite seized ancestral private and communal tracts in Chihuahua's Northwest—whose people are called Serranos, that is, "of the sierra"—consigning many to poverty. The seized properties had been in Serrano families and communities for one or two centuries. The oligarchy, moreover, controlled local political jefes and the rural constabulary, whose arbitrary conduct abused and deprived residents of their property and civil liberties.

The economic and political power that Chihuahua's oligarchy amassed during the Porfiriato—the name for the Porfirio Díaz era—finds no modern equivalent in Mexico or in the United States. The oligarchy's two leaders, patriarch General Luis Terrazas and his son-in-law, Enrique C. Creel, consolidated vast tracts of land and enjoyed a political monopoly. Luis Terrazas's cattle ranches were seven times the size of the Texas King Ranch, and Creel's were twice as large. Creel served on the board of the national railways and was the president of Mexico's largest oil company. The Terrazas-Creel clan also controlled much of Chihuahua's other commercial activity. They were both governors, Creel the incumbent and Terrazas having previously held the office for several terms. Creel was Mexico's second most powerful banker, surpassed only by the finance minister, was Mexico's U.S. ambassador, and later sat in the cabinet as minister of foreign relations. Despite having so much, Creel, especially, sought more.

When Creel became governor in 1904, he wasted no time consolidating power in his office. He made elected local officials subservient to his appointed political jefes. Those jefes also controlled the rurales, who ultimately reported to the governor. In 1905, he mandated the sale of municipal lands, an act that dispossessed many in Northwest Chihuahua. Creel directed that all lands be titled, replatted into rectangles, and sold. It was an expensive process for those of modest means, which caused many to lose lands their families had held for generations. One goal of the replatting was to establish an enforceable tax roll as the state began to tax agricultural land. Creel abhorred the idea of communal lands, promoted privatizing all resources, and continued efforts to expropriate communal properties for distribution to the already land-rich elite. Porfiriato policies nationally and in Chihuahua specifically produced vast inequality in justice, wealth, and income, making the nation unstable and ripe for revolution. Those practices, coupled with dire economic conditions Serranos faced after the Panic of 1907 and poor harvests from 1907 to 1909, set the stage for a Northwest Chihuahua rebellion and the start of the Mexican Revolution of 1910. By 1910, a combination of factors drove Serranos to resist the elite's actions and risk their lives and property to overthrow the Díaz dictatorship and Chihuahua's oligarchy. Serranos provided the national revolution with much of its initial military leadership, organization, and drive. Their direction carried the rebellion to its most important victory at Ciudad Juárez, and foremost among them was twenty-nine-year-old Pascual Orozco Jr.

The revolution presented Orozco with a menu of choices: he could support the status quo and *personalismo* in Díaz and his dictatorship or the strongman Bernardo Reyes, who followed the same mold; or he could become a Científico in line with Governor Enrique Creel and Finance Secretary José Ives Limantour. If he chose revolution, he had several options, including the moderation of Francisco I. Madero, who aspired to a return to democracy, the Constitution of 1857, the rule of law, honest elections, and competitive candidacy. Or he could support democratic rule and land and labor reform with the social revolution, especially sought by rural Mexicans who demanded a return of their communal lands and a return to their previously semiautonomous local governance, policies advocated by the Mexican Liberal Party and Emiliano Zapata. In making his selections, Orozco was not alone in radically changing the paths he would follow. Ultimately, Orozco eschewed the ideology he claimed and by his actions chose a negative personalismo—that is, adamant opposition to an individual rather than support of an individual or an idea. It was his contrarian ways that made his a conflicted and confused trail. The choices Orozco made, moreover, would undo his legacy's positive aspects.

Orozco became the hero of the May 1911 Battle of Ciudad Juárez, the pivotal event that brought down the decades-long Porfirio Díaz dictatorship and reinstated democracy and the rule of law in Mexico. Months later, the nation's first honest election in a generation saw Madero elected president, but, after only fifteen months in office, former Porfiristas assassinated Madero and his vice president in a coup d'état, killings that set off another bloody, multiyear civil war cycle. Madero's assassination shocked and traumatized Mexicans. His assassins became national pariahs, and Orozco voluntarily joined that despised group.

Along with heroic accomplishments, incidents of insubordination and rebellion riddle Orozco's military record, which Madero partisans considered acts of disobedience or betrayal. Orozco's defiance of Madero began before they met and predated the Battle of Ciudad Juárez. The Battle of Ciudad Juárez was itself a product of Orozco's insubordination, which benefited both Madero and Orozco, and three days after the battle, Orozco attempted to overthrow Madero in a violent, public coup d'état in which Orozco came near assassinating Madero, his own president and commander in chief. Theirs was a stormy and uncomfortable alliance that was doomed almost from the start. It was what happened to those coming to the revolution with different expectations and assumptions.

In general, a national uprising on the scale of the Mexican Revolution would begin in a strife-ridden, riot-plagued political capital or in an industrial urban center, a Paris, a Saint Petersburg, a Mexico City. Instead, the remote, placid farming and ranching pueblos of Northwest Chihuahua served as the unlikely setting for the start of that violent and radical insurrection. A careful examination of the area's history and its personalities, such as Orozco, shows why it was natural that the revolution began there and provides the explanation why Northwest Chihuahua would lead the rebellion.

There were, in fact, several revolutions. The heart of the Madero Revolution was the rural areas and the revolution's demand for a return to the type of government they once had, the hands-off government they had enjoyed, and the return of expropriated communal lands. The face of the government they hated was the political jefes and the rurales, who were the first targets of the revolution. Rural revolutionaries fought to reverse Díaz's political centralization and land seizures and to end abuse by appointed jefes and their rurales. Urban revolutionaries fought to end the dictatorship and to return to regularly scheduled elections with no reelection. Both groups agreed initially on the issues of elections and the dictatorship, but they were not on the same page with respect to returning communal lands or seized properties, and only the rural revolutionaries wanted to reverse political centralization. Those differences among others led Orozco to betray Madero and rise in rebellion against the idealistic president who had only been in office less than four months. Orozco's rebellion failed except that it succeeded in weakening Madero's already frail administration, which soon led to Madero's shocking assassination. Orozco's antipathy to Madero caused him to side with Gen. Victoriano Huerta, the new dictator, who unfortunately supported few of Orozco's policies. Constitutionalist forces overthrew Huerta in 1914, but within months, Porfiristas with German support and financing persuaded Huerta to end his Spanish exile and return to Mexico to restore his dictatorship. Orozco was the military head of that reactionary effort, and his attempt to cross back into Mexico brought him into the posse's gunsights.

Sheriff Morine and other possemen claimed that Orozco and his companions had stolen horses and attacked employees at the R. C. "Dick" Love Ranch in far east El Paso County, forcing ranch hands there to fix a meal and shoe a horse before they fled, actions that set off the posse's chase into Culberson County. Morine recounted how the next day, the large posse had hunted down and trapped the five men in a box canyon, where, after refusing to surrender and firing at their pursuers instead, the desperados perished in the posse's fusillade. Mexicans were incensed over the killings and accused the Americans of having executed or killed the men in cold blood. The circumstances of the killings and the nature of the deceased's wounds led others to conclude that the posse had killed the Mexicans "by foul means."[3] The controversy became so heated that U.S. officials grew concerned that Mexicans would resort to violence in retaliation, and the Mexican government called for an immediate investigation. Rather than determine what had occurred in the canyon, the coroner's inquest remained silent on most details of the killings, such as the identity of the individuals who fired the fatal shots, the number and location of the wounds the Mexicans suffered, whether the killing scene was examined, or whether there was any evidence that the Mexicans had resisted the posse.

The killing of Orozco and his men grew to be so contentious that one month after the event, a worried Sheriff Morine and the local county attorney requested that the grand jury indict the entire posse, including Morine himself, for the murder of the Mexicans. Local officials staged a trial resulting in a prompt acquittal, a process specifically intended to shield the possemen from having to answer to anyone in the future. A careful examination of the record, however, depicts a strikingly different scene than the one originally described by the posse, from the alleged Love Ranch raid, to the character of posse's leader, to the fusillade's details. The evidence in fact refutes the posse's claims and reveals the identity of Orozco's killer.

August 30, 2015, marked the centennial of Pascual Orozco's death. In reviewing his pronounced contribution to the revolution with the benefit of a century's hindsight, we can reasonably conclude that without Orozco it was unlikely that Madero would have ousted Díaz and become the president of Mexico. A review of Orozco's career shows that three events defined his legacy as he arose to become Mexico's greatest military idol. The first was the Battle of Ciudad Juárez, the second was Orozco's rebellion against Madero, and the third was Orozco's decision to join Huerta's brutal dictatorship. Thus, Orozco went from idol to ogre. His story, nevertheless, shows his leadership and why his Serrano roots took him to victory.

To understand, however, why it was northerners and Serranos who led the fighting and why Chihuahua's Northwest was the cradle of the revolution, it is first necessary to review the history of the society Serranos developed, their land tenure experiences, and the policies and conduct of the national dictatorship and regional oligarchy.

PART I

Northwest Chihuahua

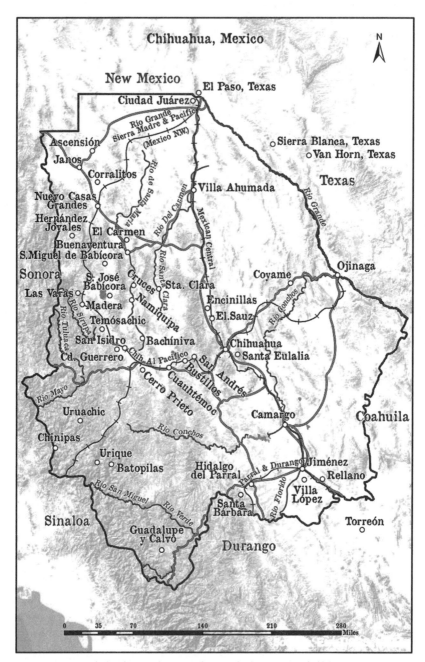

Cartography by Olga Bosenko. Copyright © 2016 by the University of Oklahoma Press.

CHAPTER ONE

The Colonial Era in Northwest Chihuahua

From near the United States–Mexico border, the Sierra Madre Occidental runs south for more than nine hundred miles along western Chihuahua and Durango and eastern Sonora and Sinaloa. The range is laced with canyons and gorges, some on par with the Grand Canyon in size and depth. The bases of its valleys have low desert or tropical climates, while its alpine highlands are fir, pine, and oak forests. Along its eastern flank and closely associated with the sierra's history and development is the adjacent foothill and highland grassland Chihuahua region, which is often referred to as the Northwest. The sierra's rugged, often impenetrable terrain prevented growth of large population centers in a mountain range that had few roads and no rail. Towns and cities provisioning and servicing the sierra arose in the adjacent highland plateau, around seven thousand feet in elevation, in places such as Guerrero, Basúchil, San Isidro, Namiquipa, and Casas Grandes. The Chihuahua portion of the sierra, called La Sierra Tarahumara after its indigenous residents, contains rich mineral deposits and forests, mined and harvested for centuries after gold and silver fever first attracted Spaniards to the area. For the Spanish, getting to the sierra and the Northwest was the easy part; staying there was a daunting challenge. Persistent labor shortages and scarce, difficult transportation impeded exploitation of resources. Even today, few roads traverse the range. Those factors, however, while significant, were not the greatest impediments to the region's development.

In the mid-sixteenth century, when only a handful of soldier-explorers had entered the region, Spain defiantly claimed ownership of Chihuahua, forcibly taking the land and willfully disregarding rights of the territory's indigenous residents. The indigenous may not have held title to the property in the manner of the Europeans, but they occupied the land and felt that it was theirs. Many Natives refused to recognize Spain's title, but with a perfect record of subjugating aboriginal people, the crown had no doubt about its entitlement and that it would be the Natives who would cede their lands and often their liberty to Spain. For its rule to prevail, however, Spain recognized the necessity of occupying the land. Therefore, along the high plains on the eastern foothills of the sierra, the Spanish crown devised strategies to attract permanent colonists. The Spanish built missions and settlements to pacify the sedentary indigenous population and to attract pioneers, but the settlers soon fled in the face of occasional violent Indian rebellions and raids, abandoning entire towns, mines, missions, and haciendas. Over and again, the Spanish rebuilt and repopulated what they had forsaken only to flee once more. Between the seventeenth and late nineteenth centuries, the crown and Mexico routinely failed to secure the area's disperse and isolated settlements from Native insurgencies and, later, from raids by nomadic tribes, especially by several mounted Apache groups, particularly the Chiricahuas based to the north in what today is southwestern New Mexico and southeastern Arizona. The Eastern and Western Apaches, along with the Navahos, had long before migrated from Alberta's Lake Athabasca area. The Western Apaches consisted of six tribes, the White Mountain Apaches, Pinals, Coyoteros, Arivaipas, Mescaleros, and Chiricahuas. Of those, the Chiricahuas were the principal raiders into Mexico, and they were divided into four bands, the Chihennes or Warmsprings, the Bedonkohes, the Nednhis, and the Chokonens. The Chiricahuas were the only Apache tribe that did not plant. They were raiders and hunter-gatherers. Raiding was not only a part of their culture; it was their livelihood. It was inconceivable that they would stop raiding.[1] The only question would be where they would raid.

In seventeenth-century Chihuahua, the mostly sedentary Tepehuans, Conchos, Tarahumaras, and other Natives, by then supposedly Christian and loyal to the crown, rebelled several times, destroying missions and pueblos and occasionally sacrificing the missionaries, not only in the sierra region but throughout the province.[2] Spain brutally repressed uprisings of sedentary tribes, driving many of the indigenous permanently into the sierra, which ultimately became their refuge.[3] While Spanish rule experienced periodic indigenous resistance throughout Mexico, only in the Sierra Madre region and the North was it so persistent. The Spanish experienced some relief in the lull of rebellions from the last Tarahumara uprising in 1694 until the time Apache raids became a major problem in the mid-eighteenth century, when the mounted raiders harassed and killed Spaniards and the sedentary Natives alike.

A century after Spain's importation of the horse, feral mustang herds dramatically proliferated and spread far into western North America. The Apaches and Comanches seized the opportunity, retamed the mustangs, and became talented and superior equestrians, the Comanches especially so. Their mobility allowed them to hunt and raid, as well as seize livestock, goods, weapons, and people. The sparse, isolated Spanish settlements were easy targets for Apache warriors, for whom the sierra and the Northwest had become a happy hunting ground. The Apaches and Comanches soon developed a society living beyond the edge of "civilization" with the ability to seize its resources through their raiding parties. Attracted south by Spanish booty and pressured there by superior Comanche warriors and increased western American settlement, Apache raiding parties increasingly rode into Chihuahua. Mexican Jesuits and Franciscans sent by the crown to pacify and convert sedentary tribes built missions, but those endeavors had no effect on the Apache threat. Presidios became the more effective Spanish response. They were manned by cavalry, but those garrisons were too few and scattered to hold such a vast, untamed territory.

In the late seventeenth and early eighteenth centuries, the first Spanish settlers began trickling into the Río Papigochi area, then under the jurisdiction of the mining boomtown Cusihuiriáchi. Among the early settlers were the Domínguez de Mendoza and Orozco families. Capitán Andrés Orozco y Villaseñor was the deputy alcalde (magistrate) for the area after 1710.[4] In the next decades, other families of future revolutionaries arrived in Basúchil and San Isidro.

The region's unreliable security restricted not only the population but also the exploitation of timber, ore, and agriculture. The Spanish were convinced of the area's potential by its peacetime productivity, and they determined to solve the Sierra Madre puzzle. To do so, Spain invested substantial resources to promote the territory's habitation and development, but the devastation continued. In 1758, the indefatigable sixty-three-year-old Pedro Tamarón y Romeral became bishop of the Durango-based Nueva Vizcaya diocese. During his ten years in office, the bishop conducted five remarkable tours and censuses of his vast province, visiting the most remote areas, including villages of Chihuahua's Northwest. In town after town, the bishop recorded the devastating path of death, destruction, and abandonment wrought by Apache raiders.[5]

Spain also sent civil inspectors to review the area and devise defense and development strategies. In 1778, intent on finding a permanent solution, Spain created the Internal Provinces, a new government for north-central Mexico, removing the area from vice-regal control and instituting a new system of land tenure. That new government, no longer based in Chihuahua or Durango but in Sonora, established a series of military villages to augment and support the presidios in places such as Namiquipa, Janos, and Casas Grandes, situated as pickets to intercept Apache raiders descending on Chihuahua.

To attract settlers, the Spanish crown allocated a 277,000-acre parcel of land to each community, a square with each side 21 miles long, an area of 432 square miles to be held by each community as municipal land.[6] In some cases, private hacendados had previously owned part of that land but had abandoned the properties in the face of Apache raids. In addition to the communal land share, the crown gave settlers a sizable house lot large enough for a vegetable garden and orchard, as well as a larger, separate irrigated agricultural land grant with water rights and a pasture for domestic animals. The settlers were exempted from most taxes. The crown paid each family two reales per day for their first year, giving families support while they settled and planted crops. That was the bait for the new residents. In return, the homesteaders had to live on and work the land for ten years, be armed, participate in the defense of the community, and resist Apache attacks. The nearby garrisons reserved the right to conscript the town's men to fight the Apaches whenever necessary. These semi-military colonies became the backbone of Northwest Chihuahua colonial life, and over time the isolated and independent people of the Northwest evolved their unique society and community. They also became the buffer zone, insulating the rest of Chihuahua from the scourge of Apache raids. They were the Mexican equivalent of Jefferson's yeoman farmers, working land and defending territory in cooperation with nearby forts.

Unlike the United States, which welcomed and absorbed people from many nations and of all faiths, Spain severely limited its pool of potential settlers by continuing to require that all immigrants be Spanish, have impeccable Catholic credentials, and have no Jewish or Moorish ancestry.[7] That policy was a monumental strategic mistake that would make it impossible for Spain to colonize vast reaches of New Spain, especially areas that became California, Nevada, Utah, Colorado, Arizona, New Mexico, and Texas. The number of qualified Spaniards willing to emigrate and resettle was miniscule in relation to the area's size. Thus, Spain could not defend territory that it claimed but did not inhabit. Its national policies of blind faith and intolerance would be its undoing in the Americas, especially North America, where the United

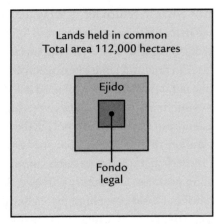

Fig. 1. Colonial Municipal Land Grants. The larger square is the common lands, *terrenos de común*, 8 leagues (33 kilometers or 21 miles) to a side. The next square is the *ejido* for agriculture, 2.5 leagues (10.3 kilometers or 6.6 miles) per side. The center square was the center of town, where each family had a house lot.

States would easily invade and take Spanish territory and where nomadic tribes could plunder scattered settlements at will. Nevertheless, when it came to the sierra, Spain actively worked to colonize the region and relaxed some of its normal practices to attract settlers.

In granting northwestern homesteads, Spain ignored the usual societal and racial castes and offered communal land shares, irrigated plots, and town residential lots to all takers, regardless of race or economic background. Unlike the hacendados, these highland settlers did not hire labor; rather, with their large and extended family relations and neighbors, they jointly worked communal and personal plots. They married within their communities, often with cousins or close neighbors, forging tight-knit social circles. They frequently took up arms as a community to fight the Apaches. Over many decades, these egalitarian, racially mixed communities developed close family, community, and economic bonds. They also became virtually autonomous, fiercely independent, and aggressive in defense of their territory and way of life.[8]

Many presidio soldiers remained after their service to live in those communities as well. Generations later, the region's armed inhabitants were largely independent of state government and close to the land they worked. So long as the Apache threat remained existential to Chihuahua, Serrano settlers were free to work their lands in return for fighting the Indian raiders and creating a protective barrier for the rest of the state. Unfortunately, the land that Serranos resided on, tilled, and ran livestock on was not as much theirs as they had believed it to be, a doubtful tenure having its own, troubled history.

Many residents of the military towns never obtained individual, documented titles to their plots or communal shares. In many cases, the government either never issued individual titles or else placed title only in the community's name. Generation after generation, these Serranos lived on their town lots in homes their families built, worked their own farms and communal lands, grazed their cattle on common pastures, and jointly harvested the common plots and forests. These families would pay a high price after the 1880s for their lack of land titles when land grabs by Chihuahua's politically powerful elite took their municipal and communal plots, seizures that became precursors to the revolution.

Aside from individual and municipal properties, there was another type of land, that owned by the Catholic Church, legally a corporation, including the immense properties possessed by the Jesuits. The viceroy had granted the Franciscans jurisdiction over the plains of Chihuahua and the Jesuits the highlands and the sierra. By 1767, the Jesuits had eighteen missions and various other properties under their control, including the one at Papigochi (Ciudad Guerrero's name before 1823). Jesuits, because of their independence, power, and alliance with the Vatican, were often in conflict with Spanish monarchs, who sought absolute power in their realms and a compliant Church establishment. In 1767, Carlos III, blaming Jesuits for internal Spanish disturbances, issued a dramatic retaliatory order to expel all 2,200 Jesuits from Spanish America. The crown handled the expulsion order as a top-secret assignment and executed it simultaneously throughout the Americas.[9] The Papigochi mission was one such Jesuit property. It took the soldiers a month to gather the priests in the sierra and highlands missions. In July 1767, royal troops appeared at the Papigochi mission door and asked for resident Jesuit priests Manuel Vivanco and José Vega.[10] Soldiers arrested the priests when they appeared. After officials and the priests made a complete inventory of the mission's properties, they marched the priests first to Parral, then, along with other Jesuits, to Zacatecas and then eventually to Veracruz where, between October of that year and January of the next, they were banished from the Americas and sent to Italy.[11]

Once the Jesuits were gone, the crown replaced the order with either Franciscans or diocesan priests. The crown turned most Jesuit properties over to Franciscans but retained a substantial portion for the government, including the mission lands near Babícora and around Papigochi, which included the village of Labor de San Isidro, later to be the Orozco's family home.[12] Over time, although they had no title, Spanish families settled on the former Jesuit land. On several occasions, the residents of San Isidro attempted to buy the land they had been working. When they could not, they simply continued to live there and work the land without title.

CHAPTER TWO

Mexican Independence and Chaos

Events in the first decade of the nineteenth century encouraged Mexican insurgents to launch their fight for independence from Spain. America's independence victory over Britain was one inspiration. Mexicans were also influenced by French enlightenment philosophers and by the French Revolution. Mexicans saw their opportunity in the massive confusion in Spain when Napoleon had imprisoned the battling Spanish monarchs and replaced the incumbent with his own brother, which left Spain with a divided government and no Spanish sovereign. In South America, Simón Bolívar had also seized the moment. Between 1810 and 1821, Mexico fought Spain for its independence. The movement's initial leadership was mostly lower-level clergy fighting under the banner of the Virgin of Guadalupe, but the Church's Mexican hierarchy and the conservative establishment were uniformly royalist, forming a natural alliance that soon defeated the insurgents. In 1821, after Spain enacted liberal reforms, conservative Mexican Catholics, the Church hierarchy, and monarchists successfully fought for independence and established a new Mexican monarchy under Emperor Agustín de Iturbide. In the Northwest, independence soon converted what had been a Spanish-Apache problem into a Mexican headache.

The Spanish had a long and successful history of conquering indigenous peoples throughout the Americas. Mostly, the indigenous died of diseases introduced by the Europeans, and for those Natives who lived to resist, the Spanish soon reduced them to near slaves. In the North, Spain's multifaceted Apache policy of the late 1700s had ultimately produced successful results, achieved with a combination of rations paid to the Apaches, communal land grants, payments to settlers, and the establishment of armed presidios. All that changed when Mexico achieved independence from Spain, which was a transition acutely felt throughout Northwest Chihuahua. The region, accustomed to receiving attention and support from the central Spanish government, soon lost it under the new and fractured Mexican government.

From 1821 when it gained its independence until 1867 when the Republic was restored under Benito Juárez, Mexico's government descended into chaos and was of little help to the people of Chihuahua. The Northwest, especially, depended heavily on federal resources to defend against Apache attacks. In the span of forty-six years (1821–67), Mexico sustained more than three hundred revolutions or uprisings,[1] two foreign invasions (U.S. 1846–48 and French 1862–67), and several coups d'etat. It also had two constitutions (1824 and 1857), four distinct republics, and was governed by two emperors, four multimember regencies, and fifty-nine presidents, including Antonio López de Santa Anna, who drifted in and out of office eleven times. Including the regencies and the emperors, that would make sixty-five heads of state, each serving an average of eight and a half months with some actually serving only a few weeks. Political fault lines formed along traditional divisions. On one side were those conservatives who believed in a strong central ruler, either a monarch or "strongman," who governed in conjunction with the Catholic Church, wealthy hacendados, and the military. On the other side were liberal reformers who believed in a federated state, limited Church power, greater personal liberty, and more widespread landownership.

Clearly, half a century of disorder, however, had important, negative consequences, one being the failure to deal with the Apache raids, which were common in northern Mexico. Indigenous nomadic tribes had been fighting each other for hundreds of years, mostly over land and hunting associated with the territory. The mounted Comanches and their Ute allies fought the Apaches. All sides took female and child captives and as many animals as possible. Both Apaches and Comanches took each other's scalps as prizes or as proof of consummated revenge. Apaches and Comanches used the same raiding methods on Spanish and sedentary indigenous settlements. Although Comanche and Apache raids terrorized much of Chihuahua, the Northwest was the Chiricahuas' favored target. Residents could expect an attack at any time and place, when traveling alone, in small groups, or in caravans with valuable cargo. Apache raiding parties usually numbered twenty to thirty braves. They often camped outside of a town and then frightened residents by galloping through town streets. Some residents fought back by throwing boiling water or oil on the raiders. Both Comanches and Apaches preferred a diet of horse or mule flesh to beef, a preference that often governed what they seized in a raid. While the settlers feared death, what they feared more was captivity, or worse, for the raiders to carry away their women and children. The warriors had an astounding ability to cover great distances, moving large herds of livestock along with scores of human captives. One Comanche raiding party that traveled as far south as the state of San Luis Potosí was found to have killed three hundred residents and had in its possession thirty-two captive children and eighteen thousand head of cattle.[2] Nomadic tribes did not keep animals in pens; they killed and consumed weak animals unable to make long treks and traded the remainder upon reaching their destination. The distances could be several hundred miles, such as taking Sonoran cattle for trade to Santa Fe's New Mexico fair.[3] The fear engendered by Apache and Comanche raids permeated Chihuahuan society for generations, causing many to abandon life in the remote Northwest. It also meant that settlers who remained were a special breed indeed, a people confident and tested in their ability to fight.

Policies adopted in the chaotic aftermath of independence from Spain upset the delicate balance and détente Spain had worked so hard to achieve with the Apaches. Internal conflicts and a depleted treasury forced the young Mexican government to end Apache rations and reduce presidio support, leaving the region once again vulnerable to attack.

The Apaches soon reacted to the new régime by renewing their raids. By the 1830s, the toll of the attacks was worse than ever, and Chihuahua had nowhere to turn for help. Northern states such as Chihuahua, which no longer expected federal assistance with the turmoil in Mexico City, opted to act on their own. They used state military and quasi-military forces to fight the Apache menace, contracting with private individuals and companies to attack the Apaches, and resorted to paying bounties to Comanches for Apache scalps and vice versa. Sonora initiated scalp and captive bounties in 1835, and Chihuahua followed in 1837 with several subsequent bounty renewals.[4] They provided cash payments for live Apache captives or their scalps. Chihuahua bounty payments varied but were usually 100 to 250 pesos for a live female and 25 to 150 pesos for a child captive. The states paid 300 pesos for live warriors or 200 pesos for their scalps. The state would pay the bounty to anyone, military or civilian, with municipal officials authorized to make payment after certifying the scalp. Scalp quality control was minimal. Given the lure of easy money, many a peaceful, sedentary Native lost his scalp, as did a number of women. Occasionally, however, officials implemented quality-control measures.[5] One rule required a scalp to have either one or two ears to prevent sellers from using one divided scalp to claim two bounties.[6] There were several Mexican and American companies working the scalp business, and Serranos soon became familiar with Apache scalp hunts. Despite private armies and scalp bounty hunters, the Apache problem persisted, and the 1840s made for the worst decade ever, but other events that were national in scope intervened in 1846 to divert everyone's attention.

From the time Texas gained its independence from Mexico to the time it became a state, Texans and Americans had never occupied the Nueces–Rio Grande territory other than some with Mexico's permission. Mexico had always claimed the territory, but Texas insisted that it was part of its state. For the United States, it was a good place to start a false dispute. In 1846, U.S. president James K. Polk saw the Nueces territory as his opportunity to seize California, the real prize he sought. Mexico was weak at that point, having had six presidents in the previous two years. Polk had decided to invade Mexico even if Mexico had not entered U.S. territory, but then, sending troops into the disputed area, Polk claimed that Mexico had invaded the United States. He created this pretext to invade Mexico.[7] The Mexican-American War was short, lasting two years from General Zachary Taylor's entry into the disputed territory in 1846 to the signing of the Treaty of Guadalupe Hidalgo in 1848. In those two years, Mexico had ten different presidents. There was hardly anyone in the presidency to lead the nation, and the government in Chihuahua was thoroughly incapable of defending its territory.

In 1847, U.S. troops invaded Mexico, including Chihuahua, remaining there from February 1847 to August 1848. Because of the war, Mexico lost half of its territory. Mexicans, however, did not forget the loss. It remained a bitter pill for them then, as it still is today.[8] The well-founded anti-American bias became more acute as the Díaz and Terrazas-Creel governments openly preferred Americans and Europeans to Mexicans. After the war, Mexico continued with its chaos, and Chihuahua's attention once again returned to the Apaches. Even amid the chaos, however, Mexico was entering into a new era and had found a new leader.

CHAPTER THREE

Benito Juárez
and the Reform Era

During the American invasion and after the Treaty of Guadalupe Hidalgo, Mexicans continued their centrist versus federalist and conservative versus liberal struggles. In the 1850s, a new leader, Benito Juárez, arose on the liberal side and was an inspiration to most Mexicans in the manner of Abraham Lincoln. Juárez, born in 1806 in Oaxaca in an impoverished Zapotec village, was orphaned as a boy and lived through an amazing struggle. At age twelve, speaking no Spanish, he walked to the city of Oaxaca to find his sister who lived there employed as a domestic worker. A lay religious man who ran a bindery took him in and educated him. As Juárez matured, he became a local, state, and national leader. He was a lawyer, law professor, judge, legislator, governor of Oaxaca, and, finally, the nation's liberal leader and president.

In 1855, Juárez and the liberals ousted President Antonio López de Santa Anna and replaced him with Ignacio Comonfort. Juárez became justice minister and later president of the Supreme Court, and his liberal colleague Miguel Lerdo de Tejada headed the finance ministry. Together they wasted no time in advancing the liberal agenda, enacting the most ambitious reforms possible, but also antagonizing the nation's most powerful forces.

In 1855, Mexico enacted the Juárez and Lerdo Laws and later the Constitution of 1857, which governed Mexico for sixty years. The laws protected personal liberties, such as freedom of conscience, speech, press, assembly, as well as other rights. By no longer making the Catholic Church the state religion, the legislation permitted the practice of other faiths for the first time and constrained the Catholic Church's powers and its right to own property. The Mexican Catholic Church held vast properties, but the new laws limited its ownership to land and buildings it used in religious services and obligated the Church to sell surplus assets that it previously owned, such as its large haciendas. Although the law's main target was Church lands, its broad terms eventually applied to all corporations and brought *ejido*, communal, and municipal lands within its ambit. It was a well-intentioned law furthering "liberal" economics, seeking to put more land into the market, and making yeomen farmers out of communal campesinos.[1] The theory favored private over communal ownership, anticipating increased productivity from individual initiative. Other laws also ended the Church's religious monopoly as well as its control over education, established the civil registry to archive vital records and perform marriages, and turned cemeteries over to state agencies. These measures addressed complaints that the Church had refused to provide burial, baptismal, or marriage services unless paid. Many in Mexico could not afford the fees. The new constitution separated state from Church and for the first time allowed the legal practice of other faiths. The reaction to those sweeping changes was immediate and fierce.

Conservatives, with Church support, launched the Reform War of 1857–61, a conflict that drove the liberal Juárez government out of the capital and into the provinces. Competing governments, liberal and conservative, ran the divided nation until 1861. After years of war and chaos, Mexico was deeply in debt. When Juárez attempted to postpone payment of the nation's debt, Mexico's creditors—Spain, France, and England—seized Veracruz to confiscate tariff revenues. When Napoleon III decided to proceed further and invade Mexico, Spain and England withdrew. Conservatives and monarchists, with the Church's support, invited the French to invade Mexico in 1863. The division continued with Juárez as president being driven farther and farther north by French invaders, who, together with the Catholic Church and conservatives, installed an Austrian noble as Mexico's monarch, Emperor Maximilian I. The French drove Juárez north to Paso del Norte (Ciudad Juárez today) on the U.S. border, as far as he could go and still be in Mexico, where he remained for nine months.

Including his stay in Paso del Norte, Juárez was in the state of Chihuahua for two years and two months. While there, he forged an alliance with Chihuahua governor Luis Terrazas, whose support allowed Mexican forces to turn the tide.[2] Juárez did not forget this assistance. Napoleon III withdrew his forces to deal with Bismarck, leaving the way open for Juárez to march south. In 1867, Juárez returned the presidency to Mexico City, restoring the republic and democracy, this time without a competing government. However, Juárez still had his problems. He had served as Mexico's president for fourteen turbulent years from 1858 to 1872, enduring an 1871 electoral challenge from Porfirio Díaz and Sebastián Lerdo de Tejada. Díaz based his opposition on the idea that there should be no reelection.[3] Juárez won reelection only when the Chamber of Deputies broke the stalemate, but Díaz refused to accept the results and revolted. The rebellion was put down, but Juárez died in 1872 and was succeeded by Sebastián Lerdo de Tejada, who had been chief justice. In 1876, however, Díaz overthrew Lerdo, became president, and went on to dominate Mexican politics for a generation.[4]

CHAPTER FOUR

Porfiriato Governance

Considering that he later rose in revolt against Benito Juárez and has been disparaged by many of those who cherish "don Benito," Díaz had much in common with Juárez. Born in Oaxaca in 1830, Díaz, part Mixtec,[1] also received a Oaxaca seminary education and later left to pursue law studies, including courses taught by Juárez. Díaz entered the military and enjoyed a distinguished career, serving in several conflicts under Juárez, receiving honors, and attaining hero status for his valiant defense of Puebla against the French on May 5, 1862, a day Mexicans everywhere still celebrate. Despite their similar backgrounds, Díaz and Juárez viewed history and government in starkly different terms. In the defeat of Maximilian and the French, for example, Juárez emphasized the victory as the triumph of law, whereas Díaz emphasized its military aspects. In their divergent philosophies and methods of governance, the rule of law guided Juárez, whereas Díaz prioritized military strength and internal order.[2] Juárez placed justice over order, while Díaz reversed those priorities.[3] Symbolically, Juárez was the man in the black suit holding aloft a copy of the constitution; Díaz was the man in a medaled, military uniform.

Díaz radiated strength and leadership, an image he carefully cultivated and guarded.[4] His expressionless face was dark, with deep-set eyes, white hair, and a large mustache. His five-foot-eight stature was soldier straight, making him appear taller than he was; his formal dress was military; his expression was inscrutable, Sphinx-like, unfathomable even to those closest to him. He was taciturn and reserved, melancholic in aspect, and tenacious in his determination. In office, Díaz strived for—and to a degree achieved—his goals, including peace, stability, internal security, economic progress, and modernization. He made Mexico a credit-worthy nation attractive to foreign investors. His achievements, however, carried a high price.

Under Díaz, Mexico lost democracy, liberty, freedom of expression and press, equality of opportunity, transparency, honest, well-administered constitutional government, the rule of law, and legitimacy. It was left with a corrupt dictatorship perpetuated in office through political and press repression and persistent electoral fraud. While Díaz was no Stalin or Hitler, he was no benign dictator either. He assassinated, executed, exiled, removed from office, or imprisoned many who peacefully opposed his rule. In governance, he mastered perfidy[5] and deceit to divide and conquer not only his opponents but also his own cabinet and ambitious politicians.[6] In his Faustian bargain, Díaz surrendered good government and Mexico's liberal democracy in return for absolute power and an indeterminate term of office. Mexicans made a similar pact and traded democracy and freedom for stability and order.

Porfirio Díaz had risen against Juárez, objecting to the concentration of power and to Juárez's multiple presidential terms, emphatically insisting that a president should be limited to one term with no opportunity for reelection. Díaz unsuccessfully ran for the presidency more than once. After Díaz took the presidency with "no reelection" as his principal promise, he proceeded to govern from then until 1911, seven election cycles, the exception being one four-year period when a handpicked straw man, his compadre Manuel González, held the presidency for him.

Writing at that time, Luis Cabrera condemned the Díaz administration for promoting *caciquismo*, local strongmen practicing violence and outrages on the populace; *la ley fuga*, political assassinations by shooting prisoners and then falsely claiming that they had attempted to escape; peonage, peasant slavery, such as the Yaqui deportations to Yucatán with forced labor on henequen plantations; *fabriquismo*, the enslavement of industrial workers, such as textile laborers; *hacendismo*, predatory landed aristocrats victimizing the poor; *cientifiquismo*, financial and commercial monopoly by big business, and *foreignismo*, preference of foreigners over Mexicans.[7] To that already long list, Cabrera could have added other serious charges, including widespread corruption, the destruction of a liberal democracy, and electoral fraud.

Díaz governance staples included dividing and conquering his opponents and playing one cabinet faction against another. By the mid-1880s, Díaz had total control and was clearly a dictator. In 1886, he amended the constitution to allow the reelection of the president and governors. He named his father-in-law, Manuel Romero Rubio, to the cabinet, and soon Romero was the cabinet's dominant force. Romero established the powerful Científicos, the group known as the positivist-influenced financial faction. Romero, who headed one bloc, packed the cabinet with his followers, and in reaction Díaz appointed ministers of a different stripe to allow him to play one group against another. Díaz pitted factions against each other to retain overall control and perpetuated a constant state of havoc and intrigue. After Romero died in 1895, financier José Ives Limantour became the Científico leader, and Bernardo Reyes headed the opposing military faction, prolonging a contest that went on for some years.[8] In that bifurcated cabinet, Chihuahua's Enrique Creel fell in with and joined the Científico faction. Governance under the Porfiriato served to implement the economic policies of the administration's Científico advisors.

Despite serving for term after term, Díaz clung to the no reelection rhetoric, presenting his candidacy with each new election cycle as the only thing keeping the nation from plunging back into a pre-1867-like chaos. His refrain was that he was old and longed to retire, but with the nation insisting that he continue serving, he had no choice but to soldier on. One successful Díaz strategy was to falsely encourage and expose those he suspected of having presidential ambitions, an approach he had used before the 1900 election with both his finance minister, José Ives Limantour, and Limantour's cabinet rival, military man Bernardo Reyes. Once Limantour went public with the candidacy Díaz had encouraged, Díaz snuffed out his race by raising the issue that Limantour was ineligible because his father was French and the constitution required both parents to be Mexican. The other candidate, Reyes, was not a Científico. With Limantour disqualified and facing the possibility of Reyes in power, Científicos saw no alternative but to insist that Díaz run again to avoid the loss of power that they saw in a non-Científico Reyes administration.[9] Thus encouraged, Díaz "reluctantly" agreed to run again. In late 1902, Limantour exposed Reyes as being behind an anti-Científico newspaper, La Protesta, which had published defamatory pieces against Limantour. To Díaz, it was an act of disloyalty that had damaged the cabinet. He punished the ambitious Reyes with exile from the cabinet and sent him to the Nuevo León governorship.[10] Setting up and knocking down straw men was a favored Díaz election strategy.

With Reyes and Limantour removed from the field, Díaz had the laws changed in 1903 to allow for his sixth reelection in 1904 and to lengthen the term of office from four to six years. Providing some pretense for having a succession plan, Díaz also amended the constitution to allow for the election of a vice president.[11] For the 1904 election, which Díaz pronounced as his last, promising to leave office in 1910, the old dictator decided that there was not to be even token opposition. Thus, he went about extinguishing another Bernardo Reyes run, making Díaz again the sole realistic choice. Díaz named Sonora cacique Ramón Corral to be his vice president. The cabinet intrigue now pitted Limantour and his Científicos against a new strongman rival, Corral.[12]

The army and the rural police, the rurales, efficiently managed Díaz's fraudulent elections. In that manner, cycle after cycle, Porfiriato elections became useless exercises with no serious opposition allowed. Given the lack of choice, Mexicans saw little need to vote, drastically reducing voter participation. Their reluctance to vote is easy to understand given that voters daring enough to buck the system risked persecution, arrest, or murder, and that Díaz agents routinely falsified individual ballots.[13] The risk of being left out or of retaliation was real, as there was no secret ballot in Mexico and votes were open records. One observer noted, "Few Mexicans have the courage to vote in opposition to the authorities."[14]

Not only was it bad for Mexico to have a dictatorship; it was worse that it lasted for so long. Díaz deprived Mexico of normal, democratic debate and competition of ideas and candidates, causing Mexico to lose a generation of democratic leadership and experience. Like many dictatorships, the persistent and interminable Díaz administration had no provision for succession, because it would not permit any successor to raise his profile. The nation expected that only death would end the Porfiriato, making civil war its succession plan, and that, essentially, is what took place.[15]

Díaz had two broad policies over economics and politics. In economics, it was development and modernization based on exports and foreign investment. In politics, it was the centralization of power in his office. Over the years, Díaz made virtually all offices in Mexico, high to low, appointed rather than elected. Those nominally elective were effectively appointed, as there was often only one candidate on the ballot—of course, the one named by Díaz. The legislative branch lost its independence and ceased being a check on the presidency. He filled congress with lackeys and did the same to the judiciary, which also ceased being an independent institution.[16] Díaz appointed and removed members of congress and the court at will. His family, of course, occupied the highest ranks in those politics. His brother-in-law sat on the Supreme Court; his father-in-law, Manuel Romero Rubio, was for years the leading force in the cabinet; his children also lived on government largesse.[17]

With each passing year of the Porfiriato, Díaz accumulated more power. He hungered for it at all costs and used several tools to succeed, including buying off possible rivals and rewarding officeholders with wealth through corruption. His explanation for rewarding others was that "a dog with a bone doesn't bark or bite." All power flowed in his direction. Díaz even controlled water rights.[18]

Díaz made corruption the fuel and glue in his administration. It became the means to power, the means to retention of power, and the element that bound the Porfiriato structure and its practitioners. By creating a massive machinery of corruption, Díaz offered wealth via public office, government concessions, and contracts to cooperative allies and public officials. Díaz decided who held governorships and political and military posts and which firms received concessions and monopolies. Trusted loyalists received monopolies and concessions, including those for tobacco, government furniture, newsprint, pulque, banking, public works, and dynamite, a monopoly in which his son participated.[19]

In return for the wealth he made possible, Díaz demanded obedience and loyalty, a choice known as *pan o palo*, "bread or the stick." The pan in the system was government-sanctioned theft by graft, usury, illegal gambling, the sale of judicial decisions, the nation's patrimony, corrupt contracts, and concessions.[20] In an illuminating and important series, a *New York Times* correspondent explained elements of Díaz corruption that routinely involved kickbacks to political insiders. Mexican states and municipalities could only issue bonds for public works with the approval of the treasury minister, ostensibly so the nation could not irresponsibly incur debt. To obtain approval, state commissions would apply to the minister. Before approving the bonds, however, the minister would suggest that only one bank could be trusted to handle the matter. When a commission approached that bank, it would dictate the terms, which the commission was obligated to accept if it wanted the loan, with the bank saying, "If you don't like [the terms] of course you can go elsewhere." The bankers would then tell the commission that they would only float the loan if a firm in which they had confidence did the work. The bankers then informed the commission that they had the firm, owned by them, that could do the work. Often the favored contractor had so much work that it sublet the contract to another firm, commonly foreign, but it would, of course, receive part of the contract price. "The [contractor] made money, the friends of the Secretary of the Treasury made money—everybody made money except the unfortunate state or municipality, which generally paid a high price for what was frequently a poor piece of work." The correspondent reported that often, to do business in the Porfiriato, you had to "see Díaz." "If, when you 'saw Díaz' he expressed himself favorably, all you had to do was to retain a gentleman of the Presidential circle, one who had access to him at all times, preferably an astute lawyer, and things would go along smoothly for a long time—perhaps forever."[21] That was the way business was done, one payoff after the next from the highest ranks in government down to the lowest local offices. Nothing happened without payment to a public official. Obviously, insiders receiving huge payoffs for doing no work thought it was a great system of government, and they would insist that their wealth was unrelated to the fact that they happened to hold a position of public trust.

The palo in the system was simple. Those not playing along would be banished from power or barred from public office, lucrative contracts, or concessions and would sometimes be imprisoned, exiled, or killed.

By centralizing power, Díaz fulfilled the conservative desire for a strongman and a strong central government. The Díaz dictatorship was close enough to a monarchy to please that element. He also satisfied the landed elite by easing the path for more land accumulation and the expropriation of communal and tribal lands. Liberals also got something from Díaz: he did not undo controls over the Church or restore Church lands although he formed a close partnership with the Church; he had effective limits on the army, the veneer of a federalist state and "liberal" economic policies.

By the 1880s, Díaz had essentially ended Mexican freedom of the press. He first tried buying favorable coverage by giving the press subsidies.[22] Later, Díaz openly censored and punished the press when it reported what the administration preferred kept secret, such as railroad subsidies granted to foreign firms. The administration jailed editor after editor, suppressed publications, or confiscated newspapers' properties for reporting the truth, including *El Demócrata, La República, El Gran Galeoto, El Explorador* (editor assassinated), *El Tiempo, El Monitor Republicano, Las Novedades, El Correo del Lunes, El Hijo del Ahuizote, Diario del Hogar,* and *El Universal,* with its staff arrested for opposing Díaz's reelection.[23] They arrested many others for offending local politicians, such as *El Correo de Chihuahua*'s Silvestre Terrazas, who was jailed by Chihuahua governor Enrique Creel on more than one occasion.

In 1893, the newspaper *El Demócrata* exposed illegal gambling houses operating under the protection of Díaz's father-in-law, Manuel Romero Rubio, then the nation's government secretary, or minister of the interior. In a controversial decision, the court held that card games and roulette were legal, because the law only prohibited "gambling" in general and was not specific. When *La República* satirized the decision, other newspapers joined in the criticism, resulting in the government closing several journals and jailing their editors.[24] Journalists were punished for criticizing not only Díaz but even the United

States.[25] Throughout all that repression of the press, the courts provided no protection. The courts heard no newspaper case, and no writ of habeas corpus ever freed a journalist.[26]

On the local level, the appointed *jefes políticos* were tyrants. The jefes along with their local police, the rurales, committed untold abuses and became a national scandal as well as one of the causes of the revolution. Among the dictatorship's abuses was the practice of la ley fuga. Rurales, moreover, were in the pocket of the landed aristocracy and industrial firms, who used them to put down labor unrest and impress workers for haciendas and factories.

CHAPTER FIVE

Porfiriato Economic Policies

Under Díaz, Mexico became a creditworthy nation with political stability and a business-friendly administration that welcomed foreign investment. Those Porfirian economic policies produced a boom with unprecedented levels of foreign investment that built railroads, factories, and ports; opened mines; drilled oil wells; harvested and milled timber; and increased export-based, large-scale agriculture. Few Mexicans, however, shared in those gains. At the dawn of the twentieth century, twenty-five years after Díaz took office, 91 percent of Mexico's 13.5 million inhabitants were poor, 8 percent were middle class, and only 1 percent occupied its tiny economic summit.[1] Among the millions of Mexicans, a mere seven hundred privileged families were the major beneficiaries of the new wealth.[2] Under Díaz, 86 percent of Mexicans were illiterate twenty years into his presidency, and public health had so deteriorated that 50 percent of children died in their first year of life.[3] Large families lived in squalid, one-room adobes. Their huts had packed-earth floors and no windows, making the dwellings dark, unventilated, and unhealthy. For furniture, they might have a table but no utensils. For clothing, they wore rags. Smallpox and measles were endemic, and Mexicans' bean- and corn-based diet meant poor nutrition. On many haciendas, such as on Yucatán's henequen plantations, workers labored in chains and were flogged, living in conditions bordering on slavery.[4]

In the Porfiriato, landownership largely became the province of the affluent. Policies that allowed seizure of Church and communal properties subsequently fueled land speculation, as did railroad construction later. The poor lost much of what they had while the prosperous few accumulated larger estates. By 1910, 96.6 percent of Mexicans owned no land in an agricultural economy. A mere 840 hacendados controlled much of the nation's land.[5]

The clear winners in the Porfiriato were Díaz political insiders, Mexico's well-to-do, and foreign investors. Díaz policies openly preferred a miniscule well-heeled community to the overwhelmingly penurious Mexican population, foreigners to his own citizens, and those of European stock over the majority indigenous and mestizo population, like himself. His policies intentionally skewed the economic scales to produce a grotesque economic disparity, promoting the unlimited accumulation of capital by the already affluent at the expense of the struggling middle- and lower-economic rungs of society, with Chihuahua serving as a prime example of that strategy. Race, caste, and economic class largely determined who was preferred. In the military, mestizos held minor posts; the European caste acquired the most important concessions and positions. It was the same for judicial decisions that favored the affluent and landed over the poor. Hacendados had freedom in the treatment of their workers and had the rurales available to them to maintain security to control any unrest. The indigenous communities got the short end. They lost their properties to expropriation and were denied justice.[6] By 1910, over 90 percent of indigenous villages had lost their communal lands.[7]

The Porfiriato attracted and preferred foreign investors and immigrants. Its bias favored European and American investors and ideas as well as the "liberal" economics recommended to Díaz by his technocratic advisors, the Científicos. Between 1877 and 1884, Díaz granted forty rail concessions, almost all going to foreign firms. By 1911, American firms had built two-thirds of Mexico's 16,000 rail miles. U.S. companies had the largest share of Mexican mineral operations and owned 78 percent of mines, 72 percent of smelters, 58 percent of oil production, and 68 percent of the rubber interests. Firms from other nations usually held much of the balance, with Mexicans left as minority shareholders in their own country. For example, Mexicans only owned 2.6 percent of Mexican mine wealth and only 30 percent of the total investment in Mexico.[8] Some Díaz policymakers attracted American investment, thinking that policy would keep America from invading Mexico again.[9]

Díaz policies not only preferred foreign capital but also gave special treatment to foreign labor. Railroads managed by Americans often denied Mexicans employment on the assertion that locals were untrained or incompetent. Americans often received higher wages for doing the same work. In some places, Mexicans had no hope of becoming mechanics or brakemen on railroads, positions held exclusively by Americans. Those and other forms of discrimination led to the 1906 strikes at the Cananea, Sonora, mine and on the Mexican Central Railroad.[10]

The economic intent of the Juárez liberal reform laws was to create a yeoman farmer class with the bulk of the population owning land, sharing in the country's prosperity, and working for the nation's progress through their increased incentive as property owners. Díaz reversed the policy, enriching the already landed elite at the expense of small landholders, a strategy that drastically reduced the number of property owners. Porfirian land survey companies seized land from small landowners by declaring their properties vacant because they lacked clear title or because the land was owned in common or held in the name of a municipality. Científicos preferred private to communal landownership and encouraged the expropriation and sale of communal and government lands to private individuals and firms. The Lerdo and Juárez reform laws' intent was the forced sale of Church lands, but its sweeping language applied to all communal properties, thus, compelling not only the sale of Church lands but also of ejido, communal, and municipal lands.[11]

The contention that society gained from putting lands into production in large, well-financed, and well-managed haciendas was incorrect. The hacienda system, in fact, was not at all efficient, and as haciendas grew, Mexico became less self-sufficient in food production. In 1892–93, the nation imported six million pesos' worth of corn, whereas it imported twelve million pesos' worth in 1909. New Díaz laws permitted vast portions of haciendas to lie fallow, contrary to stated claims that they seized land to increase productivity. Rather than blame inefficient haciendas, Científicos held indigenous people responsible and called for more expropriation. Employers called in the army and rurales to impress more indigenous inhabitants into near-slavery conditions in mills and haciendas, workplaces rampant with abuses, such as *tiendas de raya*, company stores. Because they paid workers with company scrip honored only at their store, they forced workers to buy overpriced goods, a practice that also led to debt peonage. Those and other practices threw an estimated 9.5 million Mexicans into serfdom. Thus, Mexican purchasing power plunged during the Porfiriato.[12] Because of such harsh practices, unrest also took its toll. Records note some 250 strikes during the Porfiriato, especially between 1905 and 1907. Employers often called in federal troops and the rurales to end work stoppages.[13]

By the 1880s, Mexico had vast tracts of land to which no one held legal title, called "vacant lands." The government had inadvertently created them when it left gaps that were not included within land title descriptions. People came to occupy and work those lands even though no one held title. Legally, the government, never having conveyed the tracts, retained ownership to those lands. By 1880, they amounted to 100 million acres.

In addition to those vacant lands, the government also expropriated substantial properties from the Church, indigenous communities, and municipalities, parcels that were occupied and worked. Those occupied lands were declared vacant as well. In 1883, the government, then under Díaz's compadre and placeholder president, Manuel González, determined to put those lands into commerce by allowing the creation of survey companies to identify and survey all the vacant lands they found in their allotted territory. It compensated those firms by giving them one-third of the vacant lands they found, with the government retaining two-thirds. The survey companies searched for any lands owned in common by ejidos and municipalities, declared them "vacant," and filed claims against them. While many individuals lacked clear title to the lands, settler families had worked and lived on the properties for one hundred to two hundred years and considered them theirs. The Porfiriato, however, had other plans. In that manner, within ten years, the government declared vacant 125 million acres. The government sold about 26 million acres to private individuals for a pittance, allowing payment with discounted bonds with a nominal value, in some cases as low as one centavo per acre.[14] In Chihuahua, seven land barons received 35 million acres, and one firm with operations in several northern states received a concession of 12.5 million acres. In Mexico, seventeen individuals or families received 96 million acres or 150,000 square miles, about one-fifth of Mexico's territory, or a tract almost the size of California. In exchange, the national government received only 8 million pesos.[15]

By the end of the Porfiriato, landownership had become concentrated. In 1910, in the state of Chihuahua the nineteen largest haciendas each had over a quarter of a million acres or almost four hundred square miles, and twelve "smaller" haciendas had over 100,000 acres each. In contrast, 2,615 other minor proprietors had plots of only thirty-seven to fifty acres.[16] Accompanying the large grants was the eviction of thousands of Mexicans from their homes and properties, a task often handled violently by the rurales. The new owners were sometimes the areas' political elite, a practice helping to create landed, political aristocracies, clans, and individuals such as the Terrazas-Creel family in Chihuahua, the Torres-Isábal-Corral family in Sonora, Teodoro A. Dehesa in Veracruz, and Olegario Molina in Yucatán.[17] Political leaders such as those in Yucatán evicted residents and then kept the land for themselves. In one notorious 1890 case in the Papantla Valley of Veracruz, local rurales and political leaders evicted residents from their homes. Some of the evicted who resisted were murdered. One thousand rurales arrived to clear out the residents, leaving the valley deserted.[18]

The economic and industrial boom also planted the seeds of a future revolution. The newly built rail network transported Mexican workers to the United States, exposing many of them, especially northerners, to American wages, labor unions, and ideas such as socialism, anarchism, and land reform.[19] Many of the abuses listed above were economically counterproductive, especially in the North, where workers after 1884 could migrate and work for higher U.S. wages. Workers also migrated because they were landless and had little hope of ever owning property. Most land titles issued in the later Porfiriato were for tracts greater than 25,000 acres, a practice that created larger tracts and shortchanged smaller fry.[20] Thus, the number of larger haciendas increased from 5,700 in 1876 to more than 8,000 by 1910.[21] Lack of land was one reason why in 1907 thousands of Mexican workers immigrated through El Paso, constituting the loss of a significant part of Chihuahua's agricultural labor force. As bad as it was for Mexico to lose many of its most productive workers to the United States, the mass migrations were also an escape valve, reducing pressure and discontent at home. After the Panic of 1907 and the economic downturn it caused, many of the laid-off workers returned to Mexico, where there was also no work. They became a fertile recruiting ground for Flores Magón's Mexican Liberal Party after 1909 and 1910 and a consequential force during the Mexican Revolution.[22]

The loss of opportunity was not limited to the poor. Porfiriato land and labor policies also negatively affected the wealthy. In Sonora, Yaqui deportations to Yucatán reduced the hacienda labor supply as well, causing hacendados to oppose Díaz. Many young entrepreneurs also felt frozen out, and when they tried to join the Díaz gravy train, they were often denied admittance. The phrase became *carro completo*, the carriage is full. There was no room for them. Many also began to question the legitimacy of a corrupt government that rigged elections, repressed political opponents, and eliminated civil liberties.[23]

Díaz desired to bring in new immigrants to raise what he saw as Mexicans' low productivity. To attract them in 1883, the Porfiriato issued a decree reducing ejidos to a fourth of their previous size, again allowing land survey companies to identify, inventory, and sell the balance of those tracts. These lands included the northwestern military communities of Namiquipa, Casas Grandes, Janos, Galeana, and others.[24] At the same time that the Porfiriato was making thousands of Mexicans landless and making it difficult for Mexicans to acquire small parcels of land, and rather than selling land to new immigrants, the main beneficiaries were the already landed Mexican aristocracy, large American corporations, and prosperous individuals and families. Such families included the Hearsts, who, as absentee landowners, never saw most of the Mexican properties that they owned. Now that they had completed their role as a buffer and the Apaches were no longer a menace, hundreds of Serranos lost their land and homes. Among new immigrants to Mexico were members of the Church of Jesus Christ of Latter-day Saints (LDS), also called Mormons, who were looking for new settlement sites outside the United States. Survey companies, wealthy ranchers, and merchants in league with local officials seized Serranos' communal lands in the Galeana District, and, by 1885, Mormons were living on their former properties.[25]

In 1882, the U.S. Congress passed the Edmunds Act and made polygamy and bigamous cohabitation a federal felony. Seeking refuge for their polygamous families, Mormons viewed Mexico as a possible new home. Ignoring Mexico's own anti-bigamy laws and without consulting officials in Chihuahua, Mexico's federal government encouraged the immigration of hundreds of polygamous American Mormons by arranging for their purchase of former communal and municipal lands seized in surveys of Northwest Chihuahua highlands, mostly around Casas Grandes. When Chihuahua officials learned of the sale, they tried to expel the Mormons, but the national government rescinded the action. Over widespread opposition, American Mormons purchased 160,000 acres in Chihuahua. Mormons bought land declared vacant by the Valenzuela Survey Company under the 1883 decree that reduced Casas Grandes communal lands to 69,000 acres, a mere fourth of its previous size.[26] In 1893, Díaz gave the Mormons permission to open five new settlements, which significantly increased Mormon landownership.[27]

◪

Although by 1880 Mexican and U.S. army operations had reduced Apache bands to a fraction of their earlier strength and had significantly lessened the frequency of their raids, one leader, Victorio, the head of the Chihenne or Warm Springs band of the Chiricahuas, remained a danger. Determined to end the Apache threat, Chihuahua governor Luis Terrazas sent his cousin, the veteran Apache fighter Joaquín Terrazas, and his seasoned troops on the hunt for Victorio. In October 1880, Joaquín Terrazas surprised Victorio and his band at desolate Tres Castillos in the desert north of Chihuahua City, where they killed Victorio and decimated his band.[28] The only other band of any size was that of Juh and Geronimo, Chiricahuas of the Chokonen band, which had migrated to a Sierra Madre base from which it continued attacks on Sonora and Chihuahua ranches and scattered settlements. Aside from occasional raids by Geronimo and his small band in the mid-1880s, Victorio's defeat ended the principal Apache menace in Chihuahua. Once the threat ended, so did the value of the northwestern buffer zone fortified by the Serranos' Apache-fighting capacity. Lost along with that was the tacit protection the government had given Serranos from claims against their lands.

Many often describe Apache raids and attacks by Victorio and Geronimo as irrational and senseless violence, but they were far from it. Most Americans knew but ignored that the United States continually broke solemn treaties and agreements made with Native Americans. The facade of Indian treaties and agreements was one of several strategies used repeatedly by the United States to obtain control over Indian lands. Once Americans settled on those lands, they soon demanded more. The U.S. government openly broke agreements granting Indians reservation lands and then removed the Indians so that it could take those lands as well. The U.S. government systematically practiced what is known today as ethnic cleansing by forcibly removing and deporting the indigenous from one part of the nation to less populated areas and from one reservation to another, continually moving the Indians from their homelands or reservations to satisfy the white settlers' persistent land demands. To Native Americans, that was the way the United States won the American West.

In 1872, Geronimo's band, the Chokonen Chiricahua Apaches, ended a war in southern Arizona. The Chiricahuas, led by Cochise, agreed to peace in return for perpetual title to reservation lands located in Arizona's Dragoon Mountains, their homeland. They sealed the agreement with a personal emissary of President U. S. Grant and received a signed presidential executive order, a procedure that had the force of law. Three years later, agents of the Bureau of Indian Affairs disregarded the law and unilaterally terminated the Dragoon Mountain Reservation. They transferred the Chokonens to the unpopular San Carlos Reservation some two hundred miles north. In violation of the agreement and the executive order, the bureau had consolidated various Apache bands onto the San Carlos Reservation. While the Chiricahuas did not agree to the change, most did not resist and moved to the new reservation. Feeling betrayed, however, some, including Geronimo, fought instead of moving.[29]

■

In 1886, California appointed mining magnate George Hearst to the U.S. Senate to fill the seat vacated on the death of John F. Miller. One of the benefits of being a U.S. senator was being privy to inside government information. Hearst was in Washington between March and August of 1886, but by early September, having completed the session, he was back in California when, by being a senator, he received confidential information that Geronimo and his band had surrendered in Sonora and that the army was putting him away, securely this time, in Florida. The army kept the matter confidential until it had secured Geronimo and his fragment of a band in their new reservation quarters. Hearst had already determined that land in the Chihuahua highlands was worthless with the Apache menace present but valuable without it. He wasted no time in buying land on both sides of the U.S. border, hiring a Mexican lawyer in Chihuahua to negotiate the purchase of a ranch at San José de Babícora, unseen by Hearst, which at 900,000 acres dwarfed his large California San Simeon ranch[30] at 250,000 acres.[31] Luis Terrazas, leader of Chihuahua's oligarchy, owned the adjacent Hacienda de San Miguel de Babícora. If Hearst made the purchase before word got out about Geronimo's capture, the price would be low, less than four U.S. cents per acre, for fine grazing lands. The already low price would be lower if he paid in discounted bonds. Private gain from public office was a natural characteristic of being a U.S. senator in those days and one reason the Senate was loaded with millionaires, including Hearst and his fellow Californian Leland Stanford. They profited from inside information, supported laws favoring their specific investments, and could easily buy the offices by bribing corrupt state legislators.

In September 1886, Hearst lamented over his unproductive twenty-three-year-old son, William Randolph. That May, William had attempted to reenroll at Harvard, but the school denied him admission after having expelled him the previous term for his pranks. His mother had hopes of a solid academic career and perhaps a diplomatic post for his future, but William was doing nothing and going nowhere. Growing impatient, George decided to send William to Chihuahua to organize the purchase of his Mexican ranch and run it for several months. To Hearst's surprise, William enthusiastically accepted his offer, and in days the son was on his way to Chihuahua.

William boarded a train in New York and headed for El Paso, a border boomtown on the southern transcontinental rail line, a route completed only five years before. He arrived in September 1886, and from that location William began to learn about Chihuahua and the Babícora ranch, a property less than 120 miles south of the U.S. border. Years later, writer J. Frank Dobie visited Babícora and described the tract as a "rough rhomboid" seventy-five to eighty-five miles long and fifteen to twenty-five miles wide, adding, "There is no better grassland, grama grasses dominating, anywhere than this mile-or-more high plateau-basin. It is well watered by mountain streams and by lakes."[32]

From Chihuahua City in 1886, William enthusiastically wrote to his father, explaining how they would obtain the ranch because its current residents lacked good title: "There is not only the actual government land to be obtained but a lot of land which really belongs to the government but which is claimed without good title by the parties holding it. . . . I really don't see what is to prevent us from owning all Mexico and running it to suit ourselves." Young William also gave his father advice on his coming November election campaign in the California legislature: "Have you arranged it so you are sure to get elected? . . . Have you decided how many of these doubtful [districts] are essential and have you dispensed the lubricator where it will do the most *good*. Answer Paid."[33]

William did not need to tell his father that it only took cash bribes to a select number of state legislators to buy the office of U.S. senator.[34] A few months later, Babícora title in hand, William returned to the Hearst mansion in San Francisco. His father first offered him the permanent job of managing the Babícora ranch and then the one at San Simeon, but William declined both offers. William told his father that his ambition was to run his father's newspaper, the *San Francisco Examiner*. In January 1887, as expected, the California legislature elected the elder Hearst to a full term in the U.S. Senate, and in March George took his Senate seat. He immediately named William the publisher of the *San Francisco Examiner*. In 1897, after his father's death, William and his mother, Phoebe, then Babícora's owners, expanded the already large property. Other American firms also carved out large properties on former municipal or common lands on the scale of Hearst's, such as the Paloma Land and Cattle Company and the Corralitos Ranch.

The Hearst Ranch is sometimes credited with introducing Hereford cattle into Mexico. If Hearst's Babícora was not the first, it is possible that it was an adjacent ranch, but clearly, Hearst's was a pioneering cattle operation.[35] When it came to Chihuahua cattle operations of that time, however, there was only one name that mattered: Terrazas.

CHAPTER SIX

Terrazas and Creel, Premier Chihuahua Oligarchs

The legends surrounding General Luis Terrazas are many. One was that whenever he was asked if he was of Chihuahua, he would reply that, no, "Chihuahua is mine."[1] To some Chihuahuenses, Terrazas was not exaggerating, because the grip that the Terrazas clan had on Chihuahua politics and economics was overwhelming. All Chihuahua knows the story of Luis Terrazas, not only because he was once its wealthiest citizen and Mexico's largest landowner, but also because he and his family dominated Chihuahua for well over half a century. Terrazas forged close ties with Chihuahua's elites, who served as intermediaries with foreign capitalists. The general also formed alliances through the marriages of his fourteen children, a practice he started with his own marriage. Terrazas and Kentuckian Ruben Creel, the U.S. consul in Chihuahua, married Carolina and Paz Cuilty, sisters in a prominent Chihuahua family. Ruben Creel and Paz had a son, Enrique C. Creel, who married his first cousin Ángela, the daughter of Terrazas and Carolina. Enrique Creel was thus the general's nephew by marriage and his son-in-law. That was the start of the dynasty and empire.

Deciding whether Terrazas's wealth produced political power or whether it was the reverse is not a chicken-or-egg puzzle. Political power came first and was the fountain from which their great wealth flowed. Defenders of the Terrazas clan certainly preferred everyone to believe that the family's fortune had nothing to do with its decades-long hold on political power, but, of course, everyone understood that it had everything to do with it and was the reason why the family clung so tenaciously to power. Before he entered politics, Terrazas came from a family of modest means that ran a butcher shop.[2] Creel had a mercantile store.

Terrazas became governor in 1860[3] and was in office when Juárez began to implement the sale of immense Church properties, a pool of land and haciendas so large that it might have comprised half of the nation's territory.

Sale of Church lands was to be a federal process with proceeds to go to the federal government. Initially, Juárez and Terrazas wrestled over control and proceeds from Church land sales, when Terrazas, acting for the state, sold the federal lands and kept the revenues for Chihuahua. After the French invasion, Governor Terrazas and his troops backed Juárez, and, grateful for the support, Juárez for a time ignored Terrazas's sale of Church lands. The two became close political allies, and Juárez promoted Terrazas to the rank of general, a title Terrazas used the rest of his life.

Terrazas opposed Díaz in his attempt to overthrow Juárez. There was antagonism between Díaz and Terrazas after Díaz became president. Although they were at odds at times, Díaz allowed Terrazas to do what he wished in Chihuahua. Within the state, the Terrazas family had great power as Terrazas was the governor some of the time or had political allies in the post. Terrazas often controlled the legislature, the courts, and, through appointments, state agencies. Gradually, Enrique Creel became the general's right-hand man and rose in the ranks not only in the state hierarchy but also on the national level, something Terrazas had never attempted. In the 1890s, Creel joined the national government's Científico faction, reconciled Díaz and Terrazas, and returned Terrazas to the governor's seat in 1903 after he had been out for ten years.

On the national stage, Creel had significant posts under Díaz. He was the minister of foreign relations, one of the top three cabinet positions, and before that he was U.S. ambassador, the most important ambassadorial post, holding those national positions while he still controlled the state government by being on leave as its interim or elected constitutional governor. Terrazas and Enrique Creel were the men at the top, exercising control over a vast enterprise. Their local political control worked in tandem with the immense economic opportunities that Porfirian corruption offered to top-rank politicians.

No one could doubt Creel's financial and political acumen. Creel moved with ease among bankers in New York, Paris, and Mexico City. He sat on the Díaz commission that put Mexico on the gold standard. He was among a handful of men controlling Mexican politics and the economy. The arc of Creel's influence reached its height in October 1909, the time of an important border meeting between Díaz and U.S. president William Howard Taft. Creel, then Mexico's U.S. ambassador, acted as the sole interpreter for the meeting and was the only other person present when the two presidents met in a private session. Some assumed afterward that the aged Díaz was placing Creel in line to be Mexico's president when he appointed him minister of foreign relations. Creel became second in the line of succession after Vice President Ramón Corral, but Creel had one large obstacle, the nagging question of his citizenship, and there was also the constant criticism of his opponents, led by Silvestre Terrazas at *El Correo de Chihuahua*.[4]

As governors, Terrazas and Creel controlled public institutions, such as the military, the police, and the courts, especially after 1903. Creel ran the operations of the Mexican Secret Service when he was minister of foreign relations[5] and dogged the Liberal Party. Locally, they acted through political jefes to grant concessions and seize parcels of land. They also supervised the rurales in the state, keeping local activists in check, and they supervised most of the military operations in the state since, under Díaz, governors had quasi-military powers.[6] By 1904, Creel had indeed replaced his father-in-law as the supreme power in Chihuahua.

Land was the first step in the Terrazas clan's accumulation of wealth. After he became governor, Terrazas accumulated an empire in land and invested in many commercial, financial, and industrial firms. In land alone, historians estimate that Terrazas, individually, owned 6.6 million acres,[7] or 10,300 square miles. That's an area substantially larger than eight of Mexico's thirty-one states and the federal district, larger than a combined Rhode Island and Delaware or slightly smaller than the state of Connecticut. It would take seven properties the size of the fabled Texas King Ranch to equal the Terrazas spread, which grazed an estimated 500,000 head of cattle and 300,000 sheep. Terrazas was reputedly the "largest individual cattle owner in the world."[8] Terrazas operations branded an astounding 140,000 cattle annually.[9] Terrazas, together with his sons, Juan and Alberto, and his son-in-law, Enrique Creel, owned over 10 million acres. If you include related families such as the Falomirs, Lujáns, and Zuloagas, they controlled over 15 million acres of the best grazing land in Chihuahua.

A series of laws and conditions had converged to become a land bonanza for Chihuahua's oligarchy, especially for the Terrazas family. General Terrazas came to political power in the 1860s, just when huge tracts of Church properties and lands belonging to French collaborators became available, with many of those tracts falling into the oligarchy's hands. Next, in 1880, the scourge of Chiricahua Apache attacks mostly disappeared with the defeat of Victorio, and the value of land rose as a result. Rail, however, was the main factor pushing land speculation and the increase in land prices. In 1884, rail finally connected

Paso del Norte (Ciudad Juárez) and Mexico City and later Northwest Chihuahua to the border and Chihuahua City.[10] With rail, Díaz furthered his twin goals of political centralization and economic development through exports and foreign investment. Rail enabled Díaz to send his army quickly anywhere in the country and strengthen his control, as did telephone and telegraph, which reached most areas by the late 1880s.[11] Rail made possible large-scale industrial operations in mining, timber, and lumber mills, such as William C. Greene's Cananea copper mine and the Sierra Madre Land and Lumber Company. Rail ran through Terrazas ranches, allowing the wholesale export of cattle. In other parts of the nation, rail promoted export crops grown on large haciendas, such as sugar, cotton, rubber, henequen, and coffee. These crops replaced the corn, beans, and chiles grown by small-scale farmers, triggering even more land seizures and dispossession. Rail connection determined which communities would thrive and which would wither, such as in the Galeana District, which moved its seat from Galeana to Casas Grandes because of rail service.[12]

In addition to rail, Chihuahua's oligarchy benefited from laws mandating the registry of land titles and the use of survey companies. Many families had never held title to lands they had worked for generations, or they owned an unspecified share in communal or municipal lands after common lands fell into disfavor. Terrazas amassed colossal properties in a number of ways. He bought, expropriated, or confiscated properties at deeply discounted prices;[13] he foreclosed on usurious loan contracts and used survey companies to declare and seize vacant land.[14] Terrazas used the tools available to accumulate huge ranches. The oligarchy owned already large haciendas and then claimed contiguous tracts from possessors with doubtful or no title, or they would simply fence lands and force others to fight them in court. With survey companies, lawyers, and the courts under oligarchy control, a *peón* found fighting for his lands impossible. This was particularly the case because the system placed the burden of proof on the individuals in possession, who had to prove that they had title against the claimants, who merely asserted that there was no title on record.[15] In the end, the oligarchy controlled the rural police, who would evict the dispossessed.[16]

The Terrazas family fortune began with land and cattle and expanded to meatpacking.[17] Terrazas ranches grew their own feed and had Kansas feed lots to fatten their cattle for sale. Half of the cattle raised and meat consumed in Chihuahua came from Terrazas ranches and their large meatpacking plants.[18] Many of the ranches had good access to rail, facilitating their export operations. Included in their properties were vast agricultural tracts, yielding large harvests of wheat, corn, and cotton. To handle the crops, the family built the state's largest flour mill and later developed textile mills. The Terrazas family sold 70 percent of the flour consumed in Chihuahua. It had woolen and cotton mills to make textiles and clothing. It made and sold most of the state's work clothing and ran the state's only brewery. The family produced most of the sugar in the state solely from refining its own sugar beet crop.[19]

When he was in power, Terrazas mostly made his fortune through land; Creel was more creative and brought in additional revenue streams. Under Creel's influence, the pair centralized political power through appointed political jefes and controlled tax rates, tax exemptions, concessions, and subsidies. Governor Creel raised taxes on many of Chihuahua's middle- and lower-income residents,[20] while securing lower taxes for the clan's own operations. The extended family arranged a tax structure suited to its personal benefit and to the detriment of the popular classes, providing lower taxes for or exempting grazing lands, which were the bulk of the clan's landholdings, but taxing the cultivated land that predominated among small landholders. Even then, the clan undervalued its properties to reduce its already low taxes.[21]

Under the clan's influence, the state granted the Terrazas-Creel family several subsidies and many concessions exempting its firms from state taxes between 1881 and 1910. Creel received a 685,000-peso subsidy[22] to build the rail line to Santa Eulalia and 600,000 pesos for the Chihuahua al Pacífico line.[23] Terrazas and Creel also received tax exemptions for many of their miscellaneous operations, including their telephone company, a stearin candle factory, an iron and steel plant, a pawn shop, a brewery, a sugar refinery, a meatpacking plant, the Ciudad Juárez streetcars, an iron and copper plant, a life insurance company, a metal smelter, a rail line, a serape factory, an ice plant, and a cookie factory, among others. Luis Terrazas also obtained state and municipal tax exemptions for several of his own Chihuahua City rental homes.[24]

Creel brought the finance and banking dimension into the clan's business activities. He established what became the largest bank in Chihuahua and the fourth largest in Mexico, the Banco Minero de Chihuahua. The clan had banking operations in many parts of Mexico. Creel founded two banks in Mexico City, Banco Central Mexicano and a mortgage bank. The Banco Central grew to be the nation's second largest. He was an investor in the Guaranty and Trust in El Paso, Texas. In Chihuahua, the Banco Minero did better than most because, as the clan controlled state government, it had the state's depository account and financed the state's debt and construction projects.

Creel and the clan had control over Chihuahua's credit market. Through his banking activities, Creel was second only to Finance Minister Limantour in the influence he exercised in national and international banking circles.[25]

Because the clan also controlled the state and its tax exemptions, all of Creel's banks in Chihuahua were exempt from state taxes.[26] The clan had the compliant legislature pass a law giving Chihuahua the right to charter banks, institutions that had the right to issue currency. Chihuahua was thus the sole state to issue charters. The extended family was the recipient of several bank charters that it had issued.

The Terrazas-Creel clan invested huge amounts in Chihuahua mining operations. Forty percent of miners in Chihuahua worked for the clan.[27] With more than 13,000 employees, the clan was the largest employer in the state, five times larger than the American Smelting and Refining Company (ASARCO) plants, which was a distant number two.

The family members, to be expected, were also the state's big players in rail, public transit, and public utilities. Enrique Creel sat on the board of directors of Mexican National Railways, a position paying him an annual fee of 50,000 pesos ($25,000, or more than $550,000 in 2014 dollars).[28] Creel founded the Chihuahua al Pacífico Railway to connect the Kansas City line to the Pacific, and by 1910 the line had reached the east side of the Sierra Madre. Creel sat on the board of the Kansas City, Mexico and Orient Railway. With the help of a state subsidy, he also built the Ferrocarril Mineral de Chihuahua, a spur connecting the Santa Eulalia mining center with the central Mexican rail line. The clan owned a metal foundry and the factory to make rails. Terrazas had electric trolley monopolies in Chihuahua City, Ciudad Juárez, and Parral[29] and owned the electric utility and the Chihuahua City telephone company.

The clan had oil interests in Chihuahua, but those were minor operations and not particularly fruitful. Its main petroleum interests and activities were on Creel's part. Creel, along with a handful of Científico insiders, received shares and board seats in Weetman Pearson's El Aguila Oil Company, Mexico's largest oil company, which controlled 60 percent of Mexico's petroleum market.[30] Creel not only served on the board but also became its president. He was also a large stockholder in the Compañía Petrolera del Pacífico.[31]

Many Terrazas properties and operations had company stores. One of the clearest examples of graft involved the case of the company store at the new ASARCO smelter at Avalos, just outside Chihuahua City. In April 1905, the Creel gubernatorial administration granted ASARCO a concession exempting the firm from state and municipal taxes for twenty years, a massive benefit to its Guggenheim owners. In return for the concession, ASARCO turned over the lucrative company store's management to Juan Terrazas Cuilty, a son of General Terrazas and Governor Creel's cousin, brother-in-law, and close business partner.[32]

In the Creel gubernatorial administration, Juan Terrazas received concessions for seven metallurgical plants and a cement plant in Ciudad Juárez, operations that were the precursors of today's large Terrazas-owned firms. Alberto Terrazas received concessions for railroads, gas, and hydroelectric plants.[33]

Already mentioned in passing above were the miscellaneous firms in the clan's portfolio, which included land survey companies; commission brokerage agencies; insurance companies (life and casualty); dynamite, cottonseed, and glycerin plants; coal and carbon outlets; home construction firms; timber lands; lumber milling operations; cement plants; and a broom factory, shoe factory, ice plant, glass factory, soap factory, candle factory, and cookie bakery. Creel and Terrazas were also the largest owners of urban properties in Chihuahua. They owned "hundreds" of buildings in Chihuahua in various towns.[34]

The land and investments noted, however, were only part of the picture, as the clan had vast, varied interests and held stock in any number of foreign firms holding concessions to operate in the state, many of which the Terrazas clan had granted while in power. Taking a piece of the action for no investment was what made concessions such a good deal for those in power. As expansive as were the ambitions of the general, and as much as the family owned, it was not enough, especially for Enrique Creel, a man who had national and international interests, but still had his eye on the Serranos' land. Creel exemplified the nature of an oligarchy in its similarity to a corporation: both lived to maximize profits and increase their wealth, and the notion of having too much wealth was alien to both.

Many Serranos viewed General Terrazas favorably before 1904. In earlier times, Serranos were grateful to Terrazas for having supported Benito Juárez, for having opposed the American and French invasions, for having helped them fight the Apaches, and for having been their occasional ally in resisting land grabs by hacendados. By the time Enrique Creel became governor in 1904, however, that gratitude had faded into distrust and dislike. They knew that Terrazas converted his support for Benito Juárez into a bonanza for himself, a classic case of unintended consequences for reforms designed to help poor and middle-class Mexicans but that mostly benefited the oligarchy.

After 1903, Terrazas and Creel clan were also in control of the rurales and all appointed jefes políticos in the state. Little happened without their knowledge or approval. Conditions under Creel, already bad, became worse for Serranos because many of them had been exempt from taxes until that time. Now, not only did they have to pay taxes, but Creel shifted most of the tax burden onto working people and their property while largely exempting wealth and the wealthy.

Corruption, already a staple in Porfirian Chihuahua, broadened and became more open under Creel where the political jefes, with Creel's support, joined the landed elite in expropriating Serrano properties. The *New York Times* explained the impact of those land grabs.

> Under land laws such as these families now have lived for genera-
> tions on their ranches, but who, when it came to a question of title
> deeds, could only point to the graves of their forefathers, have
> awakened to find that by due process of law their lands have been
> declared vacant, have been acquired from the national govern-
> ment by strangers, and that not only was there no chance of their
> securing their own again, but that they were liable for prosecution,
> and frequently were prosecuted for squatting on their own lands.[35]

Thus, mere months after the start of Creel's term, the discontent among Serranos became acute. The elite, the political jefes and the survey companies had been seizing land since the mid-1880s with no large-scale rebellion. Creel went after municipal lands, employing survey companies to seize individual properties as well as communal lands. By 1909, other events combined to make conditions unbearable for many Serranos. Creel's oppressive 1904 legislation increased taxes on the middle class. For example, the laws taxed working animals but exempted grazing herds. In property taxes, grazing or forested land paid five centavos per hectare compared to irrigated land at seventy-five centavos. Small landholdings tended to be cultivated, whereas the oligarchy's principal properties were large haciendas consisting mainly of grazing lands.[36] Even when paying at lower rates, the oligarchy defrauded the state. After he took office in 1911, Governor Abraham González learned that Terrazas and Creel had undervalued their properties, including one pegged by Terrazas at 800,000 pesos, when it was worth 5 million pesos.[37] The oligarchy, moreover, often did not pay the already low assessed taxes. The inequitable land taxes were the source of great discontent.[38] The wealthy, such as Terrazas, paid almost nothing in the first place, undervalued what they claimed, and often neglected to pay what they owed.[39]

Creel's policies generated an intense reaction from many Serranos. There were the brutal actions of the rurales and the corrupt, high-handed policies of the local political jefes. The jefes controlled all local government and were appointed by and answered directly to Creel. Finally, there was Creel's Municipal Land Law of 1905, one of the laws he enacted soon after he became governor. The law obligated municipalities, especially those in the Northwest that owned large communal lands given to them in colonial times, to sell those tracts to private parties. Those municipally owned lands were communal lands worked by resident families for generations. With this law, speculators and surveyors could claim grazing land, homes, and home lots. Those grazing lands were an important source of revenue to individual Serranos. Serranos who fought Creel's 1905 law became leaders in the Revolution of 1910.[40] Creel had a personal stake as an owner of a survey company and as a major landowner himself. With Creel as governor, Terrazas no longer protected Northwest landowners from survey companies or those claiming vacant or untitled lands. Thus, by 1900, most Northwest pueblos had lost their communal lands to surveyors. Casas Grandes had its communal lands intact in 1904, but by 1910 all that property and been seized and was sold to individuals or to corporations.[41]

While Terrazas, at least initially, backed the Serranos in defending their lands against hacendado land claims, Creel's sympathies were the reverse. Unlike Terrazas, Creel had no reservoir of trust with Serranos in 1904 when, only a year into his four-year term, the general handed the governorship to his nephew/son-in-law.

Terrazas was not the enlightened hacendado Madero proved to be, and the Terrazas clan had no commitment to the betterment of its employees. Clan members harbored no illusions that they were loved by their workers, for whom they ran the much-criticized company stores and for whose children they provided no schools. When considering whether he should arm his employees to protect his properties during the revolution, Terrazas opted not to distribute weapons, admitting that if he were to do so, his own peons would quickly join rebel forces and turn the weapons on him.[42]

In the latter part of the last gubernatorial terms of Terrazas and Creel, the state's debt tripled, mainly due to new infrastructure investments made by Creel. When Díaz summarily removed Governor Alberto Terrazas in January

1911, Alberto handed the state with an empty treasury to incoming governor Miguel Ahumada. The treasury had debt of 2.9 million pesos with cash on hand of only 1,725 pesos, which was less than 1,000 dollars. Of the 2.9 million pesos of outstanding debt, the state owed over 500,000 pesos to Creel's bank, Banco Minero de Chihuahua, and the state had borrowed more than 500,000 pesos[43] to give subsidies to Creel's rail construction projects. Much of the debt's balance was attributable to projects involving Creel's personal investments, such as rail and streetcars in Chihuahua, Ciudad Juárez, and Parral.[44] To cover the mounting debt, Creel raised taxes, but placed the load on the middle- and lower-economic classes.[45] Those policies and practices made Chihuahua much more open to the growing anti-Díaz, anti-Creel insurgent forces.

Terrazas and Creel certainly had their defenders—for example, José Fuentes Mares, who vehemently insisted that the Terrazas-Creel clan had come into its wealth by honest means and not through public office.[46] The records, however, told another story, according to historian Francisco R. Almada in his minutely documented books, *Juárez y Terrazas* and *Gobernadores del Estado de Chihuahua*.[47] Almada established Terrazas's start in 1862 with only 19,500 pesos in property that grew to a fortune of 100 million pesos.[48] Almada chronicled in his books what U.S. consul Marion Letcher had an opportunity to observe in the clan's operations. Letcher described how Terrazas, because of his power, purchased huge properties "for a song" and avoided paying taxes on his vast estate. Letcher dispatched a memo to the State Department:

> Backed by the prestige gained in expelling the French, and aided by his large land holdings, Terrazas built up in the course of time a dynasty in the State, and all its offices, from that of chief executive down, were held by the Terrazas family or such as the Terrazas family might find it to its interest to let be named.
>
> The Terrazas exploited the state tremendously. This seems to have been especially true during the governorship of Mr. Creel. It was hard for a concession to be gained without the influence of some member of the family; courts were absolutely dominated; a lawyer could not be induced to take a case in which one of the Terrazas family was a party. Owning nearly one-third of the State in respect to its superficial area, a very fair proportion of its total wealth, the taxes paid by the family were insignificant.[49]

In sum, there was little you could do in Chihuahua that did not involve buying or using the clan's products or services, including governmental services
that it monopolized. You could not eat, dress, travel, transport, fuel, wash,
cement, build, cool, heat, light, electrify, dynamite, insure, borrow, bank,
or sweep the floor without involving them, and woe to you if you thought
of competing against the clan. For those who opposed, there would be no
government services, advice, help or subsidies, concessions of tax exemption,
credit, or fair judicial treatment. Their power was pervasive and suffocating.
By extension, that power was felt on the local level, where it was wielded in
the same arbitrary and ruthless manner in all corners of the state by clan
surrogates, such as Joaquín Chávez, the rural police jefe in San Isidro. If you
needed something, you were forced to go to the clan or their appointed jefes
on bended knee.[50] Serranos deeply resented the clan and were running out
of patience.

PART II

The Revolution

CHAPTER SEVEN

Díaz Opposition Forms

The Liberal Party and Madero

There were several Mexican revolutionary organizations, but few rivaled the one created by Ricardo Flores Magón, which provided a significant ideological base for the revolution. Started in 1901 with a newspaper, *Regeneración*, it was one of the first movements to call for the armed overthrow of the Díaz régime. The brainchild of Ricardo and his brother Enrique, the Mexican Liberal Party (PLM), whose followers were called Magonistas, attracted an unlikely mix to its cause. Its platform was a framework of labor and land reforms with appeal to industrial workers, miners, farmers, and ranchers of the highlands as well as to those who had lost their lands or whose lands were threatened. The PLM's 1906 proposals, the most comprehensive for the revolution, called for reform of the military, no reelection, improved public education, more control over the Church and clergy, a more equitable tax system, a minimum wage, a shorter work day, abolition of child labor, and comprehensive land reform to benefit the poor and landless.

The Liberal Party was particularly active in Northwest Chihuahua, where it had a large following and occasionally took control of some municipalities, including Casas Grandes, Janos, and Namiquipa.[1] Wherever there were Mexicans who had worked in U.S. mines, the PLM was likely to be strong given the close ties between the party and U.S. unions, such as the Industrial Workers of the World and the Western Federation of Miners.

The Mexican and American governments considered the PLM to be a radical, revolutionary group and treated it distinctively from Madero's revolutionary forces. The PLM was, indeed, far more radical and insistent on armed and social revolution than was Madero. The Mexican secret service, under Enrique Creel, as well as U.S. security agencies, had Magonistas under constant surveillance and broke up several of their plots on both sides of the border. The Magonistas were first to call for a national uprising against Díaz, and in response Díaz and Creel agents worked with the United States to arrest a number of their group in El Paso in October 1906, before they could cross into Mexico,[2] and took several into custody after they had crossed into Ciudad Juárez, although Ricardo Flores Magón eluded capture.[3] Creel had his political jefes on alert, instructing them to monitor what people were reading and investigate the reason for travel to the border. Anyone reading the Magonista newspaper *Regeneración* was suspect. In the fall of 1906, Creel ordered the arrest of several individuals who had not committed any crime other than maintaining ties to the Liberal Party.[4]

Although the United States allowed Madero to buy and export weapons for his rebellion, it did not permit the Liberal Party to do the same. As their movement matured, the Magonistas increasingly occupied the left wing of the revolutionary movements but failed to generate the broad support needed to ignite their call for revolution. There is, however, no doubt about the fact that they were the first to propose an armed revolution[5] and to organize against Díaz in the Northwest. Despite the PLM's efforts to remove Díaz, the spark for Mexico's 1910 electoral fever was not the Liberal Party's revolutionary movement but rather a Díaz interview by an American journalist.

In mid-February 1908, American journalist James Creelman traveled to Mexico City to interview President Porfirio Díaz for *Pearson's Magazine*. Creelman arrived well prepared. President Theodore Roosevelt had recommended him; Enrique Creel had encouraged the interview, and the U.S. ambassador made the introduction.[6] The interview took place in an ornate salon on the top floor of the hilltop Chapultepec Castle, the official presidential residence. Díaz was in his thirty-first year as president, an office seen by most Mexicans as his for life. The setting impressed Creelman. The castle had once been a military academy, and Emperors Maximilian and Carlota had completely refurbished the building in French Empire style. The paneled, wainscoted walls were covered in red fabric, the floors were French parquet, and the rooms furnished with Louis XIV–period carved and gilded pieces. Díaz, dressed in his medal-laden military uniform, met Creelman. The journalist noted Díaz's military posture and confident, but not cocky, manner. The old president led the journalist outside for a stroll on the roof garden and then to the checkerboard marble-floored terrace, a place that guaranteed a spectacular view of the city. Viewing the city below, Díaz noted the advances Mexico had made under his leadership. He had made substantial improvements to the cityscape that unfolded before them along Maximilian's impressive Champs-Élysées–style, tree-lined boulevard renamed by Juárez as Paseo de la Reforma. It went from the Alameda, a beautiful park at the entrance to the city's historic center district, to the foot of Chapultepec's hill.

Creelman's article was hagiographic, a puff piece, but, in fairness to the journalist, it conformed to the style of the day. The article's headline read, "Thrilling Story of President Díaz, the Greatest Man on the Continent, Visited and Described by James Creelman." Creelman wrote,

> I, who had come nearly four thousand miles from New York to see the master and hero of modern Mexico . . . watched the slender, erect form, the strong, soldierly head commanding, but sensitive, countenance with an interest beyond words to express. . . . Such is Porfirio Díaz, the foremost man of the American hemisphere. What he has done, almost alone and in such a few years, for a people disorganized and degraded by war, lawlessness and comic opera politics, is the great inspiration of Pan-Americanism, the hope of the Latin-American republics.[7]

Díaz and Creelman continued the interview, when, with no warning and in an offhanded manner, Díaz said, "No matter what my friends and supporters say, I retire when my present term of office ends, and I shall not serve again. I shall be eighty years old then. . . . It is enough for me that I have seen Mexico rise among the peaceful and useful nations. I have no desire to continue in the Presidency. This nation is ready for her ultimate life of freedom."

When published in March, Creelman's article was sensational and caused a political earthquake in Mexico. It was not the first time Díaz had mentioned retirement, but perhaps, given his age and his earlier promise to quit in 1910, it rang true for a change. Years of pent-up frustration and demands for democracy, fair elections, and open candidacy exploded into the open.

As soon as Díaz announced his retirement, his Científico advisors and supporters, sensing that they would be losers in a new régime, once again rushed in to convince the old dictator that Mexico could not survive and would again plunge into chaos without his leadership. It was an election ploy Díaz had used before to get around his no reelection pledge, his well-worn rendition of Louis XV's warning of bedlam, "After me the flood." On May 30, 1908, two and a half months after he told Creelman that he would be retiring, Díaz announced his candidacy for another term in 1910. This time, when Díaz announced that he was running again, there was no going back. The country may or may not have been ready for democracy, but several individuals immediately showed interest in promoting candidates for the presidency, including a studious and earnest farmer-rancher from the northern state of Coahuila, Francisco Ignacio Madero, recently involved in forming the Anti-Reelection Party and author of an anti-reelection book.

Francisco I. Madero was born in 1873, the year after Juárez died in the presidency, and he was only four years old when Díaz first took office. He was the eldest of fifteen children born to his parents Francisco Madero[8] and his wife, Mercedes González. By the time of Francisco's birth, the family enjoyed great wealth, a fortune started by his grandfather and family patriarch Evaristo Madero, who began as a muleteer and became one of Mexico's ten wealthiest men. The family had a broad range of financial interests, including an oil company, cattle ranches, cotton fields, iron mines and smelters, metal processing facilities, the Bank of Nuevo León, sugar cane and rubber plantations, textile mills, coal mines, flour mills, timber properties, distilleries, and vineyards.[9] The Maderos had deep, long-standing ties to Mexico's financial institutions and elite and were part of the nation's top rank with close ties to Díaz and the Científicos. Evaristo Madero had served a term as Coahuila's governor from 1880 to 1884 and was a close friend of Treasury Secretary José Ives Limantour.[10]

Educated in Mexico, the United States, and France, Francisco returned to his family's Coahuila ranches, where he developed into a progressive, innovative, and successful rancher and cotton farmer, occupations he pursued for sixteen years until 1903, when he saw police violently crush a peaceful political demonstration opposing powerful Nuevo León governor Bernardo Reyes. Madero, steeped in democratic principles and ideas from his education abroad, vowed to fight for democracy by forming the Benito Juárez Democratic Club in his Coahuila hometown. His stay in France also exposed him to other ideas, such as spiritism,[11] Eastern religions, and other beliefs that made his views unorthodox in northern Mexico. He was also a teetotaler and a vegetarian, an oddity in a family that owned vineyards, distilleries and cattle ranches.[12] There was a lot about Madero that fit no mold.

Months before the Creelman article, Madero worked to organize forces against reelection, especially opposing the prospect that Sonoran vice president Ramón Corral might be on the ticket again or might run for the presidency. Díaz's advanced age made a non-Científico Corral presidency likely. Although Madero called himself a fervent anti-reelection disciple, he, along with many in Chihuahua, was open to another term for Díaz so long as Corral was gone.

Corral had become controversial and was blamed for several of the excesses of the Díaz régime, including Yaqui mistreatment and their forced deportation. In the months after the Creelman interview, Madero wrote an important book, *The Presidential Succession in 1910*, a publication that elevated him to the leadership in Mexico's anti-reelection movement. In May 1909, he proceeded with others to form the Anti-Reelection Party and ran a national campaign to recruit candidates for the 1910 election under the slogan "effective suffrage, no reelection."

Meanwhile in Chihuahua, forces combined to create a toxic brew for the Porfiriato. The hardy, independent people of the Northwest were seething with anger over their condition, which had deteriorated over the years. Yet, time after time, despite all their problems, they did not revolt. It was hard to understand how a handful of elite in the oligarchy could hurt such an independent and forceful people unless one examined the shocking wealth and economic and political control that oligarchs such as Terrazas and Creel had amassed. An example of one community that had felt the force of the clan's power was the former military municipality of Namiquipa.

CHAPTER EIGHT

Namiquipa and Northwest Chihuahua

Between 1907 and 1910, much of Chihuahua's Northwest grew into a hotbed of discontent, and this was especially true in Namiquipa. Namiquipa was the same as other northwestern military settlements founded by the Spanish to thwart the Apaches with large municipal and communal land grants. Namiquipa developed several socioeconomic classes: the mostly absent hacendados who owned the cattle ranches; the resident, well-to-do ranchers who had operations large enough to sustain their families; and the more numerous small operators who lived in their ancestral town homes, farmed small, irrigated agricultural plots, and had grazed their cattle for generations on what they considered their communal lands. For the latter group, most of their home lots and irrigated plots were on communal or municipal lands, the same as the communal grazing lands. Their small plots did not sustain the family; rather, they supplemented their primary family income brought in by outside work as muleteers, carpenters, ranch hands, or miners in Mexico or the United States. This group started the migration pattern that continued for generations, providing the United States agricultural and industrial labor.[1]

Before the railroads arrived, towns of the Northwest, such as Casas Grandes, Namiquipa, and Guerrero, supplied provisions, services, and transportation to the sierra and the region, as well as to towns and mines in New Mexico Territory, including Deming, Las Cruces, and Santa Rita. Each sierra community organized a semiannual caravan to sell what it had grown and made. The caravan travelers provided their own security en route, a trek that often took three to four weeks. In meat and agricultural products, they were vertically integrated, being growers, transporters, and traders. They raised the cattle and crops, such as wheat, corn, chiles, and lentils; harvested them; processed them; transported and sold them. The travelers were traders and transporters accustomed to living on the road with their *trocas de mulas*, mule-drawn wagons. Those on caravans lived on dried meat, potatoes, beans, chiles, coffee, and pinole. After rail arrived in Chihuahua in 1884, they took the shipments east to the Villa Ahumada station.[2]

Namiquipa's residents appeared content with their way of life. They had their farms and ranches. For long periods, many of the men worked in the mines, lumber mills, or larger ranches, often leaving the women alone to handle farming and ranching chores. Family life and routine varied depending on the time of year and the productivity of their small farms. Several developments years earlier, however, had complicated the lives of small northwestern ranchers. For generations, they had run their cattle on open, common grazing land, but after 1883, the law forced municipalities to sell those lands to private parties. By 1898, more than 96 percent of the common land in Namiquipa's district had been expropriated from the community and sold to private owners.[3] Even then, however, in a mutually beneficial practice followed by Luis Terrazas on his ranches, the large ranchers still allowed the small operators to graze their herds on their large pastures in return for labor and security. That all changed around 1897, when barbed wire made fencing inexpensive, permitting the large operators to enclose their lands, denying access to the small ranchers, and thus severely reducing the number of cattle they could graze. On Terrazas's lands, the change occurred abruptly when Terrazas handed ranch management over to his son Alberto, who instituted practices he had studied in the United States.[4]

Fencing land was one reason why General Terrazas lost the goodwill and respect he had experienced in the Northwest. Loss of common grazing lands left the small ranchers only their homes and irrigated family plots. More than ever, they relied on salaried work outside their properties to subsist. These men were often *hacetodos*, jacks-of-all-trades, providing skilled labor to ranches, towns, mines, and firms in the area. Each year, many men from Namiquipa left home to work in the mines nearby in Chihuahua and Sonora, or in Arizona and New Mexico Territories. They preferred working on nearby farms and ranches, but those daily wages were too low at seventy-five centavos, including their meals. Mine work in Chihuahua paid more than double that at 1.75 pesos per day, or 2.50 pesos in the U.S., including room and board, a wage differential that attracted many Mexicans to U.S. mines and smelters, especially during the 1901–1907 boom.[5] Those higher wages allowed them to make a decent living when supplemented with income from their irrigated farms. Events after 1907, however, caused that unstable house of cards to crumble.[6]

Mexicans working in the United States picked up more than wages for their work. They also absorbed ideas and local culture. Many northern Mexicans soon dressed like U.S. ranchers, wearing khaki and denim pants, wide leather belts, flannel shirts, western boots and sporting Stetsons rather than pointed-crown, wide-brimmed sombreros.[7] After working a few years in U.S. mines, many grew sympathetic to labor unions, such as the Western Federation of Miners, the Industrial Workers of the World ("Wobblies"), and the PLM, the left-leaning, anti-Díaz, pro-labor party. Some Mexican miners were both union men and members of PLM clubs they established. Many of their relatives and friends worked at the American-owned copper mine at Cananea, Sonora, the scene of a 1906 PLM-led strike. Their ties with the Liberal Party grew stronger as threats of seizure against their lands increased. Chihuahua's Northwest became a PLM stronghold, and the party designated the Galeana District and Casas Grandes as one of its central bases. The PLM had been active in the area since 1905 and produced some of the revolution's important leadership.[8] Their fellow Serranos joined or supported the PLM and its plan and created an unusual political union, because many of these workers were both vaqueros and industrial workers. For those who were ranchers, anyone against the Díaz and Creel land policies was an ally. It was a real, if incongruous, mix. The same man who was a cowboy and ranch hand part of the year was at other times a left-wing union, pick-and-shovel hard rock miner. A well-known example of such a rancher-miner was José Inés Salazar from Casas Grandes. Salazar was a member of Magón's Liberal Party and fought in some of its early engagements. He was also at the 1906 Cananea Copper strike and became a principal Orozco military leader.[9]

For these northwestern families, supplemental wages from outside work, such as mining, allowed many small landowners to get by. So long as they found good salaried work, families could make do, even with the loss of grazing land. Their balanced family revenues, however, fell dramatically with the combined effect of the Panic of 1907, drought, early freeze, and Creel's policies and legislation.

Luis Terrazas retired in 1904, and in his place in the governorship, Serranos now had Creel, his banker and Científico son-in-law. Creel was already one of the largest landholders in Chihuahua, but he aggressively pushed for more Serrano land seizures. Creel forcefully backed the questionable claims of *latifundista* Enrique Müller that the free, military villagers of Namiquipa were squatters wrongfully occupying his lands. Creel backed similar claims in other northwestern communities. When Terrazas retired and handed Creel control over the Chihuahua government, times changed for the people of the Northwest. Creel wasted no time once he became governor. A new Creel law eliminated elected mayors and placed local power in new jefes políticos appointed directly by the governor and under the governor's direct control, rendering futile appeals to local officials. The elected officials of the past had long been the first line of defense for Serranos in trying to keep others from seizing their land. Those whose lands had claims against them first appealed to their local elected officials, including the mayors. Creel eliminated that support by making those officials subservient to local appointed political jefes.

Claiming that he wanted to fix what he saw as a chaotic land title system and the lack of a proper property tax roll, under Creel's direction, the legislature enacted the Municipal Land Law of 1905. It required municipalities to subdivide, replat, and sell their communal lands, including residential lots, homes, and small, irrigated plots. The residential town lots included orchards, vegetable gardens, and areas for domestic farm animals. The municipality would issue new titles for the properties.[10] It was an expensive process for those of limited means and pitted them against those with resources and lawyers.[11] Creel demanded recognition of Müller's and other claims and ordered that the occupants vacate the properties. Residents of Namiquipa protested in 1908, 120 of whom signed a letter to Porfirio Díaz stating, "The government of this state has shown its contempt for us by stealing our lands, our pastures, and our woods, which we need in order to practice agriculture and livestock raising."[12] The elite filed similar claims for adjudication throughout the state, but were most active in the Northwest, especially in the Galeana District, which was also a national center for the PLM.

Namiquipa residents called on Díaz to keep the promise that he had made to them in 1889 to support their title to the property. They held demonstrations, protested the state's actions, and regularly wrote letters published in *El Correo*, a reaction Creel called "monstrous." Díaz was going to investigate complaints against the Terrazas-Creel clan, but Creel convinced him to forget the matter, telling Díaz that those complaining were malcontents and socialists. Díaz would later rue ignoring those complaints, as many who would later remove him from office were those "whose farms he had allowed to be stolen away from them."[13] There were similar scenes in Janos and other military communities. In Janos, Creel cut off the community's water supply.[14] Ironically, as bad as Díaz was, many in the Northwest looked to him for protection from Creel once Luis Terrazas was out of the picture.[15] For them, Creel had become the face of Porfiriato abuses.

A Chihuahua City land survey company along with Creel's appointed Namiquipa jefe, Victoriano Torres, made claims against Namiquipa homes and farms, and the people had no resources to resist.[16] Soon after the claims were filed, they evicted residents from the homes and land their families had owned and worked for over a century. Residents had only fifteen days to protest a claim, and they often lacked the resources to do so. Even if they had the funds to hire attorneys, the deck was stacked against them since the political jefe and the administration were against them and the oligarchy controlled the courts.[17] To many Serranos, this turning point was the end of life as they had known it. The same thing was happening to thousands across Mexico.

A drought in 1907 and 1908 and then an early freeze in 1909 devastated Serrano agriculture, but worse was the depression of 1907. It began with the U.S. panic and crash with commodity prices falling dramatically, causing the closure of U.S. and Mexican mines and smelters, putting thousands of migrant Mexican laborers out of work. When migrant laborers returned home to Chihuahua, there was no work there either, and the weather had ruined their harvest. Although people tolerated the cost of Creel's policies before 1907, the combined effect of those policies plus depression, then drought, and then losing their land was too much. Adding to the unrest was the information uniting the disaffected through the activities of PLM Magonistas, through Liberal Party newspapers and others, such as *El Correo de Chihuahua*, the Chihuahua daily, and later with *El Grito del Pueblo*, the insurgent Anti-Reelection Party newspaper. All that activity helped to create an anti-Díaz, anti-reelection fervor, with the principal focus being on Enrique C. Creel.

The oligarchy had assembled those huge ranches at the expense of many who had previously been members of the middle class or part of what had been a comfortable, working-class group that had now been thrown off its customary, self-sufficient perch into abject poverty and dependence. Resentment became a fact of life in the Northwest. The people of San Isidro had long felt diminished by their fellow Serranos from Ciudad Guerrero, a mere four miles away. They felt that folks from Guerrero looked down on them as country folk. The people of the Northwest felt the same way toward those from Chihuahua, the big town, the capital. Northwesterners were inclined by their resentment to follow their own path. That independence made the region a fertile ground for revolution and for being open to another religion.

CHAPTER NINE

The Orozco Family, Chihuahua Protestants

Members of the Orozco family serving in military posts had arrived in the Northwest by 1710. Capitán Andrés Orozco y Villaseñor served as the Papigochi-area deputy under the mayor of Cusihuiriáchi.[1] Tomás Orozco y Villaseñor had served as Papigochi's deputy mayor and captain of the militia in 1772,[2] and his son, José Roque Orozco y Villaseñor, later held the post.[3] In 1765, José Roque married María Antonia Domínguez de Mendoza, granddaughter of Juan Mateo Domínguez de Mendoza, who was among the earliest Spanish settlers in the area.

The crown had expelled the Jesuits in 1767, and their San Isidro lands were passed on to the local indigenous inhabitants, but they too abandoned the property, fleeing from Apache raids. In time, along with others, including the Caraveo, Frías, and Abitia families, the Orozcos moved onto the former Jesuit lands around San Isidro. They continued to live on the lands without the benefit of title. They attempted to purchase the property, but they could find no owner. A century later, the Orozcos and other families were still living on the old Jesuit properties at San Isidro, including José Ignacio Orozco, the grandson of José Roque Orozco and María Antonia Domínguez de Mendoza.

In 1882, twenty-five years after Mexico's Reform Laws opened the nation to other faiths, the energetic Methodist preacher James "Santiago" D. Eaton arrived in Chihuahua City determined to establish a new congregation. Catholics met him with suspicion, but he was enthusiastically greeted by many liberals, including the mayor of Chihuahua, who told Eaton that the people were open to liberation from the "ecclesiastical tyranny" that had oppressed Mexicans for centuries. Eaton was surprised at the number of prominent Chihuahuenses who self-identified as infidels or atheists.[4] The preacher was thus introduced to Mexico's liberal, reformist, Masonic, and anticlerical element, which welcomed any counterweight to the conservative Catholic Church. In time, Eaton put a cart to a horse and toured Chihuahua, selling Bibles and making converts. While he won over several well-educated Chihuahuenses, he focused his principal effort on tradesmen, teachers, shopkeepers, and the growing middle class. He spent little time on wealthy or indigenous people, seeing them as too closely connected to Catholicism.

In the mid-1880s, Eaton traveled to San Isidro and the nearby Hacienda de Santa Inés, where he met Pascual Orozco Sr. and Albino Frías, who was married to Orozco's cousin. Eaton sold the families Bibles and a new faith. He baptized Orozco's infant son, Pascual Jr., a Methodist, and nineteen years later Pascual Jr. would marry his cousin Refugio, Albino's daughter. With close family ties, converting one prominent member of the family produced other converts. In time, Eaton's seed bore fruit, as 10 percent of San Isidro residents became Protestants.[5] Eaton also developed a small congregation in Guerrero under Jesus Grijalva, a journeyman preacher newly arrived from Sonora. Eaton was not overtly political and enjoyed cordial relations with Chihuahua's conservative elite, but you could not say that about his flock, which was overwhelmingly pro-reform and openly anti–Porfirio Díaz. The Magonista Liberal Party had a substantial number of Protestant members, who also became enthusiastic participants and leaders in the various anti-reelection clubs springing up around the state after 1909. Eaton was wise and lucky to tap into families with deep northwestern roots, folks who had an independent streak that left them open to challenge the establishment and the status quo.

Pascual Orozco Merino and his wife, María Amada Vázquez, had five daughters and two sons, including Pascual Jr. Over time Orozco Sr. and the family prospered, ran pack mules, and owned land and a store. Pascual Jr. worked in his father's store from the age of ten and later began his own transporting businesses with a pack of mules mainly hauling for Sierra Madre mining companies. One company, the Rio de la Plata in Guazapares, paid him three hundred pesos a month to supervise its mule trains taking silver bars to smelters. In time, Orozco had up to thirty mule trains working the mines. He also opened his own store and owned a mine. He was trusted and well regarded by mine operators, who hired him to transport ore and bullion. Mine operator Price McKinney worked for years with both Orozcos and found them to be honest.[6] Orozco learned to speak English in dealing with Americans, such as McKinney. Orozco was strong, muscular, and a natural athlete. He had been active in gymnastics as a boy. He also became a known marksman in the area being able to hit a target at two hundred meters.[7] Orozco married Refugio Frías when he was only nineteen, and that family worked hard and prospered as well. By the time of the revolution, Orozco was a man of some means.

There was an indication that, along with many Serranos, the Orozcos might have been attracted to the ideology of the Liberal Party and were accused of reading its materials. The Orozcos were thought to have been involved with José Inés Salazar in the purchase and importation of weapons in 1909 as part of the Flores Magón efforts.[8] Without a doubt, there was affinity between the San Isidro group and the Magonistas in the Galeana District in Casas Grandes and Janos. Much of the Orozco family, including both Pascuals, became politically involved in anti-reelection activities in San Isidro, joining Albino Frías, Orozco Jr.'s father-in-law. In San Isidro, the newly formed anti-reelection Ignacio Orozco Club, named in honor of Orozco's granduncle, met at Albino Frías's home or that of his brother, Graciano, where members gathered for Sunday afternoon political discussions, sharing experiences and commenting on the news in the latest edition of *El Correo de Chihuahua* or in *El Grito del Pueblo*, the Anti-Reelection Party's newspaper. In that manner, they became acutely interested in, then later involved in, anti-Díaz politics.

CHAPTER TEN

The Short 1910 Campaign
and a Call to Revolt

Well before the 1910 election, Enrique Creel was successful in working with Americans to crush attempted PLM uprisings in Ciudad Juárez. The PLM threat ended once its leaders were either in U.S. exile or in Mexican prisons. During the first half of 1910, Madero had refused to support armed insurrection against Díaz and criticized groups such as the Liberal Party for having done so.

For the 1910 election, Díaz chose Ramón Corral as his running mate, freezing Bernardo Reyes out and leaving him few options. Once again, Reyes, the perennial presidential candidate and northern strongman, raised his profile. The leader of the Democratic Party and governor of Nuevo León, he had a following that concerned Díaz. Díaz then began reducing Reyes's power. Reyes, faced with annihilation for his presidential ambitions, was forced by Díaz to renounce his candidacy, resign as governor, and accept a European exile. The path was then clear for Francisco I. Madero to be Díaz's main 1910 opponent, a battle that initially did not worry Díaz.[1] Seeking to broaden his party's appeal, Madero sought to bring in the Reyistas once their standard-bearer had been exiled. Many of them were members of the Reyes Democratic Party.[2] Ready to mount a challenge, members of the combined Anti-Reelection and Democratic Parties prepared to attend their April 15, 1910, convention in Mexico City. The resulting united Anti-Reelection Party held its convention in the capital's Tivoli Theater, where the party chapters from all over Mexico assembled to nominate their candidate. The choice was obvious. They overwhelmingly selected Madero as their presidential candidate over the Democratic Party candidate, giving him 86 percent of the vote, and Dr. Francisco Vázquez Gómez, Díaz's former personal physician, for vice president, with 57 percent of the vote.[3] Serrano Abraham González, a native of Ciudad Guerrero, led the Chihuahua delegation and heartily supported the insurgent choices.[4] Once back in Chihuahua, González worked with the party to field candidates for local offices and to prepare for the June 23 presidential election.

When the campaign began in earnest, Díaz and his supporters expressed confidence that the old general would quickly and decidedly defeat Madero's amateurish effort. By using his well-worn bag of tricks, and with the election machinery firmly under his control, Díaz had won all his elections and expected no problems in winning this one. This time, however, the tide was running against Díaz. In Chihuahua, there was great enthusiasm in support of Madero and the anti-reelection effort. In the Northwest, Madero reaped the anti-Díaz, anti-Creel sentiment sown and nurtured for years by the Liberal Party. Anti-reelection clubs sprang up in many towns, including the Ignacio Orozco Club in San Isidro.[5] Serranos who had led the fight against Creel's land policies became leaders in the anti-reelection movement. U.S. public opinion also turned against Díaz. Several works, including the influential *Barbarous Mexico* by John Kenneth Turner, a PLM supporter, exposed the Porfiriato's uglier side, especially the abuse, killing, and deportation of the Yaquis and the horrible, slavery-like conditions on Yucatán's henequen haciendas. Díaz, however, was losing more than the public-relations war; he was damaged goods to elements in the U.S. business world and in the Taft administration. Oil companies that were once one with Díaz now sided with Madero in reaction against a Díaz preference for Briton Weetman Pearson. Taft had also cooled on Díaz because Mexico gave refuge to an anti-American Nicaraguan exile and because Díaz refused to renew the Magdalena Bay U.S. naval lease in Baja California del Sur when he met with Taft. Americans came to see Mexico as too cozy with Japan.[6]

As the weeks passed, Díaz's early confidence ebbed into deep insecurity, leading him to resort, once again, to violent repression, intimidation, and harassment of Madero's campaign. The general's luck was running out, and he now would have to rid himself of this pest the old-fashioned way. Díaz shut down several opposition dailies, such as *El Mexicano Nuevo*, *El Mexicano*, and *El Constitucional*. The old man regretted not having arrested Madero in 1905 when he had begun causing trouble.[7] Just two weeks before the election, Díaz charged that Madero had damaged the presidency by having aided the escape of a Madero enthusiast the police were attempting to arrest. On June 5, Díaz had Madero and his associate Roque Estrada arrested in Monterrey for that violation. Two weeks later, they transferred Madero and Estrada to the San Luis Potosí Penitentiary.[8]

Mexicans were outraged over Madero's arrest and the detention of their anti-reelection leader just days before the campaign ended. On Election Day, Díaz was once again in control of the corrupt election apparatus, and the rurales knew how to handle the ballots. The outcome was predictable. Díaz claimed a superlandslide victory over Madero. In some Chihuahua districts, Madero failed to receive a single vote—or rather, none were counted for him.[9]

With the election over, Madero was released on bond. It was during his imprisonment that Madero had changed his mind about armed revolution. Mexico had already experienced several incidents in which Díaz opponents rose against him, but those remained isolated events.[10] Another reason Madero changed his mind was that his campaign had complied with and exhausted all legal procedures in contesting the fraudulent election. Petitions backed with detailed evidence had been presented to the election commission and then appealed to the Chamber of Deputies, which summarily denied the petition and confirmed Díaz's election on September 27. On October 6, disguised as a railroad mechanic, Madero escaped from house arrest and fled to San Antonio, Texas. Within days, he issued his Plan de San Luis. In the *plan*, Madero called for all Mexicans to take up arms against Díaz and rise in rebellion six weeks later, November 20, 1910. In the third point under his *plan*, Madero noted that many small landowners and indigenous communities had lost properties through abuses of the vacant land provisions. Under the *plan*, those takings would be reviewed except in cases of innocent third-party purchases made before the date of the *plan*.[11] Madero certainly did not intend to start a social revolution, but by mentioning land seizures in the context of other reforms to broaden his base, he inadvertently expanded his revolution's ideology and raised expectations.[12]

The Plan de San Luis received poor distribution at first. The party's vice presidential nominee, Francisco Vázquez Gómez, did not see a copy until the end of October,[13] but in Chihuahua, events moved rapidly. Madero supporters may have gotten the *plan* late, but they all knew that the time to revolt was set for November 20, 1910.

CHAPTER ELEVEN

Chihuahua on the Eve of Revolution

Residents of Chihuahua City were excited and concerned, as everyone knew that Chihuahua would be the main theater, pivotal to the revolution's fate and the hotbed of revolutionary activity. The PLM had earlier attempted attacks in Casas Grandes and Janos and on Ciudad Juárez via El Paso, Texas. Groups around the state in San Andrés, Casas Grandes, San Isidro, and Ciudad Guerrero were primed to revolt. Access to the U.S. border was critical, as that was where the rebels could purchase weapons and ammunition. Everyone knew that whoever controlled the border could have access to weapons and supplies. The Taft administration showed its antipathy toward Díaz and ignored arms sales to Madero insurgents along with their thinly disguised exportation. Time was at a premium. It was only a month and a half from the time Madero issued his Plan de San Luis to the scheduled start of the revolution. Meanwhile in Chihuahua, Abraham González quickly assumed the state's insurgent leadership, organizing party members and allies from around the state, distributing copies of the *plan*, and making a personal plea for Chihuahuenses to join the revolution.

In San Isidro, Daniel Rodríguez told his cousin Pascual Orozco Jr. that there was revolutionary activity afoot by the Anti-Reelection Party, and, after hearing that, Orozco ached to get involved. His motivation was not so much animus against Díaz, Terrazas, or Creel, as it was his personal hatred of local political jefe Joaquín Chávez, his bitter foe, competitor, and Creel's San Isidro political operative. Orozco and Chávez vied for mining company transport contracts to deliver provisions and supplies to mining camps and then return with ore and bullion to the rail line. When he heard that González was the man to see to join the insurgency, Orozco made the connection. They met for the first time on October 15 when Orozco took the train to Chihuahua City to meet González at the party offices, which were also the offices of *El Grito del Pueblo*, the Anti-Reelection Party's newspaper.[1] On meeting, Orozco began by telling González that they were related.[2] Orozco then offered his services to the revolution, and González gladly accepted. Orozco said that he did not know about politics and that he was not exactly an enemy of Díaz. He knew, however, that the people Creel had put in office, such as Joaquín Chávez, abused the residents of San Isidro. He added that he would personally like to remove Chávez. To signify that he had joined the party, Orozco also bought a subscription to *El Grito*."[3]

What Orozco brought to the revolution was a reputation that would attract recruits and a group of well-armed, capable individuals ready to fight. Orozco had a reputation for uncommon valor and coolness when under fire, as well as for being an outstanding marksman. He had developed that renown in fighting sierra bandits. Orozco himself had twenty rifles for his mule teams and would soon get another twenty-five.[4] At their next meeting two weeks later, Abraham González had apparently looked into Orozco's record and named the young man head of the revolutionary forces in the Guerrero area, González's home region.[5]

With González having so many meetings at his office and printing copies of the Plan de San Luis on *El Grito*'s press, Creel's many informants soon reported on González's preparations. Predictably, in early November, the police raided and searched the offices of *El Grito* and the party, shutting down *El Grito* and arresting several party officers. Around the country, Díaz rurales, police, and army easily put down scattered outbursts of revolutionary activity. It was different, however, in Northwest Chihuahua.

After Orozco returned home to San Isidro, he met with his father-in-law, Albino Frías, and the San Isidro group. In similar meetings around the nation, citizens assembled and read the Plan de San Luis just as don Albino Frías had. They knew what it meant for them. They discussed the timing for the revolution, the twentieth after 6 P.M., their arms, and their targets. They also put out a call to area allies to assemble and prepare for an armed uprising of an undetermined nature and duration. They pledged their lives to the revolution, prepared their arms, supplies, and horses; advised their families that they could be gone for a time; and agreed to meet at Albino's on the evening of November 18, 1910.

CHAPTER TWELVE

Orozco and Joaquín Chávez

While historians note Orozco's hatred for Joaquín Chávez, few examine its basis.[1] There was a common dislike of jefes políticos for Mexicans who desired a return to their former, locally elected leadership without jefes' abuses, but it involved much more in Orozco's case. An intense business rivalry alone would not explain the loathing Orozco had for Chávez. The feud was more personal and had a long family history, revealing why Orozco and others in San Isidro felt the same way toward Chávez.

The village of Labor de San Isidro was established in the early 1700s when its lands formed part of the Papigochi Jesuit mission, located where Ciudad Guerrero is now. As previously mentioned, for more than a century, those families resided, tilled the fields, and grazed their cattle in San Isidro. After the reform laws decreed the sale of Church lands, San Isidro residents claimed title under that law in 1856. One of the joint claimants representing the families was Orozco's granduncle, Ignacio Orozco, an important political leader. The other joint claimant was Tranquilino Acosta, then the richest man in San Isidro and later Joaquín Chávez's father-in-law. The residents' claim was denied.[2] During the Reform War, the men of San Isidro served in the Esteban Coronado Brigade with Ignacio Orozco as second in command and fought valiantly for the liberal cause. In 1862, the government rewarded the village by naming it a pueblo. Its lands were declared an ejido and granted to its residents.[3]

In 1859, Governor Antonio Ochoa sent liberal troops led by Colonel Ignacio Orozco to put down a conservative rebel force in Corralitos, Chihuahua. Ochoa gave Ignacio Orozco specific instructions on the demands he would make of the rebels. After he defeated the rebels, Ignacio Orozco concluded an agreement, but failed or refused to include Ochoa's demand that the rebels indemnify the state, for which the governor ordered Orozco arrested and taken to Chihuahua City. Orozco escaped from Chihuahua and went to Guerrero, where he gathered forces and fought Ochoa's government, but Ochoa succeeded in defeating

Orozco. Later, Ignacio Orozco and his followers apparently returned to the liberal camp. His insurgent action may have been directed only against Ochoa and not against the liberal cause in general.[4]

Luis Terrazas became governor in 1860 and, in 1861, ordered the sale of Church properties taken by the government under the Juárez and Lerdo Reform Laws. Under those laws, Church properties belonged to the federal and not the state government. During the French invasion and occupation of Mexico of the 1860s, the people of San Isidro again fought against the invaders, as did Terrazas.[5] In 1864, Ignacio Orozco and two others accused Luis Terrazas of disloyalty for having sold federally owned Church properties. Benito Juárez removed Terrazas from the governor's office and appointed Jesús José Casavantes from Guerrero—an Ignacio Orozco ally—to replace him.[6]

By 1900, despite the law prohibiting the sale of ejido properties,[7] Joaquín Chávez used his wife's substantial inheritance from her father Tranquilino Acosta as a financial base as well as his political power to acquire virtually the entire San Isidro ejido. The people of San Isidro were forced to buy other agricultural properties in nearby Santa Inés, where Pascual Orozco Jr. was born and where many San Isidro families moved.

During the 1850s and 1860s, Ignacio Orozco was the political leader for the Guerrero area, a military leader, member of the legislature, and spokesperson. Ignacio died in 1869,[8] and, in time, Joaquín Chávez succeeded him as the local leader.[9] Ignacio Orozco was undoubtedly an influence on Pascual Orozco and others from San Isidro. The Orozco family clearly suffered a loss with Ignacio's decline and death. They went from having one of their own as the political power to being powerless under Joaquín Chávez, an abusive political and commercial competitor. After years under Chávez, the family would do anything to fight him and perhaps regain the local power they had once under Ignacio Orozco.

That ill will, passed down from parents to children, was the main reason why the townspeople already disliked Chávez. Chávez, however, did more to earn his neighbors' hostility. He was a one-man political and economic monopoly in San Isidro. He was, by a wide margin, the largest landowner; owned the largest local store, mines, and the stagecoach line; bought most San Isidro water rights; had several mule teams servicing area mining operations; owned the area's mail transport contracts; was head of the rural police and also the tax collector; and, above all, was the political jefe, a direct gubernatorial appointee, confidant, business associate, ally, and local hatchet man for

Governors Terrazas and Creel. He ran a scaled-down version of a Creel-like political and economic conglomerate. The resentment of the people of San Isidro was caused by the political and economic power and privileges exercised by Chávez rather than by land grabs, such as was the case in other areas, including Namiquipa, Janos, and Casas Grandes.[10] Years of Chávez's arbitrary and abusive conduct toward area residents—including a murder by his sons, as well as outrages committed by Chávez-led rurales—piled onto generational resentment, made for a venomous relationship, and engendered in Orozco a desire for revenge. The history of antagonism and bad blood between Orozco and Chávez included apocrypha of Orozco standing up to the bully Chávez, including a story that Orozco had beaten a Chávez family member despite being unarmed when the Chávez man was. In another, one of the Chávez boys protested to political jefe Urbano Zea that Orozco and ten others had beaten him. Orozco responded that it was not ten, but rather he alone, as he was equal to ten men and that the ten involved were the ten knuckles of his hands.[11]

Joaquín Chávez was not, however, the only score Orozco wanted to settle. There was also unfinished business with Francisco Antillón, the mayor and political jefe in the nearby town of Miñaca and a Chávez ally. Like Chávez, Antillón was the chief of the rurales for his area. At some point, a bitter break occurred between the once close Orozco and Antillón families. Orozco was Francisco Antillón's first cousin; their mothers were sisters.[12] Francisco's father, Rafael Antillón, and Orozco Sr. were cousins, perhaps even first cousins, and they had married sisters. Signifying a closer and once friendly relationship, however, was the fact that Rafael Antillón and his wife, Paz, were Pascual's godparents, his *padrinos*, and his parents' *compadres*.[13] The relationship between godparents and a child's parents is close. Once a child is baptized, the parents are from that day on compadres or *comadres* to each other, address each other as such, and form a new and close family relationship. Often, they are close family to begin with and are then brought even closer. That relationship, *compadrazgo*, manifested close family ties, especially if it involved a couple's firstborn, such as Pascual Jr. The record is unclear when their problems arose, but the two families clearly took opposite political paths, choices that would certainly strain the relationship given the strong feelings both families had about Creel's political machine.

In 1906, Rafael Antillón was Creel's political jefe in Miñaca, and his son Francisco was jefe in Temósachic.[14] By 1906, Orozco and his father were flirting with antigovernment individuals and groups, were apparently friendly with

Magonistas, and were bitterly opposed to and resentful of political jefes and the rural police heads, such as Chávez, and by extension of their supervisor, the governor. In the fall of 1906, Governor Creel instructed his political jefes to identify political troublemakers in the state, especially those involved with Magonistas or readers of Magón's newspaper *Regeneración*. In May 1909, a political jefe reported serious activity to Creel that Orozco and Magonista José Inés Salazar were buying and importing American arms and munitions.[15] Francisco Antillón, then at Temósachi, sent several reports about local suspects to Creel. He was prepared to inform on Orozco, possibly accusing him of reading antigovernment materials.[16] Events would soon prove that the bad feelings were mutual.

Almost all the men of the San Isidro area were muleteers. Except for Chávez, others in San Isidro and Santa Inés were small landholders, but thanks to their transporting activities, they were middle-class. Under Díaz and Terrazas, but especially during the Creel administration, the government shifted the tax burden to activities that had been previously exempt from taxation. Instead of being the beneficiaries of land grants, many Serranos lost their lands to the wealthy. Serranos developed a resentment of the oligarchy and its privileges and a readiness to oppose the establishment in many ways. Their Apache, Reform War, and French invasion resistance heritage and their independent, tight-knit communities made them a uniquely historic military region. Their armed, muleteer occupation and history of organizing and running long-range, armed caravans made them a war-ready cavalry.[17] These factors, also present in other northwestern towns and villages, made the Northwest the center of revolutionary activity and provided, more than any other place, essential military forces and leadership for the revolution.

The people of San Isidro, by their nature, were independent and suspicious of those in political power, contrarians perhaps. Serranos, for the most part, did not experience the *patrón-peón* relationship; rather, they were independent, small ranchers and farmers who had no special regard for the wealthy or landed elite. That natural independence from and opposition to establish-ment institutions led several to become Protestants and to support radical antigovernment forces, such as the Liberal Party.[18] Serranos were leaders of the revolution, because they felt the sting of land seizures and Creel's oppressive politics perhaps more than anyone did, and they were armed, trained, and motivated to do something about it.

CHAPTER THIRTEEN

The Start of the
Mexican Revolution

On the night of Friday, November 18, 1910, the San Isidro rebels met at the home of Orozco's father-in-law, Albino Frías, located on the north side of the village. To the assembled, Albino read the Plan de San Luis and its call for the revolution to start on November 20. In Guerrero, federal forces, sensing an imminent attack, were already telegraphing Chihuahua for reinforcements. At Frías's meeting, it was largely family. Most in the group were connected by blood or marriage or as lifelong friends and neighbors. Frías was there with his three sons, Graciano, Antonio, and Pablo. Orozco was with his father, Pascual Sr., his uncle, Alberto Orozco, as well as José Orozco, Francisco Salido, three Caraveo brothers, and other groups of brothers and cousins. Many, if not most, of them were Methodists.[1]

Knowing that the local authorities were on alert, they made plans to ride out the next night, a day early, as permitted by the *plan*.[2] For their first target, they picked the rail station and town of Miñaca, a few miles south of Basúchil, a station on the Chihuahua al Pacífico rail line, where Joaquín Chávez had commercial interests, but mainly because it was a place headed by Francisco Antillón, Orozco's first cousin and the political jefe there. The relationship between the two families must have soured indeed to have selected Antillón as the revolution's first target.

Orozco's then fifteen-year-old sister, Serafina, recalled the night of November 19 as bitterly cold, when several members of the group met at Orozco Sr.'s home. Peeking through the transom into the room, Serafina and her sisters saw the commotion as several local friends, relatives, and visitors from the area met at the residence. The group chose her brother to lead, and then her father spoke about their mission and determination. There would be no turning back for them; they would either destroy Díaz or die trying.[3] They left the home and rode out to meet their comrades. At 7 P.M., Frías's forces of around forty-three men rode out of San Isidro in small groups so as not to attract attention, headed for Miñaca, and were joined by other forces on the road. When they arrived at Miñaca, Antillón was not there, and he was lucky to have been away.[4] Since the town was only lightly guarded, Orozco's men easily took Antillón's home and a substantial arms and ammunition cache from the rurales' supply and from Joaquín Chávez's Miñaca store. The rurales were quickly subdued.[5] It was the revolution's first action against state or federal forces.

After Miñaca, they returned to attack San Isidro and the rurales based at Joaquín Chávez's home. Early Sunday morning, November 20, the group attacked the Chávez home. Orozco enthusiastically stormed the residence and store, his prime target. He broke down the front door but found Chávez absent. Chávez's two sons and twenty-five Tarahumara guards were easily overpowered. The revolutionaries left with weapons and ammunition.[6] While there were scattered shots fired around Mexico on November 20, 1910, the most important combat that involved opposition was Orozco's. All uprisings, except those in Northwest Chihuahua, were over by the end of the month. At year's end five weeks later, Orozco was a household name; he was a Chihuahua hero and known to Díaz. Already, Orozco and his small force were standing out among all others in Mexico.

Days after the revolution's first shots, the government in Mexico City displayed an air of confidence. A *New York Times* headline on November 24 proclaimed, "Revolt Crushed, Creel Declares," quoting Creel, who was speaking for Díaz as his foreign relations minister.[7] Lord Cowdray (Weetman Pearson) told a London reporter, "Cable that this affair will be forgotten within a month," and U.S. ambassador Henry Lane Wilson wired Washington that the revolution had failed.[8]

A short distance from Guerrero, Francisco Pancho Villa opened another front for the revolution, in San Andrés. Over the next four years, Villa's and Orozco's careers would intersect, their paths occasionally converging then splitting. Orozco outranked Villa, colonel to major and, later, general to colonel. They would rise to the top rank of revolutionary military leaders even though neither had served in the military. One was a muleteer, the other a bandit.

After the San Isidro attack, Orozco's forces, now numbering 165,[9] turned toward Ciudad Guerrero, where substantial federal and state forces waited in defense. For that battle, preacher Grijalva's Guerrero troops joined the San Isidro group. Although Orozco was the clear military leader, the group stopped on the way and, in deference to his early leadership and seniority, formally elected Albino Frías to be their leader with Orozco as second in command.

The Guerrero garrison forces had cabled Chihuahua for reinforcements, and Frías suspended the attack on Guerrero while Orozco took men to cut off the incoming federal troops. The forces met on the rail line at Pedernales, where Orozco dealt the federal forces their first military defeat in the revolution.[10] The rebels then renewed their attack on Guerrero, and the federal garrison and rurales under Urbano Zea quickly surrendered on December 4, making it the first large town to fall to the insurgents. The rebels allowed the federal soldiers to leave to Chihuahua City. The next day, the aging Albino Frías handed the command over to his son-in-law Orozco.[11]

Villa was in Guerrero getting to know Orozco when Orozco received notice that another sizable group of federal soldiers was on its way to retake the town. He decided to send Francisco Salido with 240 men to ambush the federal troops on the rail line at Cerro Prieto. Orozco would try to gather more forces and meet them there.[12] Under Gen. Juan Navarro, federal forces at Cerro Prieto numbered a little over one thousand. The size of federal forces surprised the rebels. Entrenched in Cerro Prieto, Salido's group awaited Navarro.[13] When the federal troops arrived, their infantry charged Salido's group, and Navarro sent the cavalry around Salido's rear to cut off his escape route. Salido was outnumbered and could not hold the line. As Salido's men retreated, they were left exposed on the hill and took many casualties, including Salido himself, before the survivors escaped into the night.

On December 11, Orozco had a small cavalry group with him. They charged to relieve Salido's group and were met by superior federal cavalry that easily repelled Orozco's troops.[14] Outnumbered, Orozco and his men retreated, and then the federal forces captured twenty rebels, including Orozco's uncle, Alberto Orozco, Albino Frías's sons Graciano and Antonio, the Morales and Solis brothers, and also Marcelo Caraveo's brother, José, all from San Isidro. Navarro had the men taken to the Cerro Prieto cemetery, where they were all summarily executed; the healthy were shot, and the wounded were executed either by bayonet to the abdomen or else were burned alive.[15] It was a horrible massacre and a tremendous personal loss for the close-knit group from San Isidro, an act seen as even more unjust since the rebels had treated federal troops in Guerrero with compassion and had freed them. The rebels lost eighty men to the federal loss of fourteen.[16] Navarro, whose conduct at Cerro Prieto was already unforgiveable and unforgettable for Serranos, did not stop there. To set an example to communities supporting the rebels, he ordered the public whipping of several women and the execution of twenty-two noncombatants, including three men over eighty years old, acts that enraged the entire Serrano community and made Navarro the most hated man in the region.[17]

At Cerro Prieto, Orozco had started with a group of thirty and had only nine left, when, in retreat, they reached a nearby ranch called La Capilla.[18] There was also an unidentified woman with the rebels at Malpaso, who joined them in the battle. She was killed in action.[19] On December 27, in retaliation for the executions at Cerro Prieto, Pascual Orozco's men executed captives from their earlier victory at Ciudad Guerrero, among them several local officials, including jefe político Urbano Zea, and several judges.

Upon the death of Foreign Relations Minister Ignacio Mariscal, Creel was named to the post in April 1910,[20] but by December of that year Díaz finally realized that Terrazas and Creel were pariahs in Chihuahua. Also, in December, Creel had turned the governorship over to Alberto Terrazas, the son of Luis Terrazas.[21] In late January of 1911, to quell the growing rebellion with Chihuahua at its center, Díaz moved to distance himself from the toxic Terrazas-Creel clan. Díaz summarily removed Alberto Terrazas as Chihuahua governor when Terrazas had only served two months and replaced him with popular former governor, Miguel Ahumada.[22] One historian notes that Díaz removed Alberto Terrazas from the governorship in hopes of facilitating contact with Orozco, seen by Díaz as more anti-Terrazas than anti-Díaz. It was too late.[23] At that early date, just forty days into the revolution, Orozco had achieved recognition as a military leader.

In Chihuahua City, soon after November 20, editor-publisher Silvestre Terrazas, a distant clan relative and constant Creel critic, had published Madero's Plan de San Luis and its call for revolution. Creel shut down the daily, arrested Silvestre, and sent him to a Mexico City prison. Weeks into Silvestre's imprisonment, Díaz summoned Silvestre for an audience. When he asked Silvestre the reason for his opposition, Silvestre responded that his antagonism was directed not so much toward Díaz as it was against Terrazas and Creel and the abuses committed in their names. He said that Terrazas and Creel had "the monopoly of everything; of the government, of the banks, of industry and even a monopoly on hate." Not long after the interview, on February 11, 1911, Díaz released Silvestre.[24]

Among other skirmishes, there was one at Namiquipa. Rebels attacked the rurales in Namiquipa soon after November 20, killed the local rurale commander, and ran off the hated local jefe, Victoriano Torres, the man who had made claims against several Serrano properties. Namiquipa rebel Rafael López was killed, but his widow took up arms and fought.[25] In the far Northwest on December 30, 1910, Liberal Party forces led by Práxedis Guerrero attacked and captured Janos, but Guerrero was killed in the battle, and José Inés Salazar took over Liberal Party leadership in the Casas Grandes area.

In Chihuahua City in late January of 1911, Orozco's bitter foe, Joaquín Chávez, died of pneumonia. At age seventy-two, he was ill and weak and had gone to Chihuahua for medical treatment. After his death, his sons took over all his businesses.

One planned event that did not occur on November 20 was Francisco Madero's triumphal entry into Mexico to lead the revolution. Madero carefully laid out his plan and supplied his uncle Catarino Benavides with arms for several hundred men. Madero was to enter Mexico near Eagle Pass, Texas, and Benavides promised that he would recruit four hundred to eight hundred men on his own in addition to the substantial forces that they expected would desert Díaz. Madero planned to cross with a few men, meet the waiting forces, and lead an attack on Ciudad Porfirio Díaz, Coahuila (Piedras Negras today). At the designated hour at daybreak, Madero drove from a ranch fifteen miles away to the designated river rendezvous about two miles north of Eagle Pass. When Madero and his few men crossed the river to meet Benavides, instead of finding several hundred men, Catarino showed up with only four poorly armed men.[26] Federal forces almost arrested Madero before he fled across the river to Eagle Pass. The dejected Madero continued to San Antonio and then went on to New Orleans, where he remained until December.[27] Madero told Francisco Vázquez Gómez that the revolution had failed, that it was over. Vázquez Gómez replied that it was too early to say that it had failed and that there was a "spark" of a revolution in Chihuahua.[28]

The spark of revolution in Chihuahua was not Madero's; it was mainly Pascual Orozco and his men who had next set their eyes on Ciudad Juárez across the border from El Paso. Ciudad Juárez had become Orozco's singular focus, the prize on the border that would give him access to arms, money, and geography. Seeking to connect with his forces in December, Madero made his way to El Paso.

CHAPTER FOURTEEN

Orozco Heads to Ciudad Juárez

No sooner had Orozco taken Ciudad Guerrero than he set his sights on Ciudad Juárez, a high-profile border city with a substantial federal garrison and access to weapons, supplies, customs duty revenues, and a supportive cross-border population. Orozco's attention was riveted on Ciudad Juárez as he abandoned Guerrero, which federal forces under General Navarro promptly retook without a fight on January 7.[1] Once he left the Guerrero area, Orozco spread false rumors that he next intended to take Chihuahua City, but his goal always remained Ciudad Juárez. He set February 5, 1911, the anniversary of the 1857 Constitution, as the date for the battle.

Already in early February 1911, Pascual Orozco's name was coming to the public's attention. In New York, Gustavo Madero, Francisco's younger brother and the revolution's representative on the U.S. East Coast, met with the press. During the interview, Gustavo heaped praise on Orozco. The article introduced the public to Orozco and his growing reputation as the revolution's principal military leader. A *New York Times* reporter also interviewed federal colonel Martín Luis Guzmán, who had fought against Orozco at Malpaso and would later die of wounds sustained there. Before he died, Guzmán told the reporter, "I have but one regret and that is that I have never been able to shake hands with my opponent, General Orozco, the bravest man and the ablest General that I know."[2]

Before Orozco's Ciudad Juárez assault, Madero was in El Paso and planned to cross into Mexico in time to lead the attack. Federal forces spoiled the surprise when they learned that Ciudad Juárez was the target, and they brought in substantial reinforcements. Orozco waited for the arrival of other rebel forces that Madero was to have recruited, but they did not materialize, which was a repeat of Madero's November 20 failure. Orozco attempted to stop federal reinforcements from reaching Ciudad Juárez at Bauche, a location just south of the city. He engaged the federal troops, but eventually the federal forces broke through and reached the city, forcing Orozco to abandon his attack. With his forces thirsty and hungry, Orozco went around the west side of Ciudad Juárez to a point on the Rio Grande, across from the ASARCO smelter.[3] Until that point Orozco certainly considered himself commander in chief under Madero. Given his record, Orozco felt that he merited the position. On February 9, Madero's other top military men met in El Paso and organized a formal staff naming Col. José de la Luz Soto chief of staff.[4] While at his riverside camp, Orozco received a Madero delegation under Eduardo Hay that had been sent by Abraham González, telling Orozco to submit to the command of José de la Luz Soto. In the presence of his men, Orozco told the delegation that, while he supported the revolution, he would do so on his own terms. He took one look at Madero's delegates and told his staff in front of the others, "I want nothing to do with these dandies,"[5] demonstrating Serrano independence and resistance to city folks, who were "dandies" or "sissies" to them, a cutting insult in that macho world. Not long after that, Orozco left Ciudad Juárez and returned to Guerrero and San Isidro, but he did not forget what he considered to have been Madero's clumsy disrespect. On the other side, Orozco's act of insubordination in refusing to submit to Madero's new hierarchy went unpunished.

Meanwhile in El Paso, Madero and his advisors decided, without consulting Orozco, to abandon the quest for Ciudad Juárez and instead have the inexperienced Madero lead an attack on Casas Grandes. On February 14, 1911, Madero crossed into Mexico just downriver from El Paso—three days after Texas had issued a warrant for his arrest[6]—with a plan to march toward Casas Grandes and assume military command.[7] Upon entering Mexico, Madero and his advisors declared him provisional president of the republic and head of the revolution.[8] The border town of Guadalupe, earlier taken by Liberal Party–Magonista forces, happened to be Madero's first stop, as it was the logical crossing place downriver from El Paso. Although the Liberal Party allied with Maderistas in fighting Díaz, the Liberal Party disagreed that Madero had the right to declare himself provisional president. The Liberal Party had its own, different ideology. Prisciliano Silva,[9] the Magonista leader, welcomed Madero but added that he did not recognize him as Mexico's provisional president. The PLM gave Anti-Reelection Party candidate Madero no more deference than any member of their own party. Madero saw himself as the anointed leader and immediately ordered the Magonistas disarmed. The Magonistas, not wishing to be defenseless against federal forces or Madero's troops, chose U.S. exile.[10]

The March 6, 1911, attack on Casas Grandes was Madero's first military experience. By then, the Liberal Party had left the area and federal forces had retaken the town. Federal troops summoned reinforcements when the rebels failed to cut telegraphic lines. Stubbornly, even though reinforcements under Orozco were en route, Madero refused to wait and launched his attack. It was disastrous, and Madero was soundly defeated. In addition to many dead and wounded, Madero lost substantial supplies and took a superficial bullet wound to his arm. Chastened and humiliated, Madero withdrew to nearby Galeana, where he had his initial meeting with Orozco.[11]

The defeat at Casas Grandes apparently increased Madero's respect, at least temporarily, for those with proven combat records. Madero seemed determined to learn from his mistake and recognize that he was not adept at military tactics. He realized that he needed Orozco and meant to bring him back into the fold after having treated him with disrespect in El Paso and ignoring his advice regarding Casas Grandes. After meeting Orozco, Madero hoped to patch the relationship and decided to head for Bustillos to reorganize his forces. On March 21, Madero and his men, followed by Orozco's troops, set out for Hacienda de Bustillos, closer to Chihuahua City and a property belonging to the wealthy Zuloaga family, to establish a temporary headquarters there for Madero to consult with advisors and military leaders. The hacienda was friendly territory for Madero, as his uncle Alberto had married a Zuloaga and was the hacienda's manager.

CHAPTER FIFTEEN

New York Peace Talks

reasury Minister Limantour was in Paris on a financing trip in February 1911 when he surprised Mexicans with comments he made in a press interview. What he said excited everyone in Mexico as supporting land reform. While Limantour demanded that insurgents lay down their arms, he also agreed with their calls for reform and said, "The feudal system in Mexico must go and the great estates in the North, which have passed from family to family should be distributed among the people." Those were radical statements indeed coming from the top Científico, who had himself owned a large Northwest Chihuahua property.[1] The controversial interview and its thinly veiled broadside against Terrazas and Creel became the topic of many discussions at the time.

Meanwhile in Mexico City, Díaz was concerned that his government was unraveling with hardly a shot having been fired. He had already moved large numbers of federal troops into Chihuahua, and he summarily replaced Terrazas's son as governor there with Miguel Ahumada, who, following the new policy line from Díaz and Limantour, immediately proposed reforms. A cabinet change was also under way.[2] Díaz removed political jefes, and on April 1, 1911, he fired Enrique Creel as his minister of foreign relations, a shocking blow to the clan. The move exposed how concerned Díaz was over Chihuahua. Díaz accurately sensed the deep unpopularity of the Creel and Terrazas family in Chihuahua and that his relationship with the clan was helping to take down his administration, especially in Chihuahua, the revolution's main theater.[3]

By removing Creel, Díaz also changed the line of succession. If he succeeded in removing the unpopular Ramón Corral, leaving the vice presidency vacant, the next in line would be the minister of foreign relations. Had Díaz and Corral either resigned or been removed, Creel would have become the president of Mexico, something the rebels would never have permitted. To replace Creel, Díaz named diplomat Francisco León de la Barra as his new minister of foreign relations. In mere days, Creel went from second in the order of presidential succession to exclusion. Limantour took charge of negotiations with the rebels, a favorable turn for Díaz given the Maderos' high regard for Limantour.

As evidence that Díaz was listening to Limantour once Creel was out, Díaz announced new, conciliatory reform proposals tracking those earlier suggested by Limantour in Paris. After completing seven terms and thirty-four years in office, Díaz dusted off his 1872 plank and announced a new electoral law prohibiting reelection, now that he had a fresh term. Without giving more detail, he also proposed breaking up large estates.[4] The news was met with skepticism at Bustillos as too little too late;[5] Orozco, however, believed that the changes signaled a Díaz capitulation. Another sign of Díaz's insecurity was that he had several peace emissaries at work. The old man was desperately pushing all the buttons he could for relief, including having Limantour meet directly with the Maderos in New York.

Díaz urgently sought to negotiate directly with the Maderos, whom he saw as having common policy views. Resorting to a reliable method of the past, playing sides against each other and perhaps to lure Reyistas away from revolution, Díaz offered to return strongman, former military leader, and Nuevo León governor Bernardo Reyes to the cabinet. Vice President Ramón Corral was weak and controversial, and Reyes would be a more effective counterweight to the Científico influence. With the nation in peril, Díaz missed the presence and counsel of his finance minister and most trusted advisor, Limantour. Díaz instructed Limantour to return from France.[6]

In early March 1911, in the weeks before the Battle of Ciudad Juárez, the Madero family took a suite of rooms in New York's Astor Hotel on Times Square while they held talks with Limantour, whose New York stop on his return from France fortuitously coincided with the Maderos' business financing trip to the city. The Madero party included Francisco Madero, the provisional president's father, brother Gustavo, and Sherburne G. Hopkins, the Maderos' Washington, D.C., lawyer. Anti-Reelection Party vice presidential nominee Francisco Vázquez Gómez later joined the group.

The Maderos had a close, trusting relationship with Limantour and were ready to agree with Limantour's points.[7] Privately, Francisco Madero Sr. favored Limantour taking the presidency and was not originally in agreement with his son's revolution.[8] When Limantour arrived in New York, Díaz was ill and had left Limantour in charge of the negotiations. Vázquez Gómez, however, had no trust in Limantour and was not close to the Maderos. Anticipating a critical battle at Ciudad Juárez, the Maderos gave away a large bargaining chip by admitting that they would do anything to prevent a shooting war on the border, which held a high probability of U.S. intervention with stray rounds likely hitting U.S. soil, a card Limantour continually played. Limantour proposed replacing Vice President Corral, giving Madero four cabinet slots, removing fourteen governors with Madero to name their replacements, and instituting significant electoral and economic reforms. Limantour was to remain at the treasury, but he was adamant that he lacked any authority to discuss any option except leaving Díaz in office. The Maderos were ready to accept that offer, but Francisco Vázquez Gómez refused to agree to any proposal that did not include Díaz's immediate resignation.[9]

The historical record on the New York peace talks is confusing. Some wrote that Vázquez Gómez had an undisguised hatred for Díaz—unusual considering that he had been the dictator's personal physician—and a comparable dislike for Limantour, whom he had also treated for illnesses. Vázquez Gómez suggested that Foreign Minister Léon de la Barra could serve as interim president replacing Díaz. The internal argument over the Díaz resignation became especially heated and personal between Gustavo Madero and Vázquez Gómez. The Maderos also demanded reimbursement for hundreds of thousands of pesos of unsubstantiated funds they claimed to have expended on the revolution, an amount Limantour agreed to include in the negotiated payment to the Maderos. Unclear were the Madero party's negotiating credentials or identification of its leadership. They were at an impasse on the Madero side, disputing over Díaz's resignation, but, with no one clearly in charge, they lacked the mechanism to resolve it. The odd man out was Vázquez Gómez.[10] Attorney Hopkins seemed loyal to the provisional president and could not reconcile Gustavo and Vázquez Gómez. As the vice presidential nominee, Vázquez Gómez at least had an official position as a negotiator. He also had a sizable base and following in the Anti-Reelection Party, stronger than Madero had among many party members.

On the other side of the historical record, both Limantour and Vázquez Gómez wrote in their memoirs that no one raised the subject of Díaz's resignation. Indeed, Limantour said that he made no proposals and simply accepted Vázquez Gomez's written position paper that only mentioned Corral resigning along with several governors. Limantour left for Mexico three days after he arrived in New York. Whether Limantour agreed to an item or not, however, large changes occurred when he returned to Mexico City. No matter the details, the obvious result of the New York meetings was an estrangement between the Maderos and Vázquez Gómez.

In his memoirs, Limantour noted how the Maderos undercut the rebels' negotiating positions. First, Madero's grandfather Evaristo and his cousin Rafael Hernández wrote long letters to Limantour while the minister was still in France, telling him that the family was against the revolution and condemned Francisco. Evaristo even told Limantour that Francisco was insane and was inspired by spiritism. Then, when Limantour arrived in New York, even before the peace talks began, Francisco Sr. went to see Limantour at the Plaza Hotel and said that he disagreed with his son's revolution. Out of credit and funds, the Maderos were desperate and begged Limantour to be relieved of the many restrictions that had tied up their money and had frozen them out of capital markets.[11]

With rebel troops soon leaving for Ciudad Juárez, Gustavo and Francisco Madero Sr. left New York bound for Chihuahua, and Vázquez Gómez returned to Washington, D.C., to continue representing Madero there. Limantour, temporarily in charge of the cabinet, wasted no time. He had replaced Creel with León de la Barra; brought in others, such as Jorge Vera Estañol, who agreed with him that reforms were needed; and announced a constitutional amendment prohibiting reelection. Limantour next sent two emissaries, Toribio Esquivel Obregón and Óscar Braniff, to negotiate directly with Vázquez Gómez in Washington. Esquivel Obregón[12] and Braniff had approached Limantour and Díaz, volunteering to mediate with the rebels. Arriving in Washington on April 12, Vázquez Gómez demanded that Díaz resign and that the delegates be credentialed.[13] Limantour's delegates proposed giving Madero several cabinet seats and ten governorships, and Vázquez Gómez indicated interest in the proposal despite no Díaz resignation. Given that apparent moderation of his position, the delegates ended the Washington meetings and headed to Ciudad Juárez to undertake direct talks with Madero and his delegates.[14] All roads now led to Ciudad Juárez.

FIG. 2. Pascual Orozco Jr. on horseback.
Courtesy of the Otis Aultman Collection, El Paso Public Library.

Fig. 3. Pascual Orozco Jr.
Courtesy of the Library of Congress.

FIG. 4. Pascual Orozco Jr.
Courtesy of Special Collections, University of Texas at El Paso.

Fig. 5. Francisco Villa.
Courtesy of the Library of Congress

Fig. 9. Orozco's Colorado troops.
Courtesy of the El Paso Public Library.

Opposite top
FIG. 6. Enrique C. Creel.
From Álbum Conmemorativo, Visita á Chihuahua de Porfirio Díaz.

Opposite bottom left
FIG. 7. General Luis Terrazas.
From Álbum Conmemorativo, Visita á Chihuahua de Porfirio Díaz.

Opposite bottom right
FIG. 8. President Porfirio Díaz.
From Álbum Conmemorativo, Visita á Chihuahua de Porfirio Díaz.

FIG. 10. Francisco I. Madero *(left)* and Francisco Madero Sr. *(center)*.
Courtesy of Special Collections, University of Texas at El Paso.

FIG. 11. Pascual Orozco Jr. *(in dark suit)* at the start of the rebellion, March 1912.
Courtesy of the George Grantham Bain Collection, Library of Congress.

CHAPTER SIXTEEN

The Road to Ciudad Juárez

Everyone who mattered would be at the Hacienda de Bustillos. Madero had been at Bustillos a few days when Pancho Villa and his staff rode in, leaving the remainder of his forces encamped at his San Andrés base about ten miles away. At a meeting the next day, Madero conferred the rank of colonel on Orozco and made Villa a major.[1] Madero, understanding that Orozco was his best military leader, was anxious to please the Serrano and make up for his previous slights. After making Orozco a colonel, Madero promised him the rank of general if he took Ciudad Juárez. Madero was careful always to keep Villa one rank below the sensitive Orozco.

Like two fighters entering the ring, Orozco and Villa carefully eyed each other as they met again at Bustillos. At five feet, eleven, Orozco was slightly taller than Pancho's five feet, ten inches. Villa, at thirty-three, was more than three years older than Orozco. Orozco was thin with a light complexion, green eyes, and reddish-brown hair and wore a flat, expressionless look on his angular face. He dressed like a Texan and wore a Stetson. Villa found Orozco taciturn, humble in appearance, and lacking what he expected in a commander's carriage and mien.[2] When Orozco observed Villa, he saw his muscular 180-pound frame; large, protruding jaw; grin exposing stained teeth; light complexion, "almost as florid as a German"; and kinky, black, uncombed hair. Villa usually dressed in khaki and wore an eclectic selection of hats, including pith helmets, military campaign hats, Stetsons, and sombreros. Villa exuded animal energy and movement, exemplified by his expressive and ever-darting brown eyes, flashing looks ranging from anger to merriment and back in an instant.[3] To Orozco, Villa was a bandit and an outlaw, a man unfit to run a military unit. Madero, however, in his position as self-declared head of the provisional Mexican government, chose to pardon Villa for his past transgressions. Privately, Orozco indicated to Villa that he disapproved of his excessive and arbitrary violence and told Villa that the revolution was not theirs to commit atrocities.[4] Madero, in the role of a teacher reconciling two warring schoolboys, insisted that Villa and Orozco exchange a public *abrazo*, but Orozco refused to be photographed with Villa.[5] The bad chemistry between them began from the start and never changed.

Madero's forces at Bustillos quickly surpassed one thousand with other groups around the state ready to join them in battle. Their destination was no secret; it was the border city of Ciudad Juárez, Orozco's goal, one he would never change. For the first time, rebel forces would be transported by rail on the Northwest line from Bustillos north to the Las Varas station, a village about one-third of the way to Ciudad Juárez, the northern end of the lower part of the unfinished line. Then they planned to proceed by horse to the line's northern railhead. At last, after weeks of mind-numbing boredom, the troops were finally off to battle. They made their way to the nearby Bustillos rail station. Madero and Orozco's group was one thousand strong with tons of equipment and supplies. The four troop trains had passenger and freight cars for horses and equipment.

Once under way, they passed through Pedernales, La Junta, Basúchil, and San Isidro, where they stopped briefly so Madero could meet with relatives of the village's troops[6] and then continued to Santo Tomás, Matachic, and Yepomera. They reached Las Varas, and the next day they marched past Madera to Babícora near Hearst's ranch headquarters, where they connected to rail again and boarded the waiting trains to continue the trip toward Ciudad Juárez. When they passed near Casas Grandes, however, a new problem arose between Madero and Magonistas.

After federal forces abandoned Casas Grandes to reinforce Ciudad Juárez, Liberal Party Magonistas immediately retook the town and named one of their own the new political jefe there. On arriving at Casas Grandes, Madero removed the Magonista jefe and replaced him with one of his own men, and immediately six Magonista rebel officers serving with Madero resigned from Madero's forces and wrote that Madero was more of a traitor than Díaz. The Magonistas refused to join the attack on Ciudad Juárez. Madero ordered Orozco to disarm the Magonistas, including their leader, José Inés Salazar, but Orozco refused because of the sympathy and connections between his people and the Magonistas and perhaps between Salazar and Orozco. Madero asked Villa to do so instead, and he did. Madero's troops arrested and jailed the six defecting Magonistas, but they later escaped. Madero's forces sent other Magonistas to be jailed in Ciudad Guerrero. With that issue out of the way, the troops continued onto Ciudad Juárez,[7] but it was disconcerting to experience yet another conflict with PLM forces.

Late on the night of April 17, seven hundred Orozco troops left Casas Grandes to board the four troop trains taking Madero's army to battle, arriving the next afternoon at Bauche Station south of Ciudad Juárez.[8] Federally controlled, Ciudad Juárez was tense as the rebels approached. Now paranoid, Juárez police suspected many innocent noncombatants of being rebels, and Mexican immigration operations, normally dormant, sprang to life, subjecting anyone entering from El Paso to detailed examination. Gen. Juan Navarro headed federal forces there. For Orozco, Ciudad Juárez was a critical goal and with Navarro there, doubly so, as Serranos hated the general.

At Bauche, Orozco divided his forces. The unit under Marcelo Caraveo was ordered to stay at Bauche to block federal reinforcements from entering Juárez. The other troops with horses and wagons left Bauche and headed northwest around the west side of Sierra Juárez, dragging two canons and taking two days to skirt the sierra with a stop on the first night about halfway to their final camp. The next day, they trailed the western flank of the sierra and then wound their way through a canyon until dusk when they met the Rio Grande, its channel and adjacent irrigation canals full with that spring's runoff. Working in the dark under a new moon that April 20, they set up camp in a field across from the ASARCO smelter, a location three miles northwest of the centers of Ciudad Juárez and El Paso and only a few feet away from border monument No. 1 and U.S. soil. The next morning hundreds of curious El Pasoans appeared across the river from the camp, waiting for the impending battle. Poised to attack, the rebel force totaled 2,500 and surrounded Ciudad Juárez on three sides.

On April 20, 1911, Madero rode into Rancho Flores, the insurgent riverside camp, commandeered a small three-room adobe there as his headquarters, and immediately established a hard negotiating line by saying that there would be no peace talks until after the Battle of Ciudad Juárez and issued a harsh ultimatum: "I will wait 24 hours longer for Díaz to surrender his presidency, give up Ciudad Juárez and recognize Francisco León de la Barra as president."[9] In the meantime, Francisco Madero Sr. was approaching Ciudad Juárez after a long, circuitous trek from New York.[10]

The day after Madero issued his ultimatum, his father arrived on the scene, and the two met privately that Friday night, April 21, and at length the next morning in a closed meeting attended by the father and son, financier uncle Ernesto, cousin Rafael Hernández, and journalist Silvestre Terrazas. Madero also met with Limantour's delegates, Esquivel Obregón and Braniff, who joined the family in softening Madero's attitude. On facing the public immediately after the meeting, Madero reversed his tone, abandoned the ultimatum, and agreed instead, without conditions, to a four-day armistice to negotiate a possible peace plan.[11] Now adamantly opposing a shooting war in fear of U.S. intervention, Madero, apparently following his family's and close advisors' counsel, signaled favoring the eleven-point Díaz proposal, similar to Limantour's New York package, which included keeping Díaz in the presidency.[12] When Francisco Vázquez Gómez arrived in Ciudad Juárez, he insisted that Díaz name an accredited negotiator and, over the opposition of the Maderos, again demanded that Díaz resign. In the interim, rebel troops and their military leaders, such as Orozco and Villa, were anxious to attack but were under orders to wait while Madero went from one conflicting public statement and negotiating position to the next with several extensions of the armistice.[13] And wait they did, which is always a dangerous lull for a force poised to attack. As the talks dragged on, Madero warned his restless troops about the consequences of desertion, a valid concern as forces could succumb to boredom rather than bullets.

Díaz appointed his special negotiator, Supreme Court justice Francisco Carvajal, to represent him in the talks. Nevertheless, before Vázquez Gómez arrived to sit on the rebel side, Francisco Madero met with Limantour's private delegates and negotiators, Braniff and Esquivel Obregón. The Díaz delegates, who worked in close communication with Limantour, convinced Madero and secured his commitment not to demand Díaz's resignation, proving Díaz and Limantour's assumption correct that Díaz could get his way if he could only negotiate directly with the Madero family.[14] On April 29, a group of rebel leaders asked Madero about his position on Díaz remaining in office, and he replied, "I'm committed to Limantour,"[15] meaning the personal assurance he had given the Limantour's delegates. After Vázquez Gómez arrived, he met with Madero, who persisted in not demanding a Díaz resignation. Vázquez Gómez, however, kept pressing until two days later, when he succeeded in persuading Madero to agree that Díaz should resign. Vázquez Gómez drew up a negotiation position paper containing the resignation demand and presented it to Madero. Madero reviewed the document and asked for Orozco's opinion. Someone explained the paper to Orozco, who responded, "Don't consult me about these matters because I don't know about such things. If you tell me that the enemy is coming, I'll see about what I should do, but on this, you know what should be done." Orozco then turned and left the room, and Madero signed the document.[16] Others followed with their signatures, including Abraham González, Madero's father, and Orozco. The next day, with his mind changed once again, Madero called Vázquez Gómez and demanded the document so he could destroy it, contending that Vázquez Gómez had forced him to sign it.[17]

Breaking up the boredom after more than two weeks at the riverside camp, rebel troops held a Cinco de Mayo celebration, an ironic event given that they were celebrating the battle that made Díaz a national hero while they were fighting to depose him.

On May 6, Madero still resisted a Díaz resignation, but he changed his mind again and sent his delegate Vázquez Gómez to the peace talks along with his father and Yucatán governor, José María Pino Suárez, with instructions to demand the resignation.[18] While the Maderos again sent mixed messages as to whether they were open to Díaz continuing in office, Vázquez Gómez remained adamant that Díaz resign, a position Madero ultimately, although reluctantly, accepted. The resignation demand, however, once again killed the talks, as Francisco Carvajal had no authority to negotiate a resignation and gave his notice that the talks were over.[19]

Orozco's Insubordination and Possible Rebellion

May 6 marks the start of Orozco's rebellion against Madero, an accusation Orozco partisans consider defamatory. Several conflicting firsthand accounts purport to document the drama that unfolded between May 6 and 13, with historians also divided or unconvinced over the various interpretations of those events. Rather than ignoring this muddled record, one should carefully examine the parties' activities on those days to gain insight into Orozco and Madero as well as possible explanations for their ultimate, dramatic split only months later.

Elements favoring an Orozco mutiny were present long before May 6. First, rebel forces were not trained military. They were ragtag irregulars, volunteering along the way, attaching themselves to local leaders, or joining whatever band happened along. Some rebels, such as Villa, were violent, veteran outlaws. Many, such as Orozco and his San Isidro colleagues, jumped into the revolution without close supervision. They fought as they wished, armed and provisioned themselves, selected their own targets, and fought in bands in their own style and under their own local leadership. The various rebel groups cooperated, but discipline and rank were often informal. When ostensible leaders, such as Madero or Abraham González, accomplished nothing militarily or bungled a skirmish or battle, they engendered disrespect among rebels. Military victories belonged completely to irregular forces, such as Orozco's. Thus, even before May 7, Orozco had openly disobeyed Madero's order to submit to Soto's command and later refused Madero's order to disarm Magonista troops. Madero not only failed to discipline Orozco for both acts of insubordination but instead promoted him to colonel soon after the first act and to general after the second infraction. To Orozco, who perhaps thought he should have been the top rebel military leader, following Madero's orders was optional. Orozco was already set to attack Ciudad Juárez in February. He might have abandoned the challenge because Madero failed to produce troops, resulting in a delay that allowed federal forces to reinforce the city's garrison. Orozco was not a man who took orders well, and he certainly did not tolerate insults or questions about his judgment or ability. All those factors without doubt played a role in the run up to the battle at Ciudad Juárez.

Until the afternoon of May 6, the record is reasonably clear. Accounts of events after that are unclear and conflicting,[20] with the large missing piece being the absence of an Orozco memoir. Orozco's questionable conduct and insubordination relate to the start of the Battle of Juárez and his altercation with Madero on May 13. Stories of Orozco's actions range from his acceptance of payment to assassinate Madero,[21] to mere disobedience, to no improper conduct at all. Some versions have no evidentiary support, making it impossible to determine the account's veracity, but several others are corroborated. Much of the suspicion regarding Orozco's disloyalty centers on the conduct of Limantour's peace delegates Toribio Esquivel Obregón and Óscar Braniff and their relationship with Orozco.

The previous truce allowing talks to take place expired on May 6,[22] but Madero still did not order an attack. To the annoyance of his military leaders, Madero seemed to be listening to those who counseled him to abandon the attack, fearing U.S. intervention should some rounds land on American soil. Those individuals included some of the Maderos, cousin Rafael L. Hernández, military advisor and Boer general Benjamin Viljoen,[23] and Limantour's informal delegates Toribio Esquivel Obregón and Óscar Braniff.

On May 6, Esquivel Obregón and Braniff asked Madero to allow them to meet with rebel military leaders. Madero agreed, and the meeting took place at 4 P.M.[24] Esquivel Obregón and Braniff sensed that some of the rebel leaders agreed with them that they did not need to insist on a Díaz resignation. Later that evening at El Paso's Sheldon Hotel, a messenger told Esquivel Obregón that Orozco was asking if he should send a telegram of his own to Díaz and showed them the draft. In the draft telegram that circumvented Madero, Orozco said that Díaz should withdraw federal forces from Ciudad Juárez, and the rebels would agree to engage in further negotiations and to suspend further action in the rest of Chihuahua. The federal government, Orozco proposed, would pay the rebels' expenses for that time. The telegram draft did not mention a Díaz resignation but would effectively give Ciudad Juárez to the rebels. Esquivel Obregón said that he suggested that, rather than Orozco sending the telegram, he would send it in his own name, which he did the next morning, May 7, by sending it to Limantour. Esquivel Obregón heard nothing from Limantour for most of that day.[25]

With rebel troops clamoring to get on with the assault, Madero, instead of attacking on the seventh, ordered their camp raised and canceled their planned attack. He ordered a retreat to an unspecified location south of Ciudad Juárez, where, he said, they could later fight federal forces free from the threat of intervention.[26] Some forces, particularly those under Viljoen, were already under way south when Orozco, Villa, and Garibaldi met with Madero at the adobe headquarters.[27] They argued against the retreat and for the attack. Madero called for other commanders to give their opinion, and all were in favor of attacking. Madero relented and consented to allow the attack to start that night at midnight.[28] Later on the seventh, however, Madero forces received word that Díaz had issued a proclamation stating that he was prepared to resign *provided* that there was peace and that the people still wished for him to resign.[29] Madero either did not understand the declaration and its proviso, or he received an altered document, or bad advice. In any case, Madero interpreted the proclamation as being tantamount to a Díaz resignation and once again immediately called off the attack and ordered Orozco and Giuseppe Garibaldi to withdraw their troops from Ciudad Juárez, saying that they would go south and fight there another day.[30] Frantically trying to buy time, the wily and duplicitous old dictator was once again playing games, confounding the easily flummoxed Madero with his "yes I will, no I won't" declarations. Again, Madero restarted peace negotiations, this time with Esquivel Obregón and Braniff, who had replaced Carvajal.[31] The Limantour-friendly Madero family was willing to keep Díaz in office and continually pulled Madero in one direction while Vázquez Gómez and military leaders, such as Orozco and Villa, demanded the removal of Díaz and his administration. Hours before dawn on May 8, Madero and the Díaz delegates agreed to yet another cease-fire, which was to last until 4 P.M. the afternoon of May 8.

Esquivel Obregón recounted, however, that during the evening of May 7, Orozco telephoned him and asked whether Limantour had responded to the telegram. Esquivel Obregón said that Limantour had not. Orozco explained that, without a response from Mexico City, his course was set, and his forces would begin the attack. Orozco said that his troops were in crisis and that he would not be humiliated by withdrawing for a second time from Ciudad Juárez. Orozco's response surprised Esquivel Obregón, who was aware that Madero had called off the attack.[32] Villa lends support for this part of Esquivel Obregón's version. Villa said that late on May 7, Orozco went to visit him and asked what they should do about the attack. Villa said that he was the one who proposed the attack's plan to Orozco, who agreed. Villa suggested that the next day José Orozco and some of his men should provoke federal troops into firing and the battle would so begin. Villa and Orozco planned to cross into El Paso to spend the day, so they could claim no responsibility for the attack. If Madero asked them to stop the shooting, they would agree to do so but in fact would permit the firing to continue,[33] and so it happened.[34]

Others, unaware of the true plan, attributed the shooting on the eighth to another incident. During the cease-fire on that morning, a flier signed by federal colonel Manuel Tamborel circulated among rebel troops referring to the rebels as cowards who were good at raiding unprotected ranches and stealing chickens but who were not brave enough to fight, repeating an insult Tamborel had been hurling for days.[35] The Tamborel affront prompted more profane exchanges between the forces, a trench warfare staple.[36]

After eighteen days of waiting, rebel troops had finally had enough. That morning of the eighth, during the agreed upon cease-fire, a rebel squad attacked federal lines.[37] When Madero learned about the attack three hours later, he first thought that federal forces had started the exchange and called Navarro to have his troops stop firing. When he learned from Navarro that it had been rebel troops who had violated his cease-fire, Madero was furious and saw it as a breach of honor. Madero wrote to Orozco ordering that the shooting stop and noted that Navarro had promised that his troops would abide by the cease-fire.[38] At 12:30 P.M., Madero sent a note to Navarro, calling the shooting accidental. Madero ordered the unit's retreat, and his soldiers responded, "To hell with you. We will remain where we are until we die if no help is sent to us." Madero mounted his horse and went to Peace Grove, which was relatively close to the area where the advanced rebels were and gathered the troops there. He told them that violating the cease-fire was a breach of faith, and he would have none of it. The troops cheered Madero, but within minutes after Madero left the scene, the rebels ran to reinforce the advance units.[39] Madero asked for an explanation for the unauthorized attack, but it was too late, because the shooting had become general—that is, everyone was involved, and it was no longer isolated. There was no going back, as his troops told Madero that they would not abandon the advance squad while it was inside the city. Madero sent Navarro a demand that federal forces surrender, but, after Navarro refused to capitulate, Madero resigned himself to the shooting war and approved the ongoing attack. That evening, Madero issued a lengthy statement explaining why he ordered the attack to commence.[40] He then took his wife, crossed into El Paso over the small pedestrian suspension bridge, and went to the Sheldon Hotel[41] to wait for the battle's outcome.[42]

That the rebels engaged in shooting on Monday morning is a fact, and most observers and historians agree that the rebels provoked the battle, as Villa later admitted. He and Orozco intentionally violated Madero's orders and started the attack. Various historians agree that the attack was intentional and planned, including Francisco Almada, who wrote that Orozco and Villa gave the order and that one of José Orozco's men initiated the firing.[43] Nellie Campobello explained that Orozco and Villa left instructions for their troops to start the attack, went to El Paso, and then returned in mock surprise when the shooting started.[44] Carleton Beals wrote that Orozco and Villa, tired of Madero's continuous vacillation and changes, ordered the attack and ignored Madero's orders to stop the shooting.[45] Madero confidant and advisor Roque Estrada concluded that the attack was an act of insubordination.[46] Although the evidence is conflicting, it seems clear that Orozco and Villa ordered the attack. Both were anxious to start the battle, neither was inclined to obey Madero, and both were tired of his contradictory and dilatory positions and statements.

CHAPTER SEVENTEEN

The Battle of Ciudad Juárez

At 4:30 on the morning of Tuesday, May 9, the Madero-authorized rebel assault began in earnest. Under fire, federal forces quickly abandoned the first trenches, freeing the rebels to move southeast downriver to occupy the levee. Attackers at Ciudad Juárez always knew to attack with the river at their backs, forcing defenders to shoot north and possibly into El Paso. The position reduced the defenders' ability to fire. A rebel machine gun occupied an adobe home south of the Stanton Street Bridge, which connected the two cities. The gun's placement kept the area to the south clear of federal troops, allowing the rebels, under Orozco, to enter homes near the border and proceed south toward the city's center.[1] The rebels entered the heart of the city on foot, pushing south toward the customs house, Guadalupe Mission, and jail area, with their final goal being the garrison. They advanced using heavy steel digging and wrecking bars, which they used to breach adobe walls and make holes that would allow an individual to pass through. Thus, the rebels moved south, house by house, in relative safety, until they came to cross streets. In homes, while troops punched holes, the other soldiers sat in living rooms and played phonographs and used telephones to call the Sheldon Hotel to report on their progress. Residents of Juárez often fed and gave water to the rebels, support they denied the federal forces,[2] because a clear majority of the populace sympathized with the rebels. General Navarro later noted that some four hundred residents of Ciudad Juárez had joined the rebels in firing at federal troops.[3]

Whenever they reached the end of a row of homes, the rebels were exposed to federal rifle, mortar, machine gun, and artillery fire, and they took many casualties. Homes and buildings burned, emitting acrid smoke and drastically reducing visibility. Rebels progressing south had no time to stop and fire weapons, other than on the run, until they reached the customs house. At that point, the field opened, with wide streets and the nearby central plaza facing the mission, giving the rebels a place to stop, take cover, and fire. Hidden or protected on roofs, in the church, in its bell tower, and in the jail, federal machine guns, snipers, mortar, and artillery had the edge on firepower and an elevated, protected location. The rebels found cover where possible and returned the fire. Although the federal forces had the superior position and firepower advantage, they did not hold, and rebel units advanced steadily until nightfall on the ninth.

As the rebels approached Guadalupe Mission and the jail, they saw the battle's devastation. It was as though a great storm had hit the city. Buildings burned and were riddled with bullet holes. Broken and splintered windows and door frames, battered walls, and torn awnings littered the streets and walks. Telephone lines dangled from poles, and the streets were filled with the battle's debris and detritus. The rebels had taken many casualties. The *El Paso Herald* reported bleeding wounded lying out in the open and more than one hundred dead, "shot to pieces, brains scattered, vital organs blown out, the dead [lying] where they [fell],"[4] often the gruesome casualties of dynamite bombs.[5] On the ninth at 6:30 P.M., an agreed-upon cease-fire allowed removal of the dead and wounded.[6] Combatants, unfortunately, were not the only casualties. Civilian curiosity also took its toll.

On the American side, five onlookers who got too close to the action were killed, and fifteen were wounded in the day's battle. Noncombatants at home or work in El Paso were shot or experienced near misses. One, a judge sitting on the bench, had a bullet fall on his desk. In a well-known photograph showing observers on the Paso del Norte Hotel rooftop, the caption mistakenly described the perch as safe. It was not. Several individuals were shot at sites farther away than that location, including one in San Jacinto Plaza. On the streets of El Paso, newspaper vendors cried out, "Extra! Extra! Read all about the battle in Juárez!" as local newspapers cranked out edition after extra edition. The *El Paso Herald* alone printed at least nine extra editions on May 8, seven on the ninth and six on the tenth, each reporting events in Ciudad Juárez with detailed reports of El Paso deaths, injuries, and property damage.[7]

Federal forces also gained at least one unanticipated and unwitting supporter. Philadelphian James Monaghan, a Swarthmore student, caught more action than he planned when he went on a Sunday sightseeing tour of Ciudad Juárez the day before the shooting started. Federal forces arrested him as a spy and jailed him. After the battle started, they put Monaghan to work with other inmates ferrying water to the troops on the jailhouse roof.[8]

On Wednesday morning, May 10, rebels reached the perimeter of Guadalupe Mission, grounds where federal gun placements on high ground dominated the area. Rebel "artillery" targeted the federal battery there, tossing dynamite sticks with devastating effect. Rebels found forty rurales defending inside the mission. When they finished with them, fourteen were dead. Rebel troops under José de la Luz Blanco successfully attacked the jail during the night. One bomb blasted a huge hole in the jail wall through which they freed the prisoners, many of whom joined the rebels. Taking the jail placed rebels next to Guadalupe Mission, a federal stronghold, where rebels clambered onto the roof and took out federal snipers perched in the bell tower and hidden behind roof parapets. Rebels seized abandoned federal machine guns and artillery pieces. Another rebel squad veered east to join Garibaldi's troops converging on the bullring, another federal stronghold. Villa and his 650 men came up from the south along the rail line. They used nail-filled pipe bombs on the federal troops.[9] From his El Paso vantage point, Madero watched his troops making progress through the streets of Ciudad Juárez.[10]

Although federal troops had a location and firepower advantage, their lines gave way, and they began a retreat to the garrison. It was not difficult to understand why federal troops folded given their composition. It was the reason why Díaz and Limantour were both anxious to negotiate a peace agreement before any serious fighting took place. They had no faith that their troops would prevail. Díaz was a soldier, a lifetime military man, yet he had no confidence in his own forces. He knew and had long known that his army was a thoroughly corrupt institution, good against the weak, but untested against a worthy foe. Early on, Díaz fashioned a militaristic state, but one he could always control, where he could keep the weak down and help the powerful. There was an officer corps, but it was ineffectual. Some infantrymen were "recruited" via forced conscription, "la leva." Troops were found by emptying prisons or jails or by kidnapping young men, sometimes hundreds at a time. In one instance, the military appeared as a bullfight crowd was leaving the arena and simply seized most of the young men in the crowd. The military handed each of them a uniform and a rifle, and off they went. The song, "You're in the Army Now," was never so true. It was therefore natural that the expectations for that sort of army were low indeed. Desertions were common. Throughout the revolution, many of the federal soldiers sympathized with the rebels and either feigned combat or else shed the uniform entirely and went over to the enemy.

Orozco and Villa, two highly regarded combatants, may have missed the fighting of May 8 if they spent the day in El Paso. There are few reports detailing their activities that day, and there were few accounts of their activities during the remainder of the battle.[11] As for the battle on the ninth and tenth, Orozco and his troops went south down the center of the city toward the mission, and Villa came up from the south along the rail line.[12]

The morning of Wednesday the tenth, federal troops, outnumbered and exhausted, lacking water and food,[13] retreated to their final refuge, the garrison in the southern part of the city, allowing the rebels to advance, racing to the garrison and reaching it before noon. Hundreds of rebels attacked the stronghold, now filled with federal troops. Rebels fired away with abandon, and the federal forces took heavy casualties, also losing many horses stabled inside. Finally, near midday, the federal forces raised the white flag of surrender. After entering the garrison, Orozco, with a look of hatred on his face, witnessed the surrendering General Navarro hand his sword to Giuseppe Garibaldi, commander of Madero's foreign legion.[14] No one needed to tell Garibaldi that Orozco and his people wished to execute Navarro.[15] In fact, they demanded that Navarro be tried for war crimes, but they expected an execution either way. Garibaldi kept Navarro close to him and protected him for five hours as they waited for Madero to arrive. Navarro also surrendered 480 soldiers, including 120 wounded.[16] After the surrender, many federal troops shed their uniforms out on the street, so it looked like a used clothing market with many soldiers walking down the street in their underwear toward the corral, where they were held as prisoners of war. A significant number of federal soldiers enlisted in rebel ranks. Inside the garrison, they found the body of its former commander, Manuel Tamborel, dead from at least a dozen bullets. He was the commander who had continually taunted and ridiculed the rebels before the fighting began. After rebel troops stormed the garrison, they seized mortars, two field artillery pieces, half a million rounds of ammunition, seven hundred Mausers, and hundreds of horses. They were now well supplied to confront any force Díaz might send from Chihuahua and were prepared even if the United States prohibited the supplying of weapons in El Paso.[17]

Roque Estrada had an opportunity to visit with Orozco and Villa after the victory in Ciudad Juárez. A careful observer and note taker, an early Anti-Reelection Party operative, and the man Díaz had arrested along with Madero, Estrada found Orozco to be a sensitive man, honest and possessed of great energy. He saw him discipline a soldier and found Orozco's manner to be a little short of harsh, judging him a hard commander. Villa, of course, came across as an unusual character. He wore a long coat, black pants with yellow leggings, and a Stetson. His dark brown eyes darted about as though he was surprised and stirred up.[18]

Given the importance of the battle to the revolution and to Orozco's and Villa's careers and reputations, there is little in the literature describing their activities on those days.[19] What we do know is that Orozco and Villa warrant credit for initiating the successful attack rather than walking away from it as Madero had wanted to do on several occasions.

CHAPTER EIGHTEEN

A Spoiled Victory Celebration

Once the battle was over, huge crowds amassed in the center of Ciudad Juárez. Hundreds of joyous and incredulous Juarenses filled the streets. After three days of fighting, Ciudad Juárez was in rebel hands. Coming from El Paso, Madero triumphantly entered the city and went directly to the corral, where, as his first act, he commended the federal prisoners for their bravery. On the evening of the tenth, after the day's tumult, Madero issued a conciliatory statement. Rather than gloat, he was anxious to conclude peace talks. With the people perhaps accurately sensing who was responsible for the successful attack, there were as many if not more shouts of "Viva Orozco" as one could hear for Madero on the streets of Ciudad Juárez that victorious day. Orozco was clearly the hero of the day.[1] The *El Paso Herald* reported, "The street is full of people calling 'Viva, Orozco, Viva Orozco.' There are few 'Viva Maderos.'"[2]

The next day, May 11, Madero commandeered the city hall behind Guadalupe Mission for his headquarters and declared the nearby customs house the nation's provisional capitol, an honor the city and customs house had not had since Benito Juárez's refuge there during the French invasion. As provisional president, Madero announced appointments to his cabinet and called for its first meeting. Showing an intense interest in Madero's cabinet choices, Orozco expressed disappointment over most of the selections. The cabinet seats went to Francisco Vázquez Gómez to foreign relations, Federico González Garza to Gobernación—the equivalent of interior minister in European governments— Pino Suárez to justice, Gustavo Madero to finance, Manuel Bonilla to communications, and Venustiano Carranza to war. Madero named J. Guadalupe González to head the military. Orozco looked with approval on the appointment of Francisco Vázquez Gómez, the vice-presidential nominee, but to Orozco and his father, the galling nomination was Venustiano Carranza, a Madero ally from Coahuila, as war minister. Orozco's father and others said that the war post belonged to Orozco. Instead of a top military post, Madero appointed

Orozco head of Chihuahua's rurales, which paid only eight pesos a day and was a relatively minor post for a military leader with national ambitions. Orozco opposed appointing anyone to the cabinet, such as Carranza, who had not fought in the revolution.[3] If Madero was intent on reducing the influence of the military on Mexican government and subjecting the military to civilian control, his appointment of Carranza to the War Ministry and González to be military commander would make sense. Carranza had spent the war either in the United States or, more recently, in the comfortable Sheldon Hotel in El Paso.[4] Also annoying to Orozco was Madero's preferential treatment of General Navarro. Madero lodged Navarro safely in Madero's quarters and appeared deaf to the pleas of rebel troops for a Navarro trial and to Albino Frías's personal plea that Madero should force Navarro to visit the widows and children of the men he had executed at Cerro Prieto.[5]

Again bypassing Madero and his staff of advisors, on the night of May 11, Orozco went to the Sheldon Hotel to meet privately with Limantour delegates Toribio Esquivel Obregón and Óscar Braniff. Orozco—further corroborating that he initiated the attack on Ciudad Juárez against Madero's orders—explained to the delegates why he felt that he had no choice but to attack Ciudad Juárez. It was to lift the morale of his troops, to maintain personal honor and reputation by not retreating from the attack they had so publicly announced, and to provide his men pay, food, and clothing. He desired peace, but he felt it out of reach because Madero was under the influence of men with poor judgment. Madero, Orozco said, was a good man, but surrounded himself with those who would spoil his work. The delegates agreed with Orozco's sentiments. Orozco again expressed his desire to restart peace negotiations but noted that his troops still needed to eat and might react out of need. The delegates proposed that as part of an armistice they would work for a provision to cover interim rebel troop needs at government expense, a condition they had proposed in their conversation of May 7, and which they now hoped rebel leaders would reconsider.[6]

If Orozco's betrayal of Madero began on May 6, 1911, its high point occurred on May 13, a memorable and controversial day indeed, and the subject of many conflicting accounts written by those who witnessed its events.[7] Several occurrences on May 12 set the scene for May 13. There was the routine, as when Madero issued a notice for Orozco and other military commanders to appear at the headquarters at 9:00 the next morning as well as an order to Luis Aguirre to provision the troops.[8] While Madero apparently arranged to feed the troops, he did not pay them as he had promised Orozco and Marcelo Caraveo the previous day.[9] Esquivel Obregón wrote that on the afternoon of May 12 he happened to be in Ciudad Juárez to deliver a newspaper to Navarro when he ran into Orozco. He asked Orozco to show him the artillery pieces the rebels had seized from federal forces. Orozco did so, and while he was showing Esquivel Obregón the guns, Venustiano Carranza visited the same location and saw them together.[10]

At five that afternoon, Villa recounted, Orozco invited Villa to meet at Orozco's quarters, where they could privately discuss a sensitive matter. Once Villa arrived, Orozco reminded Villa that Navarro had executed several members of their families.[11] Orozco proposed that they take and execute Navarro and that if Madero opposed the execution, they would disobey Madero and kill Navarro regardless. Villa agreed with the plan, and Orozco told Villa to meet him at the headquarters the next morning at 10:00, when they would present their demand to Madero.[12] After his meeting with Villa, Orozco went to the garrison, where he met at 6:00 P.M. with one of his officers, Heliodoro Olea Arias. He told Olea that he needed for him and thirty of his best men to report in front of the headquarters early the next morning. He also told Olea to tell José Orozco to do the same along with thirty of his best men. Olea delivered the order to José Orozco, who asked Olea the reason for the order, and Olea answered that he did not know, that perhaps Madero was going somewhere and needed his best people.[13]

Very early on the morning of Saturday, May 13, Orozco went to Esquivel Obregón's room at the Sheldon Hotel. It was so early that Esquivel Obregón was not yet fully dressed. At some point, they were joined by Braniff. Orozco explained that he was upset over the cabinet appointments. Orozco thought that Madero's cabinet choices were impromptu and poor and would hinder relations between the government and the revolution. Because his troops were starving, and Madero's cabinet was losing the revolution, Orozco was willing to remove the cabinet and even arrest the new ministers. While he had affection for Madero, he would oppose him in a dramatic manner. Ultimately, Madero would realize that he would benefit from this act of insubordination, like the attack on Ciudad Juárez. Madero would win, and the revolution would gain prestige. Orozco asked the delegates whether they were sure that the government would accept the conditions necessary to guarantee the principles of the revolution, and they responded that the government was open to providing all manner of assurances to the revolution. As soon as they agreed on an armistice, they would propose government support for the rebel army's upkeep. Orozco complained that his men could starve during armistice negotiations at which time Braniff said that he, together with Ernesto and Francisco Madero Sr., would provide one thousand pesos to cover immediate expenses. During the conversation, Orozco expressed his concern that others might misinterpret his conversation with the delegates and its mention of money. Esquivel Obregón said that Orozco emphasized that he sought no personal benefit. Orozco, nevertheless, was uncomfortable over his father's possible opinion of his actions.[14]

Esquivel Obregón wrote that, after Orozco left, he and Braniff considered their options regarding Orozco's shocking plan. It was nothing short of a coup d'état for a military man to remove the cabinet and arrest its members. How else could a sitting president see such an act? The delegates, Esquivel Obregón later wrote, pondered whether they should report the matter to authorities or whether they should convince Orozco not to take his proposed action. Esquivel Obregón concluded that they did not hesitate in letting Orozco do what he intended while they remained silent about the plan.[15]

At sunup on May 13, Heliodoro Olea Arias and his men lined up at the headquarters. Orozco then arrived with a few men, followed by Madero, who arrived later with his ten-man personal guard detail headed by Máximo Castillo. Madero entered the building and proceeded to meet with his new cabinet. Villa arrived with fifty men. Despite the ongoing cabinet meeting, Orozco and some of his men barged into the room. According to Madero, Orozco told him that he was under arrest and had been overthrown. While that was going on, Orozco's men grabbed and jostled members of the cabinet.[16] Madero attempted to go outside, and Orozco, his pistol drawn, kept insisting that Madero give himself up. Villa attempted to hold onto Madero to pull him back inside, but Madero, helped by part of his guard, made it outside. Once outside, Villa insisted on Navarro's custody and grabbed Madero as well, surprising Madero, who shouted, "You too!" and then Madero ordered Villa executed. Madero went to his car, followed by Orozco, who still had his pistol drawn and was still insisting that Madero submit to his arrest.[17]

Orozco or his partisans made three demands: pay and provisions for rebel soldiers,[18] removal of the cabinet, and custody of Navarro. Madero went outside and into his waiting car, which Orozco's troops had surrounded. The foreign legion, acting as Madero's security detail, was prepared to shoot. Orozco followed Madero to the car, jumped on the car's running board, and stood next to Madero. His face flushed with emotion, Orozco told Madero to give himself up as a prisoner and added, "You are useless, incapable of feeding the people. How can you be president? You are a liar, you lie that your brothers spent funds on the revolution when they haven't spent a cent."[19]

As they exchanged heated words, Orozco had his pistol out and put it to Madero's breast, declaring again that Madero was under arrest. Madero looked at Orozco and said, "Here I am. Kill me if you wish to." Then, addressing the crowd from the open car, Madero said, "Who was it that declared the revolution? Was it not I? Have I not maintained it with my life and fortune? If this is so, am I not the chief?"[20] Madero began to shout to the troops, asking whether they followed him or Orozco, eliciting a mixed response.[21] Red with anger, Orozco held still for a while, then slowly withdrew and holstered his pistol, avoiding Madero's public execution and what would have been a bloody street fight because Madero's security had a machine gun aimed at the scene. Madero shouted that all was well and kept offering his hand to Orozco, who, seeing that he did not control the crowd, eventually took it. Madero and Orozco walked away from the car and reentered the customs house, continuing their dispute there. Once inside, Orozco again aired his grievances, addressing pay, food, and clothing for his troops, and threatened mutiny unless Madero met his demands. For good measure, he also demanded the resignation of those in the cabinet who had not fought and custody of Navarro for trial. Madero responded that he would issue his own check immediately in the sum of 750 pesos to pay the troops,[22] that he alone had the discretion in naming the cabinet, and that by using Navarro in a prisoner exchange, Navarro was worth more alive than dead. That calmed Orozco, as he and Madero apparently reconciled and stepped outside, embracing for the crowd.[23] Orozco then rode away with his troops. Later that evening, Madero issued a statement forgiving Orozco's threats and assault.[24]

Manuel Bonilla, who had been appointed to the cabinet by Madero, provided a version of the events in his book published in 1922, which was contrary to that of Esquivel Obregón. In Bonilla's version, Orozco met Esquivel Obregón and Braniff at the Sheldon Hotel the day after the Battle of Ciudad Juárez. Braniff, without receiving authorization from Limantour, told Orozco that those who had fought, especially Orozco, to whose intelligence and valor the victory was owed, should not permit those who had done nothing to receive the high-paying positions. Braniff explained that Orozco could stop Carranza's appointment and receive the position instead. Orozco could also oust the other cabinet members. Braniff said that if Madero refused to go along, he could imprison him, execute him, or send him into exile. Bonilla added that Orozco later told Madero what Braniff had said. When it appeared that Orozco was not intent on committing treason, Braniff reminded Orozco about Madero freeing Navarro, and that changed Orozco's mind. Bonilla recounted elements of the scene described by the others, except that, in Bonilla's version, not only did Orozco and Villa arrest Madero, but Orozco also first demanded that, since the triumph was his doing, he should be named "supreme commander." Madero lectured Orozco on the impropriety of his demand, and then Orozco, backed by Villa, reduced his demand to the position of war minister. Madero proposed to put the case to those in attendance and stood on his vehicle to address the troops. Bonilla wrote that the soldiers unanimously supported Madero, Orozco was defeated, and the arrested cabinet members were freed.[25]

The riotous nature of the scene coupled with the understandable emotion and bias on the part of Madero, Orozco, and Villa partisans produced a conflicted and inconsistent record.[26] Nevertheless, there are sufficient, corroborated statements to discern much of what occurred. Whatever plan Orozco had in creating the mêlée, unfortunately for him, he communicated little of it to those he expected would support him, and he recruited some who were unlikely allies. Orozco's plan was shaky and unsure and went down in confusion. We can be reasonably sure that his plan constituted an attempted coup d'état. The nature of the confrontation in drawing a weapon on the provisional president, persistently attempting to arrest him, dragging him around, and telling him how worthless he was; demanding the cabinet be fired; and arresting some of the appointees amounted to nothing short of an attempted coup. Madero had the absolute right to have had Orozco tried and perhaps executed for his conduct and should have, at a minimum, cashiered the hero, but Madero kept him on as if nothing had happened.[27] Madero partisans were convinced that Orozco had indeed attempted a coup, and several were sure that Esquivel Obregón and Braniff had goaded Orozco into that course.[28] Roque Estrada wrote that while he believed that Orozco intended a coup, it was limited to deposing the cabinet and not Madero.[29] Nevertheless, assuming Estrada was correct, the coup was in fact deposing Madero. How could it be anything but a coup when Orozco arrested the new ministers and declared that they were out? The May 13 incident was especially painful for Villa. Villa insisted that he was there to ask for Navarro's head.[30] He was unaware of the wider plan to depose Madero and his cabinet. Villa later became convinced that

Esquivel Obregón and Braniff paid Orozco to assassinate Madero, and that Orozco had set Villa up to take the fall. During the assault, Orozco ordered Villa to disarm Madero's guard.[31] Villa was not alone in seeing a conspiracy between Orozco and the Limantour delegates. Federico González Garza and others became suspicious after Orozco was seen meeting Esquivel Obregón and Braniff on several occasions. González Garza thought that Orozco was crude, uneducated, and politically ambitious and thus fell into the delegates' trap.[32] While the multiple clandestine meetings with Orozco were certain to raise suspicions that Díaz delegates conspired with Orozco, it is impossible to determine the precise role that Esquivel Obregón and Braniff played in the event. Although Madero professed to accept the delegates' denial that they had conspired with Orozco against him, Madero issued an order declaring the pair unwelcome in his camp and denied them passes to cross into Ciudad Juárez, thus effectively ending their service there.[33] The delegates' self-serving denial was also to be expected. Had they been implicated in the plot, they could have been tried and executed. Whether they suggested the precise plan is unknown, but they certainly encouraged Orozco's disdain for Madero. That Orozco went directly from a meeting with them to attempt a coup is also significant. Given Esquivel Obregón's admission that the delegates agreed to remain silent even after they had knowledge of Orozco's plan to overthrow the cabinet, it is not much of a leap to think that they, at a minimum, tacitly encouraged the coup or even Madero's possible assassination. The evidence indicates that it is likely that they were, at a minimum, accessories to the attempt if not, indeed, its authors.

Manuel Bonilla's account was an indictment of Braniff and Esquivel Obregón as instigators and Orozco as the actor in a failed coup. Several elements in Bonilla's version, however, do not ring true. One was that Orozco changed his mind about proceeding when he was reminded that Madero had freed Navarro. The key conversation in question with Orozco occurred on May 11, and the record shows that Madero did not free Navarro until shortly after the altercation on the thirteenth;[34] therefore, freeing Navarro could not have motivated Orozco to change his mind. Also, there is the minor claim that the crowd on the thirteenth was unanimously with Madero. Orozco probably had the largest number of men present, with Villa also having a significant number of troops. It is unlikely that those troops would have gone against their leaders. Others, however, corroborate the more controversial elements of Bonilla's rendition. Villa especially was of the view that the delegates wanted

Orozco to execute Madero. Bonilla later became a Villista, and perhaps Villa was a source for part of his version.

However it happened, the altercation reflected poorly on Orozco. He was duped or acted clumsily on his own. Regardless of the different versions of the episode, in its planning and execution, the attempt was treacherous and inept and became another act of insubordination that went unpunished.

There is no question that Orozco already had a bad opinion of Madero. Orozco had made up his mind about Madero for his inability to recruit forces on November 20 in Texas; his February refusal to attack Ciudad Juárez; his clumsy attempt to subordinate Orozco's command; his premature and disastrous attack on Casas Grandes; his vacillation and conflicting orders over attacking Juárez in April and May; his willingness to leave Díaz in office; and his rescue of war criminal Navarro. Others unfairly demeaned Madero for some of his physical traits, such as his high-pitched voice and short stature. All those factors combined to erase any respect Orozco might have had for Madero, who continually stumbled and demonstrated weakness and indecision, characteristics Serranos found incompatible with those of a leader. Orozco, seduced by popular adulation, believed that he merited a national post, including that of secretary of war. For his part, Madero could not bring himself to confer high civilian office on a man he considered unlettered, even if Orozco had undeniable leadership and military talent, and perhaps Madero indeed believed in subordinating the military to civilian rule.[35]

Later, Madero ignored his implied promise to use Navarro in a prisoner trade. On May 13, Madero drove the general to a place along the Rio Grande, gave him a horse, and saw the old man cross safely into the United States, where he was a free man and would never be held to account.[36] In freeing Navarro, Madero violated an important clause of his own Plan de San Luis stipulating that any Díaz commander found executing captured soldiers must himself be executed within twenty-four hours. Madero might have had political reasons for giving Navarro his freedom, but under his own law, Madero was wrong, and Orozco had a basis for demanding Navarro's death.[37]

Although most considered Madero the winner in the conflict of May 13, the incident exposed troubling faults in Madero's governance. Madero and Orozco tried to minimize the event and the severity of their breach. They exchanged conciliatory letters on May 15 and had them distributed to the public in a leaflet.[38] Months later, however, Madero rendered his true opinion of Orozco's attempt and his view of Esquivel Obregón's role. Madero, of course, knew that it had been a coup attempt, and he was convinced that, at a minimum, its intellectual author was Esquivel Obregón. Interviewed by the Mexico City daily *El Heraldo* on March 29, 1912, Madero spoke about Orozco's conduct on May 13. Orozco, he said, "is a man who gave me his word of honor, who cried with me, after I broke up his coup d'etat in Ciudad Juárez, begging me after, 'Allow me to prove my loyalty.'" In March 1912, the daily *El País* was demanding a change of cabinet ministers and suggested that Esquivel Obregón be appointed. Madero questioned how he was going to appoint as minister the man who had suggested that Orozco betray him.[39]

Although Madero put on a brave face to minimize the attempted coup, in fact, its impact was profound. It was a watershed event that changed relationships and created different perceptions of the parties. Madero did not execute Villa as he had ordered, but he paid the profusely apologetic colonel ten thousand pesos and mustered him out of service.[40] From that day, Villa would remain loyal to Madero and an enemy of Orozco's. Orozco and Villa would never work together again or be on the same side. Madero kept Orozco in his service, but at a great price, and others, such as Chihuahua's oligarchy, now saw Orozco as someone who might betray Madero. Certainly, after he carried on clandestine negotiations with Limantour's handpicked delegates, freely engaged in anti-Madero commentary, and attempted a violent insubordination, Orozco was a man whom the oligarchy was anxious to court.

CHAPTER NINETEEN

The Treaty of Ciudad Juárez and Its Aftermath

With respect to the peace agreement, the remaining contentious issues hinged on one item, the Díaz resignation. There was no dispute over Corral's departure or that Madero, ultimately, would sit in the presidency. Carvajal, Díaz's official representative, was upset that Vázquez Gómez rebuffed his private assurances that Díaz would eventually resign. Vázquez Gómez would settle for nothing less than the actual resignation, making relations between Vázquez Gómez and the Madero family venomous. Their mutual dislike now bordered on hatred. Vázquez Gómez held the upper hand because he had an official title, was more determined, and had the support of most in the rebel military and the public.

There was tension between the rebel military, those such as Orozco and Villa, and the Maderos. The two sides came to the revolution with different perspectives, with divergent goals and expectations. Madero's goals were political, a return to the Benito Juárez constitution and elections, while Orozco's demands were political, regional, and socioeconomic, including land and labor reforms. Orozco desired regional autonomy and more local control. Many also wanted vast estates expropriated with lands returned to the individuals, towns, and communities that had lost property during the Porfiriato. Orozco fully expected that Madero would reward those who had fought. He was adamant that the victors, meaning those who had fought, were entitled to the spoils.

Despite expecting imminent peace, Díaz remained in the presidency and ordered defensive reinforcements to Chihuahua City. Losing patience and perhaps addressing the issue before American media, Madero wrote a harsh note in English to Díaz, demanding that Díaz and Corral resign.[1] On May 21, Orozco's troops left Ciudad Juárez by train for Casas Grandes to prepare for the attack on Chihuahua City.

By the time Navarro surrendered, rebel peace negotiators were already close to reaching a global settlement with Díaz peace delegate Francisco Carvajal. A draft of the short document was prepared. Carvajal was ready, but Díaz vacillated over his resignation. He had health issues and was feeling rotten, saying he would resign one day and then saying the opposite the next, continuing in that vein for days. They were also waiting for Corral's resignation to arrive from Europe. Carvajal knew the end was near, and so the negotiators drafted a four-point peace agreement stipulating that, by the end of May, Díaz and Corral would resign their posts. On May 21, the peace delegates had a draft of the Treaty of Ciudad Juárez and agreed to sign.

Signing the agreement was a major event, a national historic milestone. Villa and his troops assembled on the night of the twenty-first to witness the signing at the customs house. They were all there and ready at 10:30 P.M., but they could not enter the building. The door was locked. Apparently, no one had thought to advise the people who had the key to the building. They stood outside in the dark while Vázquez Gómez banged on the door. Finally giving up, they resorted to signing the document on the building's steps. With two automobiles in front, headlights shining into the space, it was there on those dimly lit steps that Carvajal signed for Díaz and Madero and Vázquez Gómez signed for the rebels. Madero immediately sent telegrams to all rebel organizations ordering a cease-fire and adherence to the agreement.[2] The revolution was over and won, or so they thought on that night.

The ink had not dried on the Juárez peace agreement before further, serious discontent arose in Madero's coalition. The rebels already controlled twenty-six of the thirty-one states, with more to come their way.[3] With the Díaz government rapidly crumbling, Madero still granted the old régime substantial rights, including an interim presidency, two cabinet posts, and several governorships. More importantly, Madero left intact the bureaucracy, the military command hierarchy, and the Supreme Court. Several of the rebel leaders, including Villa, disagreed with the peace treaty, preferring unconditional surrender because the government was rapidly falling and would soon capitulate. His opposition was no great matter, as he was retired by Madero in Ciudad Juárez.[4] Days after the treaty was signed, Villa was back in his San Andrés home, where he married Luz Corral.

Madero's revolution had taken the nation to a new place and unleashed a pent-up demand for reform, and neither Madero nor anyone else had the power to return the country to its prerevolutionary days. The largely urban middle class was the country's most stable element and was Madero's political base. Madero shared its modest political expectations, such as returning to the Juárez 1857 Constitution. However, Madero was unwilling to unwind the Porfiriato's huge land expropriations, its extravagant concessions to foreign firms, or its political centralization. To Madero, the purpose of the revolution was a return to free elections and a rotating presidency. Despite implied or explicit reforms in his Plan de San Luis, he had no interest in social revolution. The revolution's heart, however, was the rural masses, who wanted a return of their lost lands, social reform, and their old local government.

Landless rural peons, industrial laborers, the wealthy, and conservative Catholics were each of a different mind. For them, the Madero Revolution would be either a weak half-measure or too radical. Liberal Party Magonistas had long before parted ways with Madero, but many former socialist Magonistas had joined Madero. Emiliano Zapata in Morelos soon split and openly fought Madero. Sentiment among Orozco's troops tracked the Magonistas and Zapatistas, for whom a revolution that did not expropriate land from the wealthy and redistribute it to the peasantry or restore lands lost to those who had lost their properties to survey companies was not a revolution at all. Three days after the treaty, Liberal Party leader Ricardo Flores Magón issued a lengthy manifesto imploring the revolution to continue. He reminded Magonistas that simply having Madero sit in the presidency was not the object they had sought. Magonistas ignored the treaty and continued their military operations in Chihuahua that summer.[5]

Orozco and his troops left Ciudad Juárez and waited for several days in Casas Grandes for orders to attack Chihuahua City. The attack became unnecessary when, prompted by near riots in Mexico City demanding their ouster, Díaz and Corral officially resigned the afternoon of May 25.[6] The public had suspected that Díaz was playing a game, and they demanded his removal. The Díaz cabinet and his closest aides wanted Díaz out of office and pleaded with the ailing dictator to step down. The Chamber of Deputies immediately accepted the resignations and designated Foreign Minister Francisco León de la Barra to be provisional president to succeed Madero, who promptly resigned as provisional president in accordance with the Treaty of Ciudad Juárez.

Díaz announced that he would leave Mexico for Spain. He left his home on Calle Cadena to spend the night at a friend's residence, and then at dawn the next day, he went to the San Lázaro Rail Station, where two trains waited to take his party to Veracruz.[7] Once in the port city, Díaz stayed at Weetman Pearson's home for three days. On May 31, with a large crowd in attendance, Díaz bade a tearful farewell to Mexico and closed the Porfiriato. An honor guard led by General Victoriano Huerta, a Díaz favorite, presided over the ceremony. Huerta made the nation's farewell speech to the old dictator. In tears, Huerta said that the army was the only part of the country that did not abandon Díaz. With the ceremony over, Díaz, his family, and his staff boarded the German steamer SS *Ypiranga* and departed for Europe.[8]

Meanwhile, in El Paso, Madero and his family were going from one feast and celebratory banquet to the next. Perhaps the largest one took place at the Toltec Club, honoring both Madero and Navarro. The two honorees sat at the head table with the mayor of El Paso seated between them.[9] On June 1, Madero went to the Sheldon Hotel in El Paso with two of his staff members to meet with Navarro. The subject of their meeting was unpublicized, and reports noted that the meeting was "cordial."[10] Two days later, ending nonstop festivities in Ciudad Juárez and El Paso, Madero and his party went to El Paso's Union Station and boarded a train bound for Eagle Pass, Texas, and then on to Mexico City. Among the dignitaries seeing Madero off was General Navarro, with whom Madero once again exchanged a warm abrazo and engaged in pleasant conversation. Madero was either clueless or cared not at all how his own troops felt about Navarro, a man considered to be the butcher of Cerro Prieto, a man Madero courted more than he embraced his own forces. In fact, Madero was not clueless. He was intelligent and knew exactly what Navarro had done and how the rebels felt about it. He embraced Navarro, fully understanding how Orozco and the other Serranos would see that act. Navarro had needlessly and brutally killed two of Orozco's brothers-in-law and his uncle Alberto, as well as other close friends and relatives in a manner that was contrary to law and that merited immediate execution under Madero's Plan de San Luis. Perhaps the embrace was symbolic and indicated to Serranos, Magonistas, the working class, and the landless that little would change under the incoming régime.

On Madero's triumphal trip to Mexico City after the Battle of Ciudad Juárez, throngs, tens of thousands, greeted his train at its stops en route to the capital. He stopped in Torreón, his hometown of San Pedro, Zacatecas, Aguascalientes, León, and San Juan del Río. Early on the morning of his arrival in Mexico City on June 7, a strong earthquake rocked the city, killing sixty-three and injuring hundreds.[11] Nonetheless, the large crowds seemed unfazed when they greeted Madero as he arrived. The day belonged to Francisco I. Madero, Coahuila farmer and reformer.

By leaving the mostly pro-Díaz state legislatures intact, Madero had difficulty putting his people, such as Abraham González in Chihuahua, into office. Provisional president León de la Barra announced presidential elections for October 1, and great care had to be taken that incumbent provisional governors did not campaign for office and thus violate the no-reelection provision, the most sacred of Madero's planks. Madero himself resigned as provisional president once León de la Barra was sworn in. Back in Chihuahua, Terrazas-Creel supporters still controlled the assembly, and González was not sworn in until June 11, with the election scheduled just weeks away.[12]

In the meantime, Orozco and his troops remained bivouacked forty miles north of Chihuahua City at El Sauz, waiting for orders to enter the capital.[13] While Orozco rested at El Sauz as the guest of Luis Terrazas at his hacienda, his troops, following his lead, took to grumbling over the food, lack of pay, and poor conditions, complaints Orozco had presented to Madero with increasing frequency and vehemence. Orozco's troops were also dissatisfied that Madero had failed to address land reform, an omission they took as a denial of their demand. Madero's Plan de San Luis clearly declared that properties expropriated under the vacant land provision would be reviewed. The land clause in the *plan*, however, left a huge loophole. It exempted lands purchased by "innocent" third parties who had bought land *before* the *plan*'s date and left unmentioned lands taken by other means. The troops harbored a deep suspicion that Madero would maintain the status quo, an unease that Orozco shared. Orozco and his father believed that no cabinet position should go to someone who had not fought in combat. Orozco and many revolutionaries had formed a credo from their view of the nation's history that to the victors went the spoils. In this case, the rule held, but only for the Maderos and a favored few. Most of those who fought were paid a meager ration and were mustered out on June 15,[14] while those in the losing army kept their jobs, as did the officer corps and members of the bureaucracy. The Madero family received the presidency, the most important financial positions in the cabinet, and reimbursement, perhaps excessive, for their financial contribution to the revolution. The Maderos appeared to emerge as clear winners while the Orozcos felt shortchanged.

Orozco then entered a new and, for him, confusing period. He was the subject of both public adulation and anti-Madero intrigue. Orozco hero-worship after the Battle of Ciudad Juárez bordered on the extreme: a mountain near Ciudad Juárez was renamed "Mount Orozco"; an El Paso jewelry company made and sold "Orozco souvenir spoons"; and civic clubs and other organizations were named in his honor.[15] Few twenty-nine-year-olds could control their egos after receiving such acclaim. Following Orozco's public altercation with Madero in Ciudad Juárez, anti-Madero groups, including old Porfiristas and those on the left, automatically saw in him the leader of a counterrevolution or new radical insurrection—that is, someone who would turn against Madero. From then on, virtually every anti-Madero uprising or conspiracy, left or right, would name Orozco its leader or member. Chihuahua City elites went to see Orozco at El Sauz, flattering and urging him to run for governor in the place of an expected González bid. Following a Díaz model, they had Orozco believing that only he could save the state and nation from chaos.[16] Ramón Puente wrote that Orozco, barely literate, was unqualified to aspire to be governor.[17] Madero paid Orozco 50,000 pesos for his services, but, according to Puente, Orozco Sr. was insulted with the payment and thought it insufficient. That issue engendered in the father a "cruel and implacable hatred" for Madero.[18] Months later, perhaps to show that the Orozcos were seeking financial gain from the revolution, the Madero administration made public the invoice that Orozco and his father had presented to the administration for their services from November 19, 1910, to the Battle of Ciudad Juárez. Orozco and his father each billed 50,000 pesos for a total of 100,000 pesos. The receipt, signed by Orozco Sr., noted that the pair received a total of 50,000 pesos.[19]

The oligarchy-dominated Chihuahua legislature created a dilemma for Abraham González when it accepted the resignation of Governor Miguel Ahumada and appointed González as provisional governor. Under the Madero Plan de San Luis, the basic law of the new régime, one could not be reelected to any top office, including that of governor. González could not therefore be a candidate for governor if he held the job in the interim.

Despite the prohibition against a sitting governor running for the same office, González proceeded to take the oath of office on June 11 and within a week proclaimed important economic reforms. He vowed to end concessions given to foreign firms granting monopoly power and prohibited the controversial company stores, tiendas de raya. González charged that concessions were normally accompanied by huge payoffs and kickbacks to politicians. He added, "For years Mexico has been exploited by foreigners, until the great body of the people have nothing. We were on the verge of becoming a nation of paupers. Now all special privileges shall cease if we can accomplish it."[20] González outlawed gambling, stopped the sale of municipal lands, and promised property titles at no cost to those who possessed and worked their properties. He also proposed mandatory arbitration of labor disputes by commissions with management *and* labor representation.[21] To Serranos, these reforms meant a reversal of old expropriations and the return of lands to their previous occupants. The González reforms shocked the Terrazas-Creel establishment, which saw itself as having been forced to appoint a man as governor who was now threatening to end their lucrative business practices, tax preferences, and system of open graft.[22]

Once in office, González called for Orozco's troops to enter Chihuahua City. On June 21, massive, jubilant crowds greeted Orozco and his 3,500 troops as they marched into Chihuahua City.[23] The troops proudly rode behind Orozco as they made their way south down the main streets of Chihuahua City toward the Palacio de Gobierno, the state capitol. At the parade's conclusion, Orozco and González stood side by side on the capitol's ceremonial balcony, where the cheers from the crowd below were clearly louder for Orozco, the greatest hero Chihuahua had ever produced. The people always cheered more for Orozco. Serranos were totally committed to Orozco, and to them, Orozco and not Madero was the revolution's personification.

PART III

Orozco's Rebellions and Death

CHAPTER TWENTY

Elections and Discord

The stage was thus set for the 1911 state and national elections scheduled for 21 August and 1 October. Two days after Orozco enjoyed the celebration alongside Abraham González, anti-Madero elements formed the Independent Club, a group composed of dissidents from both the right and the left. The group encouraged Orozco to run for governor. They feted Orozco at a social event held at the casino and then one at the gun club.[1] Orozco—perhaps letting his ego be swayed by the roars of "¡Viva Orozco!"—agreed to run for governor. Although he was entitled to believe that González would not be eligible for reelection as he was the sitting governor, Orozco had no sooner announced his run for office than he felt the sting of criticism and cries of treason coming from Chihuahua's Maderistas and González partisans who considered Orozco's act disrespectful and disloyal. Orozco's candidacy distanced him from the Maderista camp and threw him in with his former enemies, the Porfiristas. Madero issued a personal plea that Orozco abandon the race. Orozco was reminded that the state constitution required governors to be at least thirty years old, and he was months short of that. Under heavy pressure, Orozco withdrew from the race on July 15, insisting that rumors that Porfiristas supported him were a "false alarm" and without basis.[2] The state held elections as scheduled and results confirmed in August that Abraham González, as sitting governor, was reelected to a four-year term to begin on October 4.[3] Once again, Orozco felt disrespected. He must have let those around him know that he was unhappy with Madero and Maderistas because by mid-October, word was out that he was upset.[4]

On the national scene, Madero prepared to campaign, but he too had a problem. He was the nominee of the Anti-Reelection Party, and Francisco Vázquez Gómez was his vice presidential running mate. Vázquez Gómez was popular with the party's reform base and perhaps more popular than Madero in Chihuahua.[5] Madero's family, however, especially Gustavo Madero, then the newly appointed provisional secretary of the treasury, refused to accept Dr. Vázquez Gómez for vice president. In referring to Vázquez Gómez, Gustavo said, "*Este indio no será vice presidente.*"[6] Francisco Madero adopted the same attitude, but he could not unilaterally drop Vázquez Gómez because he was the party's nominee. To solve that problem, Madero, without requesting anyone's approval, dumped the Anti-Reelection Party by dissolving it, formed the new Progressive Constitutionalist Party, and recommended that it nominate Yucatán's governor José María Pino Suárez for vice president.[7] Madero also recommended that interim president León de la Barra remove interim minister Emilio Vázquez Gómez, Francisco's brother, from the cabinet, promptly resulting in his resignation and enmity.[8]

In Chihuahua, where Francisco Vázquez Gómez was popular, the matter quickly turned into a disaster. During the meeting of the new Progressive Constitutionalist Party in Chihuahua, the convention instructed delegates to cast their votes for Vázquez Gómez at the coming Mexico City convention. Once in Mexico City on the floor of the national convention, Chihuahua delegates, pressured to go along with Madero, voted instead for Pino Suárez, who came out on top over Vázquez Gómez. On September 5, Chihuahua political clubs met to condemn and expel the disobedient delegation upon its return. Governor González tried to walk a fine line in his attempt to reconcile the bitterly opposed factions. One of those for keeping Vázquez Gómez as vice president was Braulio Hernández, González's close associate and the old party's organizational head. González made the mistake of telling each side what he thought it wanted to hear and in the end pleased neither. He failed in his efforts to unite the parties behind Madero and Pino Suárez.[9]

Then there was the matter of González having violated the Plan de San Luis's prohibition against reelection. He wavered on resigning before the election. At one point, he filed his resignation, but he changed his mind and withdrew it on August 8.[10] In the end, he did not resign, which was a clear violation of the revolution's most important plank—that no one could be reelected or run for reelection to an office. Madero's support for González's reelection resulted in loss of popularity and political power for both men.[11]

While the Vázquez Gómez affair took its toll on González and Madero, it also divided and upset the anti-Díaz masses just when they should have been celebrating their historic military and political successes. The controversy set the stage for the cascade of conspiracies, rebellions, and uprisings that were to flow from Madero's missteps in his embryonic administration.

In July elections, later confirmed on August 24 in the second round, González was elected to a four-year term as governor. The evening before the national election, Orozco arrived by train in Mexico City. Once again, he attracted great crowds at the station and at his hotel. During that visit, provisional president León de la Barra appointed Orozco head of the rural police in the state of Sinaloa, a move seen as an attempt to marginalize Orozco and distance him from the border, where he could aid in putting down any insurrection. In Chihuahua, anticipating a rebellion under the persistent Nuevo León strongman Bernardo Reyes, the transfer drew heavy protests by people who felt that Orozco was the only force up to dealing with Reyes.[12]

On October 1, a massive majority handed Madero the presidency, defeating Reyes, who had emerged as Madero's principal election opponent. Pino Suárez was elected vice president in a victory over León de la Barra and Vázquez Gómez. When the electors met to confirm the vote, they found that Orozco had received three votes for vice president.[13]

After the election and before he took office, Madero traveled to Chihuahua City to diffuse the backlash from his change of parties and elimination of Vázquez Gómez as his vice presidential running mate. Arriving on October 30, he stood with González on the state capitol's ceremonial balcony to address the large crowd assembled below. He tried to explain why he had dropped Vásquez Gómez,[14] but the crowd would have none of it, chanting, "*Pino no, Pino no.*" Madero said that if they did not care for Pino Suárez, then they should treat him, Madero, the same way. The crowd responded, "*¡Viva Madero, Pino no, Pino no!*"[15]

The next day, Madero insisted that González, Orozco, and other prominent Chihuahuenses accompany him on the inauguration-bound train to Mexico City.[16] Days later, after Pino Suárez refused the post of government or interior minister, Madero asked González to take leave as governor and become the government minister. It was an unpopular practice, especially during the Creel administration, when Creel moved several times from the governorship to federal posts, leaving Chihuahua in the hands of a series of inconsequential, interim governors. While the minister of the interior was a key cabinet position that included supervising the rurales, including Orozco in Chihuahua, the negative for Chihuahua was that it removed González from the state before he had any opportunity to solidify his administration or implement his progressive reforms.

In Mexico City on November 6, Madero took office in a joyous but simple ceremony.[17] Orozco and Roque González Garza led Madero's escort from his home on Calle Berlin to the National Palace and then to the Chamber of Deputies, where he took the oath. Madero's carriage left the chamber with the mounted Orozco at its side. Music, confetti, and flowers rained on the parade. Once at the National Palace, the Zócalo was a sea of humanity. Madero stood on the ceremonial balcony with León de la Barra at this side. Nothing could be heard over the crowd.[18] Multitudes jammed the main square and streets. Cheers for Madero were not as great as they had been on June 7, when he first entered the capital, nor were they unanimous. On Madero's inauguration day, "Orozco received the most enthusiastic applause and vivas."[19]

After the ceremony, Madero immediately met with his cabinet and other top officials. Following a pattern he had established earlier, he named several members of his family to top posts, including his financier uncle Ernesto Madero to be the nation's new treasury secretary, replacing his brother, Gustavo, who was elected to the Chamber of Deputies and was named new head of the Progressive Constitutionalist Party; his first cousin, Rafael Hernández, as head of the department of economic development (Fomento, Colonización e Industria)[20] and other relatives to high provincial offices. Such open nepotism, in naming his relatives to the posts controlling the nation's finances, did not sit well with many Mexicans and only served to resonate with charges that the Maderos were "in it for the money." With a history of state government being handed from one Terrazas relative to another, Madero's nepotism was especially disconcerting to Chihuahuenses, who had expected better.

The Madero administration also gave the impression that it would continue the status quo. In an interview given that fall, Enrique Creel expressed confidence that the Madero cabinet was not radical because it contained at least two Científicos, one being Ernesto Madero, who was Creel's partner in several joint ventures.[21] Vázquez Gómez had earlier complained to Madero that the cabinet had only three revolutionaries and five Científicos. He regarded Francisco Madero, his father, and brothers all as Científicos.[22] Only two members of the cabinet had been active in the Anti-Reelection Party. Another observer wrote, "Madero desired minimal change that would not risk the political stability that he felt was a Porfirian heritage. In other words, without being aware of it, without being conscious of it, he desired a Porfirismo without Porfirio, a revolution without revolution."[23] With the Christmas season approaching, disappointment among the revolution's rural supporters and the lower and middle classes was palpable. Meanwhile on the other side, Creel had every reason to be reassured that little would change with the Díaz bureaucracy, army hierarchy, and Científico Supreme Court intact; Científico Maderos in charge of economics; and the reform-minded González gone from Chihuahua. Things were as good as they could get for the losers in the fight. The revolution's middle- and lower-class winners did not fare as well.

Political and socioeconomic unrest in Mexico caused the revolution. Madero, Carranza, and other well-to-do Mexicans looked to reform the political side, ending the dictatorship and returning to regular, honest elections. They were satisfied with the end of the Porfiriato and return of elections. Madero ignored the expectations of the clear majority of Mexicans and leaders of the revolution, who fought for land and labor reform and a social revolution. The Díaz defeat pacified the social unrest for a few months, but Madero's failure or refusal to address those needs resulted in several rebellions soon after he took power.

Madero quickly rescinded Orozco's Sinaloa transfer. Orozco had hardly unpacked his bags in Sinaloa when Madero sent him instead to command the rurales in Ciudad Juárez. Then, like clockwork, Bernardo Reyes's anti-Madero rebellion arose in Texas but, not surprisingly, found meager support. As could be expected, Orozco's name was associated with that uprising, a connection he adamantly denied. The Reyes plot was exposed with the El Paso arrest of fourteen Reyes sympathizers on charges of violating the neutrality laws. The group was to have invaded Ciudad Juárez in early December 1911. Searches turned up documents linking the group to Magonistas, as well as five alleged Orozco letters to Reyes offering his services.[24] Orozco insisted that the letters were forgeries, but, of course, suspicions about his involvement continued to be raised, because Reyes backers had previously named Orozco as a supporter and possible leader. Orozco had declined the offer.[25] In a reprise of Madero's embarrassing entry into Mexico on November 20, 1910, Reyes's invasion a year later was even worse. Rather than being met by large forces, Reyes found only a handful of men. After wandering the Nuevo León hills for several days, a hungry, cold, and humiliated Reyes surrendered to a lonely rurale, and by Christmas, Reyes was in Mexico's military prison at Santiago de Tlatelolco, which ended that phase of the uprising.[26]

Emilio Vázquez Gómez, brother of the jilted Francisco, led another anti-Madero movement. On October 31, Emilio, who had left the provisional cabinet, issued his Plan de Tacubaya, declared himself provisional president, and went to San Antonio, Texas, to organize his uprising.[27] Several anti-Madero groups attached themselves to Emilio over the months, all loosely working under the Vazquista label. On November 15, a week after Madero took office,

Braulio Hernández resigned his post as government secretary for Chihuahua and declared for Vázquez Gómez. Hernández was a key Chihuahua player. Along with Abraham González, he was a cofounder of the Benito Juárez Anti-Reelection Club,[28] the first and most important anti- Díaz club in the state; he was editor of *El Grito* and the party's principal strategist and organizer. He was a teacher and a Protestant who had joined the anti-reelection movement in its infancy and who then turned against Madero and González.

The unraveling continued. In Morelos, Emiliano Zapata, already at war against government forces, continued his uprising after Madero entered office. Zapata never had faith that Madero would implement the land reforms he demanded. On November 28, 1911, he issued his Plan de Ayala, declared his refusal to recognize Madero's presidency, and named Pascual Orozco as chief of his liberating revolution.[29] Ricardo Flores Magón continued with his rebellion, announcing in a September manifesto that he was a committed anarchist. His influence by that time was miniscule, and his military was not a factor. Many of the socialists who were former Magonistas became Vazquistas. Magón's brother Jesus served in Madero's cabinet. Seeing so much rebellion, the Madero administration encouraged the Americans to enforce the neutrality laws.[30]

In the weeks from mid-December 1911 to mid-January 1912, Orozco remained outwardly loyal to Madero by helping put down Reyista and Vazquista uprisings in the state. In mid-January, Madero summoned Orozco to meet with him in Mexico City so that, the press reported, Madero could commission Orozco to combat Zapata.[31] They met on January 19 with conflicting reports about what occurred in the conference. Historians agree that it was an unpleasant meeting, culminating in Orozco's resignation a week later. One source said that the breach occurred when Orozco refused Madero's request for help in persuading the Chihuahua legislature to extend Abraham González's leave of absence from the governorship to allow him to continue as interior or government minister.[32] Another story based the conflict on Orozco's refusal to fight Zapata's revolt. Still another rumor had Chihuahua Porfiristas upset that Madero ordered Orozco to combat Zapata while they instead wanted Orozco in Chihuahua indefinitely so that "local Científicos could live in peace in the presence of the man who was indispensable to them."[33] Orozco was outwardly ideologically in tune with Zapata, was sympathetic to his movement, and had never declined Zapata's declaration naming Orozco chief of his movement.[34] Furthermore, the press had reported that the purpose of the meeting was for Madero to place Orozco in charge of federal anti-Zapata forces.[35] While it would have been odd for Orozco to be putting down a revolution that named him its leader, he had done exactly that previously with the Reyes and Vázquez Gómez uprisings. Orozco resigned on January 26, but Madero insisted on extending his service until March 1.[36]

On February 2, a group headed by Braulio Hernández widened its breach with Madero by publishing its Plan de Santa Rosa. Intending a Vazquista alliance, they swore to and did take up arms against Madero, supporting the Plan de San Luis, which they alleged Madero had betrayed. Moreover, they were dismayed over his alliance with Científicos.[37] Under the banner of "Tierra y Justicia," Hernández and his group pushed for radical land reform measures under which the government would own the land and rent it to those who worked their plots.[38] In early February, Madero began to address the issue of land reform. He did not confront the matter of seized properties, but rather indicated that the government could make large properties available for distribution in several Chihuahua districts. Alberto Madero, moreover, wrote that it was possible to sell the Bustillos hacienda to the state on reasonable terms so lots could be sold or distributed to the public.[39]

In early February, Orozco's rebellion was already being reported a month before his service to Madero was to end, one of many reports and rumors predicting Orozco's disloyalty.[40] On February 7, a group under José Inés Salazar and Emilio P. Campa revolted in Casas Grandes under the red Magonista banner of the Liberal Party and named Orozco its leader.[41] Campa later said that he had every expectation that Orozco would join his group on its march from Ciudad Juárez to Mexico City. These were strong indicators that Orozco was already aligned with their Vazquista-Magonista effort.[42]

On February 16, González returned to resume his Chihuahua governor's office and issued a new agrarian plan to redistribute lands, buy large haciendas for distribution, and fund irrigation improvements. His decree authorized the expropriation of lands to form new or to reconstitute old ejidos.[43] Old Porfiristas and the oligarchy vowed to resist González. Naturally, considering these events, everyone in Chihuahua was waiting to see what Orozco would do after he left his Madero post.

CHAPTER TWENTY-ONE

Run-Up to Orozco's Rebellion

The months of February and March 1912 were a mass of confusion throughout Mexico but especially in Chihuahua, where a multitude of forces were arrayed against the hapless Madero. The turmoil was due to the Zapatistas in the South and Magonistas, Vazquistas, Braulio Hernández, and eventually Orozco in Chihuahua. And that was only the opposition from the left. On the right, Madero had Reyistas and Felicistas (followers of Porfirio Díaz's nephew Félix Díaz) and the ever-present machinations of the oligarchy intent on stirring unrest against him. For Madero, the nation was spinning out of control. He had lost control over Chihuahua, with Governor González away in the cabinet and the unreliable Orozco over its military. If Madero found it difficult to follow chaotic events in February and March, it was impossible for the confused populace to understand the multiple uprisings. Orozco would also find it complicated to control his unruly coalition, which contained incompatible ideologies housed under his umbrella. Here, anyway, was how Orozco's Colorado Rebellion unfolded.

The more unpopular Madero became, the more anti-Madero activists sought someone to depose and replace him. For months, the most popular choice to do so was Pascual Orozco. As he approached the end of his service in March, interest in Orozco intensified nationally, and more so in Chihuahua, the most active area against Madero. One writer noted, "All eyes are on Orozco: if he goes over to the enemy, Madero loses; if he remains loyal, the government might be saved."[1] Not only did Magonistas and Vazquistas want Orozco to join them; their ideological opposite, the oligarchy, saw Orozco as *its* only hope despite his leftist rhetoric and alliances. Orozco had what they all needed: a man with a proven military record, broad popular support, and an ability to recruit, organize, and lead a military force. He was the package, except that he lacked the intellectual, educational, and emotional attributes to navigate complicated political waters. He was everyone's choice for a military leader, but aside from his core support group (*su gente*), he was not a universal choice for a political chief.

Orozco attracted diverse and mismatched pockets of support. One group was comprised of disaffected old reform Maderistas, as well as Magonistas and Zapatistas, folks with values ranging from the middle to the left, and the others were those personally loyal to him along with Catholic Party members, former Porfiristas, and the oligarchy, which looked to Orozco to protect its economic interests. It was a shaky and unreliable coalition. Many were choosing sides and were waiting to see the direction Orozco would take. The choices Orozco ultimately made were poor: he would reject a large bloc of his leftist support and would instead embrace a controversial ally, Chihuahua's oligarchy.

Orozco understood that to depose Madero, a rebellion needed troops and arms along with significant financing to attract and support his army. Orozco could supply the men; and the oligarchy could provide the money. The problem with the union, however, was its divergent goals: Orozco and his supporters demanded labor and land reform and the return of seized properties while the oligarchy wanted a return to a Díaz-like economy.

The oligarchy had begun courting Orozco within days after his personal conflict with Madero in Ciudad Juárez on May 13.[2] They were convinced that Orozco was a military leader and was anti-Madero. After the Battle of Ciudad Juárez, Orozco enjoyed good relations with General Luis Terrazas and supported his claim for damages by certifying the harm done by revolutionary forces to his San Lorenzo and El Carmen haciendas. On his way to Chihuahua City after the Battle of Ciudad Juárez, Orozco stayed at Terrazas's El Sauz hacienda for several days and then a night at Terrazas's splendid Quinta Carolina on Chihuahua City's northern outskirts.[3] Members of Chihuahua's oligarchy had visited Orozco while he was Terrazas's guest at El Sauz. Within two weeks after the Treaty of Ciudad Juárez, it was already public that Chihuahua's conservatives were wooing Orozco. On June 11, the *New York Times* reported, "Not all, but some of the Cientifico group who still have large money resources have, as is well known, tried to purchase the allegiance of such chiefs as Orozco, who commanded the Chihuahua contingent in the army of the north."[4] The attempt to turn Orozco against Madero started in June, continued after Orozco marched into Chihuahua City, and intensified into early 1912.[5]

In February 1912, Chihuahua's oligarchy feted, toasted, and honored Orozco at several social and elite events, including banquets, dances, and fiestas. Orozco tasted a slice of society that he had never experienced before, and he was pleased to have become a part of it. Despite finding society with the anti-Madero oligarchy, Orozco gave the impression that he was still loyal to the president.[6] By early February, faced with persistent rumors that he would betray Madero, Orozco stoutly denied any intent to revolt or have Chihuahua leave the union.[7] Behind that facade, however, Orozco was busily working to strengthen his own future position rather than Madero's. Orozco mustered out 25 percent of rurales, those whose loyalty he questioned, replacing them with people faithful to him. The discharged troops were unhappy and joined others in creating disorder,[8] including a riot in Ciudad Juárez and a raid on the Chihuahua penitentiary, where they freed prisoners including Antonio Rojas.[9] Making further preparations for his future needs, Orozco requisitioned more weapons and supplies from Mexico City.[10] When Chihuahua's interim governor, Aureliano González, resigned, the legislature offered Orozco the post, but he declined it even though Madero had urged him to accept.[11] In the meantime, in his last two weeks of service, Orozco helped extinguish more than one uprising in Northern Chihuahua, including the Ciudad Juárez riot.[12]

In late February, during the waning days of Orozco's Madero service, conservatives and elites continued their "assiduous" courting and cultivating of Orozco.[13] Their overtures must have worked, because before the end of the month, the record shows that Orozco had openly decided to turn against Madero and side with the oligarchy. However, Orozco had an impossible task. He needed oligarchy funding for his revolution, but he had to conceal its source and keep his leftist supporters in the dark that he had received oligarchy financing. For confidentiality and deniability, Orozco and the oligarchy used an intermediary to communicate, receive, and administer Científico funding, and that man was Gonzalo C. Enrile.[14]

Organizing a civil war such as the Mexican Revolution involved many components, including recruiting fighters; assembling supplies, arms, and munitions; transporting men and supplies; securing finances; gathering intelligence; generating support from the media and the public; developing positive international relations; and conducting military operations. Civil wars and large rebellions created a demand for certain skills, held out an opportunity for fortune and excitement, and thus invariably drew into their orbit adventure seekers, profiteers, spies, reporters, photographers, merchants, mercenaries, prostitutes, smugglers, gun dealers, murderers, thieves, and rank conmen. Madero had placed several dubious characters on his staff, including Washington lawyer Sherburne G. Hopkins and German spy Felix Sommerfeld.

To the consternation of Orozco's longtime staff, Gonzalo Enrile, an ambitious and devious minor ex-Díaz consular officer, mysteriously arose from nowhere to become Orozco's principal policy advisor, spokesperson, financial agent, and nexus to the oligarchy. To some observers, Enrile's role was so large that it appeared Enrile was the one in charge. Orozco made Enrile central and indispensable to his rebellion in raising and handling money, in administering the rebellion, in making policy, and in managing press relations. The U.S. consul reported that Enrile became "the soul of the revolution."[15] In Orozco's hierarchy, Enrile also became the center of intrigue and skullduggery. Selecting Enrile to administer and become the face of his revolt would become one of Orozco's major mistakes, perhaps his worst. Although Enrile's role within the short-lived rebellion was central and his influence on Orozco profound, the record contains virtually nothing explaining why, when, or how Enrile's appointment came about. Whatever Orozco saw in Enrile,[16] he should have heeded the many warning signs surrounding the man.[17] Perhaps it was obvious that it was not what Orozco saw in Enrile, but rather what Enrile brought to Orozco: money, and lots of it. Others, perhaps Orozco himself, could have raised significant amounts of money, but Enrile's timing must have been key. He presented himself to Orozco with fast talk and some quick money at the precise moment when Orozco needed financing and conservative support. Enrile, however, brought along with him a history and views that would become problematic. Enrile's colorful past is relevant in explaining Orozco's subsequent conduct and policy statements, some of which bore Enrile's distinctive mark. What follows is a sketch of Enrile, the man Orozco would choose to run his rebellion, a choice that sealed the fate of his revolt and a good part of his historical legacy.

Gonzalo Carlos Enrile Villatoro was born in Guanajuato in 1867 and served in the military as a young man.[18] In October 1891, Enrile was a clerk in the Ciudad Juárez post office, where authorities accused him of stealing checks from the mail. A codefendant converted the checks into cash for Enrile.[19] A court found Enrile guilty of the charges and sentenced him to serve six years in prison, but before they could lock him up, he fled the state.[20] He is next found in Campeche, where he married in 1897 and soon moved to the state of Mexico, where he obtained a local government post in Zumpango, a small municipality just north of Mexico City.[21] In 1898, the governor of the state of México appointed Enrile the political jefe for the municipality. Within a year, several residents complained of Enrile's arbitrary and abusive conduct.[22] Enrile then moved into national politics in Mexico City. At least by 1902, Enrile was in Mexico City serving as an editor of the newspaper *La Protesta*, a journal controlled by Bernardo Reyes and his son Rodolfo. *La Protesta* made its name promoting Reyes and, although pro-Díaz, in harshly denigrating Científicos and especially their leader Limantour, as well as other Científico cabinet members.[23] *La Protesta*'s chief complaint against Científicos was that they favored foreign investors and were Wall Street puppets. Limantour exposed *La Protesta*'s Reyes connection by showing Díaz original manuscripts written by Rodolfo Reyes. On December 22, 1902, Díaz confronted Reyes over his perceived disloyalty, and the meeting resulted in Reyes's banishment from the cabinet and demotion to the governorship of Nuevo León.[24] Following Reyes's demotion and loss of power, authorities immediately arrested Enrile and other *La Protesta* staff and confined them in Mexico City's notorious Belén prison on charges of having defamed Limantour. Authorities may have also been holding Enrile for other unspecified property crimes.[25] *La Protesta*'s high profile and controversy may have been fateful for its editor, Enrile, a man on the lam for whom a low profile would have been prudent. Anonymity, however, was incompatible with Enrile's outrageous persona. Chihuahua officials learned that Enrile was in custody and demanded that Mexico City authorities remand the fugitive there to serve his pending six-year prison sentence. The daily *El Tiempo* also noted that Enrile had been stealing more than checks from the mail and had taken valuable diamonds as well.[26] The Mexican Supreme Court quickly disposed of Enrile's spurious claim that the statute of limitations had run on the Chihuahua crime because of the ten-year time lapse caused by his escape after his sentencing.[27] In March 1903, a court found all *La Protesta* staff guilty of criminal conduct against Limantour, namely defamation, sentenced the group to time served, and released all except for Enrile, whom they held on other pending charges.[28] In late May 1904, after a year and half in custody, the court released Enrile from the dreaded, fetid Belén.[29] Inexplicably, Enrile never served the prison time he owed Chihuahua.

It was lore in Mexico City that if you were not a criminal when you entered Belén, you would learn to become one once inside its walls. Before Belén, Enrile was already an ex-convict with a theft record and a charge of obtaining merchandise without paying.[30] Once out of Belén, records note several incidents and charges against Enrile for ordering merchandise and refusing to pay, or simply taking someone's property, including stealing a waitress's tips in a bar he owned. He was also accused of taking a court file while in custody and rejecting the judge's order to return it. He later demanded the case against him be dismissed because the evidence had disappeared from the file. Not long after that, he and his codefendant faced charges for destroying evidence.[31] He and his codefendants harassed the judges assigned to hear their cases and made bogus claims against the judges to have them recused. As horrible as Belén was, Enrile would return there several times. Records show that Enrile was once again in Belén for much of 1906 and 1907 on several theft and fraud charges.[32]

In preparation for the 1910 election, Bernardo Reyes attempted to position himself for vice president against an expected bid by the Científico incumbent Ramón Corral, and Reyes supporters formed the Democratic Party to promote his candidacy.[33] After he was out of Belén, Enrile reemerged and reengaged in pro-Reyes politics in that effort. He attended a small organizational meeting for the party in December 1908, with Reyista luminaries in attendance.[34] Three days later, the Ministry of Foreign Relations appointed Enrile the Mexican consul in Puerto Cortés, Honduras, the start of Enrile's consular career.[35] Although Enrile was a consistent Reyes supporter, Reyes was no fan of Enrile's.[36]

Enrile's background is unclear except that he was a Porfirista of Reyista stripe and became the oligarchy's connection to Orozco. Unconfirmed reports noted that Enrile had served in consular posts in Brussels, Costa Rica, Philadelphia, and finally in Clifton, Arizona Territory. If his last post was indeed Clifton, he was surely a minor consular official. In March 1911, then no longer in consular work and as rebel troops prepared to advance on Ciudad Juárez, Enrile announced to the press and American officials the non-existent position that he was Díaz's envoy to Francisco León de la Barra, Mexico's U.S. ambassador and the new minister of foreign relations. Enrile claimed that the Madero insurgency would be over within a month.[37] Two months later, in May, at the time of the Battle of Ciudad Juárez, Mexico City news reports that mentioned Enrile noted that a concerned public there was avidly reading placards warning that Madero had foreign mercenaries in his army and had sold out to and was a puppet of U.S. business interests. The signs bore the name "Enrile."[38]

In late February 1912, U.S. authorities identified Enrile as the author of an anti-American, anti-Taft leaflet attack based in Ciudad Juárez. The fliers contained a manifesto blaming Taft and the United States for many of Latin America's problems. The manifesto called for Madero's ouster and advocated the appointment of General Gerónimo Treviño as provisional president and Pascual Orozco as governor of Chihuahua. Enrile, as will be seen later, had a fondness for Treviño, an old Porfirista general. The proclamation asserted that American firms, including the Waters-Pierce Oil Company, had financed the Madero Revolution, a repeat of the charge that certain Mexicans were Wall Street puppets.[39] Enrile admitted that he was the manifesto's author and called for El Paso Mexican consul Enrique Llorente to surrender Ciudad Juárez to the rebels at a time when Orozco was still working under Madero. The news also noted an unconfirmed report that Orozco had already joined the anti-Madero revolutionary movement.[40] Enrile was the author of another similar anti-American manifesto he distributed in San Antonio, bearing the title "La Venta de la Patria" ("The Sale of the Nation").[41] In it Enrile declared that the new movement was "backed by the Cientifico element in Mexico and added that authority for issuing the manifesto came from 'higher up.'"[42]

With Magonista-Vazquista troops—overall under José Inés Salazar and specifically led by Emilio P. Campa—planning an attack on Ciudad Juárez, the United States warned Madero and Campa against engaging in battle in Ciudad Juárez, which could injure El Paso citizens. In heed of the warning, Madero ordered federal forces to reinforce Ciudad Juárez but to do so thirteen miles south of the city, and for that purpose sent Col. Marcelo Caraveo and his forces to block the rail line between the city and the rebel stronghold of Casas Grandes. Orozco countermanded Madero's instructions, and, instead of defending Ciudad Juárez, Orozco ordered Caraveo's forces withdrawn from the area and moved to Chihuahua City.[43] As expected, Salazar and Campa quickly took the lightly defended Ciudad Juárez on February 27, 1912.[44] Salazar's forces had earlier declared Orozco their military leader and Emilio Vázquez Gómez as their provisional president.[45] Ciudad Juárez went under the control of a Magonista-Vazquista union with Orozco as a possible partner. Several revolutionary forces were converging upon Chihuahua City, causing great anxiety among Chihuahua's oligarchy. At that point, Orozco clearly seemed to have one foot in the Magonista-Vazquista camp and the other in the oligarchy's.

A leftist force had taken Ciudad Juárez, the most important border city. The Magonista element always raised the specter for the United States of a violent, popular socialist uprising; therefore, the United States resisted that faction. Furthermore, Enrile's anti-American manifesto caused consternation in Washington, a fear further whipped up by Madero's energetic El Paso consul, Enrique C. Llorente.[46] Washington responded with threats of intervention as Congress considered an embargo on Mexico. While Enrile was enraging Americans, he was soon to be the oligarchy's point man in running Orozco's anti-Madero operation and helping to rid Chihuahua of González and his reform agenda. In late February, Salazar, apparently unaware of the close connection Enrile had with Orozco, arrested Enrile in Ciudad Juárez for stirring up trouble with Americans and for antirevolutionary activities.[47]

Failing to have the Chihuahua legislature extend his leave, Abraham González had left the cabinet and returned to Chihuahua in mid-February as governor to resume his reform agenda. The oligarchy there remained opposed to his reform program, which included progressive taxation on landholdings and collection of back property taxes, policies that would strain the oligarchy's ability to hold on to its massive properties. The Terrazas had their properties assessed at low values, failed to pay even those low taxes, and thus owed years in back taxes.[48]

Orozco left government service on March 1, issuing his manifesto stating that he was leaving his post and politics but would return to work with his group if the people called upon him to do so.[49] In an unlikely coincidence the next day, as though answering that call, demonstrations broke out in Chihuahua City. Conrado Gimeno noted that about four hundred demonstrators, mostly paid park vendors, appeared along with a band across from the capitol. Members of the legislature went out to the balcony to inquire about the demonstration's purpose. Demonstrator Antonio Cortazar demanded that Abraham González resign and that Orozco replace him. Another demonstrator called out for the people to renounce Madero. González appeared on the balcony and said that because the people elected him, he would not yield to the opinion of a few demonstrators who were sellouts. The demonstrators then went to a cantina and later left to search for González, who had hidden in fear of imprisonment or assassination.[50]

González and others detected the hand of the Terrazas-Creel clan in the demonstrations, as demonstration leader Antonio Cortazar was the brother of Creel's son-in-law, Joaquín Cortazar, and had joined other Chihuahua conservatives and Científicos in the mêlée. While he was under attack, González summoned Villa, who was at Bustillos with six hundred men, to Chihuahua City to provide security.[51]

On the evening of March 2, Chihuahua elites feted Orozco as guest of honor at a high society dance at the Teatro de los Héroes. Early the next morning, still at the dance, Orozco learned that Villa was on his way to Chihuahua City.[52] The people at the dance implored Orozco to save the city from depredation by Villa's forces. Historian Francisco Almada wrote that Chihuahua conservatives and elites prevailed in convincing Orozco to rise, using the false claim that Villa was about to plunder the city. The oligarchy was in a desperate state. González was returning to promote his reform agenda; Villa was ordered into the city by González; and the leftist forces of Salazar and the Vazquista–Liberal Party alliance that had taken Ciudad Juárez was headed for Chihuahua City. There were rumors that Braulio Hernández and his radical rebel forces were bound for Chihuahua as well. There was only one man who could save them from all those attacks, and that was Orozco. To recruit Orozco, the elite were willing to allow his alliance with Salazar.[53] The incongruous alliance coming together for Orozco was confusing enough. Adding to the mess was a succession of events that made it difficult, if not impossible, for observers to make sense of the chaos that overtook Chihuahua from February to April of 1912. The uncertainty and the mix of rebel groups rising in rebellion with several prominent radical leaders made the American administration very nervous, so much so that Taft advised Americans to leave dangerous areas and to refrain from involvement and warned that violations of U.S. neutrality laws would be prosecuted.[54]

On February 22, a Bureau of Investigation agent in El Paso reported that Orozco had already turned against Madero and would control the state for Vazquistas within ten days.[55] On the day of Orozco's resignation, March 1, Salazar and his Magonistas announced that they were bound for Chihuahua City and did not expect opposition from Orozco. A member of the Vázquez Gómez junta also announced that Orozco would command Vazquistas in Chihuahua.[56] Those were just a few of several signs that led many to conclude that Orozco had long before been in league with Salazar, Vazquistas, and others in the ongoing revolt against Madero, who had been in office a mere four months. Orozco and his supporters created a narrative that Orozco was committed to enter retirement and tend to his business and that it was only his sense of obligation to save Chihuahua from the ravages of Villa's violent troops that forced him to oppose Villa, González, and Madero. Unfortunately, the evidence ran in the other direction.

CHAPTER TWENTY-TWO

Orozco's Colorado Rebellion

Early on March 3, 1912, Orozco declared his allegiance to the anti-Madero rebel groups, withdrew his support for and recognition of the Madero government, and took up arms against Madero in an uprising called the Colorado or Orozco Rebellion.[1] The public knew Orozco's people as the Colorados, or Red Flaggers, for the red banners in their hats and for their red flags bearing the slogan "Reform, liberty and justice." Orozco went that morning to the Chihuahua garrison he had left only two days earlier and ordered the troops there—no longer under his command—to follow him. Since June 1911, there had been no federal troops in Chihuahua and Orozco's rural forces had been in control. Colonels Agustín Estrada and Marcelo Caraveo refused to join the rebellion at that time.[2] Enrique Creel's brother Juan became a standard-bearer and captain for Orozco, another indication of an Orozco alliance with the oligarchy.[3] Also on that day, Orozco claimed to have engaged in his first combat on the outskirts of Chihuahua City. In the encounter, Orozco ran off Villa's forces as they attempted to enter the city. Villa's troops retreated after scattered firing, unaware that they had faced Orozco's troops.[4] Chihuahua's business community immediately congratulated Orozco on his victory.[5] Orozco insisted that he fought to save Chihuahua City from Villa and his violent troops,[6] and immediately summoned Salazar's anti-Madero and Vazquista forces to Chihuahua City.

In his afternoon telegram, the U.S. consul in Chihuahua City, Marion Letcher, summarized the tumult of March 3: "All the reports from border are alarming. Excitement high here on account intervention rumors resulting from meager news arriving from Paso del Norte of President's proclamation advising Americans to keep out of danger zone. This is construed as warning to leave country and private messages give color to this construction. Governor has disappeared. Villa is attacking Orozco, a few miles from town, this morning. Former for Government and the latter against."[7]

On March 4, awash in Chihuahua's adulation over his questionable confrontation with Villa, Orozco boldly announced that in four days his army would march south to take Mexico City.[8] Orozco not only ran Villa off but also ran González and his reform administration right out of town to the joy of the Porfirista elite. Due to Orozco's timely intervention, González's exile lasted months, and his progressive reforms were suspended.[9] Orozco thus stopped González's program, which included many of the same reforms that Orozco and his followers had advocated, and instead turned the state government over to reactionaries. Within days of taking over the state, the oligarchy's involvement in Orozco's camp became evident. The U.S. consul wired the State Department: "Entire [Orozco] movement here openly promoted by adherents of old [Díaz] régime. Money is being openly solicited and contributed for extending military operations to Mexico with Orozco as commander in chief."[10]

On March 6, Orozco convened a meeting at the meatpacking plant on the northern outskirts of the city, where the junta named him chief of the revolution and rebel leaders agreed to submit to Orozco's orders.[11] He took the oath of office and named his staff, including Gonzalo C. Enrile as the secretary general of the revolution and Lieutenant Colonel Alfonso Castañeda as his chief of staff.[12] Enrile was now officially the administrative head of the Orozco Revolution although he was then in custody in Ciudad Juárez. Orozco issued his *plan*[13] outlining his policies and then triumphantly rode into Chihuahua at the head of his troops. Orozco was so much in control that the consul described Chihuahua's state as a "dictatorship."[14]

It was obvious that Orozco had turned against Madero at least before February 22, as that was when he was obviously on the same side as the anti-Madero Magonistas led by Salazar and allowed their easy capture of Ciudad Juárez. Orozco had reversed Madero's order to send Caraveo to defend the city.[15] The mystery over when Orozco engaged the services of Enrile deepened. Whatever connection Enrile had with Orozco in late February, even Orozco's close friend and ally José Inés Salazar seemed unaware of it. In Ciudad Juárez, with rebel forces in control, Salazar's subaltern, General Rojas, arrested Enrile on March 1 and tried to execute him for stirring up trouble with Americans and for antirevolutionary activities.[16] Even on March 6, as Orozco announced that Enrile was the secretary general of his revolution, as well as its administrative and financial executive, Enrile was still in Salazar's custody in Ciudad Juárez, creating the odd circumstance that Enrile was the prisoner of the forces he was officially administering. It was not until March 15 that Salazar took the arrested

Enrile to Chihuahua City to see Orozco.[17] Obviously, Orozco and Enrile must have been in close touch well before Orozco named Enrile secretary general on March 6, and Salazar was not acquainted with or was in denial of Enrile's well-publicized appointment. Since Enrile was in Ciudad Juárez days before March 1 and was in custody after that date, Orozco and Enrile had clearly been planning the revolt well before March 1. These circumstances are more evidence that, contrary to his claims of loyalty, Orozco was betraying Madero well before he left his service on March 1. Thus, Villa's troops marching into Chihuahua on March 2 was the pretext for and not the cause of Orozco's rebellion. By that time, in intent and preparation, Orozco was long down the road to rebellion. One headline on March 6 noted, "Trusted Chief Turns Traitor." Few were surprised by the betrayal when it was announced. Sources friendly to Madero expected as much after Madero denied Orozco's pay demand for 100,000 pesos.[18]

Immediately after Orozco's March 6 parade into Chihuahua, the oligarchy-controlled legislature met and joined the Colorado Rebellion against Madero.[19] The uprising forced González to flee the city to save his life. The legislature, however, claiming that González had abandoned his office for more than four days, deposed him and installed a new interim governor, Felipe R. Gutiérrez.[20] As a fact, Orozco became the supreme power in Chihuahua. On March 8, three of his military leaders, José Inés Salazar, Braulio Hernández, and Emilio Campa issued a hubristic proclamation that Orozco was not politically ambitious, as he was accused of being, and would settle for the position of vice president with Francisco Léon de la Barra as president.[21]

Orozco based his rebellion on two assumptions. He was confident that if he could supply and arm his forces, he would defeat Madero. Another was that he could obtain arms and ammunition from the United States in the same manner that Madero had,[22] but he needed substantial financial support to do so, funds he did not personally have. The reason why Orozco named and kept Enrile as his top administrator soon became evident. Enrile had become Orozco's connection to substantial financing for his rebellion.[23] Enrile had inserted himself in the key position controlling Orozco's lifeline—money. Enrile tapped oligarchy financing in two ways: first, openly as official acts of the state issuing bonds, making state loans or expenditures; and, second, clandestinely receiving off-the-books, elite individual contributions or loans. Orozco and the oligarchy benefited in keeping some financing confidential. Orozco did not want his anti-oligarchy friends to know that he was receiving private Científico support, and the oligarchy contributors did not want to risk Madero's retaliation.

No sooner did Orozco start receiving money from the oligarchy than he heard cries that Científicos were funding his revolution, and this occurred less than one week after he announced his rebellion. Orozco denied that he received Científico backing and said that his was an effort backed by the rich and poor alike. In the *El Paso Herald*, Orozco insisted, "It is the people and only the people who are making this revolution and it is an absurdity to say that it is the work of the Cientificos and the Porfiristas. No, a thousand times, no."[24] It was not possible, however, to conceal that which was so open—that is, the flow of Científico-oligarchy funds into Orozco's hands. Indeed, Enrile himself admitted that Orozco had Científico support. Questioned by the press about the February anti-Taft manifesto, Enrile had declared that "the new [Orozco] movement is backed by the Cientifico element in Mexico and added that authority for issuing the manifesto came from those 'higher up.'"[25] To Abraham González, hiding in Chihuahua only two weeks into Orozco's rebellion, the oligarchy's support for Orozco was undeniable and unmistakable, as indicated by Orozco's appointment of his Washington representatives, Manuel Luján, who was married to General Terrazas's granddaughter, and Juan Prieto Quemper, who was married to a niece of José María Sánchez. González said that the oligarchy's influence was evident with Orozco replacing his state employees with those from the previous Porfirista administration.[26]

The flow of funds to Orozco from the oligarchy was so manifest that on March 12, only nine days after Orozco's revolt commenced, Consul Letcher was already hearing indications of discontent among Orozco's supporters and troops caused by the oligarchy's prominent role in the revolution. There were also unconfirmed rumors of desertions.[27] It could well have been that, in addition to other information, Letcher had heard about the defection of P. O. Dávila. On March 12, a large front-page story in the *El Paso Morning Times* reported that Davila, an Orozco officer serving under Braulio Hernández, was deserting Orozco's cause. Davila claimed that he decided to leave after overhearing Orozco in conversation with an unnamed Terrazas family member, who noted that the Científicos were financing Orozco. Davila said that he later confronted Orozco and that Orozco admitted the conversation but said that he would take Científico money and then "kick them out."[28] Far from kicking them out, Orozco was keeping the promise he allegedly made to the Terrazas clan in return for an unspecified payment.

Sometime before March 1, during an event at the Foreign Club of Chihuahua, Gonzalo Enrile had connected Orozco to members of the Terrazas family. Enrile promised to deliver an unspecified amount of Terrazas money to Orozco and Marcelo Caraveo in return for protecting Terrazas properties and cattle from rebel troops.[29] Orozquista leader Máximo Castillo later broke with Orozco, alleging that Orozco had sold out to the oligarchy, receiving payments, attention, and honors at banquets and fiestas. He said, "I found out that Orozco was a traitor, a coward who had been bought by the rich."[30] Along the same lines, historian Friedrich Katz wrote:

> Castillo's assessment of Orozco was borne out when about two weeks after he joined the rebellion, Orozco issued orders, according to informants of the Bureau of Investigation, that the property of Luis Terrazas was not to be touched under any circumstances. The administration that Orozco's party appointed to govern Chihuahua went a step further and reduced Terrazas's taxes to 50 percent of what he was paying under González. This, according to González, was the major reason why Terrazas supported the Orozco revolt.[31]

On March 18, El Paso–based Bureau of Investigation agent L. E. Ross received information that "General Orozco had issued orders to Enrique Portillo in Casas Grandes that hereafter the property of Gen. Luis Terrazas would be immune and was not to be touched under any circumstances." Ross added, "It is a very well established fact that the Terrazas people are putting up money for the revolutionists here."[32] Further confirmation of Orozco's order regarding amnesty for Terrazas cattle came on March 22 when the *El Paso Morning Times* reported that Orozco forces in Ciudad Juárez had received specific orders to stop confiscating Terrazas livestock.[33] Orozco's order to exempt Terrazas cattle was unwelcome and disobeyed by some Orozquista forces,[34] as in mid-March, Orozco's troops were still taking Terrazas cattle.[35]

When Chihuahua severed ties to Mexico City, it also cut the purse strings. With the loss of federal money, Orozco immediately required funds for his troops, and in support of Orozco the new Gutiérrez administration in Chihuahua arranged a provisional loan of 200,000 pesos until Orozco obtained longer-term funding. The oligarchy's Chihuahua banks and several individuals funded that loan. Three banks, including Creel's Banco Minero, loaned 50,000 pesos and another bank loaned 20,000 pesos. Various individuals raised the balance, such as General Terrazas's son, Luis, who loaned 10,000 pesos. The oligarchy raised a total of 208,000 pesos just for that short-term loan, exceeding its stated goal.[36] Members of the Terrazas-Creel oligarchy—including General Terrazas's son Luis, Creel's brother Juan, and Manuel Prieto—were named managers of the provisional loan along with Enrile, Orozco's financial agent.[37] These were all loans the oligarchy voluntarily oversubscribed.[38] In addition to the 208,000 pesos, the state tendered to Orozco 150,000 pesos that had been sitting in the state's treasury and 65,000 pesos it held on deposit in various banks.[39] With Orozco's troops controlling Ciudad Juárez, they also received its substantial customs revenues.[40]

Having invited Orozco to lead a rebellion on the promise that he would receive generous financing, Chihuahua's oligarchy proceeded to keep its commitment. Already, the day after Orozco defeated Villa, newspapers reported total unity on the rebel side and great enthusiasm on the part of the rich to raise money. The *El Paso Herald* reported, "A million dollars have been subscribed by bankers, business men and ranchmen of this region to unseat Madero. The money power of the state is to rest entirely with Madero's former Chihuahua commander [Orozco]." The business community could not have been more delighted to fund Orozco, at least initially.[41] In addition to handing Orozco the 215,000 pesos in cash the state had on hand and 208,000 pesos from the first loan, on March 19, Governor Gutiérrez authorized the issuance of 1.2 million pesos in state-guaranteed bonds to finance Orozco.[42] Gutiérrez assured bondholders that the federal government would later assume payment of the bonds.

The business community, bankers, merchants, and private capitalists met at Chihuahua's chamber of commerce to allocate bond purchases among Chihuahua businesses and individuals. The business community agreed that it was a better business practice to issue state-guaranteed bonds instead of resorting to forced, non-guaranteed loans of questionable value.[43] Referring to Chihuahua's business community, interim governor Gutiérrez later said, "The majority of them, with the exception of three or four, purchased the bonds with apparent pleasure."[44] Enrique Creel's brother Juan Creel took his share, buying 80,000 pesos in bonds for the clan's Banco Minero.[45] Firms in Chihuahua quickly snapped up the bonds, and Orozco and his designates received the funds.[46] Orozco therefore received a total of at least 1.6 million pesos in publicly disclosed funds in addition to customs revenues and substantial undisclosed funds from individuals and firms.[47] The 1.6 million pesos was a sum much larger, perhaps double or more, of what Francisco Madero had available during his much broader revolution.[48] With the addition of undisclosed, under-the-table payments, the funds approached the million-dollar commitment the business community had reportedly made to Orozco. Orozco's funding was only for Chihuahua. Ultimately, almost all that Orozco received, under the table or over the table, was oligarchy money.

Once Orozco had declared his rebellion and his union with other rebel groups, those insurgents initially came to him, not necessarily the titular heads, but the low-ranking rebels. To attract recruits, Orozco had agreed to pay soldiers the high wage of two pesos per day rather than the customary one peso.[49] It was more than the higher wage that attracted men. Orozco was also the one with the name, the allure, and the leadership. Vazquista, Reyista, Magonista, whatever they were, they came to Orozco under the anti-Madero umbrella, including veterans José Inés Salazar and Máximo Castillo. Once the group united, it was not two weeks before Orozco controlled all of Chihuahua except for Hidalgo del Parral and Ojinaga.[50] Flush with victory and in a moment of hubris, Orozco announced that he would immediately march on Mexico City with a force of eight thousand.[51] Madero responded and sent a team offering to negotiate, a move Orozco took as weakness, and he refused to consider the talks.[52]

In one manifesto, Orozco mentioned some of the wrongs Madero had committed, including nepotism.[53] Orozco remarked that if they ever captured Madero or his relatives in government, he would try them under military law, which was a clear threat of execution.[54] Orozco, however, had his own problems, one being the lack of weapons and ammunition that he needed for the coming battles. It was in vain that Orozco controlled Ciudad Juárez and customs revenues; it did him no good in the face of the new U.S. embargo. Orozco's earlier refrain that whoever controlled the border controlled the war was no longer true.

By late March, Orozco had taken Parral by defeating federal troops under Villa, giving Orozco control over all of Chihuahua except for Ojinaga. Madero dispatched a force of two thousand under General José González Salas to stop Orozco's advance south. González Salas had resigned as minister of war to lead the defense, and was joined by six thousand more troops in Torreón, Coahuila, to total eight thousand.[55] On March 23, the federal and Orozco forces met in combat at Rellano, a remote rail station south of Jiménez, Chihuahua. The government gained the initial advantage, and Orozco's troops retreated to regroup. The federal forces were loading their trains to pursue and attack Orozco's troop train when one of Orozco's commanders, General Emilio P. Campa, sent south a dynamite-laden, unmanned locomotive, a *tren loco* or *máquina loca*. It collided with the federal train, causing a horrific explosion, many casualties, and a world of confusion. Orozco followed with an attack and was victorious to such an extent that a shamed General González Salas went to his train compartment and committed suicide.[56] Despite victory at Rellano, the future would be different for Orozco's Colorado Rebellion.

On another front, the combination of Orozco's rebellion, radicals taking Ciudad Juárez and Casas Grandes, and Enrile's anti-U.S. February screed and manifesto caused Taft's critics to charge that the president was soft on Mexican affairs, an accusation made more serious because Taft would soon face a stiff intra-party fight from formidable former president Theodore Roosevelt. Taft immediately mobilized to pressure Mexico. He first admonished Americans to avoid involvement in the country's internal affairs and then warned Americans in dangerous zones, such as Chihuahua, to evacuate and return to the United States. Then senator and former secretary of state Elihu Root led Congress to pass a joint resolution calling for an embargo on Mexico.[57] On March 14, the day when Root's resolution passed, Taft imposed a strict embargo on exports to Mexico. The embargo was so severe that it initially blocked the export of food and clothing. The ports were closed for a while, and border commerce came to a halt. Later, Taft relaxed the embargo for most items but held it ironclad for armaments and war supplies.[58] The embargo against Orozco was partially the product of Enrile's February manifesto and Enrile's authorship of Orozco's anti-American press statements. Orozco's alliance with Magonistas was an additional factor as the American administration had long before marked the PLM as a radical, anticapitalist foe. March 14, most likely, became the day that Orozco lost his rebellion, but he did not understand that until a few weeks later. Buoyed by his Rellano victory, his coffers brimming with Científico money, Orozco continued in Enrile's thrall and under his domination. Orozco's actions of March 25 showed the extent of Enrile's influence on his judgment.

On March 25, Orozco issued his Plan Orozquista,[59] a progressive plan for social, labor, economic, and land reform, his most comprehensive policy statement.[60] The *plan*, however, was much more than that. Between March 3 and March 25, Orozco issued five proclamations. The one on the twenty-fifth was a detailed social plan, based largely on Liberal Party policies. Other than the manifesto's anti-American flavor provided by Enrile, the document was heavily Magonista, so much so that Orozco even adopted the PLM's slogan "Reforma, Libertad y Justicia" and its red flag.[61] The *plan* contained thirty-seven clauses, several repeating original complaints against Madero. In Clause 29, Orozco addressed one of his pet complaints against the establishment, the political jefes. His *plan* promised to replace jefes and return to elected municipal presidents.[62] It reiterated Enrile's assertion that U.S. business, especially the Waters-Pierce firm, funded Madero and that Madero had issued 14 million pesos in bonds to repay those loans. The *plan* used anti-American language, tracking Enrile's February manifesto—so reminiscent of it, in fact, that Enrile was accused of being the *plan*'s author, which was undoubtedly at least partly true.[63] The anti-American portions of the manifesto were vintage Enrile with roots going back to his days at *La Protesta*, when he regularly accused Limantour and Científicos of being Wall Street's puppets. Enrile, now taking Científico money, simply shifted his formerly anti-Científico rhetoric to be anti-Madero. The man who went to prison for continually defaming Científicos was himself now considered a Científico.[64] The finer points of Porfirian politics got lost with time. Formerly, there were two distinct and competing lines of support for the dictator, Limantour's Científicos and Bernardo Reyes's supporters, such as Enrile.

No sooner had Orozco released his March 25 *plan* that he began to feel its negative consequences. He attempted to disown the manifesto and went so far as to deny that he signed his own proclamation. His personal envoy in El Paso, Braulio Hernández, quickly told Orozco that the proclamation, coupled with Enrile's previous manifesto, was causing harm to the revolution. Hernández said that he was forced to leave El Paso soon after Orozco issued the *plan* because of increased pressure from Mexican consul Enrique Llorente. Llorente's stock and influence with the Americans rose dramatically as the result of Orozco's embracing of Enrile and his rhetoric.

Orozco's *plan* of March 25 announced a broad social and economic reform agenda; nevertheless, historians leave no doubt that Orozco had the full support of Chihuahua elites and conservatives, people who professed to support Orozco but had no intention of backing his reform *plan*. Always perplexing was how Orozco could ostensibly occupy the left wing of a movement, fighting for the revolution and reform while simultaneously forming an alliance with Chihuahua reactionaries.[65] That was a subject dominating the conversations among many in Chihuahua. The question continued to be whether Orozco's was a true revolution or a counterrevolution.

CHAPTER TWENTY-THREE

Orozco's Decline

Despite Orozco's immediate successes in Chihuahua and his hubristic promise to march on to Mexico City, things were not going well in his camp. The impact of bad relations with Taft and the embargo was already being felt. In contrast to the warm reception Americans had given Madero, Orozco got the cold shoulder. Moreover, exposure of his cozy relations with the oligarchy and Enrile's activities had already taken the bloom off his rebellion. By the end of March, he was disappointed in the lack of enlistments and the rising desertions from his ranks.[1] There is no question that the rebels believed that they would quickly take down the weak Madero, but the popularity Orozco earlier enjoyed dropped dramatically when he grew to be seen as a traitor to the revolution and tool of Chihuahua capitalists.[2]

Madero pulled General Victoriano Huerta out of retirement to replace González Salas to stop Orozco's advance and promised Huerta a free hand in dealing with Orozco. Mexico City was in near panic over the Rellano defeat and assumed that Orozco would be marching to the capital. To the contrary, Orozco was headed north because of his munition shortage.

The arms shortage was strangling Orozco's revolution, and he was desperate to undo the damage that he and Enrile had inflicted in causing the embargo. Braulio Hernández complained that Enrile had just appeared on the scene and was unfamiliar with the people and terrain.[3] It was true. Orozco, moreover, was not previously anti-American. He had for years transported for American firms and developed a good and trusting working relationship with those companies. Orozco's recent anti-American tone and accusations were Enrile's work, but, when he went along with Enrile, it was Orozco who assumed that anti-American cast. Enrile did what he had always done in condemning the United States and criticizing pro-American Mexicans for being Wall Street puppets, but the ground had shifted under Enrile. Now his audience included the United States, and the revolution he administered depended on American armaments and supplies. Orozco attempts to reel in Enrile came too late. On April 5, Orozco sent a telegram to Taft saying that, although Enrile worked for him, Orozco had been unaware of the manifesto and found it offensive.[4] Orozco repudiated Enrile's manifesto, ordered all copies retrieved and destroyed, and apologized to Taft.[5] Orozco's effort was futile because the United States was not going to be placated. The apology changed nothing. Orozco had simply run into a perfect storm of bad luck, bad choices, and Enrile.

Four days after he apologized to Taft for the Enrile manifesto, apparently still under the influence of the undiplomatic Enrile and desperate to have the United States recognize his rebellion as a belligerency, Orozco wrote to Consul Letcher, saying that, because the United States did not recognize his rebellion, his government would no longer recognize U.S. consular representatives, and U.S. consuls should no longer address his military government.[6] Rebels had also raided a train, seizing what included consular correspondence and dispatches.[7] Under instructions, Letcher told Orozco that the consulate had national credentials and would continue its work. Three days after he sent the nonrecognition letter to Letcher, Orozco met with Letcher and apologized for the tone of his letter and for having seized consular mail and delaying its telegrams. He said that he would unofficially recognize consular functions and would no longer interfere with its duties.[8] A frustrated Orozco continued unsuccessfully to press his case that his rebellion was entitled to belligerency status as it had all the required attributes of a state and appointed Manuel Luján to be his Washington representative.[9] The embargo and the rebellion's lack of status proved to be its undoing.

It was not only the arms embargo declaration, however, but also the way it was enforced. Already, two weeks after the embargo was announced, the U.S. Department of Justice was filing criminal charges against Colorados for violating U.S. neutrality laws.[10] Orozco was reasonable in assuming that after Taft imposed the embargo, his rebels could simply import arms the old-fashioned way: they would smuggle them. Under the new embargo, circumstances changed that prevented smuggling. The United States had too few agents to control smuggling, and antismuggling enforcement was largely an intelligence operation requiring significant personnel. It was still legal for arms dealers to sell all the guns anyone wanted; the law only prohibited their exportation. A few agents could not track the multitude of weapons and ammunition sales. A series of changes brought about a highly unusual level of U.S.-Mexico cooperation to increase the number of agents and make the embargo effective.

The Mexican Secret Service had been under the direct control of the interior ministry, Gobernación, then under Abraham González, but once he returned to Chihuahua in February 1912, Madero placed the agency under the control of Washington, D.C., lawyer Sherburne Hopkins and his agent Felix Sommerfeld.[11] Hopkins and Sommerfeld persuaded American agencies to do the unthinkable and allow the Mexican Secret Service and other Mexican agents to assist the United States on the *American* side of the border, a controversial change in policy. The U.S. Secret Service admitted that it supervised Mexican agents who searched individuals on the U.S. side before they crossed into Mexico.[12] Mexican agents also participated in making arrests in the U.S. for Neutrality Act violations.[13] The following headline and story appeared in the July 19, 1912, *El Paso Herald*: "Mexican Spies Overrun El Paso; Women Are Searched."

Mexican agents and spies operating on the U.S. side reported to several supervisors, including Consul Llorente, Felix Sommerfeld of the Mexican Secret Service, and El Paso operative Abraham Molina. Mexican agents also paid gun merchant employees for intelligence on purchases. They kept watch on the stores to see who made purchases, eavesdropped on conversations, and followed anyone they pleased. The *El Paso Herald* noted the estimated number of agents to be one hundred,[14] although many of them were part-time spies. With the help of this large group from Mexico, the United States effectively shut off Orozco's arms supplies. The U.S. embargo stopped the exportation of arms, and U.S. agents strictly enforced the Neutrality Act, allowing the arrest and prosecution of those who attempted to deal in arms or to conspire to aid the anti-Madero insurgency. The Neutrality Act made it illegal to organize an action against a friendly government from within the United States, and Llorente constantly filed charges accusing anti-Madero operatives with violating its provisions.[15]

This entire operation run by Hopkins and Sommerfeld was controversial even within the Madero administration and should have been even more contentious had everyone understood Hopkins's and Sommerfeld's primary loyalties. Hopkins's main client was Henry Clay Pierce, a key player in U.S. and Mexican oil and railroad ventures. Sommerfeld was an important German spy, making one of Madero's principal advisors a German spy who ran Mexico's Secret Service. It came as no surprise, therefore, that Governor González and Consul Letcher viewed Sommerfeld with suspicion.

Before he turned against Madero, Orozco was accustomed to receiving glowing press reports. Those days were over. His battle for the public's approval was not going well. *El Correo de Chihuahua* and other pro-Madero journals

Fig. 12. Front Page, *El Paso Herald*, July 19, 1912

relentlessly pointed out Orozco's oligarchy connections, as did the persistently critical *El Paso Morning Times*. The El Paso daily referred to Orozco as "Cientifico Pascual Orozco" and "Orozco Turncoat"[16] and had reported Orozco's betrayal as early as February 7.[17] Moreover, Orozco might not have realized that, contrary to common belief, the public did have a memory. While he was still working for Madero before March of 1912, whenever the subject of his loyalty arose, Orozco declared his loyalty and insisted that he would "stick by [Madero] to the last."[18] The public did not forget those assurances, or their breach. To the consternation of many of his supporters, Orozco strengthened his alliance with the oligarchy.[19] During April, Orozco's staff was anxious to reverse his abysmal public relations, especially in Chihuahua City. They tried getting their proclamations and statements into the press. In March, Orozco's people seized copies of *El Correo de Chihuahua*,[20] and on April 16, Orozco forces entered *El Correo*'s offices and angrily confronted editor Silvestre Terrazas for not having published pro-Orozco accounts. When Terrazas refused to promise a change, the officers unsheathed their swords, paddled the editor,[21] and roughed up other employees. The editor was jailed, and, claiming censorship, the newspaper suspended publication.[22] Enrile's hand was evident in Orozco's attempts to control the press when Enrile boasted that, after El Correo's closure, he would be the one publishing the newspaper. Exercising more control, Orozco prevented the El Paso Morning Times from being sold in Chihuahua,[23] and he closed or censured other Maderista newspapers.[24]

In state government, Orozco and the oligarchy not only had deposed Governor González but also had replaced the legislature. When legislators opposing the new régime refused to attend sessions run by Orozco's group, the remaining deputies called for a new election to replace the absentees.[25] In mid-April, to break the arms block by requesting de facto recognition of his new rebel government, the Orozco-controlled Chihuahua legislature withdrew its recognition of Madero and declared Chihuahua an independent state.[26] Governor Gutiérrez decreed that Chihuahua would no longer recognize the Madero government and declared Madero a traitor to the nation.[27] Chihuahua essentially voted to secede from the Mexican republic and establish a rival state, a desperate move to elevate its international status to that of belligerency and thus possibly gain U.S. recognition rather than being a mere insurgency. All this was done to avoid the embargo. Chihuahua's government went as far as refusing to recognize federal postage stamps. Orozco gave the people of Chihuahua eight days to exchange their federal stamps or lose their value.[28]

A Terrazas-Creel friend and a U.S senator from the new state of New Mexico, Albert Bacon Fall energetically supported Orozco's effort to eliminate the embargo, but the State Department declined the request and the embargo held fast.[29]

Although Orozco controlled almost all Chihuahua, in April and May the hinges started coming off his rebellion. At a banquet held in Chihuahua City in honor of Orozco's chief of staff, Lieutenant Colonel Alfonso Castañeda, the Porfirista element in Orozco's forces once again showed its face. After toasting Castañeda, the crowd rose and began toasting Porfirio Díaz, "¡Viva Gen. Porfirio Díaz!"[30] Perhaps that manifestation of a strong Porfirista element in the upper ranks of Orozco's hierarchy caused Orozco other problems.

In April, Braulio Hernández resigned as Orozco's El Paso representative. Consul Llorente had Hernández arrested and jailed in El Paso on weapons charges. From jail, Hernández said he disapproved of Orozco's political conduct. In late

April and early May, Orozco's behavior became truly bizarre. He was already losing support from quite a few old Maderistas, such as Hernández. Next, under Enrile's influence, his actions would alienate many of his Vazquista supporters.

Back in the fall of 1911, Emilio Vázquez Gómez had announced his break with Madero, his Plan de Tacubaya, and the establishment of a provisional government with him as the president. He operated the movement with a junta based in San Antonio. The Vazquista junta later set up its new headquarters in Ciudad Juárez in early March 1912, after José Inés Salazar took the city for Vázquez Gómez. On April 24, Orozco wrote a letter addressed to Vázquez Gómez and gave it to his personal envoy for delivery. In the letter, Orozco invited Vázquez Gómez to join him in Chihuahua and become the nation's provisional president. Orozco's envoy was instructed to escort Vázquez Gómez back to Chihuahua.[31] Based on that signed letter personally delivered by Orozco's envoy with instructions to return with the envoy, Vázquez Gómez left San Antonio for Ciudad Juárez, arriving there on May 4. After Vázquez Gómez arrived, Orozco's local officials declared him provisional president, and the customs house once again became the nation's provisional capitol.[32] In Juárez, Vázquez Gómez named his cabinet, which included Orozco's father as acting secretary of war, pending his son's assumption of the office. Orozco's father graciously accepted the appointment. Vázquez Gómez went about the business of provisional president, issuing proclamations, speaking to the press and public, and so on. Vázquez Gómez publicly read Orozco's letter endorsing him as provisional president. But then in a shocking turn, three days after Vázquez Gómez arrived in Ciudad Juárez and was declared the nation's provisional president, Orozco, pressured by Enrile, announced that he did not in fact recognize Vázquez Gómez as provisional president and that Vázquez Gómez had misinterpreted his letter. Orozco ordered Vázquez Gómez to leave the country.[33] Orozco said that he had only invited Vázquez Gómez to Chihuahua for talks with his staff. The rejected Vázquez Gómez left Ciudad Juárez and returned to San Antonio. Rather than fault Orozco for the embarrassing event, Vázquez Gómez instead placed responsibility on Enrile and claimed that Enrile and the Chihuahua oligarchy would not allow him, a reformer, to become provisional president.[34] Perhaps this bad ending for the Vázquez Gómez–Orozco relationship could have been predicted. Two weeks before Orozco sent the messenger inviting Vázquez Gómez to Chihuahua to become the provisional president, Gonzalo Enrile had sent an open letter to the Mexico City daily *El Imparcial*. In the letter, Enrile complained to the press over calling Orozco's revolution a "Vazquista movement." Enrile explained that Vázquez Gómez had done nothing for the revolution, that he had been safely in San Antonio while others fought, that the rebels would not accept him or his socialist-tinged program, and that the revolution had been completely in the hands of Pascual Orozco.[35] Orozco later repeated these charges to Vázquez Gómez when he sent the former provisional president packing.

In the meantime, on May 3, Orozco tried to rein in the unruly Enrile. Hoping to mollify critics, he fired Enrile as the revolution's general secretary, but, unwilling to lose the financial support that came with Enrile, he privately retained him as paymaster, which kept Enrile in firm control over the revolution's purse strings.[36]

By being so dependent on the oligarchy for financing, Orozco was continually on the defensive. Once again, Orozco claimed surprise to learn that Enrile had received Científico money for the revolution. In a May 1912 report, Orozco conceded that he received Científico funding but insisted that he did not know that it was oligarchy money until that time. In May, a group of potential new financial backers emerged who wanted Orozco to get rid of old Porfiristas and to adhere to the Plan de San Luis, the original Madero plan. The unnamed sources gave their explanation for Orozco's confused and inconsistent treatment of Vázquez Gómez. The report continued:

> These men [new support group] declare that Enrile was the agent of Jose Yves Limantour, Gen. Bernardo Reyes and the Terrazas family, of Chihuahua, in furnishing the money to carry on the revolution and that Orozco knew it, though the troops did not. . . . They say that the men whom Enrile represented would not permit the recognition of Vasquez Gomez as provisional president and that while Orozco did send for [Vázquez] Gomez to come to Mexico, Enrile as his fiscal agent, the man who has kept the revolt on its feet, brought so much pressure to bear upon him that he had to refuse to recognize [Vázquez] Gomez when he came. They say that Enrile threatened, if deposed, to inform the army that Orozco had been accepting Cientifico gold for the conduct of his campaign and that Orozco feared he would himself be deposed if the army learned the truth.[37]

Enrile damaged the close relations Orozco had with Salazar and others who had supported Vázquez Gómez and even with his father, who had been named interim minister of war in the short-lived Vazquista cabinet. Salazar, Campa, and Orozco Sr. were against Enrile.[38] Orozco's break with Vázquez Gómez also damaged Orozco's relationship with revolutionaries far from Chihuahua, including Zapata, who removed Orozco as the head of the Morelos revolution. In a decree of June 14, 1912, General Zapata removed Orozco as head of his revolution and "told Orozco that he was 'Traitor to the people's cause' and refused to recognize Orozco any longer as Chief of the Northern Revolutionary Forces, and offered to shoot him in the back the day that he would fall into his hands."[39] By May, Orozco's Colorado Rebellion was spinning out of control, and Enrile was responsible for much of the chaos. Even those close to Orozco were opposed to Enrile's administration, and there were rumors that insiders might murder Enrile.[40] Enrile had indeed worn out his welcome in Chihuahua. On May 13, two unknown men assaulted Enrile as he walked home through a Chihuahua City park in the early morning hours. The assailants stabbed him in the left arm and shot him in the chest near his heart.[41] Enrile was in serious medical condition for some time.[42] The assault, supposedly, was the result of a dispute in Orozco forces.[43] Orozco, reports said, feared that Enrile might give the idea that they were fighting for Díaz rather than for the nation.[44] With the exposure of Enrile and Científico financing,[45] Enrile and Orozco ended their relationship, with Enrile leaving the movement.[46] Enrile went to Ciudad Juárez, where Orozco forces once again arrested him. He spent the night in in custody in the garrison, and Pascual Orozco Sr. freed him so that he could obtain medical treatment in El Paso. At the request of Consul Llorente, who accused Enrile of embezzlement, U.S. officials arrested and jailed Enrile when he entered El Paso. The *El Paso Herald* summarized:

> Enrile is known to have been the man who secured Cientifico money to aid the rebellion and when it became known among the rebels that such was the source of much of the money supporting their cause, the indignation is so great that Orozco had to remove him as financial agent of the revolution and an attempt was made on the life of Enrile by two unknown men in Chihuahua. Orozco continued Enrile as paymaster of the revolution, but he was wounded soon after he was deposed and has been in the hospital since that time.[47]

Following Enrile's exit in May, just when federal forces under General Huerta began their counterattack, Orozco's oligarchy funding began to dry up.[4]

CHAPTER TWENTY-FOUR

The End of Orozco's Rebellion

As he waited for the approach of Huerta's army in mid- to late April, Orozco counted on ten thousand men under arms. He stationed them along the rail line from Santa Rosalia de Camargo down to Ciudad Jiménez. Short of munitions and seeking to distract the attention of the coming federal forces that were being assembled in Torreón, Orozco sent Salazar east into the state of Coahuila with 1,500 of his men. Orozco planned to advance against Huerta as soon as he received the arms he expected from the United States.[1] Sending Salazar to Coahuila turned into a disaster for Orozco's forces. Reinforcing local elements, Huerta's troops defeated the tired and overpowered Colorado troops. Once he received delivery of the expected munitions, on May 8, Orozco began his move south to meet Huerta.[2] In addition to Salazar in Coahuila, he sent Campa west of Torreón into the state of Durango, where Campa engaged with federal forces. Eventually, Huerta repelled the diversionary actions, and in May he finally proceeded north to meet the main body of Orozco forces.[3]

Villa and his troops had joined Huerta in Torreón. By not having proceeded to Torreón immediately after his March victory at Rellano, Orozco had given Huerta time to set up a block there, a principal rail junction and key to the south. After Huerta fortified the area so that Orozco could not easily get through, he ordered his slow-moving entourage north after Orozco.[4]

On May 12, with comparable forces of eight thousand men each, Orozco and Huerta met in a battle at Conejos, Chihuahua. Once again short of munitions, Orozco forces disengaged and retreated north by rail[5] to the scene of his previous victory, Rellano, leaving behind artillery, rail engines, and four hundred fatalities.[6] They met again on the twenty-second in the second major battle at Rellano. By the afternoon of the twenty-third, Huerta had dealt Orozco a major defeat with political consequences. The battle raged for twenty-three hours, and Orozco forces suffered 650 casualties to federal losses of 140. Orozco also lost some of his few artillery pieces. From that point forward, Orozco would be in retreat, bleeding from desertions, and always low on arms and ammunition. Orozco headed north thirty-three miles to Ciudad Jiménez, abandoning more and more territory to Huerta's federal forces, hesitating only to destroy rail and bridges.[7] Eventually, Orozco found a more suitable site to make a stand farther north along the rail line at Bachimba Canyon south of Chihuahua City. At that location, Orozco placed his six thousand troops and his remaining four pieces of artillery. On July 3, his once again demoralized, under-armed troops lost to Huerta and retreated. Federal artillery continued to make the difference, pounding Orozco's forces mercilessly with Orozco unable to respond. Orozco fled farther north, not bothering to stop to defend Chihuahua City and leaving it for Huerta to take.[8] Instead, Orozco headed toward Ciudad Juárez, his last refuge,[9] and Huerta replaced Orozco as a national hero.

Orozco's rebellion was dying a slow, agonizing death. In early June, having exhausted a massive sum of money, the oligarchy-controlled legislature authorized another bond issue to support Orozco. This one was for 10 million pesos,[10] but, unlike the first, this one had few takers and went largely unfunded. The oligarchy only picked winners, and they no longer saw Orozco in that category. Out of options, Orozco changed his policy and engaged in forced loans.[11] The business community was wise to refuse to buy the new bonds. When the reconstituted legislature, consisting of members who had not deposed Governor Abraham González, reconvened in July, it immediately nullified acts of the Orozco legislature, including the 1.2 million-peso bond issue. The state would never pay those bondholders.[12]

There is, perhaps, an explanation for the apparent contradictory record as to whether the business community willingly financed Orozco. Those in the oligarchy had unrealistic expectations for the rebellion and did not appreciate the magnitude of the challenge. They might have been prepared to oppose the Madero administration, but they surely did not anticipate the harsh American reaction and the embargo along with wartime economic disruption. While it appears that the Chihuahua business community initially enthusiastically invited Orozco to rebel and participated in financing his army, that was not necessarily the case for businesses based elsewhere. Officials of the Banco Nacional, for example, complained about having to buy bonds as early as March 22—that is, immediately on their issuance. The bank refused at first to accept its allotted 250,000-peso share and considered closing its Chihuahua branch and moving it across the border to Gómez Palacio, Durango. Some foreign firms, such as Krakauer and Zork, also refused to purchase bonds,[13] but they were the exception in the early days of Orozco's rebellion. Once restored to his office, González not only nullified the state's approval of the bonds but also refused to give banks credit for the state funds on hand that they had turned over to Orozco.[14] As the Colorado Rebellion weakened, so did much of its business support in Chihuahua. Enrile's oppressive hand and his increasingly threatening behavior also dampened whatever enthusiasm the oligarchy might once have had for Orozco. As the rebellion wore on, its business support waned. Enrile had presented wealthy merchants a stark choice, voluntarily take the loans and bonds, or the funds would be taken "by force of arms."[15] Once Orozco was no longer in charge and González had resumed control, the business community might also have made the self-serving claim that it had been forced to loan Orozco money.

On July 7, the restored governor Abraham González and Huerta stood together on the ceremonial balcony of the government palace as Huerta's federal cavalry rode triumphantly into Chihuahua City. The *New York Times* reported, "The people who a week ago were loud in their protestations of friendship for Gen. Orozco and his ragged and undisciplined army stood in the streets applauding the victorious Federal General [Huerta] and his columns of regulars with shouts of 'Viva Madero!'"[16] Earlier reports indicated that, well before July, the Orozco administration was unpopular. The reports began early, but certainly, by April, Chihuahuenses in growing numbers, including its early oligarchy supporters, had a negative view of the rebellion.[17]

With González back in power, Orozco faced a new reality. In the wake of the defeats at Conejos, Rellano, and Bachimba Canyon, there was bitterness, strife, and dissension among Orozco's officers. They were divided over what they thought they could accomplish and over their strategy. They were bitter toward the United States and its effective arms embargo. Orozco seemed numb, incoherent. He went from announcing a grand turnaround to saying they would disband. There was little still unifying the command other than its opposition to Madero.

Orozco's father, waiting in Ciudad Juárez for his son's arrival, announced a plan to attack the state of Sonora and take the port of Guaymas there, where they could finally obtain Japanese and German munitions and then move south to unite with Zapatista forces moving north.[18] The lack of confidence in the plan was evident in the discontent among the troops, some of whom complained about having to leave Ciudad Juárez and others who deserted.

Orozco opted to leave most of his troops at El Sauz and the remainder at Encinillas, and he continued to Ciudad Juárez along with a few men.[19] They boarded a yellow caboose attached directly to the engine and tender, which composed the entire train that took them to Ciudad Juárez, where they arrived on July 7. As he arrived in Ciudad Juárez, the defeated Orozco proclaimed unconvincingly that the change to guerilla warfare was the start of the true revolution, one to be prosecuted as Zapata had in the South.[20]

In Ciudad Juárez, the disarray, squabbling, ongoing desertions, and lack of energy all overwhelmed Orozco, such that he became despondent. Over the next ten days, Orozco conferred with his father's Ciudad Juárez command. The father had already announced that Orozco forces would head for Sonora from Casas Grandes. Recognizing that they were incapable of meeting federal forces in open warfare, they discussed breaking up into guerilla bands. On July 14, at his customs house headquarters, Orozco Jr. received the New York Times reporter whose story the next day noted, "Orozco is due to quit instead of returning to his army at Sauz or Casas Grandes. . . . The defeated rebel commander has decided to seek the first opportunity to leave the country in disguise. He has admitted that he is defeated, and says that the United States is responsible by withholding ammunition from him."[21] Whatever intentions he had in making the statement, Orozco did not quit at that time.

Southwest of Ciudad Juárez, Orozco's general José Inés Salazar harassed federal troops in the area of Casas Grandes and issued threats to the Mormon community there, including threats to massacre any Mormons remaining,[22] causing a large part of the Mormon population in Chihuahua to flee, mainly to the El Paso area, with many never to return.[23] Desperate for weapons, Orozco ordered Salazar to take arms from the Mormons, saying, unconvincingly, that if he just had arms, he could win the war in sixty days.[24]

Huerta appeared to be taking too much time to head north. In fairness to the general, however, his was not a force designed for rapid movement or strikes. The Mexican army that was tediously making its way to Ciudad Juárez, the force Madero had inherited, made war the same way it had for years under Díaz. With completion of several rail lines in the 1880s, it became possible to send large numbers of federal troops long distances. During the Mexican Revolution, there was an undetermined number of women soldiers, actual soldaderas, who fought the same as men, and some achieved command ranks. There were also women soldiers who pretended to be men or who identified as male. The Mexican army developed a tradition allowing its soldiers to take their women and families when they traveled to battle. Díaz did not invest in a quartermaster corps. Paid low wages, troops were forced to find their own food and quarters. That was his army's tradition, and that was why they used the services of many women, including wives, quasi soldaderas, and camp-follower women, who trudged along after the troops wherever they went. The women foraged and pillaged. Their children accompanied many of them, and often they too foraged and pillaged. They were a necessary and integral part of the army.

The camp-follower women, however, performed important, vital functions, akin to being the army's quartermaster corps. These women, often called "soldaderas" too, were not actual combatants, although some did bear arms and occasionally fire them. A better description would be "camp followers," an army adjunct common in fighting forces everywhere for centuries if not millennia. After battles, they could be seen doing their work on the fallen, removing weapons, ammunition, money, religious medals, shoes, and clothing—that is, anything of value. For Mexican troops, finding food was a never-ending quest. Some camp followers collaborated with specific soldiers. Others freelanced, performing services for pay. They rode whenever and wherever they could find a space on a train, often on its roof, or they walked, carrying their pots and pans, dragging their chickens, and often carrying their children on their backs. Whenever there was a stop, no matter how brief, they immediately laid out their cookware, searched for food, and prepared what they could. Soldiers' wages, paid daily, were meager. Since the army did not provide quarters or food of any kind when bivouacked in the field, many units took on the appearance of a large family camping trip. There were as many camp followers and children as there were soldiers as the troop trains lumbered toward their destination.[25] One correspondent described an army camp scene:

> Sometimes children accompany their parents on such journeys, and the writer has seen Federal troops on the way to an active encounter . . . accompanied by women carrying nursing babies on their backs. Indeed, to such an extent is this carried that in a number of cases where the humans being on troop train were counted fully half were found to be women and children.
>
> As soon as such a train halts the women immediately begin their search for food and its preparation. Without their aid the army could not exist.[26]

When the revolution began, both Villa and Orozco forces, being cavalry units, either prohibited or discouraged camp followers as incompatible with a mobile operation. Later, they both relented and allowed camp followers when train travel became the norm. In Chihuahua, Villa's camp followers were called "Adelitas." Madero's army commander tried to prohibit camp followers, but Madero overruled him because he thought that the change would be a hardship on his irregular forces.

As the caravan of Huerta's troops moved north toward the border, Orozco admitted that he would abandon Ciudad Juárez and that he would not confront Huerta's forces. Orozco was biding his time on the border, waiting for Huerta's eventual arrival. He claimed to be relaxed and in no hurry, insisting that rumors that he was suing Madero for peace were false. To him, there would never be peace so long as Madero was in office. Apparently recovered from his recent depression, he returned to saying that the fight was just beginning.[27] For days, his troops prepared to evacuate. The portion of the Chihuahua legislature backing Orozco had been meeting in Ciudad Juárez. Now it too prepared to leave. In late June, Orozco had already moved his family from San Antonio to Los Angeles.[28]

Early the morning of August 16, Orozco and his men slipped out of Ciudad Juárez, and the federal forces at Casas Grandes quickly moved in to take the city.[29] Orozco, down to 1,400 men including his father and brother, continued his guerrilla campaign in the North in the Ojinaga area.[30] In early September, Orozco forces took Ojinaga, but federal forces drove them out on September 10. Many of Orozco's troops fled into the United States, including Orozco's father and Crisóforo Caballero.[31] Within a week, U.S. authorities arrested Orozco's father based on a complaint from Consul Llorente alleging murder charges in Mexico and transferred him to El Paso, where they later charged him with having violated the Neutrality Act for unlawfully exporting weapons.[32]

Once in Ciudad Juárez, Huerta continued his habitual heavy drinking. One night at El Gato Negro, the general's favorite Juárez cantina, a drunk Huerta said that he had the power, if he so wanted, to allow Orozco to go all the way to Mexico City and depose Madero.[33] Huerta's incredibly slow pursuit of Orozco had already raised questions of his loyalty. His unhurried movement made it appear that Huerta was uninterested in ending Orozco's uprising, as prolonging it weakened Madero. Persistent rumors of Huerta's disloyalty and an Orozco collaboration made the news. There were enough warning signs that there might have been some basis for a Huerta-Orozco anti-Madero collaboration. In August, Orozco told the U.S. consul in Ciudad Juárez that Madero would soon resign and that hostilities ended under an agreement he had with Huerta.[34] A month later, the *El Paso Herald*'s headline on September 14 read, "Revolt of Mexican Army Expected to Proclaim Gen. Huerta Leader, Orozco to Be Connected with the Movement." The State Department also noted the proliferation of rumors predicting Huerta's betrayal and his collaboration with Orozco.[35]

At the September 16 Independence Day celebrations in Ciudad Juárez, the crowds had *vivas* for former dictator Díaz but apparently none for Madero. It was the same in Mexico City.[36] With strong indications that Huerta would revolt against him, Madero removed Huerta as head of the northern forces and recalled him to Mexico City. Huerta took his time in returning to the capital. He stopped on the way in Chihuahua, where business leaders honored him at a banquet. Among those in attendance was Luis Terrazas Cuilty, the general's son, the same man who had contributed at least 100,000 pesos to Orozco in his fight against Huerta and the federal army. Indicating that the oligarchy had by then abandoned Orozco and once again demonstrating its pragmatism, Terrazas spoke and, without a hint of irony, solemnly told the crowd, "So long as we have the army, there will be a nation."[37]

Even if Orozco failed in his effort, with Madero so unpopular, others were still thinking of replacing Madero, including the old dictator's nephew Félix Díaz. Vazquistas had apparently had their fill of Orozco, and some of them deposed Orozco as their nominal leader.[38] In late September, several former Vazquista and Orozquista elements set up a new junta for Félix Díaz in Ciudad Juárez. On October 16, Díaz forces attacked Veracruz, seized some boats, and held the city for a few days, but within a week federal forces put down the revolt, arrested Félix, and confined him in Mexico City.[39]

Orozco's rebellion, for all its promise and handsome financing, had a shelf life of only a few months. His unruly coalition was too unstable. Large desertions, poor munition supply, and the impaired, bizarre Enrile administration and policies did it in. It had only one main battle, the first at Rellano, to its credit and an unbroken string of defeats once Huerta engaged. With mostly defeats, there was nothing positive to hold popular support for Orozco. Poor food supplies, a tattered war economy, significant casualties, and disrupted rail and telegraph networks took their toll and doomed the rebellion. On closing its governance, the Orozco-oligarchy Chihuahua rebellion and administration had been an unmitigated disaster.

After his defeat at Bachimba, Orozco ceased being a threat to Madero. Although Orozco's rebellion was a failure and his forces "were militarily defeated, they contributed mightily to the wreck of the Madero régime."[40] To fight Orozco, Madero had doubled the military budget, resorted to the hated leva to raise troops, and drained the treasury.[41] Both Orozco's rebellion and Madero's defense resembled a murder-suicide. Bands of Colorados under Salazar and Antonio Rojas invaded Sonora and, after some initial successes, were soundly defeated by troops organized under Álvaro Obregón.[42] With Orozco's rebellion on life support and down to a guerrilla force after August 1912, there was little hope for its revival, unless he could get the arms embargo lifted. It was a long shot, but the only hope, and the only individual who had the possibility of changing Washington's mind on the issue, was a brand-new senator from New Mexico, Albert B. Fall. Senator Fall wanted a return to a Mexico under the Científicos and the oligarchy. It was for that reason that he did what he could to assist Orozco in fighting the embargo.

CHAPTER TWENTY-FIVE

Fall Committee Hearings

American diplomatic and business interests have always had an eye on Mexican affairs. American firms often took sides in its conflicts, and Mexican partisans, especially conservative and Científico groups, courted American support and financing. The Mexican Revolution was no different, and U.S. oil, rail, mining, and industrial firms were deeply involved in the fight. When Díaz preferred Briton Weetman Pearson and essentially froze out several important companies, U.S. firms no longer sided with Díaz as a monolith. Several major firms were open to Madero's revolution as a vehicle to enhance their opportunities in the Mexican market. The Mexican Revolution thus became the intersection of competing business interests with the revolution's partisans. The possible financing of the Madero Revolution, especially from oil companies such as Standard Oil, interested U.S. senator Albert Fall, who hoped that Orozco's rebellion might bring about a counterrevolution. He was friendly with many prominent Mexicans, including Terrazas and Creel. Above all, Fall wanted a return to the Porfiriato.[1]

Within three months after he entered the Senate, Fall had the Senate schedule hearings on Mexican affairs during the revolution and had incidentally gained a seat on the prestigious Foreign Relations Committee. He quickly became the Republican point person regarding U.S.-Mexico policy. In his position, Fall did what he could to damage Madero and impede the Mexican Revolution. He was a bitter opponent of the arms embargo and sought to overturn it. The subcommittee's stated mission was to determine whether the Madero Revolution had received any U.S. corporate financing, especially from oil companies. The hearings were to take place in El Paso just as Orozco's Colorado Rebellion was collapsing, mostly due to the U.S. arms embargo.[2]

The ostensible purpose of the hearings was to expose any American businesses that financed the Madero Revolution, in hopes of proving the Maderos guilty of the same type of graft Americans had encouraged under Díaz. At first, Fall and others were convinced that substantial American oil money had backed Madero, and he meant to expose it. Fall saw benefits in assisting the moribund Orozco uprising. Orozco was friendly to the Terrazas-Creel clan, and Orozco represented the best opportunity to depose Madero. Fall's hearings received an unexpected bonus when, after Orozco retreated from Ciudad Juárez, many of his supporters fled to El Paso.[3] That was where Orozco's father was in custody on federal charges. The subcommittee was thus able to call on several witnesses friendly to Orozco.

At the turn of the century, the petroleum business had experienced a widespread change in the United States and in Mexico. Before 1900, there was not much demand for oil, except for lighting. Then ships changed from coal to oil and transportation went from horses to cars. Suddenly, the demand for petroleum mushroomed. Mexico had no oil production before 1900. It imported all its oil from the United States. Standard Oil had a virtual monopoly in distributing that oil in Mexico and did so through Waters-Pierce, a firm managed by Henry Clay Pierce, who also owned most of the stock in Mexican rail companies. Díaz did not care for Pierce or Standard Oil and was happy to grant concessions to his favorite building contractor, Englishman Weetman Pearson, and to American Edward L. Doheny, so that they could explore for oil in competition with Waters-Pierce/Standard Oil.

Texas hit the first big oil strike in 1901 with Spindletop, a major well that produced 100,000 barrels daily and set off a boom in Texas. At the same time, Doheny, who was exploring in the Tampico area, hit a gusher like Spindletop. Later, Weetman Pearson also struck it big doing business with his El Aguila Oil Company. Not only did that end the Waters-Pierce/Standard Oil monopoly; it put them at a competitive disadvantage and out of the petroleum business in Mexico. Suddenly, oil went from being a small business to being one of Mexico's largest revenue sources. The government's petroleum development policies immediately became the subject of intense interest for foreign firms.

Weetman Pearson had a history with Díaz. He ran his family's large construction company, which built the Hudson Tunnel in New York. He suffered from depth sickness in working in the tunnel and went to Mexico to recover. Díaz was about to build the Gran Canal, a huge drain and flood control project in Mexico City, and needed British bonds to finance it. The bondholders wanted a British contractor, and Weetman was there. He built the canal, and then Díaz gave him contracts to build the harbor at Veracruz and the Tehuantepec Railway, connecting the gulf and the Pacific at the isthmus. During those projects, Pearson became friendly with Díaz, but Pearson also knew that to be successful in the Porfiriato, he needed to buy influential Mexicans in the administration. Weetman clearly saw Creel as being influential, so he put Creel and Díaz's son, Porfirio Jr., on the board of El Aguila. Creel and the others received stock in El Aguila, and Porfirio Jr.'s wife's family was able to sell property to Pearson. Pearson spread a lot of money around, as others did in Chihuahua during the Terrazas-Creel years when politicians enriched themselves, legally or otherwise.[4] That was the way they did business in the Porfiriato.

To be fair, Mexico was not alone in doing business that way. They did it that way too in the United States, although in Mexico, those in political office had more than an advantage; they enjoyed a monopoly, running the equivalent of a toll road. If you wanted to do something, you had to hire them or their relatives, pay or give them a share to get contracts and concessions, just as Pearson had done. In Mexico and the United States, people went back and forth between government and private firms, the familiar "revolving door." As far as policy was concerned, there was little difference in the results between outright bribery, always present, and the seemingly honest dealings short of bribery. Officeholders, essentially on loan from private firms to which they invariably returned after serving in government, had the belief that the nation's interests were the same as those of their former corporate employers. They continued to own stock in firms that benefited from their government policies. They did not use blind trusts.[5] Taft's attorney general, George W. Wickersham, and Taft's brother Henry W. Taft were members of the same law firm, and both served on the board of El Aguila. The firm also represented Weetman Pearson's Mexican rail interests. From a policy standpoint, it made no difference whether the companies bribed policy-making public officials or whether those officials were former corporate officers on loan to the government. The company always won, and the public lost either way. The proper course, rarely followed by U.S. or Mexican officials in those days, would have been to abstain in cases where, for example, the official had represented a firm, had been a board member, or was a significant shareholder.

The El Paso hearings recessed on October 12 and resumed in Washington on December 10. At that session, the senators took the testimony of the most interesting witness they heard, Washington, D.C., attorney Sherburne G. Hopkins. Long involved in supporting revolutions in Latin America, Hopkins had helped the Maderos navigate Washington political waters. He also worked for Henry Clay Pierce and the Waters-Pierce Company, big players in Mexican oil and rail. It was no coincidence that the Maderos chose the same attorney who represented Waters-Pierce, the company allied with Standard Oil. Hopkins claimed that, except for Limantour, Científicos, such as Creel and his colleagues, had received large sums in graft for having granted government concessions to businesses. Hopkins said that Creel and several associates were each given $200,000 in El Aguila stock as well as seats on its board, putting its competitors at a disadvantage.[6] In that manner, Weetman Pearson, who exercised influence with Díaz, placed the cooperative Creel on several boards, including that of the Mexican National Railways. That system of graft in exchange for generous business concessions became the modus operandi in the Porfiriato,[7] making public office a lucrative venture, with Creel serving as its premier practitioner on the national stage.

During the fall of 1912, Madero continued to fight Zapata in the South and remnants of Orozco forces in the North. Fall was unable to rescind the embargo, and Orozco's rebellion was left to wither. The year 1913, however, was to bring a more serious challenge.

CHAPTER TWENTY-SIX

La Decena Trágica

In June 1912, after Huerta's Rellano victory, Pancho Villa came under his command. Federal forces took Ciudad Jiménez, and Villa requisitioned horses in the area, a common practice. Among those they took was a fine mare belonging to a wealthy Jiménez woman, the wife of the area's most prominent merchant, Marcos Russek. Villa liked the mare enough to want her for himself. Russek complained, and Huerta had Villa arrested on charges that he stole the mare and for insubordination when Villa delayed responding to Huerta's charges. Huerta ordered Villa executed and had him in front of the firing squad when Emilio Madero fortuitously heard about the planned execution, went to the scene, and intervened. Francisco Madero ordered Villa's life spared and sent him instead to Lecumberri Prison in Mexico City, where Villa languished for months. He complained bitterly about the injustice of his detention and about dreadful prison conditions.[1] In late November 1912, Villa got his wish in a transfer to the military prison, Santiago de Tlatelolco, where he continued his unsuccessful attempts to prove his innocence to Madero. On Christmas Day, Villa cut through the cell's bars, donned a suit a complicit court clerk had given him, covered his face while feigning a conversation with the clerk, and walked out of Tlatelolco. He made his way to Mazatlán, then to Arizona, arriving in El Paso in early 1913.[2] From El Paso, Villa continued to press his claim for clemency from Madero.

In September 1912, Orozco was wounded in combat in Ojinaga and fled to the United States. When Orozco's forces fled and crossed the river into Presidio, U.S. forces arrested many of them, including Orozco Sr. Mexican officials and Cónsul Llorente quickly prepared charges so that American authorities would hold them.[3] Between September and November of 1912, Orozco's forces were in Ojinaga, where they defeated the federal forces and made their headquarters until January of 1913. The speculation was that General Huerta was allowing Orozco's revolt to continue because he had his own plans to overthrow Madero.[4] Eluding American federal charges, Orozco Jr. traveled to Saint Louis and then to Los Angeles.[5] By mid-November 1912, Orozco was back in Chihuahua but was ill and not leading his forces, and he was also reported hiding in El Paso. Orozco forces were being led by Marcelo Caraveo, Antonio Rojas, José Inés Salazar, and Juan Porras, although there were reports that Orozco and Salazar were estranged.[6] By January of 1913, Orozco's guerrilla forces were once again threatening Ciudad Juárez.

That same month, Madero attempted to initiate peace talks with Orozco, but Orozco responded by insisting on Madero's resignation and the naming of a new interim president and cabinet. The individuals listed by Orozco as his proposed government were mainly old Porfiristas and conservatives, including General Gerónimo Treviño for president, once again exposing the influence of right-wing, anti-Madero groups over Orozco.[7] Orozco was so inflexibly anti-Madero that one report had him agreeing with the opinion of some in the oligarchy that Mexico's best course lay in American intervention.[8] Madero, having put down several uprisings in his first months as president, now had the confidence that he could deal with the weakened Orozco as well. The main impact of Orozco's Chihuahua-centered revolt was that Madero was forced into combat in the North, which left Zapata free to widen the southern conflict. The 1912 Orozco Rebellion also broadened the base for anti-Madero forces until its ties to the oligarchy were clearly exposed, causing many liberals to abandon its ranks.[9]

In Chihuahua, the general criticism of Madero was that he was not a "true revolutionary," that is, he did not intend to change the established order of the Porfiriato but was merely interested in putting the Madero family into the control group. Seen as naïve, Madero kept the same pro-Díaz military commanders, retained the same bureaucracy, and refused to initiate economic and social reforms demanded by most in his revolutionary army. He also lost support through several actions, such as freeing General Navarro; ignoring those who fought for him, such as Orozco, and rewarding many who did not; failing to pay and support his troops; and failing to restore lands that many had lost unjustly. Madero was repeatedly warned, even by his mother,[10] that the army and reactionaries he retained would overthrow him, and he was specifically warned about Huerta's plans for a coup d'état. When confronted, Huerta's response was to dismiss disloyalty charges with a curt retort that he was not Orozco. Madero continued to pledge his faith in the old Porfirista general, but he nevertheless removed Huerta from the northern command and sent him back to Mexico City. Madero was attempting to unite the nation and heal the revolution's divisions before he had gained control over the government and while defending himself from revolts. Instead of purging his enemies, he embraced them while giving many of his allies the cold shoulder.

On February 9, 1913, in Mexico City, General Manuel Mondragón and two thousand federal troops and military cadets revolted against Madero. Rebel troops initially took the National Palace and then lost it to the loyal general Lauro Villar. Another group of rebels freed imprisoned presidential aspirants Bernardo Reyes and Félix Díaz, who then joined the assault on the National Palace. In the revolt's pecking order, Reyes most likely outranked Díaz. When Reyes approached the National Palace, loyal army forces repulsed the attack, killed Reyes, and sent Mondragón's forces along with Félix Díaz in retreat to the Ciudadela, an old fort and prison in the city. With Reyes dead, Díaz inherited the rebellion. General Lauro Villar, however, had been seriously wounded in the National Palace skirmish. Madero gathered his guard and cadets and proceeded toward the National Palace. Before Madero reached his destination, Huerta, in civilian clothing, joined the group and offered Madero his services. Ignoring warnings of Huerta's treachery from Gustavo Madero and Carranza and with his military commander wounded in the skirmish, Madero named Huerta head of the armed forces and put him in personal command against the revolt.[11] On February 15, Vice President Pino Suárez was told that Huerta was in on the rebellion, and, hearing of that, Huerta went to Pino Suárez's home to assure him of his loyalty.[12]

Fighting raged in the center of Mexico City for days, but the rebels were confined to the Ciudadela and were not making progress. On February 17, with artillery fire shaking the center of the city, a frustrated Madero asked Huerta when he would stop the fighting. Huerta assured the president that it would be over the next day. What Madero did not know, though, was that Huerta was already in collaboration with U.S. Ambassador Henry Lane Wilson, who was deeply involved in the revolt. Wilson, openly pro-Díaz, wanted Madero ousted and assured Huerta that, if he overthrew Madero, the United States would recognize his government. Under Wilson's plan, Huerta would become interim president with Félix Díaz slated to become Mexico's new president, reinstituting the Porfiriato. Huerta went along with Wilson's plan. Huerta withdrew his recognition of the Madero government and then made an agreement called Pact of the Ciudadela, a plan that was immediately renamed Pact of the Embassy for Wilson's open involvement in the coup. In fact, Ambassador Wilson was acting on his own in fomenting the coup.[13]

Under the pact, Huerta joined Félix Díaz's revolt against Madero.[14] On the afternoon of the eighteenth, the shooting stopped, just as Huerta had promised. At Huerta's invitation, he and Gustavo Madero were eating together in a downtown restaurant when Huerta told Gustavo that he had to attend to an urgent matter and rose to leave. He felt under his jacket and returned, telling Gustavo that he had forgotten his pistol. Huerta asked Gustavo to give him his pistol, which Gustavo did. No sooner had Huerta left than soldiers arrested Gustavo. Gustavo asked, "On whose orders?" and the captain replied, "From my general Huerta."[15] Soldiers took Gustavo to the Ciudadela to be held by rebel forces there.[16] Two hours later, as Madero was descending in his private elevator in the National Palace, federal officer Aureliano Blanquet put a gun to Madero's chest and placed him under arrest. Federal troops also arrested Vice President Pino Suárez and confined him and Madero to a reception room of the National Palace.[17] Meanwhile at the Ciudadela, rebel soldiers beat and tortured Gustavo Madero. One soldier stabbed Gustavo in his one eye with his sword and blinded him, before he was executed by some twenty soldiers there.[18] Huerta claimed that Gustavo, who was unarmed and blind, was killed while attempting to escape. La ley fuga was back in vogue.

Coerced to do so, both Madero and Pino Suárez resigned, and the congress appointed Huerta interim president. In addition to Francisco and Gustavo Madero and Pino Suárez, Huerta had also arrested Madero loyalist General Felipe Ángeles and others. While Huerta held them, Mexicans and the diplomatic corps in Mexico pleaded with Huerta to spare the captives' lives since Madero had previously accorded safe conduct to Díaz and his staff. Ambassador Wilson assured Taft and the world that he had Huerta's word that Madero would not be harmed[19] and that there was a plan to take Madero to Veracruz and have him board a ship to exile in Cuba. Huerta, however, rescinded the order for Madero's deportation, shutting the door on a safe exile for Madero.[20] Fortunately, the history of these events is documented. Cuba's ambassador to Mexico, who spent the night of the eighteenth with Madero and the other prisoners, was present at several meetings called by Ambassador Wilson regarding the events and was intimately involved in efforts to spare Madero's life and provide a Cuban exile.[21]

Late on the night of February 22, Madero and Pino Suárez were abruptly wakened and told that they were being transferred to Lecumberri Prison. They left General Ángeles in the palace, and the rurales took Madero and Pino Suárez to Lecumberri in separate cars. On the way, the troops suddenly stopped on the back side of the prison next to its high walls, removed Madero and Pino Suárez from the vehicles, and executed them.[22] Rural Major Francisco Cárdenas, who rode with Madero, was his assassin, and Rural Corporal Rafael Pimienta killed Pino Suárez.[23] Believed by few, Huerta expressed shock and promised a full inquiry into the killings. His official explanation was that Madero supporters had assaulted the two cars to free the men while en route to the prison, and the prisoners were shot as they attempted to escape.[24] The brutality and brazen aspect of the arrest and murders of Madero and Pino Suárez repulsed Mexicans and the world. It also made Madero a national martyr.

Ambassador Wilson's plan was for Huerta to assume the interim presidency and then be succeeded by Félix Díaz.[25] That never happened; Huerta retained the presidency. Huerta remained in office, and, in the name of the United States, another democratically elected government was replaced by a newly minted dictatorship, this one under Huerta. Thus ended the first stage and began the second stage of the Mexican Revolution, a bloody war lasting years and killing tens of thousands of Mexicans.

Opposition to Huerta immediately arose, mainly in the northern states of Sonora under Governor José María Maytorena, Coahuila under Governor Venustiano Carranza, and Chihuahua under Governor Abraham González. Huerta demanded declarations of loyalty from all governors, but the three from the North did not respond. On February 22, the same day that Madero and Pino Suárez were assassinated, federal troops arrested Chihuahua governor Abraham González at his office in the state house on charges that González was plotting a revolution.[26] On March 6, 1913, under military guard, González was put on a train to be imprisoned in Mexico City. En route, the train was stopped forty miles south of Chihuahua City at Bachimba Pass, where the escort took González off the train, executed him, and then had the train run over his body. He was buried at that spot.[27] The official explanation was that González was killed while his supporters were trying to help him escape.[28]

On February 27, five days after Madero's assassination, Orozco formally consented to join forces with Huerta, the man seen as Madero's assassin,[29] but the record is clear that Orozco had been on board with the coup since even before Madero's assassination. Historian Francisco Almada wrote that Orozco may have been trying to reach and ally with anti-Madero rebel elements under Félix Díaz even before Huerta became involved in the coup.[30] On February 19, during the coup and three days before Madero's assassination, Orozco's father was advocating for León de la Barra as president. On February 20, Orozco Jr. sent Félix Díaz, the then presumed provisional president after the expected Huerta resignation, his congratulations.[31] Díaz responded, asking Orozco to rush to Mexico City to confer.[32]

Huerta immediately dispatched a peace commission north to bring Orozco and other northerners into his camp. Manuel Garza Allape, a member of Huerta's new cabinet, led the delegation. The commission met with Orozco Sr. in Nuevo Laredo on February 28, and they spoke at length. Immediately afterward, Orozco Sr. said that Orozco forces were recognizing Huerta, and the next day, Orozco Jr. formally recognized Huerta's government.[33] The peace commission then left to confer with Orozco in Villa Ahumada, Chihuahua. There were indications that sometime after Orozco's forces were defeated in Ojinaga in September 1912, Orozco may have taken refuge in El Paso and might have been ill. Whatever illness it was, he was apparently well when he emerged to join Huerta.[34]

Orozco readily agreed to fight for Huerta, and Huerta immediately agreed to Orozco's conditions, including land reform and making Orozco's troops federally paid rurales.[35] Alberto Terrazas and Enrique Cuilty, son and nephew of General Terrazas, respectively, became colonels in Huerta's Chihuahua forces,[36] and a number of other Orozquistas left San Antonio for El Paso soon to return to Mexico.[37] Of Huerta's promises to Orozco, the only one kept was the promise to recognize the military ranks that Orozco had conferred on his troops. Huerta ignored all the rest, including land reform.[38] Once again, Orozco expressed liberal reforms but in fact acted in support of regressive elements.[39] Some Orozco partisans note that, given the options, Orozco had no choice but to join Huerta, as his relations with Carranza were vile. Those Orozco defenders neglect to mention the option of doing nothing. Orozco could have gone into exile as many had done during the revolution, but he established his historical legacy instead by joining the reviled Huerta. Chihuahua's oligarchy joined Orozco in welcoming Huerta.[40]

In early March, Orozco returned to Mexico City on the special train with Huerta's "Peace Commission." On the train with Orozco as it entered Mexico City was Gonzalo Enrile.[41] With as much trouble as Enrile had caused for Orozco, Enrile continued to have a strong hold on the general. On March, 17, Huerta commissioned Orozco brigadier general[42] and requested his help in bringing Zapata to their side. Rather than go himself, Orozco instead sent his father to win Zapata over. After Orozco Sr. arrived in Morelos, Zapata had him and the other peace commissioners arrested and tried for treason. Zapata later had Orozco's father executed. Zapata joined many in calling Orozco a traitor and removed him as titular head of the Zapata revolution and named himself its leader.[43] Among the Mexican left, Zapata thus sealed Orozco's reputation as a traitor and ally of Mexican reactionaries. Zapata wrote to Orozco, "If Madero betrayed the revolution, you have done the same. You don't offer liberty to the people—you offer chains. Huerta represents the defection of the army. You represent the defection of the revolution."[44] Against all evidence, Orozco and his close advisors continued to see themselves as leftist, reform-minded revolutionaries.

Contrary to Ambassador Wilson's promise that the United States would recognize Huerta's régime, neither Taft in his last month nor Woodrow Wilson after his March 4, 1913, inauguration recognized Huerta's coup d'état government. Failure to obtain U.S. recognition would shorten the Huerta administration's life. Huerta's anger with the United States would also make him more receptive to German overtures.

The fall of 1913 was a confusing time for everyone. Battles were raging in the North, the United States had not recognized Huerta, and Mexican presidential elections were set for October 26. If Huerta were to follow the no reelection rule, he could not run, and he implied as much. He had, after all, promised to yield to Félix Díaz in the coup deal. Members of his cabinet and those from competing factions and parties announced their candidacy, including Félix Díaz, Federico Gamboa for the Catholic Party, and Jorge Vera Estañol for the liberals. In the congress, the liberal faction was doing everything it could to thwart Huerta's régime.[45]

In October 1913, Huerta and the congress engaged in a complicated civil battle over several issues. In one, the congress, convening as a grand jury, was insistent on investigating corruption on the part of Limantour and was stopped by the courts from doing so. The congress determined to defy the courts, claiming that it was a congressional prerogative. In another, Huerta appointed a member of congress to the cabinet, and when the liberals in the chamber refused to grant the member an after-the-fact, but routine, leave of absence so he could serve, Huerta began to threaten the deputies. Several deputies and senators complained, with Chiapas senator Belisario Domínguez being particularly forceful and vocal in his criticism.[46] Domínguez soon went missing, causing the congress to pass a resolution questioning the disappearance and threatening to suspend the congress or to move its sessions to a secure locale. Huerta demanded that the resolution be withdrawn, and, when the congress refused, on October 11, Huerta arrested 113 of the offending deputies and had them imprisoned.[47] After some senators met with him to support the deputies, he had those senators arrested as well. The arrested senators included the well-known Rodolfo Reyes, son of Bernardo Reyes, Jorge Vera Estañol, a former member of Huerta's cabinet, and others. As the very prominent legislators were being marched down the streets of the capital to the prison, walking along with them and in custody was the ever-present Gonzalo Enrile, about to add yet another entry to his already lengthy "rap sheet."

Senator Domínguez was later found assassinated and became another Huerta martyr. After he arrested most of the congress, Huerta dissolved the legislature and officially became a dictator, adding another controversy to his already contentious administration.[48] For the scheduled October 26 election, Huerta created a mass of confusion and obfuscation. Three days before the election, Huerta gathered the diplomatic corps and reminded members that the constitution prohibited him from running for the presidency, rendering his candidacy null and void. He also reminded them that he had promised to resign.[49] Even as he told the public that he was not running, he instructed federal employees and the military to get the vote out for his ticket.[50] Huerta, nevertheless, put himself up as a candidate with Aureliano Blanquet as his running mate. In a fraudulent process, Huerta claimed a landslide victory and was elected, but the process was later invalidated by the congress because less than half of the electoral districts had submitted returns. Huerta nevertheless remained in office, claiming a semblance of democratic support.[51]

Nine months before Huerta dissolved the congress, from his exile in El Paso, Pancho Villa learned of Madero's assassination and González's arrest and vowed to fight Huerta. Villa paid his El Paso hotel bill, borrowed nine horses, bought nine weapons, and, on the night of March 6, 1913, along with eight others, crossed into Mexico in the early days of the second stage of the Mexican Revolution. In one of the most improbable, Phoenix-like rises and in one of history's greatest demonstrations of leadership, Villa, the uneducated former bandit, went on to amass the largest army in Mexico in less than one year and took the state of Chihuahua for the constitutional, anti-Huerta forces.[52] Never passing up an opportunity for revenge, when Villa took Ciudad Jiménez in April 1913, he burned down La Vencedora, the large mercantile establishment owned by Marcos Russek, the husband of the woman who caused Pancho's imprisonment and near execution.[53]

In November of 1913, Villa's constitutionalist forces defeated federal Orozco forces at the Battle of Tierra Blanca, Chihuahua, a decisive win putting virtually all the state in Villa's hands. Orozco was the main military man for Huerta in the North, but he could not get along with General Salvador Mercado, Huerta's other general in the area and military governor of Chihuahua. Their break came in late November 1913, when Mercado left Chihuahua City defenseless, allowing Villa to walk into the city. The fear of Villa plunder was so great that hundreds of residents, including Mercado and Orozco, marched toward Ojinaga and possible refuge in the United States.[54] Orozco's request to Huerta to allow him to bypass Mercado's command was denied. In December, Villa took Chihuahua City and days later took Ojinaga, the last federal stronghold in Chihuahua, sending thousands of federal soldiers and refugees streaming into the United States, including Orozco and much of the Terrazas clan. The massive column of refugees that had left Chihuahua City then left Ojinaga bound for El Paso, including thousands of federal soldiers, who were headed for internment at Fort Bliss.[55] Those who did not flee were captured by Villa, but Orozco eluded capture, slipped into the United States, and later made his way back to Mexican territory and to Torreón.[56]

On January 10, 1914, Villa forces controlled the entire state.[57] Orozco's whereabouts for a period after January 10 were a mystery. After Huerta's fall and exile in July in 1914, Orozco was sought by U.S. authorities. Reports of the Bureau of Investigation mention that Orozco had been indicted on April 15, 1912, for violating U.S. neutrality laws.[58] The bureau had labeled Orozco a fugitive and kept his family and friends under watch. The bureau monitored Orozco residences and put a mail cover on them, which allowed the agents to determine who was communicating with the family. Orozco was reported to be in several Texas sites, including Mineral Wells, San Antonio, Fort Shafter, El Paso, and in Las Cruces, New Mexico; Santa Ana, California; and New Orleans. He was clearly moving around, avoiding capture.[59]

After Villa had all Chihuahua firmly in his hands, Huerta attempted to devise a strategy to control the ever-difficult state. In early 1914, after federal troops and hundreds of refugees had fled from Ojinaga to the United States, Huerta pushed the congress and the state legislatures to amend the constitution to permit the division of rebellion-prone Chihuahua. He separated several northern districts to be the new territory of Bravos with a capital in Ciudad Juárez, and other districts in the southern territory of Jiménez with its capital at Hidalgo del Parral. The balance in the center was to remain as the state of Chihuahua with Chihuahua City to continue as its capital. Huerta also appointed a military governor over each of the three, with Orozco being named the military governor of Chihuahua. The constitution was thus amended, with Orozco nominally over Chihuahua, José Inés Salazar over Bravos, and General Carlos García Hidalgo over Jiménez. All of this was for nothing, as none of the new governors was ever in control to take office and the laws were nullified after Huerta was deposed.[60]

By February 21, 1914, Orozco, nominally military governor of Chihuahua, was back in Mexico City to testify against Mercado for having abandoned Chihuahua. He was also there to organize his forces under the new divided Chihuahua, and Huerta promoted him to the rank of division general.[61] Later, Villa was on the move and took the key city of Torreón on April 19.[62] At that time, Orozco and his forces began their march north to confront Villa. Orozco himself, however, met up with retreating federal forces and joined their march back to San Luis Potosí.[63]

Huerta's was a difficult presidency, at least what there was of it. The constitutionalist forces arrayed against him held Sonora, Chihuahua, and Coahuila and then marched south under Obregón, Villa, and Carranza. The going was rough for the Constitutionalists, but they got a boost when, in February 1914, Woodrow Wilson eliminated the Taft arms embargo, allowing armaments to flow.[64] In fact, the embargo was only lifted for Carranza and not for Villa.[65]

There was bad blood between Carranza, the first chief of the Constitutionalists, and Villa, a tension that would soon reach a breaking point. Villa, head of the Northern Division, and his special troops, Los Dorados, were strong in the northern states of Chihuahua and Durango. It seemed that nothing could stop Villa, as all armies marched toward Mexico City, with Villa marching down the center; Obregón, down the west; and Carranza, down the east. Ordered by Carranza to split his forces, Villa disobeyed and sent all his troops to Zacatecas. In a massive victory, Villa took the city of Zacatecas on June 24, 1914, and there was little anyone could do to stop him, not even Orozco.[66] Zacatecas was the bloodiest battle of the revolution. The federal army suffered six thousand dead and three thousand wounded. The Constitutionalists suffered one thousand dead and two thousand wounded. The battlefield was a dreadful sight.[67] There was, however, still the matter of Villa's insubordination and a need to clarify the chain of command. In July 1914, Villa met with other military emissaries and agreed to recognize Carranza as first chief, and Carranza agreed that Villa would head the northern army. It was, however, a shaky truce.[68]

By that time, a mere year and five months after he had grabbed power, Huerta was finished and submitted his resignation on July 15, 1914. Within days, Huerta boarded the German ship SS *Dresden* bound for Spain and exile, settling in Barcelona. Former Díaz peace delegate Francisco Carvajal, by virtue of his position as sitting president of the Supreme Court, became interim president. By then, Orozco knew that his army days were over as well. Two weeks after Huerta left Mexico, Carvajal fired Orozco.[69] Orozco left the army with four thousand men. They fought in León and later moved to San Luis Potosí with the Constitutionalists in pursuit. By September, it was over. With only a handful of men still with him, Orozco slipped across the border into Texas.[70] For the first time in years, Orozco found himself without a military fighting force under him.[71] His options, once again, were limited. He could not go to Carranza, Obregón, or Villa, all enemies since Orozco had betrayed Madero. He probably never considered returning to San Isidro to run mule trains. He did what many defeated Mexicans had done: he went to the United States in hope of building up his forces for a fourth time.

In September, revolutionary and constitutional leader Carranza became Mexico's president. However, unlike Díaz, who remained in exile, this was not the last to be heard of Victoriano Huerta.

CHAPTER TWENTY-SEVEN

A New Huerta Plot

The nation that Venustiano Carranza inherited in August 1914 was still torn by revolution. Although the Constitutionalists had defeated Huerta, they had split the country into zones under three leaders, Villa, Zapata, and Carranza. Carranza, from Coahuila, resembled Madero in many ways. His family had acquired a fortune in Coahuila land when his father, Jesus, a mule transporter, supported Benito Juárez against the French. Venustiano Carranza was a gubernatorial candidate in 1909, but after Díaz supported his opponent and Carranza lost, Carranza repudiated Díaz and allied with Madero. When Madero came to power in 1911, he named Carranza provisional minister of war for a short period, and Carranza soon left the post to become governor of Coahuila. Carranza was Madero's opposite in several ways, including his six foot, four stature, which, together with his impressive mustache and goatee, made him memorable. When Huerta became president in 1913, Carranza refused to recognize him and rebelled. Carranza declared himself "Primer Jefe" of the Constitutionalist Army, a title Villa and Zapata refused to honor. After the Constitutionalists defeated Huerta in August 1914, Carranza controlled less territory than Villa and Zapata held together.

To resolve differences between Carrancistas on one side and Zapatistas and Villistas on the other, Carranza called for a convention to meet in Aguascalientes in November 1914.[1] It was the radical Conventionists, Villa and Zapata, against the Constitutionalists, the more conservative elements supporting Carranza. In a futile effort to mend the split, Carranza allowed the adoption of Zapata's radical Plan de Ayala.[2] There was, however, to be no peace, for Villa and Zapata split with Carranza, and they spent the next several months in 1914 and 1915 fighting Carranza's forces led by Álvaro Obregón. In battle after a pivotal fight, Obregón relentlessly drove Villa steadily north and out of power in Chihuahua. Orozco took no part in the fight between the right-centrist Carranza forces and the leftist forces of Villa and Zapata. Orozco had long before split with his former allies of the Madero Revolution, and he was no longer part of the debate over the reforms Mexico would adopt.

Back in September 1914, however, with Huerta exiled in Barcelona, Orozco had few options. He had only a fraction of his previous supporters, and, if captured, he would surely face a Villa or Carranza firing squad. Carranza had a list of those who would be tried for treason if found, a threat that drove prominent Mexicans into a U.S. exile, including Creel, Félix Díaz, and many others.[3] Orozco quickly declared himself in revolt against both interim president Carvajal and his successor, Carranza. Orozco was not about to join Carranza, the man who, after all, had taken the cabinet post he thought was his; moreover, Orozco had been fighting on Huerta's side against Carranza and Villa. One of the few to join Orozco in his uprising against Carranza, because he too had run out of options, was Francisco Cárdenas, the man who had assassinated Madero and Pino Suárez.[4] Orozco was at the bottom of the barrel. He was in the United States with occasional forays into Mexico, working to unify the large number of exiles in El Paso and other areas of the United States against Carranza. During the fall of 1914, Orozco was hard at work organizing forces and building up an arms cache. U.S. authorities noted that Terrazas and Creel were financial supporters of Orozco's group.[5] Orozco traveled to New York City in December 1914, where he met with other dissidents and purchased arms.[6] At the same time, the press was reporting that Germany had sent a high-ranking naval intelligence officer, Captain Franz von Rintelen, to the United States to stir up problems in Mexico. Reportedly, von Rintelen had $30 million at his disposal.[7]

Intending to organize a new force, in the fall of 1914, a group of anti-Carranza exiles formed a junta based in San Antonio. Claiming to be a peace effort (Mexican or San Antonio Peace Assembly[8]) consisting of varied political views, its cast was mostly Científico-Porfirista, with support from the Catholic Party.[9] Orozco was its military leader, but the junta lacked a political head. At that moment, several forces were converging on Huerta and Orozco, including the San Antonio junta, German efforts to create problems in Mexico for the United States, and stirrings of revolt among Mexicans in Texas.

By 1915, Mexico was supplying one-fourth of the world's oil production with Weetman Pearson providing most of that. The British navy ran on Pearson's Mexican petroleum.[10] With World War I under way, Mexico was thus critical to the allies and to the Germans, who, moreover, were interested in creating Mexican problems for the United States that would keep America out of the conflict. It was a simple choice for the Germans, and it was not an idle exercise for them given the enormous pressure within the United States to remain out of the conflict. Whichever side had U.S. resources and armed forces on its side would likely have the advantage. Because the United States would not likely ally with Germany against Britain, Germany's best option was to keep the Americans away from Europe by creating so much trouble in Mexico and on the border that the United States would have to keep its resources home and possibly intervene in Mexico.[11]

In early 1915, two of the forces joined in reaching out to Huerta. The first was the German military. In February, Germany sent von Rintelen to Spain to visit Huerta. Huerta had been at his Barcelona exile only a few months when von Rintelen arrived. Historian Barbara Tuchman detailed the intrigue that ensued in her book *The Zimmermann Telegram*. Von Rintelen offered German financing to back Huerta in a coup to oust Carranza and for Mexico to start a war against the United States.[12]

The American government was already deeply preoccupied with the Mexican Revolution and the various armed groups crossing into the United States. The other force approaching Huerta was the San Antonio junta. On its face, the junta consisted of a peace assembly that first convened in San Antonio in early February 1915.[13] In late March 1915, intersecting with the German effort, the San Antonio–based junta decided to launch a revolt against Carranza with Orozco as its military leader, but it still needed a political chief. Historian Michael C. Meyer wrote that to solve that problem, Enrique Creel was sent to Spain to persuade Huerta to return, lead a revolution, and retake Mexico.[14] According to Meyer, Creel also took an odd plan to present to Huerta, which was based on an obscure proposal that had first surfaced a few months previously in November 1914, titled "Los Hijos de Cuauhtémoc, Hidalgo y Juárez en Tejas," signed by a Francisco Álvarez Tostado.[15] "Los Hijos de Cuauhtémoc" was a precursor of the January 1915 Plan de San Diego, which called for Mexicans living in Texas and the Southwest to revolt against the United States, secede, form a new republic, and study possible annexation by Mexico.[16] Huerta, persuaded by Creel that the junta had presented the elements it needed for a successful rebellion, financing, and strong leadership, agreed to return to Mexico and sailed for New York, where his party arrived on April 12.[17]

Despite their efforts, Mexican officials in the United States were unsuccessful in keeping Huerta from landing.[18] In April, Von Rintelen also made his way to New York, where Huerta, with Creel's approval, entered into a pact to receive substantial German financing and munitions for the mission. The Germans immediately deposited almost $1 million in Huerta's account and promised as much as $12 million along with ten thousand rifles.[19]

In early May, Orozco went to New York to confer and coordinate the revolt with Huerta, leaving no doubt of the existence of a right-wing Huerta-Creel-Orozco alliance.[20] Orozco told Huerta that forces under Campa and Salazar were gaining ground in Northern Chihuahua. Huerta and his allies selected June 28, 1915, as the day to ignite the new revolution.[21]

With German agents meeting with the Huerta-Creel-Orozco junta, American security agencies were on high alert and had Huerta and his allies under close surveillance. Agents had an eye on Orozco and his family, whose residences and mail they scrutinized in El Paso, San Antonio, and other places.[22] In New York City, three sets of agents tailed and spied on Huerta and the Germans. U.S., British, and Mexican intelligence agencies had Huerta under watch at his New York hotel. At one point, agents slipped into Huerta's Manhattan Hotel meeting room, installed microphones in the draperies, and ran wires into the adjoining room, where agents listened to conversations. By doing so, they learned in detail about the German connection and support and of Huerta's plan to return to Mexico and lead a revolution against Carranza.[23] Although Huerta denied that he intended to lead a revolution in Mexico,[24] several military and political people headed for an El Paso rendezvous with Huerta and Orozco.[25]

Seemingly oblivious to the spies hovering around him, and claiming to be on his way to the San Francisco world's fair, Huerta boarded a westbound train.[26] El Paso officials learned that Huerta changed trains in Kansas City, Missouri, and, instead of going to San Francisco, he boarded a train bound for El Paso,[27] where agents were ready to confront him. Rail employees tipped off El Paso customs collector Zachary Cobb that, rather than alighting in El Paso, Huerta's destination was Newman, New Mexico, an isolated stop twenty miles north of El Paso on the Texas–New Mexico border.[28] Cobb quickly organized a detail of Justice Department agents and officials and a detachment of army troops to meet the train. Early on Sunday morning, June 27, the day before the revolution's scheduled start date, Huerta's train arrived at Newman. The train station was one hundred yards inside New Mexico, so federal officials instructed the engineer to stop the train over the Texas line, as they mistakenly thought that they had no authority in New Mexico.

When Cobb arrived at Newman, he did not expect to see Orozco there and found him hiding behind mesquite bushes. Orozco and Huerta's son-in-law, Major Luis Fuentes, had driven to Newman and were waiting for Huerta.[29]

Cobb and an agent of the Bureau of Investigation boarded the train, went to Huerta's compartment, and invited Huerta and Orozco to accompany them to the federal courthouse. Huerta continued to maintain vacation pretenses after going with the agents.[30] Once at the courthouse, federal neutrality charges were filed against both Huerta and Orozco. The case caused great excitement. El Pasoans mobbed the courthouse whenever Huerta and Orozco made appearances.[31] Carranza quickly instructed his staff to request Huerta's extradition to Mexico for Madero's assassination. Staff at the Ministry of Foreign Relations considered extradition, but it was not possible because the United States did not recognize Carranza's government and there was no extradition treaty in place.[32]

Huerta and Orozco were both arraigned and released on bond,[33] but, taking no chances of a quick escape by the pair into Mexico, guards were placed at their homes. Orozco resided with his family at a rental home. Orozco's sister Serafina recalled that on July 3 she happened to go into the kitchen for water and saw Orozco putting on his black Stetson, getting ready to leave. He signaled for her to remain quiet. The military guard posted at the rear of the home—one of six on guard at all times—was drunk and asleep. Serafina said that she saw Orozco quietly leave, step gingerly over the sleeping guard, proceed into the alley, and walk away.[34] The next morning officials learned that Orozco had escaped.[35] The court revoked Huerta's bond and remanded him to custody. There were several reported Orozco sightings over the next few weeks, but there was no confirmation. In addition to Huerta's people, a Felicista group supporting Díaz's nephew Félix Díaz was active in their attempt to organize a force. Both groups were active in the United States and Cuba.[36] For some time, Orozco and his people had been accumulating a large arms cache in El Paso. One source noted fifty machine guns, five thousand rifles, and 1.5 million rounds of ammunition. The same source said that, over time, he had crossed arms and some six hundred men, and on July 3 was to have crossed the fugitive Orozco, who was expecting 1,400 men on the other side.[37]

CHAPTER TWENTY-EIGHT

The Death of Pascual Orozco

Federal agents were on the lookout for Orozco all that summer of 1915. They knew that he was preparing yet another attack on Ciudad Juárez. He and his associates had been working for months recruiting men and buying and storing arms for the coming battle. Orozco was not one who abandoned rebellion. On August 4, 1915, twenty-four Orozco soldiers were arrested about thirty miles east of El Paso while attempting to cross into Mexico.[1] Surely, Orozco had been in the area, and the day of battle was approaching. On August 26, 1915, Bureau of Investigation agents were certain that Orozco had visited his family at their new El Paso residence on Montana Street. They searched the home and found indications that he had been sleeping in the basement. The family later admitted that he had been there.[2] On August 31, newspapers and wire services carried stories reporting that Orozco had been found the previous day one hundred miles southeast of El Paso. A sheriff's posse, stories reported, had cornered Orozco and four companions in a box canyon in the High Lonesome Mountains of Culberson County, Texas, where the Mexicans perished in a hail of bullets fired by the large, well-armed posse. The popular story of Orozco's final hours appeared in the *New York Times* the next day.

> After a raid on the Dick Love ranch yesterday, Orozco and four companions were pursued from the Sierra Blanca country into the foothills. Orozco died at dusk tonight. . . . According to reports the raiders led by Orozco arrived at Dick Love's ranch near Sierra Blanca, yesterday, and forced the cook to supply them with dinner while they made a ranch hand shoe their horses.
>
> While they were eating, Dick Love and two cowboys were seen by the raiders approaching the house, and the Mexicans fled, shooting as they rode, pursued by Love and his companions, who delayed only to arouse the surrounding country by telephone. The

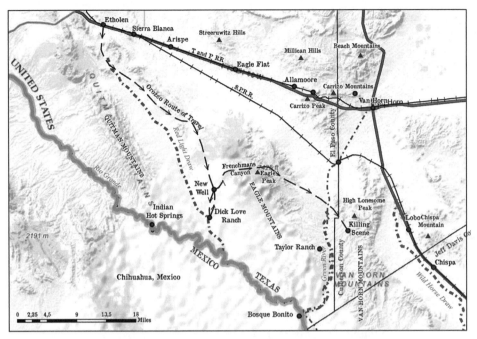

Orozco's Route of Travel. Cartography by Olga Bosenko.
Copyright © 2016 by the University of Oklahoma Press.

posse was formed hurriedly and the running fight, which ended
when the last raider was killed, continued until dusk this evening.
Four bullet wounds were found in the body, positively identified,
according to reports, as that of the Huerta General.[3]

The final shootout took place in a canyon near the Taylor Ranch. The next
day, members of the posse took the bodies by wagon to the ranch house and
from there by motor vehicle to the Culberson County Courthouse in Van Horn.
Outside the courthouse, Sheriff John A. Morine and his deputies displayed
the bodies for the press and the public to view. Later, El Paso undertaker J. J.
Kaster arrived in Van Horn, where he embalmed and prepared the bodies for
burial and then had them transported to El Paso by train. On September 2,
Orozco's coffin was taken to his family's home at 1218 Montana Street, where
family and friends held a wake and paid their respects.[4]

On September 3, with a Methodist minister officiating, the family buried Orozco as three thousand El Pasoans looked on.[5] The *New York Times* reported, "The funerals of General Pascual Orozco and four companions killed in Texas last week were held today. The bodies, on a float, passed through streets lined with thousands of somber Mexicans, with heads bared and each carrying bouquets. Villa's Chihuahua government granted permission to bury Orozco in Mexico, but the family declined."[6]

Among officials immediately summoned to the Orozco death scene on August 30 was Culberson County justice of the peace T. R. Owen, who immediately commenced a coroner's inquest into the incident. He arrived at the location the next day, the thirty-first, and began taking testimony from relevant witnesses. The nature of the multiple homicide required a justice of the peace to determine the cause of death and to rule whether the deaths were due to an unlawful act, in which case the report could form the basis for a prosecution. Before Owen arrived, the posse was sure that Orozco was among the dead. Completing the inquest when he returned to Van Horn the following day, Judge Owen filed his minimal findings. First, he identified the bodies and found that Orozco, Delgado, Caballero, Sandoval, and Terrazas "came to their death" in a canyon two miles south of High Lonesome Peak in the Van Horn Mountains of Culberson County, Texas. They died from gunshots fired by members of the combined El Paso and Culberson County posse. The ruling included no other findings—no description of the location or number of wounds of the deceased, no identification of who fired the lethal shots, and no finding whether unlawful acts caused the deaths.[7]

Because there were no survivors on Orozco's side, the only witnesses were members of the posse and a few others, who assisted with determining the location of the killings and identifying the deceased. Several of the most important witnesses never gave statements or testified, most significantly Sierra Blanca deputy constable Dave Allison, the appointed head of the combined posse.[8] Two of the most important witnesses were Dick Love Ranch employees August Fransel and Joe Thomson. They were the only witnesses and victims of the alleged raid at the Dick Love Ranch headquarters and the only ones to have contact with the Orozco group, and neither gave the judge a statement. The only sworn testimony regarding Thomson and Fransel is contained in the statement given by El Paso County deputy sheriff W. H. Schrock, who repeated what Thomson and Fransel had told him. Schrock was a member of the posse who claimed to have been the first law officer to arrive at the Dick

Love Ranch. The Love Ranch was then in El Paso County (today it would be in Hudspeth County). Schrock's statement read, verbatim,

> I first heard of Mexicans when I drove up to R. C. [Dick] Love's Ranch about 1 o'clock P.M. 29 Aug. 1915, when August Fransel and Joe Thomson told me that two well armed men had rode off from the Ranch in a hurry in direction of the Dick Love new well, Joe also said that five Mexicans were camped at this new well and they had several horses, Joe said he was hunting horses and saw some loose horses and rode to them when these men rose up and spoke to him in English saying "Come here," He said he went to where they were camped, they asked him what he was looking for, he said he was looking for horses and asked them what they wanted with him, they told him they wanted some chuck, he said "All right come with me to the ranch and I will get you some chuch [*sic*]." Two of the men, one with black leggings and the other with a black eye, Kaki suit and tan bootees went with him to the ranch, when they got to the ranch one of the two men told Joe to shoe his horse, Joe did so. They went into the ranch house to eat and while eating dinner they were constantly on the watch and during the meal one of them spied three men coming toward the house and said in Mexican "There comes three men, let's go." They jumped up grabbed their winchesters, which they had brought in, ran, jumped on their horses and ran toward the new well.[9]

That testimony is the only official account detailing what occurred before the posse undertook its chase of Orozco and his companions. There was no raid. There was no mention of stolen horses or untoward conduct on the part of the Mexicans. They were not called bandits. There was no shooting; there were no threats. They said that they were hungry, and Thomson invited them to eat at the ranch house. They asked for a horse to be shoed and apparently paid for the service.[10] They were suspicious and fled when others approached the ranch.

Deputy Schrock said that he and five other men arrived fifteen minutes after the two Mexicans fled from the Love Ranch house. They saddled up and began to pursue the Mexicans. Underway, the pursuers soon found where the five men had been camping. The Mexicans were then seen headed north then east from that camp at a full gallop toward the nearby Eagle Mountains. It was when the Mexicans reached the Eagle Mountains, with the posse a quarter of a mile behind, that the Mexicans allegedly fired at the posse, the possemen reported. No one from the posse side stated that they fired at the Mexicans before the final battle.

As night fell, the posse trailed the men as far as Frenchmans Canyon in the Eagle Mountains. The next day, August 30, the posse again picked up the Mexicans' fresh trail at two in the afternoon several miles east of the Eagle Mountains across the Green River valley in another mountain range, the Van Horn or High Lonesome Mountains, due south of High Lonesome Peak. The chase was now at the eastern border of El Paso County and the western edge of Culberson County. Given the direction of the chase, Dick Love sent a telegram by phone to Culberson County sheriff Morine: "Look out for five Mexicans in Eagle Mountains, well armed, are going your way." Other telegrams noted that the Mexicans had a fight with rancher Dick Love.[11]

In the statements of two members of the posse, a Taylor ranch hand had seen the Mexicans and told the posse where they were located. They found the Mexicans that afternoon, August 30, camped in a box canyon in the High Lonesome Mountains. Once there, Sheriff Morine split the posse split into two groups,[12] each climbing the opposite back sides of the hills of the canyon until they reached the rim and surrounded the Mexicans. They fired at the Mexicans and killed them. There was no mention of calls for surrender. No member of the posse was wounded in the "fusillade." The five Mexicans each had a horse, a substantial unspent ammunition supply, and "some fresh jerked beef supposed to have been part of a calf butchered by them the evening before."[13]

In inspecting the Mexicans' camp after the killings, Dick Love told Morine that he recognized one of the five horses as his and two others as belonging to Joe Marshall, a railroad water pumper based at the Etholen rail stop a few miles west of Sierra Blanca. Schrock said that, after the shootings, they found the Mexicans to have the two Marshall horses and a horse belonging to Bob Love, which had been in the same pasture. Sheriff Morine also said that the Mexicans had jerked meat from a freshly slaughtered calf taken from the Bob Love Ranch. Judge Owen carefully noted that, although the El Paso County line was nearby, the site of the deaths was on the Taylor Ranch, one mile inside Culberson County.[14] It was a fact that Judge Owen carefully documented.

To posse partisans, such as the *El Paso Morning Times*, incursions by Mexican bandits in remote areas had to be stopped. Mexican horse thieves and cattle rustlers were fair game if caught. Orozco and his comrades were uniformly portrayed as bandits, cattle rustlers, or *mal hombres* in the vernacular of Western magazine stories of the event. To many, members of the posse, the killers of the Orozco group, became heroes.[15] Even so, given the allegations, others, including the anti-Orozco *El Paso Morning Times*, insisted on a full investigation of the event.[16]

In the months between Orozco's escape in July and January 1916, the earlier threat to Carranza posed by Huerta had evaporated. Villa's army collapsed, and Orozco was killed, leaving Carranza in an unassailable position. Huerta remained in El Paso in custody or under house arrest. He had been remanded into custody after Orozco escaped. He had been ill but seemed to have improved as time when on. When Huerta learned of Orozco's death, he became depressed. He took to drinking heavily again, and his health rapidly deteriorated. Huerta joined many Mexicans in believing that Americans had assassinated Orozco.[17] On January 13, 1916, Huerta died from complications of cirrhosis of the liver and from a post-surgical internal hemorrhage. Huerta was buried in a vault next to Orozco's. Both men's families planned to reinter their remains in Mexico.[18] Although they buried Orozco, that did not end the speculation over the details of his death.

CHAPTER TWENTY-NINE

Controversy over Orozco's Death

Some had a view of the killings that differed from the posse's account, such as Alfonso Taracena's unsourced chronology: "On August 30, 1915, Pascual Orozco, dies from a shot to the head by ranchers named Lob [Love] who dragged him from the scene to make it appear that Orozco was taken by surprise while stealing horses along with other Mexicans. When ranchers discovered that Orozco had a large quantity of dollars on his person they killed him for that reason."[1] Luis Cabrera wrote to Carranza that Orozco and his companions were assassinated while asleep. Huerta, he added, feared that he would have the same fate.[2]

The circumstances surrounding Orozco's last days and death became the subject of controversy. Orozco's enemy, President Carranza, demanded an explanation and an investigation.[3] To many Mexicans, Orozco's killing was wanton, an execution, something akin to ley fuga executions they knew very well. When the remains arrived in El Paso, Mexicans were upset, and officials took measures to avoid trouble.[4] The *El Paso Morning Times* noted, "Considerable feeling was evident here yesterday among the Mexicans over the Orozco death. This feeling was increased by the issuance of an extra edition of a Mexican paper, 'La Justicia,' in which it was declared 'Orozco was assassinated.'"[5] The *New York Tribune* reported that Mexicans charged that "Orozco and his companions were massacred and that there was no evidence that they were looting any American ranches."[6] In one news account, the posse was called cowardly for having shot men who were fleeing and apparently posed no threat, an act seen as a murder and a stain on America. The article further noted, "The shots fired by thirty 'American Rangers,' and the entry wounds show that Orozco as well as his companions were shot in the back."[7] Another article in the same issue explained, "Even when the Americans assure that Orozco died in combat, no one believes this because of the location of the wounds as well as the fact that none of the attackers [possemen] received a single wound, and Orozco and his companions were notable shots."[8] Mexicans were convinced that the posse's story was false and that Orozco and his group were shot at point-blank or contact range and executed.

El Paso mayor Tom Lea, a lawyer who was representing both Huerta and Orozco, was so worried of possible violence that he requested army troops and artillery. El Paso customs collector Zachary Cobb wired the mayor's message to Washington, adding, "Bitterness among Mexicans here over Orozco's death very intense. Their agitators assert and Mexicans generally seem to feel that he was assassinated."[9] In San Antonio, articles critical of the posse in two local Spanish language newspapers alarmed Bureau of Investigation agents, who thought that the pieces might incite violence. The agents summoned the editors for a counseling session and received assurances that similar articles would not be published again.[10]

The killings raised many questions. The possemen claimed that they did not know until after the killings that Orozco was among the victims, which meant that they were unaware that one of the Mexicans was a fugitive. They did not know until after the killings that horses had been stolen, and they knew nothing about the men. All they knew was that several well-armed Mexicans had asked for a meal and for a horse to be shoed, that both requests were voluntarily granted, and that the men had fled.

Soon, the posse suspected that one of the desperados they had killed was Orozco, and, given the questions raised over the killings and claims of assassination, authorities in Culberson County feared reprisal from Mexicans. One report said that they were so fearful of attack that "American inhabitants and the border patrol are spending the night under arms."[11] The proximity of the killing to El Paso County and the chase's clear initiation there caused their concern about a possible investigation or criminal charges in El Paso. The public, especially the Mexican community there, was incensed over the killings. Although many El Pasoans were unsympathetic to Huerta and Orozco, Orozco had still had a large following there. Many among those who were against Orozco also were offended by the nature of the killings. There were accusations that the posse members shot the Mexicans in the back or at close range, intentionally executed them, killed them while they were sleeping, or killed them for the money they carried. They also suspected that the Mexicans had not returned the posse's fire and may have been sleeping and unarmed at the time. The contentions immediately raised questions:

How many wounds did each man have?

Where were the wounds?

Were they each shot in the back of the head?

Were they shot at close range?

Were there gunpowder burns?

Was there gunpowder residue?

Were they running away when they were shot?

Were some of the men asleep when shot?

Were the men tied up or restrained?

Were the Mexicans given an opportunity to surrender?

Who fired the fatal shots?

Where were the bodies first found in relation to each other?

Where were the Mexicans' weapons in relation to their bodies?

Had the bodies been dragged?

How many spent cartridges were near the dead men that would
   definitively show whether and to what extent they fired at the posse?

How much money did the Mexicans have?[12]

Was the location of killings changed?[13]

These were some of the uncomplicated questions raised about the killings, questions that were also on the minds of U.S. officials who were deeply concerned with possible disorder, violence, or reprisals on the part of Mexicans upset over the killings. These were not questions requiring modern technology. These simple questions could and should have been answered. The inquest, however uninformative it was to start with, was never supplemented, although it begged for more information, such as a cursory examination and description of the scene, of the bodies, and a minimal examination of the witnesses.[14] Posse supporters in Sierra Blanca and Van Horn appeared uninterested in finding out whether the posse had murdered the Mexicans. They were more concerned about Orozco's popularity in El Paso's large Mexican community than they were about answering the questions raised. Ranchers in the area armed themselves in fear of revenge and joined officials in appeals for military and state protection.[15] Unconfirmed reports had one hundred Mexicans crossing the border and entering the area.[16]

As the tension mounted, posse members, apparently aided by Culberson County attorney A. L. Green, devised a strategy to prevent any action by El Paso authorities and to avoid answering any further questions. On October

5, a month after Orozco's funeral, the grand jury convened at the Culberson County Courthouse. Three witnesses appeared—Sheriff Morine, Justice of the Peace Tom Owen, and county attorney A. L. Green. Attorney Green and Sheriff Morine asked the grand jury to indict Morine and thirteen posse members for the intentional murder of Orozco and his four companions.[17] The grand jury immediately returned a bill of indictment for murder. Charged with murder were Morine, two of his deputies, two El Paso County deputies, a federal customs officer, and several ranchers and ranch hands. An *El Paso Morning Times* editorial gave assurances that the indictment and the expected trial would bring out the facts as it had demanded. It read,

> As a matter of fact, Sheriff Morine of Culberson county requested that the indictment be returned. The possemen will now be tried and acquitted, but at the trial the facts will be brought out that the Orozco band had been rustling cattle and that when surprised by the Americans, opened fire and sought to make their escape. . . . The trial will bring out the details of the battle and will undoubtedly put a quietus upon the stories which have been told by Mexicans that Orozco was wilfully [*sic*] murdered by the possemen without having had a chance to defend himself. These stories were circulated with the purpose of creating feeling between Americans and Mexicans, but they carried little weight. Glib-tongued Mexicans are much too common hereabouts now and their efforts to create disorder in El Paso have repeatedly failed.[18]

Authorities in Culberson County knew that the indictment, rather than lead to a fact-baring trial, was instead an instrument intended to conceal the evidence, immunize the defendants, and prevent anyone from asking further questions.[19] There was a union of the prosecution and the defense, a misuse of the legal system whereby the object of the prosecution became a quick verdict of acquittal. At the unusual trial, few facts were elicited because no eyewitnesses were called.[20] As for the evidence produced at trial, a news report noted that the saddles, guns, and other items were admitted.[21] No eyewitnesses could be called to testify at trial, because they had all been indicted. The judge and prosecutor left their normal places, and all sat, figuratively, at the defense table, working as a team to undermine the friendly indictment. It was among the speediest murder trials. During the course of one day, October 8, only three days after the indictment, the defendants were arrested, arraigned, tried, and acquitted before a twelve-member jury, with El Paso–based district judge Dan M. Jackson presiding. Although fourteen were indicted, the prosecution dismissed charges on three defendants, who apparently were not at the killing site, and only eleven proceeded to "trial."

Normally, especially in murder prosecutions, lawyers conduct a detailed examination of a panel of prospective jurors, allowing the parties either to indicate their preferences for specific jurors or more likely to exercise peremptory challenges—that is, to "strike" or mark out the names of jurors they do not want. Each side was allotted a set number of challenges to exercise at their discretion. The jury panel would be large enough to allow the exercise of peremptory challenges, excuse those who could not serve or who were disqualified as a matter of law, and leave at least enough to seat twelve jurors remaining on the list who had not been excused or challenged. Those remaining on the list would be the ones who would serve on the jury. It should have been a panel numbering at least around thirty individuals. The record in this case shows that the prosecution and defense received identical jury lists that contained the same twelve names and only twelve names. There were no names in reserve to be scratched or excused, and neither the prosecution nor the defense exercised a single challenge. The entire panel had twelve names and both prosecution and defense thus agreed to the same twelve jurors. The obviously uncontested process raised the questions of whether there was any examination of the panel, whether some of the proceeding's records were hastily created after the fact to document something that had not taken place, and whether there was a prosecutor present at all. It is likely, given the nature of the sham trial conducted, that the jury panel only had twelve individuals who both sides knew would summarily return a not-guilty verdict. It appeared that no trial participant was on the prosecution side.

The names of the prosecutor and defense lawyer[22] do not appear, but the prosecutor for the Thirty-Fourth District would have been El Paso–based, as was the judge. Although the court noted that evidence was presented, the record failed to note the witnesses who appeared. Judge Jackson read the indictment and instructed the jury, and the jury promptly returned a verdict acquitting all defendants.[23] Once the accused were acquitted, Judge Jackson dismissed the indictment and ordered the return of two horses, tack, money, guns, and supplies to the families of the deceased.[24]

It was a radical act for a grand jury to indict their own law enforcement officers for the murder of five Mexicans, a fugitive and alleged horse thieves—

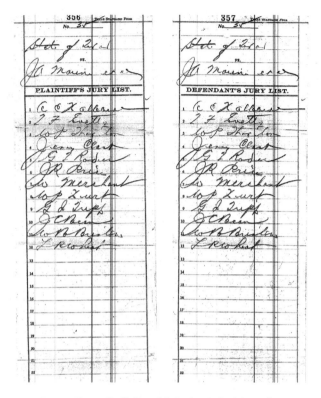

FIG. 13. Plaintiff's *(left)* and defendant's *(right)* jury lists,
State of Texas v. John A. Morine et al., Culberson County, Texas.

charges that lend weight to the contentions and suspicion, especially among Mexicans, that the trial was a charade with the posse insistent on being indicted to prevent El Paso charges or further inquiry. The only reason for the posse members to resort to such an extreme measure as asking to be indicted was that they could not afford to answer any questions or allow any formal inquiry. Morine and his defense counsel, Green, knew what had occurred at the death scene, and they were anxious to keep the facts of the shooting under wraps. The much-choreographed "trial" had one obvious purpose: to prevent anyone else from retrying the members of the posse under the double jeopardy clause.[25] Jeopardy attaches once a jury is sworn in. Thus, the object there was to empanel and swear in a jury, read the indictment and the instructions to the jury, and close the case.

The tainted proceedings indicated the existence of a conspiracy to cover up the facts surrounding the deaths, a scheme in which many participated. Indeed, the furtive and unethical nature of the case invited criticism over the handling of the matter. All those involved in Culberson County—lawyers, judges, officers, and grand jury members—worked overtime to undermine the judicial system in this instance.[26] The result of these aborted proceedings left a tainted, incomplete, and unclear record, allowing for almost any interpretation of the facts.

CHAPTER THIRTY

The Lynching of Pascual Orozco

"Lynching" is a term applied to the wanton killing of an individual by a mob—that is, summary or extrajudicial punishment. It is not limited to hangings. The definition includes extrajudicial homicide by lawmen. In Texas lynching incidents, lawmen were sometimes part of the mob. The killing of suspects by law officers is not a modern phenomenon. It has been around as long as there have been lawmen. It is relatively easy. Suspects are restrained; law officers are armed and can execute a suspect if they so choose. In Mexico during the Porfiriato, these killings were known as la ley fuga. In all but rare cases, the lawmen get away with it. Usually the only other witness was dead. Some law officers grew impatient, did not trust the machinery of criminal justice, and took shortcuts. The strong emotions, anger, and mob mentality that lead to a lynching may be understandable, but it is illegal, and, for a law officer, it is the ultimate mark of unprofessionalism. The object for a professional officer is to remain unemotional and detached and to bring suspects to justice.

The 1915 Plan de San Diego was a fanciful idea of dubious origin, calling for Mexicans in the United States to rise in rebellion, retake the Southwest, form a new state, and seek annexation by Mexico. It called for the killing of all adult Anglo males. The *plan*, given the name of a small town in South Texas, never got anywhere, but it created fear among many Anglos, especially in South Texas border areas, and certainly provoked local and Texas law enforcement to overreact against innocent Mexicans. The Mexican Revolution frequently spilled into the United States in the form of raids for food, guns, cattle, and horses. As with most borders, traffic also went in the other direction. There was always a thriving market on the United States side for stolen Mexican cattle and horses, an activity in which many border ranchers participated. Mexicans had long complained that cattle taken in Apache raids and by rustlers found a ready market on the United States side of the border. Buying stolen cattle was a profitable practice for border ranchers. Cattle rustling, by Americans or Mexicans, remained a problem in 1915, but the United States' response to Mexican cattle rustling and horse theft was different. Furthermore, as part of the Plan de San Diego, Mexicans raided several South Texas communities and ranches, especially after July 1915. Some blamed pro-Huerta groups for the raids; others said it was a Carranza ploy to obtain U.S. recognition.[1] Although most of the raids were ineffectual, the fear and hatred they produced radiated far from the border. All along the border, the presence of unknown, armed Mexicans alarmed many.

It is now established that several Texas Rangers of that time lynched innocent people, lied about it, and acted illegally as a group; and many of their victims were Mexicans. Texas law officers executed or lynched an undetermined number of innocent Mexicans, perhaps three hundred, as suspected bandits.[2] Although lynching was a well-known practice in the United States, especially in the South, in the lynching of Mexicans in Texas, "local authorities and deputized citizens played particularly conspicuous roles in mob violence against Mexicans,"[3] and Texas Rangers most prominently. The Culberson County posse included two former Rangers, Herff Carnes and Dave Allison.[4] Historian Walter Prescott Webb wrote,

> The situation can be summed up by saying that after the troubles developed the Americans instituted a reign of terror against the Mexicans and that many innocent Mexicans were made to suffer. The Americans found sufficient cause in the raids, murders, and thefts for vigorous action, but when they learned that the Germans were supplying the Mexicans with arms and ammunition, the I.W.W. with incendiary literature, that Japanese were accompanying some of the bands and manufacturing crude bombs for them, and that plots were being made by the Mexicans, with the aid of Germans and Japanese, to take Texas and other Southwestern States, their anger was lashed into fury. Of bandits they asked no quarter and gave none. In the orgy of bloodshed that followed, the Texas Rangers played a prominent part, and one of which many members of the force have been heartily ashamed.[5]

Fear stirred up by the Plan de San Diego, along with the recent killing of some lawmen, could explain the strong reaction against suspected Mexican raiders and bandits by the posse against the Orozco group. Although the possemen had no information about the group, they apparently assumed that they were Mexican raiders who were there to steal. They did not know that they were dealing with a group of Mexicans who were trying to return to Mexico to fight in a revolution. The *New York Times* incorrectly tied Orozco to the farfetched Plan de San Diego, reporting, "He was one of the leaders of the raiders, the active head of a preposterous and impossible scheme to regain Texas for Mexico."[6] There was no evidence that the Orozco group was attempting to incite local Mexicans, and allegations that it was so are implausible.

Violent incidents and banditry had indeed occurred along the border, and some residents there were determined to put a stop to it. It was probable that before Orozco ever set foot in the Sierra Blanca area, law enforcement and the cattle association there were primed to deal violently and summarily with any suspected banditry, using an ask-no-questions, take-no-prisoners approach, a practice that was evident two years later at the Porvenir massacre.[7] One Sierra Blanca resident expressed the sentiment that bandits should be dealt with summarily and implied that the problem left residents with no option but execution: "Cattle stealing and the running off of horses by Mexican thieves and adventurers must stop. The rangers haven't time to take prisoners and the cowboys have no place to put prisoners even should they take them. But the thieving must stop."[8]

It did not take much to raise suspicions and jump to a conclusion when folks at the R. C. "Dick" Love Ranch stumbled on five well-armed Mexicans, who immediately fled from the scene and set off the chase. A number of individuals have attempted to sort out the circumstances of Orozco's last days and death, with each contributing a theory of the case.[9] The principal accounts were the "official" report of the inquest witnesses, the report of Inspector Carnes to his superior,[10] the accounts of E. A. "Dogie" Wright and Ed Love, and later books about the incident by writers Bob Alexander and Robert Bolling. Alexander, Dave Allison's biographer, largely accepts the official account as factual. He also mentions other possible motives of the posse, including a determination to deal with Mexican incursions and violent assaults on law enforcement officers, such as the killing of two area law officers in May and June of that year.[11]

The record lacks documentary material normally found in death cases, including death certificates, autopsies, or postmortem descriptions. Despite a coroner's inquest, no death certificate was issued or filed. Rather, the Culberson County clerk's record has mere notations of the deaths, but no mention of their cause.[12] In those days, undertakers often aided coroners in determining the cause of death and occasionally conducted autopsies. El Paso undertaker J. J. Kaster promised customs collector Zachary Cobb a postmortem report, but none is found in the record.[13]

A detailed work by writer Robert Bolling explains much of what the official record fails to note, but other than referring to interviews he conducted, his work omits naming specific sources. Nevertheless, it is evident that Bolling, "Historian of Sierra Blanca," interviewed several individuals for his account, as did Bob Alexander and E.A. Dogie Wright for theirs. Dogie Wright's unpublished account is valuable because it is based on his interviews of several posse members over the years.[14] Ed Love, the son of George Love and Dogie Wright's brother-in-law, gave an account that was mainly in agreement with Wright's.

At this point, any rendering of the events is incomplete. The official inquest report is especially suspect, given the part it played in the cover-up in suppressing rather than finding evidence. In reviewing the available evidence, however, a reasonable partial account emerges. First, the deceased Mexicans included Orozco, a rebel general working to reenter Mexico to overthrow the Carranza régime. There was another general, José F. Delgado, who had served as President Huerta's private secretary and then as Huerta's representative on Orozco's staff. He was a professional military man with a long career in which he held important posts. There was Crisóforo Caballero,[15] a major in Orozco's forces, an Orozco confidant and former head of the customs guard in Ciudad Juárez. Andrés Sandoval was also an Orozquista soldier. Several accounts described Miguel Terrazas as a soldier assigned to General Eduardo Salinas. Salinas was on the Mexican side waiting for Orozco's group. Alexander described Terrazas as a guide for the Big Bend area.

It was improbable that the mission of the group was horse theft and banditry. When authorities arrested them at the Newman station, Orozco and Huerta were en route to meet with the Salinas forces waiting for them in the Bosque Bonito area on the Mexican side of the Rio Grande, south of Van Horn and about ten miles south of the killing location.[16] These men were resuming the original June mission. They had one object on their minds—to fight Carranza in Mexico and Villa in Chihuahua. They had spent months planning an attack on Ciudad Juárez.[17]

So how was it that these men with that mission came to be on Dick Love's ranch, riding three stolen horses?[18] First, it is not clear that the Mexicans stole any horses, although it is indeed likely that three of their horses were stolen. Ed Love, son of George Love and owner of a ranch just south of Etholen, believed that Orozco and his companions had contacted a "crooked rancher" who lived near the rail line who had sold three of his own horses and two horses stolen from Bob Love to Orozco and his group. Moreover, Ed Love said that all five Mexicans arrived by rail and would have had to obtain horses somehow. This part of Ed Love's account is likely wrong because the Mexicans owned two of the horses, a fact verified by the judge's order returning those two horses to the families. Additionally, none of the possemen claimed that those two horses were stolen. It is likely that the Mexicans had seven horses altogether and abandoned the two spare horses as the chase began. So, three or four of the five Mexicans arrived by train. Once in the area, they purchased three horses from the "crooked rancher." Regardless of whether three of the horses were stolen, the posse was unaware that any had been stolen until after they had killed the Mexicans, and the Mexicans were probably unaware that three of the horses were stolen.

Another scenario, taken mostly from the Bolling account,[19] suggested that the group's guide, Miguel Terrazas, was sent by General Eduardo Salinas from Bosque Bonito on the Mexican side to meet the other four at the Etholen rail stop west of Sierra Blanca, some forty miles from Bosque Bonito. The group of four would have boarded the train somewhere east of El Paso, perhaps at Ysleta or Fabens.[20] They carried their own saddles and tack as well as weapons and ammunition. Bolling wrote that Terrazas, who was sent to meet the group, had at least two horses and one saddle. He was to bring supplies for the trip of perhaps two days, as well as either three more horses or a wagon. Somehow, perhaps in crossing the August-swollen Rio Grande, Terrazas lost his food supply and either three horses or a wagon. Either scenario is credible, with the horse loss being more likely. At any rate, in Bolling's account, having only two horses, Terrazas continued to the prearranged meeting point, Etholen, a railroad water station four miles west of Sierra Blanca. There were several Love family ranches in the area; the one owned by Bob Love was just north of the river and on the route to Etholen. If the Mexicans stole the horses, then Terrazas likely stole a horse belonging to the Bob Love Ranch and continued. He would then have had three horses and would still have been short two horses and had no food. Given that situation, Terrazas, alone or in the company of the group after its arrival, addressed the problem by stealing two more horses from Joe Marshall's corral at the Etholen rail water stop, where four of the Mexicans likely got off the train.

Or, it could have been as Ed Love said. They could have bought the horses from the crooked rancher, who apparently was known to sell stolen livestock.

The evidence is overwhelming that Orozco and his group either bought or stole at least three horses. If they did steal horses, they did so out of necessity and not because they went to the area with a plan to steal. These were high-ranking officers headed to a rendezvous and a revolution, and it was unlikely that they would be taking the time to steal horses with an army waiting for them.

Orozco's group arrived at Etholen on August 29 when there was a three-quarter moon, making night travel easier. When Joe Thomson found them at midday on the twenty-ninth at the new well on the Dick Love Ranch, they had traveled some twenty-five miles from Etholen. The narrative from the time of their discovery to the "fusillade" has several renditions and discrepancies, but those details are not essential to understand the controversy over what occurred at the final encounter and over whether a lynching took place. From Deputy Schrock's statement, it is known that although Orozco's group had indicia of mal hombres and desperados—and the men of the posse thought that they did—when the chase began, the pursuers knew of no of criminality. You could not legally kill those who had done nothing wrong, especially when they were fleeing to get off your property and posed no threat. Given the circumstances, Orozco's group might have had the justification to shoot to keep its pursuers and attackers at bay. Orozco's men had no way of knowing that it was a posse on the chase. If there was shooting on the chase, it is doubtful that the Mexicans were the only ones firing their weapons before the final encounter, and there is no way to determine which side shot first. It is also doubtful that there was any shooting during the chase, given that the posse only approached the riders at the start of the chase and were more than 1,500 feet distant.

The major conflict among the various interpretations is about the final encounter on August 30 in the box canyon, where all five Mexicans perished. The various accounts regarding the final shooting scene are those of the possemen, Dogie Wright, Ed Love, and Bolling.

The Posse Report

This account appears in the report that customs inspector Herff Carnes made to his superior as well as in Sheriff Morine's inquest statement and his statements to the press. In it, the posse was chasing armed bandits who had assaulted ranch hands at the Dick Love Ranch. The posse chased and trapped the men and killed them in their cross fire. Carnes reported that the Mexicans had ignored calls to surrender and instead returned fire. To the posse, it was a fair fight. The subsequent finding of three stolen horses, fresh jerked meat from a butchered calf, and a pilfered horseshoe hammer confirmed the men's suspicions.

The Dogie Wright History

Wright was a contemporary and knew most of the posse well. Following in the footsteps of his father, he had been a Texas Ranger. Later he was a career border patrol inspector and a three-term Hudspeth County sheriff, among other posts with law enforcement agencies.[21] He wrote, "I knew all of these [posse] men personally and talked over this chase with them a good many times." He had married Mabel Love, the daughter of rancher George Love, who was one of the indicted possemen. Wright was a good friend and colleague of Inspector Carnes and was himself an ex-Ranger. Wright added, "We naturally talked over many things and among them the Orosco [sic] chase."[22] From the information that he had gathered, Wright said that when the posse arrived near where the Mexicans were camped, his father-in-law, George Love, told the posse precisely where the Mexicans were located. On hearing this, Allison, without waiting for anyone, immediately mounted his horse and galloped off alone toward the Mexicans. George Love, whose mount was not as fresh, attempted to follow. As Allison and Love approached the ridge ahead of the rest of the posse, Love's horse fell into a hole. Allison did not stop and continued alone and was the first to reach a position to fire at the Mexicans. Wright wrote that Allison alone killed four of the Mexicans before any of the other possemen had arrived or got in a position to shoot. Wright does not mention any calls to halt or to surrender; rather, Allison started shooting the moment that he laid eyes on the Mexicans and immediately shot four of them.[23] However, Wright added this note, in the words he typed himself:

> There was one man out of the Orosco bunch that escaped but was picked up by the posse coming up they brought him into where Dave Allison was and Dave began to question him when his gun went off and killed the mexican. Dave claimed this was an accident. . . . Ever one of these mexicans was shot in the head or neck apparently ever time one stuck his head up to fire Dave a dead shot let him have it. This posse never knew who they were after until after this fight and the leader identified as General Pasqual Orosco.[24]

Dogie Wright's description, based on his interviews with the possemen, especially with George Love, differs dramatically from the official and other pro-posse renderings. Instead of the Mexicans being surrounded and dying in the posse's cross fire, Allison was the lone triggerman. There was no cross fire, no fusillade. Allison shot four of the Mexicans before any of the other possemen fired a shot. In Wright's words, "When the posse heard the shooting [Allison's] they fell off [their] horses and went to fireing but they were not in a position to do any killing."[25] Wright said Allison was "hired by numerous ranches as a fighting man." Under Wright's account, it is difficult to imagine circumstances that would exonerate Allison. The posse had taken a captured Mexican to Allison, surely unarmed and restrained. How could it be that this Mexican, the same as the others, died of a gunshot to the head? Was Allison waving his pistol around the man's head as he conducted the interrogation? Although Allison was the undisputed leader of the combined posse, and by Wright's description the sole triggerman, he never testified, never gave a statement, was never placed under oath in the case, and might never have been questioned in the inquest. Allison was not a man burning for utterance—not in court, that is.

Wright was a longtime friend of the possemen, the son-in-law of one of them, a fellow officer and a natural supporter, lending weight to the charge that at least one Mexican was killed while in custody and that Allison was the triggerman. One or more of the posse members, perhaps Allison himself, told Wright how Allison shot one Mexican who was in custody. If members of the posse admitted killing one captured Mexican, we can see why others concluded that all of them were executed by a gunshot to the back of the head. That would be the Bolling account.

The Bolling Book

Bolling's unsourced report and the posse accounts agree that the posse surrounded the Mexicans in the box canyon but differ as to what happened after that. Bolling wrote that the large posse held the high, protected position and had a vast firepower advantage, putting the Mexicans in a hopeless, defenseless position. Bolling wrote,

> Further resistance was futile and they threw up their hands and surrendered. The battle only lasted a few minutes and after the firing stopped, the posse members worked their way to the bot-

tom of the canyon and confronted the Mexicans. Handcuffs were placed on the five and the camp was then inspected for stolen property. Two of the horses taken from Joe Marshall at Etholen were identified and a third horse carried Bob Love's brand.

Because the Mexicans had been caught with stolen horses, La Ley Fuga demanded that they should die. There was no disagreement among the posse as to what must be done, and several of their number stepped forward to administer the golpe de gracia or death blow. They drew their revolvers and went along the line of Mexicans, shooting them at close range, and watching their bodies fall.[26]

Wherever Bolling got his information, the wounds that his scenario would have produced are consistent with accounts of one or more individuals who saw the bodies on display, including young Alice B. Cummings and rancher Vivian McAdoo.[27] McAdoo told his son-in-law that he saw the bodies when they were on display and could see that the men had been "killed by foul means." It made him nervous to be around the bodies, and he quickly left the area in fear that Mexicans would retaliate. Allison's biographer wrote that accepting other accounts, such as Bolling's, would have involved a massive conspiracy among the lawmen and ranchers to withhold the truth, something that he claimed was inconceivable.[28]

The Ed Love Oral History

Citing his father, rancher George Love, as his source, Ed Love said that his father was with the lead group just before the killings, but that his horse fell on the trail, and he followed on foot at the end. He said that the "other bunch" was already shooting at the Mexicans when they found them at three or four that afternoon. He reported that the Mexicans were asleep where they had eaten lunch and had no lookout when the posse found them. "When they got there, they were running up the mountain toward them. And this fellow Allison shot them and that was the last of them, killed all five of them." George Love also said that Allison killed all five of them. There was no mention of the Mexicans firing at anyone or of warnings being given.[29] Wright placed George Love the closest to Allison when the shooting started and said that Allison was the only shooter. The evidence indicates that Allison was the sole killer, but other, more direct, evidence removes any doubt about Allison's role.

About the time of the Culberson County posse trial, young Second Lieutenant George S. Patton, the same man who would become a World War
II four-star general and hero, was stationed at Fort Bliss in El Paso. He was
detailed with a few others to man the army outposts at Sierra Blanca, perhaps
in response to calls by Sierra Blanca residents for more security after the
Orozco killing. About a week after the jury had acquitted him of murdering
Orozco, Allison met Patton. Enamored of guns and gunfighters, Patton was
impressed by the fifty-four-year-old Allison, the undisputed leader of the
posse and "a gunslinger with a colorful past." Although Allison was reticent
during the legal proceedings surrounding the Orozco killings, he lost no time
at all in boasting to Patton that, indeed, he alone had killed all five Mexicans,
confirming that part of Dogie Wright's history. It was unlikely that Allison
would have bragged to the young Patton that he was the sole gunman if it
were not true. Given that the possemen all lived in the area and the recent
shooting would have been a frequent topic of conversation, Allison's boast
would likely have been contradicted if untrue. It appeared to be the case that,
as Allison alleged, he rightfully owned the bragging rights to being the lone
shooter. In an October 20, 1915, letter to his wife, Patton wrote, "I met a Mr.
Dave Allison yesterday. He was a very quiet looking old man with a sweet
face and white hair. He is the most noted gun man here in Texas and just at
present is Marshall. He alone killed all the Orosco [sic] outfit five of them about
a month ago and he kills several Mexicans each month. He shot Orosco and
his four men each in the head at sixty yards."[30]

According to one writer, some of Allison's fatal shots might have been closer
to six inches rather than sixty yards, as "Orozco's close friends maintained that
there were powder burns on the dead bodies shot at close range and that the
Orozco party was actually shot while they slept."[31] Normally, bragging that he
killed several Mexicans a month would be considered an exaggeration, but in
Allison's case, maybe not. He was a braggart, but he was indeed a notoriously
mean hired gun who was constantly on the hunt for Mexican bandits and
rustlers. He had certainly killed several Mexicans on August 30 and did not
hesitate to claim credit, adding, as it did, to his reputation as a gunslinger, an
image Allison clearly loved and burnished.

Who was William Davis Allison? He was, to say the least, the type of
lawman popular frontier Western stories love, a man who neither gave nor
asked for quarter. He was a gunslinger with a badge. He also did not cut his
corners square when it came to the specific division of duties parceled out

by the criminal justice system. Under the judicial system, the job of officers was to arrest suspects, bring them to court, and have the courts determine guilt and then mete out punishment, if any. Allison occasionally bypassed that process. A former multi-term Midland County sheriff, Allison left that job for embezzling ten thousand dollars. He had a serious gambling problem and was arrested and convicted in Midland for gambling, for which he gave up his law enforcement commission. He was apparently fired as an Arizona Ranger due to his continued gambling.[32] Later, Allison resigned as the chief of police in Roswell, New Mexico, after he was indicted for attempting to bribe the district attorney. He was acquitted of the charge but left Roswell. He then floated around, going from job to job, landing in Sierra Blanca at least by 1914[33] to work as a "deputy constable" but in fact was being paid by the area cattlemen's association to stop cattle rustling. He was what was called a "subscription deputy," a quasi-lawman.[34] Allison had a troublesome law career, but he also had other problems. Two historians note that Allison "despised" Mexicans.[35]

The determination that Allison was the lone triggerman is unassailable. Moreover, at least four of the Mexicans were shot while they were asleep or getting up, and each was at some point shot in the head. The information posse members gave to Wright, coupled with Ed Love's account, makes their telling of the final event credible. Allison's boast to Patton plus the Wright and Ed Love accounts are sufficient to set aside as fiction the "cross fire–fusillade" event in the official version. The available information regarding the location of the wounds comes from Allison's comment to Patton, Wright's account, McAdoo's comments, and Alice Cummings, as well as from upset Mexicans who said that each of the Mexicans had been shot in the head, in the back, or in the back of the head.

It is possible to reconcile some elements of the Wright account with the Bolling account. It was likely that Allison shot several of the Mexicans from a distance while they were asleep, but they might not have died from the wounds. Once Allison approached the Mexicans, he might well have shot them again at close or near-contact range, just as Wright said he shot at least one of the group. That would explain Bolling's coup de grace comment.

In the George Love account as told by his son Ed, it is clear that the posse had no idea why they were chasing Orozco other than because they naturally chased armed Mexican strangers. If George and Ed Love thought the Mexicans had purchased their horses from the crooked rancher, then what was the chase all about? The only motive remaining for the chase was that the possemen routinely engaged in such "fighting trips," as Love called them. Ed Love said that the posse that gathered at Dick Love's ranch after the chase numbered around forty. The group consisted of the "usual bunch that usually went on them Mexican fighting trips," he recounted.

While some Mexicans thought that Orozco and his companions were executed along the lines of the Bolling depiction, others thought that the Mexicans were caught by surprise and without their weapons while sleeping or resting in that canyon, thinking that they had eluded their pursuers. Newspaper accounts stated that the Mexicans, "secure from pursuit," had dismounted, hobbled their horses, and made camp a distance away from the horses.[36] They most likely were sleeping. The three-quarter moon had helped their nighttime crossing over the Eagle Mountains, a rocky and dangerous ride as described in Wright's piece. They rode many miles from where the chase began, including their harrowing all-night crossing of the rocky terrain of the Eagles, slightly north of 7,500-foot Eagle Peak. From the Love Ranch, the men would have climbed over two thousand feet in elevation and then descended two thousand feet into the Green River valley. They needed to rest, and their horses were surely spent. The killings took place near Stephan's (or Stephen's) Tank near a ranch owned by Grover Stephens. A report had Stephens claiming to have watched the shooting from a distance and noting that the Mexicans were shot "in their sleep."[37] Given initial reports of the killings, Mexicans were upset that Orozco and his companions were caught essentially unarmed or asleep, given no warnings, and wantonly killed, a scenario consistent with the Wright, Ed Love, and Stephens accounts.

The lack of a postmortem is also troubling. Given talk in 1912 of a possible execution-style ending for Orozco and his companions,[38] El Paso officials, such as customs collector Zachary Cobb, were vitally interested in knowing the manner of these deaths. It was unlikely that Cobb would have forgotten his request for, and undertaker Kaster's promise to produce, a postmortem report describing Orozco's wounds.[39]

Modern accounts of the killings omit mention of the part of Wright's account reporting Allison shooting a Mexican in custody. Rather than portray Allison as having shot four men in the back while they were sleeping and one while he was restrained and in custody, the posse members made up a different narrative. Their story became that of heroic possemen running down the canyon, shouting for the five dangerous outlaw Mexicans to surrender, and then killing them all after the Mexicans, rather than surrendering, fired on the posse.[40] An example of the posse's version of events survives in this account:

> Tuesday afternoon late the posse surrounded the Mexicans in the Green River canyon, in the Eagle mountains. The Mexicans resisted and a battle ensued for hours. The Americans finally succeeded in silencing the guns of the Mexicans and upon investigation found all five dead, many of them shot full of holes. The Mexicans had replied to the fire as long as their ammunition held out and then were killed like rats in a trap for there was no escape.[41]

The posse members were surprised to learn later that they had killed such prominent Mexicans. To Bolling, the possemen thought that they were dealing with ordinary Mexican horse thieves for whom death was a matter of course. It was only when they later discovered the men's identities that the possemen grew concerned. That could well be why the coroner identified no triggerman, studiously refrained from mentioning Allison, and failed to describe the wounds. Five men shot in the head by a lone triggerman with a gunslinger reputation would certainly have raised questions the coroner wanted to avoid.[42] The inquest, indictment, and trial, unfortunately, were all exercises to shield the posse, explaining the silence on the details of the deaths. Allison would not testify or give a statement despite being the posse's leader. The men would do everything to prevent an El Paso hearing or any further inquiry.[43]

These men were not interested in stepping on their original narrative. There was no reason for Deputy Schrock not to have told the possemen that there had been no raid of the Dick Love Ranch. Given the practice of hunting down armed Mexicans as presumed bandits and thieves, it probably would have made no difference whether these men were innocent. The possemen clearly erred in subverting the legal process to protect a gunslinger, whom they unfortunately held in high regard. This posse looked for its leadership to the wrong man, and that man set them on an erroneous course.

As Dogie Wright concluded, "I believe that the Mexican people could prove to your satisfaction that Gen. Orozco was not a bandit in the true sense of the word but a man fighting for a principle and a cause to relieve the suffering of the poor in Mexico. On the other hand this posse could say well if they were not bandits they sure acted like one."[44]

The record makes it clear that Allison shot all five Mexicans perhaps in their sleep or while in his custody. Allison was not under assault and did not give the Mexicans a warning or an opportunity to surrender. He had no idea why he killed them. It was what Allison did, without knowing if men were innocent or not—chase and kill. As far as he was concerned, they might have been guilty or they might not have. Just like Allison's boast, he killed several Mexicans every month, undoubtedly adding to the toll of innocent Mexicans lynched by Texas law officers in the 1915 era. It seems clear that whether they were captured, had surrendered, or were just lying there wounded, there would be no prisoners. As far as Allison was concerned, on that day, no Mexican was leaving that box canyon alive.

Whatever the facts, the cover-up worked. That was the end of Orozco, and nothing more came of the incident.

Conclusion

The Legacy of Pascual Orozco

After Mexicans canonized the assassinated Francisco Madero and Abraham González as martyrs of the revolution, Victoriano Huerta, unable to remove the stain of Madero's murder, became the most odious figure of the times, with Orozco only a rung below him. Over time, Orozco's history evolved into a controversial, mixed record that achieved some rehabilitation.[1] In the 1930s, friends and family repatriated his remains to Chihuahua, and since 1936 his native village of Labor de San Isidro has borne his name. He is honored there with an equestrian statue and a museum located in the former rail station. In 2012, Orozco was named a meritorious citizen of Chihuahua,[2] and the village was designated a Heroic Pueblo.[3] In Mexico, several towns, boulevards, and streets carry his name. Corridos alternately call him a hero and a traitor.

At the start of the revolution, rebel leaders did not appoint Orozco to a national military post. They named him head of Chihuahua's regional group of rebel irregulars. How did an unknown mule skinner with no prior record of public or military service become the most important military leader of the Madero Revolution? Orozco became that national commander and hero because what began as a small group of men from Labor de San Isidro became the nucleus of a force that grew to take Ciudad Juárez six months later. That Serrano-dominated force was the one, out of an entire nation, that effectively took the fight to Díaz, and it did so despite Madero's attempts to discourage the attack. It was the group's courage, persistence, and audacity—and insubordination—that made Orozco the nation's hero and Madero the president. The victory would not likely have happened without Orozco—nor, perhaps, without his disobedience.

In carefully examining Orozco's history, his most dominant traits were his undoubted personal valor and leadership qualities. Later, after the Battle of Ciudad Juárez, Orozco evolved into a paradox for having promoted progressive political positions while simultaneously siding with notorious reactionaries and counterrevolutionaries. Historians struggle to explain why Orozco fought Díaz, turned against Madero, and finally allied with the reactionaries Huerta and Creel.

Before 1910, Orozco seemed to have harbored no deep animosity toward Díaz. Serranos were nostalgic for their former independence and governance, products of their colonial history and their isolation. They resented Díaz's centralization and oppressive political jefes. The clearest explanation for Orozco's rebel enlistment was his deep-seated hatred of Joaquín Chávez, the San Isidro political jefe and wealthy land and business owner.[4] In Orozco's thinking, he was attacking those who kept Chávez in power, which included Enrique Creel, who in turn derived his power from Díaz. Therefore, if Orozco wanted Chávez out, the movement already afoot to depose Díaz and Creel was the obvious vehicle. With Chávez gone—he died less than two months after the start of the revolution—Orozco may have been rudderless, having lost his only motivation. Once committed to overturning Díaz, however, he completed the work. Explaining his turning against Madero is more complex.

The record is clear that Orozco attempted to overthrow Madero on May 13, 1911, a mere three days after the victory of Ciudad Juárez. Months later, Orozco provided explanations for revolting against Madero: Madero's betraying the revolution by jilting vice presidential nominee, Vázquez Gómez; violating the no reelection rule with the Abraham González election; not pursuing land reform; and failing to pay and support his troops. Of those factors, only the latter existed on May 13. It seems unlikely that, serious as it was, failure to pay the troops was the only reason for his rebellion. The more probable motive was that Madero bypassed Orozco and made Carranza war minister, and it is likely that others encouraged his attempted coup of May 13. Certainly, lack of pay and protecting Navarro added to Orozco's anger.

Regarding his March 1912 rebellion, Orozco said that the immediate cause was to protect Chihuahua City from Villa and his troops, a force Governor González had ordered into the city. It is conceivable that Orozco was responding to the cries of Chihuahua residents who were fearful of Villa, but it was more likely that Orozco was answering calls from Chihuahua conservatives who were outraged by González's reform agenda, which included raising taxes on the wealthy and implementing land reform. Orozco was ousting González, the man with policies closest to those he advocated. Orozco was therefore motivated more by his desire to settle scores and personal slights than by policy. He was resentful of the treatment he had received from the González camp in launching a campaign for governor against a then nonexistent González bid. It is another of Orozco's claims that in removing González he was helping ordinary residents, when, in fact, he was serving the elites' interests or satisfying a personal animus.

We can also add other reasons to the mix to explain Orozco's turning against Madero, such as Madero's disrespect of Orozco during his first attempt to attack Ciudad Juárez; his attempt to place others in command over Orozco; and his decision to free the hated General Navarro, the butcher of Cerro Prieto—who had brutally executed a number of Orozco's close family members and friends, including two of his wife's brothers.[5] In freeing Navarro, Madero had violated his own Plan de San Luis, which called for the immediate execution of any Díaz officer who killed captured soldiers. Orozco's anger over Madero freeing Navarro should not be underestimated. Orozco was a man of strong loyalty toward his friends and deep hostility for his opponents. Thus, freeing Navarro could explain Orozco turning on Madero, but that would explain only his March 1912 rebellion and not the May 13 attempted coup. If Orozco ever had any respect for Madero, he had lost it and grew to detest him. His lack of respect for Madero became evident when, during the Battle of Ciudad Juárez, Orozco disobeyed Madero by launching the attack against Madero's orders and then after the battle, when he tried to arrest and perhaps came close to assassinating Madero. Several significant public acts of insubordination marked Orozco's relationship with Madero, and they began before the two had met.

As to the accusation that the elite bought Orozco, it is unlikely that money motivated him personally, but there is no doubt that the oligarchy funded his rebellion. We might accept his assurance that he could not be bought,[6] but, as a leader, he was vitally interested in financing his revolution and knew that oligarchy money was essential. By San Isidro standards, Orozco was wealthy before the revolution, and with Joaquín Chávez out of the picture soon after the revolution began, his financial future looked bright.[7] He lost much of his wealth, however, on financing the revolution and from inattention to his businesses. Nevertheless, whatever motives he had for his actions, a desire for wealth was likely low on his list.[8] A more probable explanation is that Orozco's ego got the best of him as he succumbed to the allure of power and fame.

Orozco quickly grew to believe that he was a great national leader and deserved national recognition, the governorship, an important cabinet post perhaps, or maybe even the presidency.[9] He enjoyed an undoubted national reputation for leadership, as evidenced by the fact that virtually every national anti-Madero uprising named Orozco its leader despite his not being a member of those groups. In public events, cheers for Orozco drowned out those for Abraham González and even those for Madero. Many people recognized Orozco as a national leader—except the one whose opinion mattered most, Madero. Turned down for war minister, governor, and a national military command, Orozco repeatedly felt cheated and disrespected by Madero while reactionaries flattered him.

Orozco saw Madero as weak and indecisive, surrounded by and giving recognition and power to "dandies" rather than to those who had fought. Therefore, having built up a hatred and disdain for Madero like those he had earlier borne for Chávez, Orozco had a clear direction. He would do anything to topple Madero, even if it meant allying with former enemies, such as Creel, and later the assassin Huerta. There is no question that Creel and Orozco were allies. They both wanted González and Madero out and Huerta in. They supported Huerta twice, both times after Huerta had Madero and González executed. In the pacts Orozco made with reactionaries, they uniformly ignored his written progressive manifestos, and still Orozco supported counterrevolutionaries, who, in contrast, promoted their own conservative programs and stopped any other reform plan, such as González's.

One can understand why Orozco would turn against Madero,[10] but what is puzzling is why he allied with the oligarchy and elites. The paradox of Orozco was that the oligarchy promoted and financed his revolt, but the leftist Liberal Party inspired his manifestos. The elites, who would never have stood for the implementation of a reform agenda, supported Orozco even when he espoused reform, because they knew that a broader agenda would generate support with Orozco in the lead. They also realized that in that climate, openly promoting their own policies would lead to defeat. In a risky gamble, the elites bet that Orozco would not implement reforms and would instead be clay in their hands. Events proved them correct.[11] Historian Alan Knight wondered, however, whether the elite took advantage of Orozco or whether it was the reverse. Regardless of their intent, both sides ultimately lost. Orozco never addressed his promised reforms, and the oligarchy financed an unsuccessful rebellion, although in balance the oligarchy had gained something in having had Orozco kill the González reforms and tax hikes and help Huerta into power.[12]

A review of record also shows that Orozco was plotting against Madero with leftist Vazquista and Liberal Party groups as well as with the oligarchy before he resigned as head of Madero's Chihuahua forces. Three days after Orozco left Madero's service, U.S. consul Marion Letcher wrote, "All the intrigues of the past several months have centered around Orozco, *who all the time* was plotting against the Madero government. His backing in these intrigues now stands revealed in the persons of the 'Cientifico' party who have within the last day or two openly declared themselves for Orozco and against Madero. They are now raising money to further finance the revolution, and, as well, have met in open meetings and offered their services to Orozco."[13]

A few Orozco partisans dispute whether the oligarchy supported Orozco and gave him financial and other support. The conflict is not whether the Terrazas-Creel clan furnished Orozco support, but rather whether General Luis Terrazas or Enrique Creel individually gave Orozco money.[14] It is a minor point, since the family acted in unison, and others in the family provided Orozco substantial funding. By 1912, Luis Terrazas was retired from politics and had turned management of the haciendas over to his sons. He also spent most of 1912 in California recovering from a stroke. The Terrazas-Creel family, however, was still active in Chihuahua and supported Orozco. Of that, there is no doubt. Historians writing on the matter understand that financial support of revolutions is often concealed, especially when the funding is from a group that has much to lose and is against an incumbent administration. Well-regarded historians leave no doubt that Orozco received such support. Friedrich Katz wrote, "There is widespread agreement among both contemporary observers in Chihuahua and historians that Orozco was linked to the Chihuahua oligarchy. The evidence is clear on the financial, diplomatic, social and political support that he received from both the Terrazas-Creel group and other members of the oligarchy."[15] Michael Meyer maintained, "That former supporters of the dictator [Díaz] and of the Terrazas clique lent assistance to Orozco is undeniable; if it had not been for the financial support of the aristocratic elite, the movement would have been no more dangerous for Madero than the *reyista* and *vasquista* uprisings."[16] Mark Wasserman agreed, noting, "There seems to be little doubt that the 'Terrazas organized, directed, and financed the Orozco rebellion,' which lasted from March to September 1912. One grandchild, Luis Terrazas Bobadilla (son of Luis Jr.), served as captain of artillery for the orozquistas and was wounded. Another grandson, Francisco Terrazas (Juan Terrazas's son), held the post of *juez de instrucción militar* under Orozco."[17] Several members of the family contributed substantial financing, and others served in appointed capacities, such as Manuel Luján, who served as Orozco's Washington representative.

General Terrazas's defenders say that there is little evidence that he provided money to Orozco. The general's defense was that, although he gave, he was forced to do so. Although General Luis Terrazas and Enrique Creel denied voluntarily giving Orozco financial support, there is ample, undeniable proof that Orozco received financial support from Chihuahua's oligarchy, including from the Terrazas-Creel clan. The following members of the clan and its allies gave Orozco money or purchased bonds: Juan and Luis Terrazas, the general's sons; Luis Terrazas Bobadilla, the general's grandson; Juan A. Creel, Enrique's brother; Ángel Calderón Urrutia, Banco Minero's Ciudad Juárez manager; Federico Sisniega, the general's son-in-law; Lic. Rafael Horcasitas, the general's son-in-law; and others.[18] The practical Enrique Creel was in Mexico City doing business with the Científicos in Madero's cabinet.[19] With respect to supporting Huerta and Orozco in their attempted uprising in 1915, Creel no longer attempted to hide his support for Huerta. He was, after all, the one who Michael Meyer credited with returning the old dictator to Mexico. Moreover, Creel no longer needed to hide his support, as he was not in business with Carranza as he had been with the Madero family.

Soon after Orozco forced Abraham González to leave Chihuahua City in March 1912, he and the legislature's oligarchy-dominated recess committee engineered a legislative coup d'état, deposing Abraham González and installing a new governor, Felipe R. Gutiérrez, who remained in office until Orozco lost Chihuahua months later.[20] The crowds demonstrating in Chihuahua City, orchestrated by elites, threatened González, as did the seizure of the state's armed forces by Orozco. Claiming that González had thus abandoned his office for more than four days, the legislature alleged that it was merely fulfilling its duty to name a sitting governor. The conduct of that legislature was radical indeed, including its attempt to withdraw from the Republic as well as its pushing extreme measures to stop González's reform policies.

Having invited Orozco to take over the state's military and then having cut off federal funds by severing relations with the national government, members of the oligarchy could hardly deny Orozco funding for their common forces. And they did not deny him. Through the oligarchy-controlled state administration and legislature, Orozco received 208,000 pesos in proceeds of interim state financing from banks and wealthy individuals, 215,000 pesos the state had in cash, and an additional 1.2 million pesos in proceeds from the sale of bonds guaranteed by the legislature. The local banks, merchants, and individuals in the oligarchy quickly purchased the bonds. Orozco had no trouble getting the oligarchy's money for his revolt. The loans were official acts of the state and the oligarchy.

Aside from the money itself, the clearest proof that the oligarchy supported and financed Orozco's rebellion are the statements of Manuel L. Luján. Luján was married to General Terrazas's granddaughter and was in business with the Terrazas-Creel clan. Luján was, by marriage, a prominent member of the Terrazas clan and was Orozco's appointed U.S. representative. Responding to the U.S. secretary of state regarding complaints from the State Department that Orozco's rebellion was exacting forced loans from Americans and Mexicans,[21] Luján wrote, "Deny absolutely that we have forced foreigners or Mexicans to make loans on us. Only public loan we have secured is one of 200,000 pesos, raised by voluntary subscription among bankers, merchants, and property owners of Chihuahua. Chihuahua City's chamber of commerce secured this loan."[22] Luján also testified before the U.S. Senate's Fall committee and detailed the oligarchy's financial support. To Luján, it was a not a question whether the financing was voluntary or forced. He said, the "loan was not a forced loan, and neither was it a voluntary loan, but it was one of those arrangements which was beneficial to both parties."[23] It was a practical business measure. The funds the friendly legislature gave to Orozco, a total of 1.6 million pesos, was a large amount, ranging from 150 to 200 percent of the state's annual budget expenditures.[24] It was a sum much larger than funds Madero had to fund his part of the revolution. Orozco burned through that money in only a few months. There was no need for the elites to fund him directly when they could do so with state -guaranteed bonds—and they did do so handsomely. Nevertheless, in addition to those huge sums, Orozco also received customs revenues and elite moneys of an unknown sum.[25] The oligarchy resisted funding Orozco only after his rebellion lost steam and Enrile became threatening. By then Orozco was clearly in decline, forcing him and Enrile to exact involuntary loans.[26]

There are simply too many Terrazas-Creel clan fingerprints to ignore. This clan was not known for its insubordination. It acted as a unit and profited as such. Aside from clan-related individuals who demonstrated against González in front of the state capitol and who served in Orozco's forces, there was the connector, Gonzalo Enrile. Before Orozco declared his revolt, Terrazas's emissary, Enrile, promised Orozco Terrazas's financial support—and perhaps delivered some of the money at the Club Estranjero—if Orozco would spare their properties,[27] which the Bureau of Investigation reported that Orozco ordered done.

Within two weeks of taking power, Orozco issued an order that Terrazas's properties were not to be disturbed. Under his administration, Orozco cut Terrazas's taxes in half.[28] The Bureau of Investigation also reported that the entire business community supported Orozco.[29] This prompted the defection of Orozco supporters, including revolutionary leader Máximo Castillo.[30] Another good reason why Orozco wanted to keep oligarchy funding a secret was that a good number of his followers, such as Castillo, would walk away if they learned of direct payments from Científicos. Later, when the influence of the oligarchy became undeniable, Orozco suffered substantial desertions. Orozco's defense was that he did not know that Enrile received Científico money. Enrile was the emissary, the intermediary between Orozco and the oligarchy, his paymaster, and his treasurer.[31] Under their flimsy plan, Enrile's role was to provide Orozco deniability. It is still a mystery how Orozco allowed himself to come under Enrile's spell. Given the man's record, almost anyone could have predicted the disaster that Enrile would bring to Orozco's rebellion.

When one's ego grows too large, a grounded parent might counsel humility. In Chihuahua, however, the oligarchy worked hard to convince Pascual Orozco Sr. that Madero was shortchanging his son.[32] They clearly saw the influence the father had over his son and the father's dissatisfaction with Madero. The father was as talkative and loquacious as his son was reticent and taciturn. Rather than calm his son's ambitions, his father egged him on. Indeed, his father played an important role in the drama, a close and influential family member who stoked the fires of great ambition where more modest aspirations might have been in order. The father convinced Orozco that, at the age of twenty-nine, with only a third- or fourth-grade education, and with less than six months of military service as his only experience, he should be named the nation's war minister. Moreover, the father complained that 50,000 pesos was inadequate compensation for his son's services, even though Villa received only 10,000 pesos and all other soldiers each received a mere 50 or 100 pesos, their saddle, and a train ticket home.[33]

What was it about Orozco that fired such ambition in the face of such a brief, although impressive, history? To Ramón Puente—a harsh Orozco critic—Orozco was "simple in spirit," barely able to read, of "limited intelligence," and unqualified to hold any office.[34] Nevertheless, writers who were more balanced said essentially the same thing. Meyer wrote that Orozco fell into a trap common to military heroes who are tempted by political office. He noted, "Orozco did not possess the intellectual or the legal qualifications

necessary for the office of governor or for any other high governmental post."
Regarding Orozco's support of Huerta, Meyer said, "His intellectual limitations
had again made him prey to the machinations of the vested interests."[35] This
was also the view of historian Alan Knight, who maintained that once the
Battle of Juárez was over and the politics began, it was a field in which Orozco
was "less adept" and was "prone to manipulation by literate secretaries and
advisers and, through them, by conservative interests."[36] Consul Marvin
Letcher had this blunt assessment, "'Bright and capable men' exploited the
'torpid and dull-witted Orozco.'"[37]

Was Orozco unintelligent or was he just naïve? Michael Meyer, Orozco's
principal biographer, certainly acknowledged that, while he was competent on
military issues, he was politically naïve, "duped" by the oligarchy, confused,
politically clueless, and unaware. He added that Orozco "never realized that his
[conservative] backers would not allow a reform program to become operative
if his revolt were successful."[38] For Meyer, however, being "unaware" did not
explain Orozco's choice to side with Madero's assassins. To Meyer, it made
no sense whatsoever for Orozco to have revolted against Madero for having failed to implement modest reforms while backing, to the hilt, Huerta,
who promoted none and who, in fact, wanted to undo the modest ones that
Madero had implemented. Meyer observed, "Orozco's naïveté degenerated
into intellectual incompetence and his dedication to a cause into obstinacy."[39]

Other writers have described Orozco's as a small-bore intellect, but they
might have fallen into a trap common for the urbane, wealthy, and genteel, who
mistakenly saw uneducated rural Mexicans as unintelligent. Many a country
boy has made a handsome living from such arrogance. Orozco was undeni-
ably intelligent. He could not be limited in intelligence and have organized,
recruited, armed, and led the large numbers that he commanded. A better
explanation was that his disdain for and bitterness toward Madero, as well
as Madero's refusal to appoint Orozco to a national post, made him open to
fawning and proposals from Madero's opponents. His overdeveloped ego made
him more vulnerable to flattery and appeals from the oligarchy and others.[40]

What was Orozco's motivation for turning against Madero and supporting
Huerta? One explanation could be that Orozco's reform ideology was soft,
as Máximo Castillo said, thus making it easy for him to change. It is not
satisfactory, however, to focus on one isolated comment Castillo mentions
and ignore Orozco's years of promoting reform.[41] The forces driving Orozco
appear more likely to be a mix of an outsized ego, a large but unsatisfied

ambition, bitterness, and hatred. Almost anyone would have been pleased to have become a national idol, to have international fame, and to have achieved the rank of division general when barely thirty-one, when those few who did achieve that grade arrived there late in their careers—but not Orozco, who was bitter over his fate.

Orozco had no idea of his personal limitations, because those closest to him told him that he had none, to such an extent that he might have had presidential ambitions. He felt that he could control any situation, such that he could make alliances with the oligarchy and still believe that their agenda would ultimately yield to his. We will never know whether this was true or realistic. Furthermore, Chihuahua elites also pulled no stops in their flattery of the young general. The elite feted, celebrated, and honored Orozco. They opened the doors to Chihuahua's society for him at the casino, the gun club, and other venues. Máximo Castillo said, "I found out that Orozco was a traitor, a coward who had been bought by the rich. Everywhere the wealthy people gave them dances, banquets. He became a society hero. He accepted presents of money from the very robbers who had left the poor without a foot of ground they could call their own."[42] Then there was Orozco's love of good times, women, and alcohol. One Chihuahua merchant noted, "Power went to Pascualito's head. He began attending fiestas, became a swaggering show-off, a carousing bon vivant who drank and chased women."[43]

Orozco was a natural leader. Although the San Isidro rebels initially deferred to Albino Frías, he in turn transferred the command to Orozco within days. In choosing the twenty-nine-year-old Orozco, they passed over many others with experience, including Orozco Sr. Although young, Orozco had already experienced years as a leader. He had been exercising it from a young age. His village recognized it, as did Abraham González. There were some important parallels between the life of his great uncle Ignacio Orozco and himself. It could be that Ignacio was a model for the young Orozco to follow. Ignacio was a military as well as a political leader. He fought for his village and its people. He fought for the liberal cause, but then, after he was arrested by the liberal governor for failing to follow orders, he turned and at least temporarily fought against the liberal governor and was defeated. Ignacio brought about the removal of General Luis Terrazas by Benito Juárez. He was clearly a man of great ability and independence, an individual who did not hesitate to fight injustice even if those he fought were more powerful. He also had the desire to seek revenge when he felt wronged. Pascual Orozco would develop similar attributes. He would also fight to restore the family's political power that Ignacio once held and that was lost to Joaquín Chávez.

Bitterness, produced because those in control failed to see Orozco's value, morphed into the intense hatred he could develop, perhaps "blind hatred" being an apt term. That hatred produced conduct on Orozco's part that was illogical and that appeared senseless. When hatred is a motivator, it can lead to strange alliances, exemplified by the phrase "the enemy of my enemy is my friend." It motivates an individual to act against an enemy blindly rather than by promoting desired policies. This type of negative decision-making appears illogical, as one can be thrown in with those with contrary goals or even with the odious, such as Huerta.

Given the importance of Orozco to the revolution, the paucity of material about him is impressive. It seems that each year several Villa books are released, adding to the dozens already on the shelves, but, until now, there has not been one on Orozco for almost fifty years since the publication of Meyer's *Mexican Rebel* in 1967 and none in Spanish for a century. There is much about Orozco that we do not know. We know about Joaquín Chávez, but few are aware of the reason for Orozco's deep antipathy for his first cousin, Francisco Antillón, the son of his padrinos. We are almost totally in the dark over how, when, or why Gonzalo Enrile captured the helm of Orozco's rebellion. It is unfortunate that we do not have more of Orozco's writings or memoirs.

In regarding Orozco's gaunt, angular face and frame, with its wan expression, it is difficult to imagine the magnetism that he undoubtedly possessed. Villa did not see it at first, but there was something about Orozco that drew men to him. Part of that was surely his undisputed valor and his calm under fire. His followers worshipped him to such an extent that they refused to recognize what was obvious—that around the time of the Battle of Ciudad Juárez, he was clearly in contact with and getting close to the hated oligarchy. His troops were with him when he stayed at Terrazas's grand ranches at El Sauz, Quinta Carolina, and other places. They saw Orozco socializing with the elite. A large number knew that he was taking money over and under the table from the oligarchy. Yet many continued to follow him. Some followed him to their graves. Some never acknowledged that he was doing the oligarchy's bidding even when they saw it and it became undeniable. That was how strong his hold was on many Chihuahuenses.

Orozco could promote two diametrically opposed programs because of the pathological hatred that only he could generate—against Joaquín

Chávez, against Madero, against Carranza, and finally against any surrogate of Madero's. So long as he was opposing that which he hated, he could say anything otherwise and believe it. Orozco was not alone in this paradoxical behavior, but he was its clearest and most dramatic example of that time. Orozco's denial that he was in the service of the oligarchy bordered on the pathological. It is possible that he believed he was furthering the cause for reform when he was obviously doing the reverse. Had he been on a polygraph, he could well have passed in insisting that he was promoting reform while simultaneously fighting on the same side as Creel and Huerta.

Pascual Orozco was a paradox because he advocated radical reforms and maintained friendships with leftists, such as those in the Liberal Party, Zapata, and others while he fought alongside reactionaries. Orozco had almost five years of public service, with one-third in favor of the revolution and reform and the balance in opposition. Given that contradiction in his record, ultimately, history should judge Orozco not by what he said, but by what he did—by his intentional actions and their effect on the revolution and its possible reforms. Looking at his conduct after the Battle of Ciudad Juárez in that light, Orozco was undoubtedly a counterrevolutionary. Although he often fought alongside undoubted revolutionaries such as Zapata, the Magonistas, Salazar, Castillo, and Hernández, from March 1912 until his death, he was most consistently the oligarchy's military arm. Thus, he furthered the oligarchy's counterrevolutionary policies. Yes, his proclamations and manifestos tracked Magonista reforms, but that was as far as it went. When Orozco attained positions of power, as he did for several months during his 1912 rebellion or in 1913 and 1914 during Huerta's dictatorship, he never attempted to implement the reforms he claimed to advocate in an administration run by and for the oligarchy. The impressive land reform program proposed by Abraham González on his return to Chihuahua in February 1912 was shelved by the oligarchy-controlled legislature when Orozco controlled the state as soon as Orozco ran González out of Chihuahua.[44]

In 1912, Orozco had a compliant legislature, was called a dictator, and did nothing with the power other than undo the few reforms Abraham González had begun, such as collecting and raising taxes on large landholders and initiating land and labor measures. Máximo Castillo said that Orozco took money from the oligarchy and that Pascual had admitted to him that "he did not altogether believe in the division of the land."[45] There was some corroboration for that sentiment found in the dispute between Orozco and Magonista José

Inés Salazar in March 1913. Although Orozco made land reform his principal condition for joining Huerta, when Salazar demanded immediate land reform measures from Huerta, Orozco refused to press the issue and said that he would leave the matter to Huerta. Huerta never pursued land reform, and Orozco did not complain.[46]

In contrast, showing what was possible by someone in power in those days, there was the record of Abraham González who, unlike Orozco, faced a hostile, Científico legislature. Despite that handicap and to the oligarchy's alarm, in the few weeks he was in office in 1911 and in the two-week period after he returned to Chihuahua on February 16, 1912, until he was deposed by Orozco on March 3, González pushed through the following agrarian and labor reforms: ending seizure of ejido, municipal, and other common land grants; passing land reform measures such as a six-million-peso bond issue to support irrigation, the purchase and seizure of properties to be distributed to ejidos and an agricultural bank; replacing political jefes with elected municipal government; requiring mandatory arbitration in labor disputes; outlawing company stores; and passing equitable tax laws to provide for fair taxation of large properties that had been paying only five centavos per hectare; and progressive rates for large properties increased from one to four pesos per hectare.[47] González proposed or decreed all these measures in the first few days in office.

In another example, Villa became Chihuahua governor on December 8, 1913. Four days later, he ordered the confiscation of Terrazas and Creel properties and began preparing for their distribution. In the same decree, he ordered the restitution of improperly acquired lands.[48] It may have been an arbitrary decree, but Villa's action was what many rebels expected from Madero and Orozco and did not receive. One can point to no similar effort on Orozco's part despite his complete military and political dominance and the invitation by the Madero administration to start land distribution in Chihuahua.[49]

The people Orozco appointed to high positions in his Colorado Rebellion are illuminating. Orozco was powerful; he could have appointed anyone he chose. Although his field commanders were faithful rebels from the past, such as José Inés Salazar, Marcelo Caraveo, and others, his choices to administer his revolution, to make policy and its pronouncements, were decidedly Porfirista. Those men included Enrile as his top administrator, spokesperson, and policy maker; Lieutenant Colonel Alfonso Castañeda as his chief of staff; and Manuel Luján and Juan Prieto Quemper as his Washington representatives, among others. His stated presidential preferences were General Gerónimo Treviño, Francisco León de la Barra, and Huerta, all Porfiristas or Reyistas. Orozco's history, then, is clearly one of having fought against Madero's and Carranza's democratic régimes and having supported the oligarchy, Huerta's dictatorship, and Huerta's attempted restoration. Fortunately, for history, by the time Orozco joined the oligarchy's side, his major accomplishments were behind him.

Assessing the impact of Orozco's conflicted record and chameleon character is more difficult. He left no meaningful ideological legacy as his was mostly secondhand and unimplemented. His could have been a national movement, but he abandoned the ideology that could have made it so. He spoke *magonismo*'s words but not its governance. Had he continued to fight for reforms, this history would be different, and his legacy most certainly would be. He abandoned his professed ideology and pursued instead a negative personalismo, promoting himself as a leader but making his only program a reaction against his enemy du jour, thus rendering his a historically insignificant movement. He caused no progress and only damaged what he claimed to advance. His was not Zapata's consistent fight to recover communal lands lost to sugar plantations. Unlike Orozco, who chose the oligarchy and a dictator as allies, Villa was uniformly on the side of the revolution and the peón. Villa in that sense did lead a program national in its potential, but he took on more than he could handle. Had Villa solidified his Chihuahua base, he might have grown his movement. Orozco had no economic program of his own and largely supported the oligarchy's anti-Madero reaction.

Orozco's main contributions were military accomplishments and development of leaders. He led a group of men who became important leaders themselves, such as José Inés Salazar, Marcelo Caraveo, and Rodrigo M. Quevedo—the latter two would become Chihuahua governors. Orozco, however, led them down an erroneous path against Madero and in support of the dictator Huerta. The flawed road Orozco chose was detrimental to his community, to his disciples, and to his own legacy.

Francisco Madero can be honored for having called for a revolution and for having been so committed to the restoration of democracy. There was purity and naïveté in Madero's struggle to return Mexico to its constitutional ideal and in his open and too-trusting personality. Despite the enormous opposition he faced, he mostly kept a free press and free, clean elections and permitted his opponents' loud voices in legislatures and the press—an environment that produced a cacophony of constant criticism that helped destroy his popularity and administration.[50] It was a fleeting, fifteen-month flirtation with the ideal that Mexico would never experience again.

Despite Orozco's failings, to him and the people of Labor de San Isidro must go the recognition for having started the revolution and for having driven the movement's first phase to success, something Madero would not likely have achieved without Orozco. The people of Labor de San Isidro can be justifiably proud that their tiny hamlet produced sons and daughters who made the sacrifices that achieved a victory few could dream about, making the village deserving of the honor in being named a Heroic Pueblo. To their leader, Orozco, goes the credit for having deposed the despot Porfirio Díaz. Orozco's positive contribution was so great in its consequences, therefore, that it outweighs the negative policies that he later pursued and the questionable associations that he made. As for whether Orozco was a principled military hero and political reformer or was instead a sellout to the oligarchy, a politically ambitious traitor to the revolution, and an eager ally of a brutal assassin and dictator, the record reflects that, at various times, Pascual Orozco was all of those things.

Epilogue

Following is a summary of salient issues and personalities in this account.

Francisco I. Madero. Madero was a decent if odd character, principled, well-intentioned, and deeply loyal to and influenced by his family. The Panic of 1907 and the crash of metals and commodity prices nearly bankrupted the Maderos. They were deeply in debt, faced foreclosure of several of their properties, and were under pressure to regain access to Mexican capital markets.[1] Politically, Madero's focus and passion was always a return to liberal democracy under the reform Constitution of 1857, and he did not advocate a social revolution.

It is beyond question that Madero would have tolerated another Díaz presidential term, a position he supported as late as the Battle of Ciudad Juárez. Madero called for revolution only after he was imprisoned during his 1910 campaign. Anxious to gain widespread support for his revolution, he broadened his reform agenda to include modest land reform measures. After he became provisional president, however, he shed or ignored much of his reform agenda. By appointing his Científico relatives to important cabinet posts, overseeing finance and economic development, he signaled a move away from reform and left the Madero family open to charges of profiting from the revolution.[2] He sent the same message in dumping his vice presidential running mate, Francisco Vázquez Gómez, a man popular with reformers. Whether he was tone-deaf or received poor advice, Madero completely mishandled the aftermath of his Ciudad Juárez victory. In short order, he lost the trust and support of important leaders, such as Orozco and Francisco Vázquez Gómez. He had never enjoyed the trust of Ricardo Flores Magón and Emiliano Zapata, who knew that Madero was not their type of revolutionary. For Madero, it was a case of overpromising what he intended to deliver. Mexicans joined the revolution with different expectations, and

Madero's overly ambitious Plan de San Luis unreasonably raised the hopes of those who fought for him. Madero's goals were largely fulfilled with his election—that is, in ending Díaz's dictatorship, returning to normal electoral terms of office, and restoring the constitution's civil liberties. Zapata, Flores Magón, and other revolutionaries wanted significant land, social, and economic reforms and a reversal of land grabs by the wealthy and large plantations as well as a reversal of overgenerous Díaz concessions given mostly to foreign firms, all goals not shared by Madero and his mostly conservative cabinet.

Madero was reckless in reconciling too early with Díaz sympathizers and in retaining the Díaz military, government bureaucracy, and judiciary. He gained nothing by freeing and then socializing with the hated Navarro. Thus, he angered one group of supporters after another while retaining and rewarding his enemies. He kept close those who would be his assassins while cavalierly brushing off allies who had fought honorably for the revolution. Madero was naïve and too trusting. He repeatedly disregarded warnings from his closest and principal advisors, including his mother, Mercedes González, and Gustavo, his brother and closest confidant,[3] and from his close advisor, Felix Sommerfeld.[4] He was indecisive and vacillating, traits that contributed to his downfall and assassination. On the eve of his death, he recognized his two main weaknesses, his efforts to please everyone and inability to rely on his friends. He seemed to have recognized his faults too late following the assassination of his brother Gustavo, who had vainly warned of Huerta's treachery.[5] Still, the public and the nation were correct in honoring Madero's contributions. He made the ultimate sacrifice to return Mexico to democracy, and for that he is rightfully credited with a special place in Mexican history. He is interred in Mexico City's Monument to the Revolution.

Porfirio Díaz. President Díaz, exiled from Mexico in late May 1911, initially went to Spain but soon settled in Paris. He died there four years later on July 2, 1915, and is buried in Montparnasse Cemetery, where even today his tomb usually has fresh flowers. The Mexican government allowed his widow, Carmelita, to return home but denied the family's request to repatriate the dictator's remains.[6] Díaz's legacy continued indefinitely. Although he is not solely to blame, his intentionally corruption-filled, multi-decade administration built on Santana's record of a government and military permeated with dishonesty, practiced with bribes, kickbacks, and lucrative government contracts, depriving Mexicans of efficient, honest government and the rule of law. Mexico continues its perennial battle to eradicate such endemic corruption, a legacy of the Porfiriato, from its national DNA.[7]

Abraham González. For many in Chihuahua, Abraham González became the hero of the Mexican Revolution. Yes, González sinned for having violated the rule against reelection in running for the governorship while holding the office. It is understandable why he did not resign in the face of a legislature controlled by his oligarchy opponents, but he erred nonetheless. You cannot run with your main plank being "no reelection" while you are violating the promise. Beyond that significant misstep, González tirelessly promoted the goals of the revolution, the ones the people of Chihuahua fought for, such as passing land and labor reform,[8] expropriating lands acquired unfairly by the elite, and insisting on fair taxation on the wealthy and democratic government. González fought for those principles in the face of an organized and armed Chihuahua elite. He had barely begun to fight when Orozco's 1912 revolt forced him into exile and prevented the implementation of his reforms, an agenda González would never again be able to revive. It could be that, as Consul Letcher observed, González "was too trustful, too easygoing, and too unalert to cope with the coterie of shrewd and cunning politicians who had grown up around the court of olden days."[9] González had been back in office only a few months when Huerta's coup took his life as well as Madero's. Huerta had him executed for his refusal to recognize his presidency.

Months after his execution, González's impromptu grave was rediscovered. In February of 1914, Villa had the remains moved to the government palace in Chihuahua City, where the people of Chihuahua honored González's memory. After a major parade, they reinterred his remains at the Panteón de la Regla. Later in 1914, the Chihuahua government arrested and charged the Huertista troops who had taken custody of González. The soldiers confirmed that they had executed González on direct orders from Huerta. In 1956, the remains of Governor González were placed in the Rotunda of Illustrious Chihuahuenses.[10]

Gonzalo C. Enrile Villatoro. Few readers would believe that even the serious multiple gunfire and stab wounds Enrile sustained in the Chihuahua City assault, followed by an immediate arrest in Ciudad Juárez, incarceration in El Paso, and hospitalization with several serious surgeries would be the end of the story for the irrepressible Gonzalo Enrile. And, of course, that was not the end of this fascinating and manic conman's life. Enrile was part of Orozco's administration for less than four months, when at the age of forty-five he left Orozco in June 1912.[11] In July, he was released from El Paso's jail after forty days and made his way to the East Coast of the United States. In early 1913, he was in Paris unsuccessfully attempting to persuade Porfirio Díaz to return to Mexico.[12] Enrile returned from Europe in late February,[13] and, as soon as he heard of Madero's assassination, he rushed back to Mexico and accompanied Orozco as Orozco traveled to Mexico City to join Huerta's forces in March 1913. As mentioned earlier, in October 1913 Enrile was arrested along with most of the members of the Chamber of Deputies. He was imprisoned, but eventually obtained his release. Enrile's long-suffering wife pleaded for her husband's freedom, insisting that he had not been involved in politics.[14] To the contrary, very soon after he returned to Mexico City with Orozco in March 1913, Enrile had become involved in party politics. Enrile was a solid Reyista, and Rodolfo Reyes was his former employer. Once Rodolfo Reyes resigned from Huerta's cabinet, he returned to the congress, where he joined the opposition.[15] Enrile most likely attached himself again to Reyes. The record is unclear why Enrile, not being a member of the congress, was arrested, but that he was walking in custody along with Reyes is an indication that he was in some manner involved. After their arrest and release, many former Porfiristas who had joined Huerta's opposition fled the country. They could not live there with possible death sentences under Huerta or Carranza and thus emigrated to the United States, Cuba, or Europe. Enrile went to all three.

Around April 1914, during Huerta's dictatorship, Enrile was in Saltillo, Coahuila, where he had already made a name for himself, with one observer noting of him, "Gonzalo Enrile, famous in Saltillo for his exploits there." Immediately before Huerta's federal troops abandoned the city and Villa's forces moved in, Enrile had become interested in two wealthy women, the Señoritas Zamora. The women had made a fortune in a mine, and as they received its income, they secretly buried the money in their patio. Armed with this information obtained from a former servant of the Zamoras, Enrile devised a plan to seize the Zamora cache by persuading a military chief to assign a squad to search the property. On hearing about the proposed search, the public raised a scandal over the matter, such that the governor ordered the search suspended.[16]

By mid-1915, Enrile made his way to Cuba, where he was again deep into intrigue, apparently gathering arms for Orozco,[17] and later left for Berlin to work on disrupting U.S.-Mexico relations.[18] In 1916, he became a member of another anti-American and anti-Carranza conspiracy based in New Orleans and Havana. Referring to Enrile as "famous" and "pernicious," the Mexican consul in Havana worked unsuccessfully to have Enrile extradited to Mexico; instead, Enrile escaped to Spain to gather German financing and support to involve the United States in Mexico.[19] One writer claims that some of that effort involved Villa's March 1916 raid on Columbus, New Mexico, part of a plan hatched by Enrile and encouraged by the Germans.[20] Borrowing from the Plan de San Diego, as Creel had done the previous year, and now claiming to have been a colonel in the Porfiriato, Enrile traveled to Berlin in April 1916. Once there, he claimed alliances with Villa, Félix Díaz, and Zapata and assured the Germans that he could overthrow Carranza and get Mexico to recover Texas, New Mexico, Arizona, and California. Enrile spent almost a year unsuccessfully selling that plan. Elements of Enrile's far-fetched, borrowed plan, however, found their way into the famous Zimmermann Telegram.[21] In May 1917, Cuban authorities arrested Enrile in Havana in possession of pro-German documents.[22] After his Havana arrest, the U.S. State Department noted that the United States had a case pending against Enrile for conduct in Saltillo, Coahuila, in the "Maass" incident.[23] In 1919, Enrile was arrested in Coahuila for murder and on other charges.[24] Never far from the action, in 1920, Enrile was in Mexico City, where he and Vito Alessio Robles prepared to engage in a duel, which was apparently stopped by the authorities.[25]

In May 1921, Enrile organized the Oaxaca-based Restoration Movement, a pro–Félix Díaz plot to overthrow Obregón's régime in a multicity rebellion whose nominal head was the grandson of Benito Juárez, José Sánchez Juárez. Enrile, however, called himself the "General in Chief" of the revolution.[26] In June 1921, newspapers reported the death of the fifty-three-year-old Enrile. Enrile had been arrested, and officials alleged that he was killed while attempting to escape[27]—a victim, one historian noted, of "*la Ley Fuga.*"[28]

General Luis Terrazas. Unlike Díaz, when Luis Terrazas said that he was retiring from active politics in August of 1904, he kept his word. He and his son-in-law Enrique Creel became unpopular during the revolution as symbols of the excesses and corruption of the Porfiriato—falling so out of favor, in fact, that Díaz jettisoned Creel from the cabinet and summarily ousted Terrazas's son as Chihuahua's interim governor.

A century after the end of the revolution's first stage, some still debate over whether Díaz, Terrazas, or Creel were corrupt. There is no need, however, to apply contemporary ethical standards retroactively to find the Díaz, Terrazas, and Creel administrations corrupt. Díaz openly allowed corruption to flourish as one method of retaining control over the rich and powerful, and those in power around the nation, especially in Chihuahua, were enthusiastic participants in the system. Terrazas began his public life as a man of modest means, but only the most naïve would assert that the massive fortune Terrazas amassed over his time in office was unrelated to his complete control over Chihuahua politics for much of half a century. Without doubt, the fountain from which the Terrazas and Creel fortunes flowed was public office used for private gain. What the families received they invested well, and that allowed them to accumulate more. Much of their fortune came to them by their passage of legislation and the granting of government contracts, concessions, and subsidies from which they personally profited. They also controlled appointments to public posts, the courts, and agencies that prevented any opposition, political or economic. Chihuahua's government, a personal cash cow for the Terrazas-Creel clan, was for sale, mainly to outsiders, and was closed for business to most of its own citizens.

During much of the decade of 1910–20, especially the period after the Orozco Rebellion failed, General Terrazas lived in exile in El Paso or in California. For much of his time in El Paso, he lived in the mansion owned by Senator Albert B. Fall. Terrazas lost much of his property to expropriation, especially under Villa in 1913–14, and he later dedicated himself to recovering a portion of it and restoring it. He persuaded President Venustiano Carranza to return the properties, but Álvaro Obregón overthrew Carranza before the effort succeeded.[29] Luis Terrazas died in Chihuahua City on June 15, 1923, at the age of ninety-three, and he is buried in a tomb conspicuously placed almost at the front entrance to the Sanctuario de Guadalupe. The Terrazas family continues its prominence in international, national, and Chihuahua business circles.

Oil and the Revolution. In 1900, Mexico had zero oil production. In 1906, it produced half a million barrels. That grew to 12.7 million barrels in 1911 and to 25 million two years later in 1913, making Mexico the third largest producer in the world seemingly overnight.[30] The big winners in oil production during the Porfiriato were Weetman Pearson and Edward Doheny, who together by 1918 controlled over 60 percent of the Mexican oil market.[31] Creel attached himself to Pearson's El Aguila Oil Company, becoming its president. With so much at risk, oilmen contributed to politicians. As an example, oilman Doheny testified to the Fall committee that he gave Carranza $685,000 as an "advance on future taxes."[32]

Enrique C. Creel. This was a man with many portfolios: banker, rancher, politician, governor, legislator, ambassador, minister of foreign relations, business executive, industrialist, intermediary between foreign capital and the Mexican government. Like his father-in-law, General Luis Terrazas, Creel spent much of the revolution in exile in California, where he continued to be active in business. Working with Orozco and Germany, he tried unsuccessfully to return Huerta to power in 1915. He returned to Mexico in 1920 and served as an economic advisor to President Obregón. Creel died in Mexico City in 1931 at the age of seventy-six. His family continues its prominence in business and National Action Party (PAN) politics.[33]

Francisco "Pancho" Villa. After he helped the constitutional forces defeat Huerta, Villa did not get along with President Venustiano Carranza and fought him instead. Villa and Zapata captured Mexico City, forcing Carranza to retreat to Veracruz. Eventually Carranza's most capable military man, Álvaro Obregón, drove Villa north and defeated him. From that time, Villa was largely ineffective. To avenge what he saw as American policy favoring Carranza, Villa attacked Columbus, New Mexico, in 1916. President Wilson sent American troops under General John J. Pershing to hunt Villa down, but they never found him and withdrew to fight in Europe instead. After Carranza was assassinated in 1920, Villa approached President de la Huerta and proposed an accommodation that was accepted. De la Huerta gave Villa a large Durango hacienda south of Parral, as well as a handsome pension. In his life, Villa had narrowly escaped death an impressive number of times, but in July of 1923, his luck abruptly ran out when some of his old enemies ambushed and murdered him in Parral.[34] Villa's remains were later moved from Parral to Mexico City and now lie in the National Monument to the Revolution along with the remains of Francisco Madero and Venustiano Carranza.

Marcelo Caraveo Frías. Mentioned in this work, Caraveo, cousin and supporter of Orozco, San Isidro native, and fellow Colorado, followed Orozco in his revolt and his alliance with Huerta, who promoted Caraveo to general. He later became a Zapatista, fighting against Carranza. He was elected governor of Chihuahua in 1928, but during his term, he revolted against interim president Emilio Portes Gil and was replaced as governor. He died in El Paso on March 15, 1955, and is interred in Chihuahua City.[35]

Albert Bacon Fall. Fall continued to play an important role in United States–
Mexico policy for the remainder of his time in Washington. He served in
the Senate until March of 1921, when he was confirmed to be secretary of the
Interior in the Harding administration and may have been the principal reason
why Harding delayed recognizing the Obregón government.[36] During his
Washington years, Fall continued to enjoy his homes in Washington, El Paso,
and his beloved ranch at Three Rivers, New Mexico, situated 120 miles north
of El Paso on the western flank of the snowcapped, 12,000-foot Sierra Blanca.
After less than a year in office, President Harding transferred jurisdiction
over strategic naval reserves from the War Department to the Department of
Interior. As Interior secretary, Fall soon executed controversial no-bid leases,
one over the California Elk Hills oil field with Edward L. Doheny and another
for the Wyoming Tea Pot Dome formation with oilman Harry F. Sinclair. A
later investigation disclosed that Fall had received several hundred thousand
dollars from Doheny and Sinclair, sums Fall insisted were loans to improve
his Three Rivers ranch. Fall was convicted of bribery and served time in the
federal penitentiary. Doheny was acquitted, and Harry Sinclair was found
guilty of contempt of court for having shadowed members of the jury sitting
on his aborted bribery trial. Because Fall was the only one of the trio who
was imprisoned, the term "took the fall" is still used when one individual is
punished for a group's crime. The Tea Pot Dome scandal remained the defin-
ing national political scandal until Watergate, and Fall was the first cabinet
member to go to prison for in-office misconduct. After serving his sentence,
Fall returned to El Paso, where he died in 1944 at the age of eighty-three.

Ricardo Flores Magón. Revolutionary leader and thinker, Magón was the head
of the Mexican Liberal Party (PLM). The party's platform and plan deeply
influenced others, such as Pascual Orozco, and the drafters of Mexico's 1917
Constitution. Magón's writing also inspired radical American labor groups,
such as the Industrial Workers of the World ("Wobblies") and the Western
Federation of Miners. In later years, the Liberal Party fractured into ideological
factions, anarchists versus socialists. Many socialists eventually deserted the
movement, whose influence and following waned. In 1917, the United States
charged Ricardo Flores Magón with sedition for impeding the war effort, for
which he was sentenced to serve twenty years. Just before he was to be released
from prison, he died in his Leavenworth Prison cell on November 21, 1922. A

compatriot and prison mate insisted that he was murdered, but the evidence indicates that he died of natural causes.[37]

The Posse. Dave Allison left Sierra Blanca in 1919 and went to Post, Texas, where he served as a deputy sheriff. In 1923, Allison and fellow cattle inspector H. L. Roberson went to Seminole, Texas, to present a case to the grand jury. They were both murdered by the two suspects they were to help prosecute.[38] Customs inspector Herff A. Carnes remained a career customs patrol inspector and was killed in 1932 in El Paso by suspected smugglers.[39] Descendants of the Love families continue ranching in Hudspeth and Culberson Counties. Sheriff John A. Morine resigned his office in 1916. He went to Socorro County, New Mexico, where he served as a deputy U.S. marshal for several years, and he died in 1968 in Sierra County. The judge in the case, Dan M. Jackson, went to Washington, D.C., to work for Albert Fall and was the clerk or secretary for Fall's subcommittee in 1920.

Orozco Court Cases. Federal agents had earlier followed Orozco as he moved about the United States. Agents considered him a fugitive as they surveilled his family members and checked their mail. Orozco only faced a court in June 1915 on the joint Huerta-Orozco indictment. Orozco fled and jumped bond on those charges. He would never face a court again after his initial appearances in El Paso.[40]

The 1917 Constitution. On February 5, 1917, Mexico adopted a new constitution at the convention held at Queretaro. The constitution was deeply influenced by the Juárez reforms as well as by the ideas of Ricardo Flores Magón and other intellectuals. It remains in effect today. Radical delegates dominated the constitutional convention, holding 132 seats to 85 for Carranza. Among its provisions are Article 27, returning to the rule that the government owns the land, including the subsurface; Article 123 on labor, which abolished child labor, mandated reasonable salaries, profit sharing, and an eight-hour day; other clauses providing for strict controls over the clergy and ecclesiastical property, including forbidding the wearing of clerical clothing in public, restrictions on religious education and public religious ritual, and requiring the public ownership of all churches. The constitution also strengthened the executive branch, weakened the legislative branch, and made the judiciary more independent by giving judges lifetime appointments.[41]

Survey Companies. On January 5, 1924, the Chihuahua state government issued an order published in the *Periódico Oficial*, canceling the land survey concession it had granted to Jesus Valenzuela & Co. in 1882 for five million acres and declared null and void all titles based on the concession.[42] The communities of Galeana and Santo Tomás also recovered their ejidos in 1925 and 1926.[43]

William Randolph Hearst. Among the titles affected by the revocation of the Valenzuela land survey concession was that for the Hearst's San José de Babícora ranch. In 1926, William M. Ferris, the manager of the ranch, published a memorandum detailing the problems Hearst had in fighting government efforts to expropriate the property. The manager insisted that the attempted expropriation of Hearst's interest was illegal and unfair and that Hearst had done everything by the book. Ferris wrote that Hearst was generous in "giving" property to nearby residents to form an ejido. Much of the Hearst land was initially expropriated from an ejido community. Hearst employees spent years working on the problem and were only partially successful in revalidating the Hearst's title. Squatters occupied most of the farmland, leaving the ranch with only grazing land. Operations were reduced to a fraction of those in earlier times.[44] It is possible that the entire property was sold to the Mexican government in 1953.[45]

Hearst had a fickle relationship with various Mexican administrations. In April of 1910, he strongly supported Díaz,[46] but by 1914 he was supporting Villa when he controlled Chihuahua. In 1915, however, Hearst turned against Villa. One historian attributes Hearst's change of mind to Villa's plan to impose higher taxes on the ranch.[47] After Villa lost power and was roaming Chihuahua, he ordered the ineffectual expropriation of Babícora.[48] Chihuahua's government, however, pursued Babícora's expropriation for several years. New state laws limited properties to 100,000 acres, meaning that Babícora would have to dispose of 800,000 acres. An agreement was finally reached to divide the property among its various directors to bring ownership within state limits.[49]

It could not be determined how many families lost their homeland for the Hearsts to take possession of their Chihuahua ranches at Babícora and Las Mulas. In exchange for dispossessing and eliminating the livelihood of a significant number of Mexican families, Mexico sold its patrimony and valuable land for a pittance to the most absent of absentee landlords, for whom the land was nothing more than a balance sheet entry. J. Frank Dobie wrote that

William Randolph Hearst never visited Babícora, although there was a rumor that he might have once flown over it.[50] It seems more likely that George and Phoebe Hearst never visited the property and that their son William visited at most twice, once in 1886 and then again in 1910. There is no record of any Hearst having seen Las Mulas.

Hearst had a larger-than-life personality (which was the inspiration for the lead character in the film *Citizen Kane*) and a lifestyle scandalously extravagant even for the Roaring Twenties, exemplified by his castle at San Simeon; several large, sensationalist newspapers rumored to have brought about the Spanish-American War through yellow journalism; two terms in Congress; candidacies for major offices in New York; and a run for the presidency. Hearst died in Beverly Hills in 1951 at the age of eighty-eight.

Members of the Church of Jesus Christ of Latter-day Saints. The LDS, or Mormons, remain in Chihuahua. At least one has been elected to political office there.[51] George Romney, former governor of Michigan and 1968 presidential candidate, was born near Casas Grandes, Chihuahua, and left as a child in 1912, when his family abandoned Mexico during the revolution. His son is Mitt Romney, former Massachusetts governor.

Namiquipa. In March 1913, under Villa-controlled Chihuahua government, the village council of Namiquipa voted to take property expropriated under Creel's 1905 Municipal Land Law and divide it among the traditional Namiquipa residents. On March 26, 1925, the state of Chihuahua granted to Namiquipa 282,000 acres, territory slightly larger than the 1744 grant for the Namiquipa communal lands, in complete restoration of the lands lost through adjudications.[52] The nearby village of Cruces also recovered its ejido on August 5, 1926.

Joaquín Chávez's Land. On February 17, 1921, the Mexican president issued a decree expropriating all the land owned by Joaquín Chávez that was formerly part of the Labor de San Isidro ejido, that is, communal lands, returning that property, about five thousand acres, to the 169 families who had lived there before Chávez took ownership.[53]

By those acts, the government reversed, at least in part, several of the more egregious events that brought about the Mexican Revolution.[54]

Appendix

Following is a transcription (complete with the Culberson County court's typos) of the inquest conducted regarding the deaths of Pascual Orozco and his four companions.

In the matter of the death of Pasqual Orozco, Jose F. Delgado, Christoforo Caballero, Andreas Sandoval and Miguel Terrazas in Culberson County, Texas, on the 30th day of August 1915, the following proceedings were had at the inquest held by me on the 31st., day of August and 1st., day of September 1915.

THE STATE OF TEXAS   )
                           (
COUNTY OF CULBERSON)

In the matter of the death of Pascual Orozco, Jose F. Delgado, Christoforo, Andreas Sandoval and Miguel Terrazas.

August 30th., 1915.

On this day information was given me by John A. Morine Sheriff of Culberson County that the above named parties had been killed in said County in a canon 2 miles South of the High Lonesome Peak in the Van Horn range of Mountains; that their death was caused by gun shots fired by a posse of officers and citizens of El Paso and Culberson Counties. I viewed the bodies of these men on the ground where they fell in the fight with the posse and of my own knowledge know that the statement made by John A. Morine to be true.

August 31st., 1915.

On this day I held a partial inquest upon the dead bodies of the men at the ranch of D. Taylor by taking the testimony of Will H. Schrock and the inquest not haveing been completed was adjourned until the following day when it would be resumed in Van Horn to which place the bodies were to be carried.

Sept. 1st., 1915.

This day the inquest was resumed by me at Van Horn by taking the testimony of John A. Morine, A. B. Medley, John Russell and A. Hermosillo and the inquest having been completed from the evidence adduced I find that the said Pascual Orozco, Jose F. Delgado, Christoforo Caballero, Andreas Sandoval and Miguel Tarrazas [sic] came to their death in Culberson County, Texas, on the 30th., day of August 1915, by gun shots fired by officers and citizens of El Paso and Culberson Counties, Texas.

TESTIMONY OF W. H. SCHROCK

I first heard of Mexicans when I drove to R. C. Love's Ranch about 1 o'clock P. M. 29th Aug. 1915, when August Fransel and Joe Thomson told me that two well armed Mexicans had rode off from the Ranch in a hurry in direction of the Dick Love new well, Joe also said the five Mexicans were camped at this new well and they had several horses, Joe said he was hunting horses and saw some loose horses and rode to them when these men rose up and spoke to him in English saying "Come here", He said he went to where they were camped, they asked him what he was looking for, he said he was looking for horses and asked them what they wanted with him, they told him they wanted some chuck, he said "All right come with me to the ranch and I will get you some chuch". Two of the men, one with black leggings and the other with a black eye, Kaki suit and tan bootees went with him to the ranch, when they got to the ranch one of the two men told Joe to shoe his horse, Joe did so. They went in to dinner and while eating dinner they were constantly on the watch and during the meal one of them spied three men coming toward the house and said in Mexican "There comes three men, lets go". They jumped up grabbed their winchesters, which they had brought in, ran, jumped on their horses and ran toward the new well. About fifteen minutes later myself and five other men were saddled and ready and took their trails, we trailed them to where they had been camped when we got within half mile of their camp we could see them going east towards the Eagle Mountains, and they were 'Beating them on the tail too'. They reached the Mountains about ¼ mile ahead of us and began shooting at us. I lost my hat about that time and don't know what happeded for a while, they fired about 15 or 20 shots which turned us back. They stayed where they did the shooting for about 2 hours, then went into Frenchmen Well Canon, we trailed them into said canon above Frenchmen Well and darkness stopped us. Next morning we picked up the trail where we left it, followed them through the mountain and on to where we found them about 2 o'clock P.M. Aug. 30, 1915, in the foot hills of the Van Horn Mts., almost due south of Hogh Lonesome Mts., and about half mile from Stephens Tank. There our posse surrounded them and they made fight and fought until they were all dead, hiding behind rocks and shooting with rifles. They were all armed with practically new 30-30 Marlin Rifles, they also had one and perhaps more pistols. After the battle we found in their possession about 1000 rounds of 30-30 cartridges, we also found in their possession 2 horses belonging to J. E. Marshall, G. H. & S. A. Ry., Pumper at Ilaska Texas, one horse owned by Bob Love taken from same pasture. They had only five horses with them so far as I know.

Signed, W. H. Schrock.

TESTIMONY OF GEO. G. KIRTLEY.

About 2 o'clock yesterday Aug. 30, 1915, Bertie Bristow and Hardy Mershon came by and told me that a posse was hunting a bunch of Mexicans. I helped to bring in the dead Mexicans this morning, know where they were picked up. It was in Culberson County, Texas, about one mile east of the El Paso and Culberson county line.

Signed, Geo. G. Kirtley.

TESTIMONY OF JOHN RUSSELL, OF EL PASO, TEXAS.

I am acquainted with the bodies in the other room, Pascual Orozco, Christoforo Caballero, Jese F. Delgado, Sandoval and Terrazas, I have known Orozco personallu since 1912, I have known the other four about six months, Orozco and I were just friends, that is all he is a friend to my father. My father died just a few months ago. My father was Orozco's best friend, after my father died Orozco's family invited me to come and stay at their house, his family was in El Paso and I brought my mother to stay at this house in El Paso. The last time I saw Orozco was in Ojinago in 1914, he did not invite me personally he told his family to invite me, he had told my father before, when my father had been over to see him. I saw Christoforo Caballero about one week ago in El Paso, It was a week ago yesterday, about the 24th day of August, I took supper with him, he was alone. I am not sure what he was engaged in. He lived in El Paso, he was my father's friend. My father recommended me to him as a friend, when I first met him before my father died. I met him in Presidio, I do not know what his business has been at anytime, I do not think he has been associated with Mexican Officers. Sandoval, I saw him in El Paso, I did not associate with with him much, he was not a close friend with my father, I met him in El Paso, I do not have the least idea when I met him but it has been a week or two. Jose Delgado, I have known him about six months, I haven't seen him for some time, I last saw him in El Paso. Terrazas, I haven't seen hin for some time, he is not a relative of General Lewis's family. I do not knwo what his business was, he might have been employed by some one to work, they are all poor men, I do not know whether they are employed by and of the Mexican Officers or not, I have never seen any two of the men together at any time. I do not know what they were out for. I do not know where they were headed for, of course, immagination is all a fellow can give, I suppose they were going to Palaris.

Signed, John Russell.

TESTIMONY OF A. HERMOSILLO,

I am acquainted with the men in the other room, I have known Orozco fro some years, I lived in the same town a short distance from his family, it was about 10 or 15 years ago, it was in Sanlsedro, Chihuahua, I am not related to any of his familu, I have a house rented at the same place they stay. Christoforo Caballero, I think I have known him one or two years, when I knew him he was employed by the Police force in Jaurez, he guarded the town when Jaurez was under Madero, when the Orozco revolution began. Sandoval, I went out one day to ask for Pasqual Orozco and they said Sandoval was the one I talked to. I have not seen them since Orozco got away at Wyoming St., I do not know what their reason was. I can only imagine, I do not know absolutely what their reason was at all, I think they wanted to cross the line and they came across this way to get there.

Signed, A. Hermosillo.

TESTIMONY OF JOHN A. MORINE,
Sheriff of Culberson County, Texas.

The first think I knew of these Mexicans was when I received a telegram from R. C. Love, which was phoned to Sierra Blanco, and addressed to me at Van Horn, which read as follows viz;

> 3 Jn J.B. Cm 13 pd.
> Sierra Blanco, Texas, 8/30/;5.
> John Morine,
> Van Horn. Texas.
> Look our for five Mexicans in Eagle Mountains,
>   well armed, are going your way.
> R. C. Love

It was from other telegrams that was received here, one from Mr. Mellard and one from Tom Yarbro in which it was stated that Dick Love and two of his companions had, had a fight with these Mexicans and that they were going to the Eagle Mountains and that a posse of officers and ranchmen were in pursuit. I immediately obtained assistance and made preparations to leave, I received a phone message from Dave Allison, Constable at Sierra Blanco, El Paso County, Texas, from D. Taylor's ranch that a Cusom Officer, H. A. Carnes was on the trail and that the Mexicans had passed about three quarters of a mile South of Taylor's ranch, at which place myself and two deputies took the trail about 1 o'clook the same day. Just as we found the trail there appeared ten other men also on the same trail, Will Schrock of Sierra Balnco being one of the number, we immediately struck a gallop and overtook Constable Allison and Custom Officer Carnes, then we all hastened on the trail. Myself and Joel Fenley being on fresh horses took the lead as we neared the Culberson County line where the trail of the Mexicans led to a point about two and onehalf miles south of the High Lonesome Peak in the Van Horn range of mountains, where we engaged them in battle. The place the Mexicans were in, was hidden from our view in a rincon at the head of a very rough rocky canon and after acting upon a plan to surround them I was to take the right hand swing and appear above then and the other part of the posse to swing to the left but before arriving at my positon the Mexicans evidently suspicioned something for the[y] immediately grabbed their arms and fired on the left hand party as soon as they made their appearance. We all closed in about the same time and after a fusilade of shots all the Mexicans were killed. Upon making an examination of the Mexicans camp we obtained five horses, three of which I am positive were stolen horses, also five saddles, bridles and blankets, five 30-30 Marlin Octagon barrel safety rifles, one Smith and Wesson 44 Special Revolver, one 45 Colts Revolver and approximately between 1000 and 1500 rounds of 30-30 cartridges, There was also found in the damp some fresh gerked beef supposed to have been a part of a calf butchered by them the evening before on George Love's ranch; also a number of other articles I hold ion my possession subject to order of the Justice's Court. Three of the captured horses being thoroughly identified were turned over to their owners one of these horses belonged to Bob Love and the other two to Joe Marshall both of Sierra Blanco, Texas, and the other two horses I hold in my possession with five saddles and equipments subject to the order of the Justice's Court. Upon returning to the ranch of D. Taylor on the head of the Green Rover draw, I immediately phoned for the Justice of the Peace and the County Attorney so that a proper inquest might be held. The Justice of the Peace and the County Attorney immediately came out and the following morning were taken to the scene of the killing. After viewing the bodies of the Mexicans on the ground the Justice of the Peace ordered them to be taken to Van Horn where they are now lying in the Court House embalmed by undertakers sent from El Paso, Texas.

Signed, John A. Morine,
Sheriff, Culberson County, Texas.

TESTIMONY OF A. B. MEDLEY, of Van Horn, Texas,
who accompanied John A. Morine as a deputy sheriff
in the pursuit of Mexican outlaws.

John Morine asked me if I would go with him to catch some desparadoes that were coming his way. I went with hin in an automobile to the Taylor Ranch where we got horses and took up the trail with the Sierra Blanco boys. We then trailed the Mexicans up to where we overtook them at a point right south of the High Lonesome Mountains in D. Taylor's pasture. When we overtook them they at once gave battle and we also made fight in which all of the Mexicans were killed five in umber. We then went directly to their camp fire. The nearest man to the camp was about 30 yards away angling from there across the ridge it was about 150 yards where the fartherest one of the men lay from the damp fire.

Signed, A. B. Medley.

On the 30th day of Aufust, 1915, a telephone message was sent from D. Taylor's ranch on the head of Green River in El Paso Co. Texas, by Jno. A. Morine, Sheriff of Culberson Co., to A. L. Green County Attorney for Culberson Co., asking him and myself to come to the Taylor ranch at once, and stated in the message that his posse and one from El Paso Co. had killed five Mexicans about nine miles in a Southeasterly direction from the Taylor ranch. Immediately on the receipt of this message Mr. Green and I started in an Automobile for Taylor's ranch where we arrived a little before dark, at this ranch we met nearly all of the posse from both El Paso and Culberson Counties, who took part in the fight with the Mexican outlaws.

On the morning of August 31st., 1915, Mr. Green and I accompanied the entire party of officers and ranchmen who took part in trailing up and killing of Pascual Orozco, Jose F. Delgado, Christoforo Caballeo, Andreas Sandoval and Miguel Tarrazas to a small rincon in the head of a steep rocky canon, a tributary of Green Rover where we found the bodies of the above named parties lying where they fell in battle that was fought the evening of 30th of Aug. After I had made a careful examination of all the bodies and gathered up such things from among the baggage and clothing scattered over the ground as I thought would help to identify these men I ordered all the bodies to be carried to Taylor's ranch.

Mr. D. Taylor carried his wagon over to the scene of battle and it was in this that the bodies were carried to his ranch. After retunring to the Taylor Ranch I took the testimony of W. H. Schrock who was in the party who first encountered these Mexicans near Dick Love's ranch, so that he might retunr to his home from that place, I also took the testimony of Geo. G. Kirtley who is working a Mica Mine about two miles from where the fight ocoured in order to ascertain definitely whether this killing took place in El Paso or Culberson County. Mr. Kirtley has lived at the Mica Mine several years, had his land surveyed and knew within a very short distance of where the County line ran. About 2 o'clock in the afternoon all the bodies of he Mexicans were loaded in Mr. Greens Automobile and accompanied by Mr. Yarbro, Mr. Holzman and the Van Horn party we all returned to Van Horn.

On the 1st., day of Septmeber, 1915, I finished my examination in the cause of the death of parties whose names are given in the first part of this statement by taking the testimony of John A. Morine A. B. Medley, John Russell and A. Hermosillo at Van Horn, Texas. Hermosillo and Russell were sent to Van Horn from El Paso for the purpose of identifying the bodies of the men killed in the fight on Green River wgich they did beyond all question of doubt.

On the night of the 31st., of Aug. 1915, Mr. J. J. Kaster an undertaker of El Paso, was sent to Van Horn for the purpose of embalming the bodies of the men killed in the Green River fight and carrying them to El Paso for interment. On the request of Mr. Louis Holzman, Custom Inspector at El Paso, I turned over to Mr. Kaster the five bodies brought from the battle field on Green Rover and took Mr Holzman's receipt for them.

T. R. Owen [signature]
Justice of the Peace.

THE STATE OF TEXAS   )
                        (
COUNTY OF CULBERSON)

I, T. R. Owens, Justice of the Peace of Precinct No. 1, of said State and County, do hereby certify that the above and foregoing contains a full and complete copy of all the proceedings had before me at an inquest held upon the dead bodies of

Pascual Orozco, Jose F. Delgado, Christoforo Caballero, Andreas Sandoval and Miguel Tarrazas, in said County and State on the 31st day of Aug. and the 1st day of Sept. 1915.

Witness my hand his 1st day of Sept. 1915.

T. R. Owen [signature]

Justice of the Peace, Precinct No. 1,

of Culberson County, Texas.

Abbreviations

AGN   Archivo General de la Nación, México, DF

AHDN   Archivo Histórico de la Secretaría de la Defensa Nacional, México, DF

ATJ   Archivo del Supremo Tribunal de Justicia de Chihuahua, Chihuahua, Chih.

BNM   Biblioteca Nacional de México, UNAM, México, DF

BOI   U.S. Bureau of Investigation (later to become the Federal Bureau of Investigation in the Department of Justice)

CEHM   Centro de Estudios de Historia de México, México, DF (See also CONDUMEX.)

CONDUMEX   Centro de Estudios de Historia de México, México, DF

INEHRM   Instituto Nacional de Estudios Históricos de las Revoluciones de México

RDS   Records of the U.S. Department of State

SCJN   Suprema Corte de Justicia Nacional

SRE   Archivo Histórico de la Secretaría de Relaciones Exteriores, México, DF

STP   Silvestre Terrazas Papers, Bancroft Library, University of California, Berkeley

UACJ   Universidad Autónoma de Ciudad Juárez

UNAM   Universidad Nacional Autónoma de México

USGPO   U.S. Government Printing Office

UTEP   University of Texas at El Paso

Notes

Introduction

1. There were two Pascual Orozcos, father and son, both officers in the revolutionary forces. Any reference to "Pascual," "Orozco," or "Pascual Orozco" indicates the son, Pascual Orozco Jr., and the father will be referred to as "father" or "Sr."
2. Knight, "Caudillos y Campesinos," 32–33, 46–47.
3. Jarvis Vivian McAdoo told his son-in-law, current Hudspeth County attorney C. R. Kitt Bramblett, that he was in Van Horn the day the bodies were on display. He said that he saw the bodies and could tell that "they had been killed by foul means." McAdoo was uncomfortable with the scene and quickly left because he thought there would be reprisals by angry Mexicans. Bramblett, interview.

Chapter 1

1. Mort, *Wrath of Cochise*, 25, 32–33.
2. Chihuahua experienced Tepehuan, Tarahumara, and Concho uprisings in 1606, 1607, 1616–17, 1618–21, 1621–44, 1650, 1651, 1689, and 1694. Galaviz de Capdevielle, *Rebeliones Indígenas*, 119–27.
3. Nugent, *Spent Cartridges*, 40.
4. Almada, *Cantón Rayón*, 16; Márquez Terrazas, *Memoria del Papigóchic*, 304–305; Brondo Whitt, *Patriarcas del Papigochi*, 39.
5. Tamarón y Romeral, *Demostración*.
6. Lloyd, "Rancheros and Rebellion," 110, 111; Nugent, *Spent Cartridges*, 44.
7. Spain failed to encourage emigration by Spanish farmers. Meyer and Sherman, *Course of Mexican History*, 169.
8. Lloyd, "Modernización y corporatividad," 223–56; Nugent, *Spent Cartridges*, 42–47.
9. Lister and Lister, *Chihuahua: Storehouse of Storms*, 69–73.
10. The last Jesuit entry in the parish journals was on July 3, 1767, by Joseph de la Vega for a baptism at Basúchil.
11. Márquez Terrazas, *Memoria del Papigóchic*, 281.
12. Almada, *Resumen de Historia*, 119.

Chapter 2

1. Romero, "Philosophy of the Mexican Revolution," 13.
2. Smith, "Scalp Hunter," 14.
3. Chavis, "All-Indian Rodeo," 5, 6.
4. Álvarez, *James Kirker*, 83. Álvarez said that the scalping practice began with tribes on the U.S. East Coast, spread to the Europeans (against the Indians), and was then brought west by Americans and passed along to Chihuahuenses by the Santa Rita copper mine management.
5. Márquez Terrazas, *Terrazas y Su Siglo*, 40.
6. Smith, "Scalp Hunter," 18–21.
7. Historian Louis Fisher wrote that Polk's claim of a Mexican invasion was false: "The [Nueces] territory did not belong to the United States." The author also notes that even Polk later backed away from his original claims. Fisher, "Law: When Wars Begin," 173–174. Lincoln introduced the "Spot Resolutions" to determine whether Mexicans had killed Americans on U.S. soil as Polk alleged. On January 3, 1848, the U.S. House censured Polk for having started the war unnecessarily. *Congressional Globe*, 30th Cong., 1st Sess. 96 (1848). See also Fisher, "Mexican War and Lincoln's 'Spot Resolutions.'"
8. It was not only Mexicans against the invasion. In addition to Abraham Lincoln, others such as John C. Calhoun and U. S. Grant saw through Polk's pretexts. Grant wrote, "Generally the officers of the army were indifferent whether the annexation [of Texas] was consummated or not; but not so all of them. For myself, I was bitterly opposed to the measure, and to this day regard the war [with Mexico] which resulted as one of the most unjust ever waged by a stronger against a weaker nation." Grant, *Personal Memoirs*, 22–24.

Chapter 3

1. Lloyd, *Cinco ensayos*, 227; Sandels, "Antecedentes," 394.
2. Salmerón, *Juárez*, 164–67.
3. His manifesto was *Plan de la Noria*. Meyer and Sherman, *Course of Mexican History*, 410.
4. This time Díaz called his manifesto Plan de Tuxtepec, and it also had no reelection as its principal base. Meyer and Sherman, *Course of Mexican History*, 414.

Chapter 4

1. The record on his racial background is conflicting except that he was certainly part Mixtec on his mother's side. Krauze, *Porfirio Díaz*, 67–68. Krauze has Díaz's ethnicity as half-indigenous, half-Spanish.
2. Krauze, *Porfirio Díaz*, 8, 16–21.
3. Those were also the differences between Miguel Hidalgo and the royalists. Luna, *Miguel Hidalgo*, 75.
4. Díaz also worked hard at developing a cult of his personality. He exercised, lifted weights, and took daily cold baths. With his medaled uniform, he resembled Bismarck. Krauze, *Porfirio Díaz*, 52, 77.

5. Protasio Tagle, a cabinet member familiar with Díaz's machinations, referred to don Porfirio as "don Perfidio." Krauze, *Porfirio Díaz*, 35.

6. Krauze, *Porfirio Díaz*, 35, 45, 65, 74. Excepting foreign adventures, the Díaz style resembles the common press description of Russia's Vladimir Putin today, including a vain strongman image, absolute power, no tolerance of opposition, a veneer of democracy, limited civil liberties, no free press, and a pampered oligarchy made wealthy through state-sponsored corruption that enabled its accumulation of spectacular fortunes from government resources.

7. Beals, *Porfirio Díaz*, 274, 396.

8. Ibid., 280, 316–19.

9. Iturribarria, "Limantour," 252–56.

10. Taracena, *Verdadera Revolución (1901–1911)*, 47; Beals, *Porfirio Díaz*, 351, 357.

11. Iturribarria, "Limantour," 260–63.

12. Beals, *Porfirio Díaz*, 365, 368.

13. Ibid., 296.

14. RDS, Lind to State Dept., December 15, 1913, File No. 812.00/10196.

15. Sandels, "Antecedentes," 390.

16. Krauze, *Porfirio Díaz*, 43–45. Díaz often appointed his friends to Congress. In 1886, 62 of the body's 227 members were from Oaxaca. Members were appointed to represent districts they had never lived in.

17. Beals, *Porfirio Díaz*, 291–93.

18. Ross, *Francisco Madero*, 30.

19. Beals, *Profirio Díaz*, 337.

20. Ibid., 286.

21. Stephen Bonsal, "The Mexican Revolution as Seen from the Inside," *New York Times*, June 25, 1911.

22. Under Díaz, his supporters established *El Imparcial*, a government-subsidized Mexico City newspaper. The Díaz-supported journal purchased new, efficient printing presses that allowed the publishing of huge editions of around 100,000 copies that could be sold at prices so low that others could not compete, causing their closure. Iturribarria, "Limantour," 251.

23. Beals, *Porfirio Díaz*, 267–72.

24. Ibid., 315. See also Iturribarria, "Limantour," 250.

25. Beals, *Porfirio Díaz*, 347.

26. Ibid., 295.

Chapter 5

1. Raat, "Ideas and Society," 33.

2. García Moisés, *Madero*, 68.

3. Ross, *Francisco Madero*, 28; Krauze, *Mexico: Biography of Power*, 219.

4. Beals, *Porfirio Díaz*, 306; Krauze, *Mexico: Biography of Power*, 219.

5. Cockcroft, *Intellectual Precursors*, 29; Hackett, "Mexican Revolution," 340–41.

6. Beals, *Porfirio Díaz*, 298, 302.

7. Ross, *Francisco Madero*, 31.

8. Marion Letcher, *Daily Consular and Trade Reports*, No. 155 (July 2, 1912), 316.

9. To appease the United States, Mexico ignored a favorable international tribunal decision on its Chamizal land claim. Beals, *Porfirio Díaz*, 347.

10. Ibid., 396; Sandels, "Antecedentes," 395.

11. González Navarro, "Ideas raciales de los científicos," 572–73.

12. Beals, *Porfirio Díaz*, 302–305.

13. Raat, "Ideas and Society," 38.

14. Beals, *Porfirio Díaz*, 300.

15. Ibid.

16. Sandels, "Antecedentes," 392.

17. Beals, *Porfirio Díaz*, 371.

18. Ibid., 301–302.

19. Ross, *Francisco Madero*, 32.

20. Sandels, "Antecedentes," 401.

21. Krauze, *Mexico: Biography of Power*, 219.

22. Sandels, "Antecedentes," 397, 402.

23. Raat, "Ideas and Society," 38.

24. Lloyd, "Rancheros and Rebellion," 110–11.

25. Among the settlers was Miles Park Romney, great-grandfather of U.S. presidential candidate Mitt Romney.

26. Lloyd, *Cinco ensayos*, 165–66.

27. Lloyd, *Distrito Galeana*, 78.

28. Lister and Lister, *Chihuahua: Storehouse of Storms*, 163–64.

29. Davis, "Our 'Prisoners of War,'" 356–67; Blount and Bourke, "Apache Campaign," 20–38; Seymour and Robertson, "Pledge of Peace," 154–79.

30. San Simeon, famous today, is the site of Hearst Castle.

31. Wasserman, "Oligarquía e intereses extranjeros," 306. See also Ferris, "Land Title Difficulties," 13–22.

32. Dobie, "Babicora."

33. George and Phoebe Apperson Hearst Papers, 1849–1926, University of California, Bancroft Library. https://archive.org/details/bancroft_appersonhearst_3002_6.

34. The buying of a Senate seat was an open secret, so much so that it led to the Seventeenth Amendment to the U.S. Constitution in 1913, which provided for the direct election of U.S. senators, a move to end the corruption associated with Senate elections.

35. Brand, "Early History," 136. Other large American-owned ranches beside Hearst's operation, such as Corralitos, also took ejido lands. Lloyd, "Rancheros and Rebellion," 126.

Chapter 6

1. Almada, *Gobernadores*, 269.

2. Terrazas's 1862 property valuation showed his property to be worth 19,500 pesos. Almada, *Juárez y Terrazas*, 332.

3. On September 20, 1860, Terrazas became substitute governor upon the resignation of José Eligio Muñoz. The following June, Terrazas won election to a four-year term. Márquez Terrazas, *Terrazas y Su Siglo*, 73.

4. Consul Letcher had this assessment of Creel: "Able, progressive and immensely wealthy he was ambitious, and he was not content to remain out of national politics." RDS, Letcher to State, October 17, 1913, 812.00/9484.

5. Creel's intelligence network was even broader than his agency. He may have been part of a binational, bicultural spy and law enforcement web with Creel receiving reports from the U.S. State Department. Raat, "U.S. Intelligence Operations," 616.

6. Wasserman, *Capitalistas, Caciques*, 95.

7. Almada, *Revolución*, 1:58; Sims, "Espejo de Caciques," 379–99.

8. *Amarillo Daily News*, March 6, 1912; Brand, "Early History," 136. Stephen Bonsal wrote that Terrazas was "oppressed with an insatiable land hunger." "The Mexican Revolution as Seen from the Inside," *New York Times*, June 25, 1911.

9. Almada, *Gobernadores*, 269.

10. Rail became so important to trade that by 1885, 75 percent of Mexican exports passed through El Paso. Lloyd, *Distrito Galeana*, 68.

11. Ibid., 50–51.

12. Ibid., 47–48.

13. Terrazas, for example, purchased the valuable Hacienda de Bustillos with his relative Pedro Zuloaga for a mere 7,200 pesos. He also purchased the Hacienda Terrazas at a low price, and it was sold in 1920 for 13 million pesos. Almada, *Gobernadores*, 271.

14. Almada, *Juárez y Terrazas*, 322–27.

15. Lloyd, *Distrito Galeana*, 243.

16. "Rise and Fall of Royal Families of Chihuahua," *New York Sun*, April 5, 1914.

17. Almada, *Gobernadores*, 268.

18. Wasserman, *Capitalistas, Caciques*, 102–103.

19. Ibid., 126.

20. Taxes increased 800 percent between 1892 and 1911. Knight, "Caudillos y Campesinos," 49.

21. Stephen Bonsal, "The Mexican Revolution as Seen from the Inside," *New York Times*, June 25, 1911. Bonsal wrote that Orozco paid more taxes on his little ranch than Terrazas did on his huge properties. See also "Rise and Fall of Royal Families of Chihuahua," *New York Sun*, April 5, 1914.

22. Almost $8 million in 2014 dollars.

23. Almost $7 million in 2014 dollars.

24. Almada, *Revolución*, 1:64–80.

25. Ibid., 1:120–22.

26. Wasserman, "Enrique C. Creel," 651.

27. Almada, *Revolución*, 1:120–22.

28. Wasserman, "Enrique C. Creel," 654.

29. Wasserman, *Capitalistas, Caciques*, 102, 133.

30. Attorney Sherburne Hopkins stated that to entice Creel and other directors to sit on El Aguila's board, Weetman Pearson gave Creel and each board member $200,000 in preferred stock. In addition, they received board seats on the lucrative Mexican National Railways. Testimony of Sherburne G. Hopkins, in U.S. Senate, Committee on Foreign Relations, *Revolutions in Mexico, Hearings*, 772, 776, 779.

31. Wasserman, *Capitalistas, Caciques*, 36.

32. Almada, *Revolución*, 1:72, 73.

33. Meyer, *Mexican Rebel*, 12.

34. Almada, *Gobernadores*, 269.

35. Stephen Bonsal, "The Mexican Revolution as Seen from the Inside," *New York Times*, June 25, 1911.

36. Ibid.

37. Sandels, "Antecedentes," 399.

38. Stephen Bonsal, "The Mexican Revolution as Seen from the Inside," *New York Times*, June 25, 1911.

39. Terrazas claimed that his properties were worth 1 million pesos when their value was 24 million pesos. With Abraham González in power, Terrazas was assessed almost 5 million pesos in back taxes. See also "Rise and Fall of Royal Families of Chihuahua," *New York Sun*, April 5, 1914. The newspaper *El Padre Padilla* noted, "It's about time." Almada, *Juárez y Terrazas*, 329.

40. Lloyd, "Rancheros and Rebellion," 105.

41. Lloyd, *Cinco ensayos*, 243–56.

42. Wasserman, *Persistent Oligarchs*, 25.

43. This figure appears low in as much as Creel received over 1.2 million pesos in rail subsidies.

44. Almada, *Gobernadores*, 443; Sandels, "Antecedentes," 399–400.

45. Wasserman, "Enrique C. Creel," 651.

46. Fuentes Mares, . . . *Y México Se Refugió en el Desierto*.

47. Almada, *Juárez y Terrazas*; Almada, *Gobernadores*. In his scathing critique, Almada accused Fuentes Mares of fraud and of making false statements. Regarding Fuentes Mares's defense of Terrazas over the Encinillas Hacienda, Almada said the account "contained not one truthful word and that it was all the author's literary fantasy." *Juarez y Terrazas*, 327.

48. Almada, *Gobernadores*, 268.

49. RDS, Letcher to State Dept., March 20, 1912, 812.00/3424.

50. Wasserman, *Capitalistas, Caciques*, 98.

Chapter 7

1. Lloyd, "Rancheros and Rebellion," 117.

2. Almada, *Revolución*, 1:112–13.

3. Albro, *Always a Rebel*, 66–67.

4. STP, Creel correspondence, Folders 8a–8c, Box 83.

5. Cockcroft, *Intellectual Precursors*; Cumberland, "Precursors," 344–56.

6. Beals, *Porfirio Díaz*, 274, 389.

7. Creelman, "President Diaz," 231.

8. Any reference to "Francisco Madero" or "Madero" refers to President Francisco I. Madero and not to his father, also Francisco Madero, who will be indicated as "father" or "Sr.," or others in the family who will be otherwise identified.

9. Skirius, "Railroad, Oil," 35.

10. Cockcroft, *Intellectual Precursors*, 61.

11. Madero became a faithful follower of spiritist Allan Kardec. An anecdote has Madero playing with a planchette, a Ouija board–like device, which he said wrote out the message that he was to be president of Mexico. Ross, *Francisco Madero*, 7, 8; Mayo, *Metaphysical Odyssey*, 50.

12. Butterfield, "Situation in Mexico," 653–54.

Chapter 8

1. Lloyd, *Cinco ensayos*.

2. Lloyd, *Distrito Galeana*, 64–67; Lloyd, "Modernización y corporatividad," 231, 235, 255.

3. Lloyd, "Rancheros and Rebellion," 109, 110.

4. Lloyd, "Modernización y corporatividad," 245. Alberto Terrazas was Creel's first cousin, brother-in-law, and his son-in-law from Alberto having married his niece, Creel's daughter.

5. Ibid., 252, 254.

6. Lloyd, *Distrito Galeana*, 155.

7. Ibid., 57–58.

8. Ibid., 15.

9. Cockcroft, *Intellectual Precursors*, 179; Vigil, "Revolution and Confusion," 146–47.

10. Nugent, *Spent Cartridges*, 68.

11. The filing fee was the equivalent of one and one-half months' salary in a time when work was scarce. Lloyd, *Distrito Galeana*, 234–36.

12. Katz, *Life and Times*, 32.

13. Stephen Bonsal, "The Mexican Revolution as Seen from the Inside," *New York Times*, June 25, 1911.

14. Katz, *Life and Times*, 32–38.

15. Sandels, "Antecedentes," 391.

16. Nugent, *Spent Cartridges*, 69–71.

17. Stephen Bonsal, "The Mexican Revolution as Seen from the Inside," *New York Times*, June 25, 1911. Bonsal wrote several lengthy reports for the *Times*. He reported hearing of many law cases in Chihuahua alleging that Luis Terrazas stole land from his neighbors, but with the courts under Terrazas's control, no cases were ever heard. It was the same with the federal courts, where hundreds of cases were on the books but were never processed or heard.

Chapter 9

1. Almada, *Cantón Rayón*, 15. A Capitán Andrés Orozco y Villaseñor served at Papigochi in 1710. He was still serving in 1717 and died in 1718.
2. Orozco, *Tierra de Libres*, 34.
3. Orozco's great-great-grandfather, José Roque Orozco, served as *capitán de milicias* and *alcalde local*, under a 1937 Orozco family tree.
4. Eaton, *Life under Two Flags*, 87, 121–24.
5. This figure is based on the 1930 Mexican census.
6. Testimony of Price McKinney, in U.S. Senate, Committee on Foreign Relations, *Revolutions in Mexico, Hearings*, 804.
7. Serrano, *Episodios*, 54–57.
8. Meyer, *Mexican Rebel*, 17. Orozco's pre-November 1910 Magonista activities, however, are unclear, with Orozco only clearly emerging as a revolutionary force just prior to the start of the revolution.

Chapter 10

1. Beals, *Porfirio Díaz*, 411–12.
2. Blanco, "Toribio Esquivel," 808.
3. Vázquez Gómez, *Memorias Políticas*, 28, 31.
4. Meyer, *Mexican Rebel*, 13.
5. *El Correo de Chihuahua*, January 14, 1910.
6. Beals, *Porfirio Díaz*, 412–13, 425.
7. Krauze, *Mexico: Biography of Power*, 249.
8. Vázquez Gómez, *Memorias Políticas*, 45.
9. Almada, *Vida, proceso y muerte de Abraham González*, 27–28.
10. Several incidents are noted as being precursors of the November 20 revolution. The first armed incidents were under the PLM Magonista banner in Cananea during the 1906 strike against the Cananea Consolidated Copper Company, the 1906 arrest of PLM insurgents in El Paso as they prepared to attack Ciudad Juárez, and the 1908 attack on Palomas. There were also events in 1910, including Tlaxcala in May; Sinaloa in June; Valladolid, Yucatán, also in June; Toribio Ortega's defiance on November 14 in Cuchillo Parado, Chihuahua; the well-known Aquiles Serdán incident in Puebla on November 18, and several others. Sánchez Lamego, *Historia Militar*, 1:13, 17–19, 24–29, 45; Katz, *Life and Times*, 60.
11. Almada, *Revolución*, 1:159, 161–69.
12. Raat, "Ideas and Society," 40–41.
13. Vázquez Gómez, *Memorias Políticas*, 59.

Chapter 11

1. Puente, *Pascual Orozco*, 25.
2. Whether or not Orozco knew it for certain, it was true. Like many whose families had lived in the area for several generations, they probably had several common direct ancestors, and certainly both were direct descendants of Juan Mateo

Domínguez de Mendoza—as were Albino Frías and Marcelo Caraveo among others.

3. Meyer, *Mexican Rebel*, 17–18; Puente, *Pascual Orozco*, 26–27. Orozco said this about removing Chávez: "Si lo liquido y triunfa la revolución, no vayan ustedes a cobrarme ese muerto" ("If I kill Chávez and the revolution triumphs, don't you go charge me with that").

4. Puente, *Pascual Orozco*, 27.

5. Meyer, *Mexican Rebel*, 18.

Chapter 12

1. Victor Orozco, for one, provides an explanation.

2. Orozco, *Tierra de Libres*, 38.

3. Orozco, *Estado de Chihuahua*, 247.

4. Almada, *Resumen de Historia*, 255–57; Almada, *Gobernadores*, 198; Terrazas, *Memorias*, 22; Orozco, *Tierra de Libres*, 38. According to Almada, Ignacio Orozco appeared to have switched sides by issuing a declaration with conservative undertones and joined the conservatives in the rebellion against Ochoa. Victor Orozco contends that Ignacio Orozco always remained a liberal.

5. Not everyone was against the French. Captain Reyes Orozco fought for the French in Chihuahua and was later imprisoned for treason. The residents of San Isidro petitioned for his pardon and release, which were granted. Almada, *Gobernadores*, 244.

6. Ibid., 235, 291.

7. Orozco, *Pascual Orozco (San Isidro)*, 19–20; Orozco, *Tierra de Libres*, 39.

8. Orozco, *Tierra de Libres*, 39.

9. Orozco, *Pascual Orozco (San Isidro)*, 15, 18, 21–22.

10. Ibid., 24.

11. Serrano, *Episodios*, 56–57.

12. Caraveo, *Crónica de la Revolución*, 39.

13. Baptismal record of Pascual Orozco, Parish Baptismal Records, Nuestra Señora de la Purísima Concepción, Ciudad Guerrero, March 30, 1882.

14. In a report to Creel dated October 20, 1906, Francisco Antillón, then political jefe in Temósachic, said that his father was jefe in Miñaca and that his brother Elias had a position in San Isidro. It indicates that the Antillón family was closely tied to Creel and to Chávez. STP, Folder 8a, Box 83.

15. Meyer, *Mexican Rebel*, 17, citing a May 18, 1909, report from Félix Bárcenos to Creel.

16. Antillón's report to Creel noted that an unknown individual in San Isidro was reading a newspaper critical of the government and that one or two individuals accompanied that man. The report noted that one of the individuals might have been Pascual Orozco. It did not specify "Jr." or "Sr." STP, Antillón at Temósachic to Creel, October 20, 1906, Creel 1906 Gubernatorial correspondence, Folder 8a, Box 83; Meyer, *Mexican Rebel*, 17.

17. Orozco, *Pascual Orozco (San Isidro)*, 24, 26.

18. Orozco, *Tierra de Libres*, 36–41; Siller Vázquez, *1911: La historia*, 1:51. See also Orozco, *Estado de Chihuahua*, 245–48.

Chapter 13

1. The individuals who rode out of San Isidro were Pascual Orozco Vázquez, Pascual Orozco Merino, Albino Frías Chacón, Francisco Salido, Marcelo Caraveo, Samuel Caraveo, Albino Frías, José Rochín, Luis Solís, Graciano Frías, José Caraveo Frías, Antonio Frías, Leonardo Solís, Ramón Solís, Alberto Orozco Varela, Cruz Márquez, Victor Solís, Jesús Domínguez, Jesús María Frías, Joaquín González, Jesús Antonio González, Fidel González, José González, Jesús Morales, José Morales, José María Márquez, Felícitas Márquez, Ascensión Enríquez, Hilario Díaz, Emilio Valenzuela, Eduardo Hermosillo, Flavio Hermosillo, Reydesel Hermosillo, Ramón Aragón, Abelardo Amaya, José María Peña, Ramón Estrada, Agustín Estrada, Laureano Herrera, Tadeo Vázquez, José Aragón, José Chacón, Camilo Valenzuela, and Tomás Orozco Vázquez. Victor Orozco, "Los comienzos de la Revolución," *El Diario de Juárez*, December 2, 2012. The record is in conflict regarding the number of men in the original San Isidro group. The only member to have written a memoir was Marcelo Caraveo. He wrote that twenty-some odd men were in the force, and he named twenty-nine of them. Caraveo, *Crónica*, 38. San Isidro historian Victor Orozco named forty-three individuals as noted above. Given his careful study of the subject, this is the most credible estimate. Michael Meyer wrote that the estimates varied from seventeen to forty-one, and he found credible the estimate of forty-one noted by Amaya, *Madero y los auténticos revolucionarios*, 167. Meyer, *Mexican Rebel*, 191.

2. *Diccionario histórico y biográfico*, 2:486; Sánchez Lamego, *Historia Militar*, 1:46.

3. Serafina Orozco interview, in Martínez, *Fragments*, 42.

4. Antillón's luck ran out two days later when he was arrested on November 21. A news story reported that he was made to ride a horse between rebel soldiers, who shouted "Down with Díaz!" He was forced to pay a $2,000 ransom for his liberty. Another report said that he escaped by using a disguise. "Excitement at Chihuahua and Many Reports of No Trouble," *El Paso Herald*, November 24, 1910, 2; "No Harm Coming to Americans," *El Paso Herald*, December 1, 1910, 11. Antillón later took refuge in El Paso, where he sold groceries, but he was back in Chihuahua by 1917.

5. Meyer, *Mexican Rebel*, 19.

6. Almada, *Revolución*, 1:171–72.

7. "Revolt Crushed, Creel Declares," *New York Times*, November 24, 1910.

8. Beals, *Porfirio Díaz*, 423.

9. *Diccionario histórico y biográfico*, 2:564.

10. Sánchez Lamego, *Historia Militar*, 1:48–49.

11. Ibid., 47.

12. It seems more likely that Villa was not there. Meyer, *Mexican Rebel*, 22. Katz, *Life and Times*, 849n117, covers the conflicting reports on Pancho and Cerro Prieto. Most likely, Villa was not at Cerro Prieto either because he quarreled with Pascual or else because he left the area with Pascual's approval. See also Taibo's discussion in *Pancho Villa*, 63, 74.

13. Orozco, calling himself first in command, ordered Salido to attack federal troops. Orozco also noted that José de la Luz Blanco and José Rascón had disobeyed and were only involved for the money. RDS, Orozco to Salido, December 11, 1910, in United States, *Foreign Relations of the United States, 1911*, 412, File No. 812.00/875.

14. Report of General Navarro on Battle of Cerro Prieto. AHDN, Navarro to Rodríguez, December 12, 1911, exp. XI/481.5/61, folio 1151.

15. Meyer, *Mexican Rebel*, 23, 52–53; Caraveo, *Crónica*, 44.

16. Sánchez Lamego, *Historia Militar*, 1:57–58.

17. Siller Vázquez, *1911: La historia*, 1:52.

18. Marcelo Caraveo wrote that they retreated to Chopeque. Caraveo, *Crónica*, 42.

19. Orozco, *Pascual Orozco (San Isidro)*, 42.

20. Almada, *Vida, proceso y muerte de Abraham González*, 24.

21. Katz, *Life and Times*, 79. Nepotism was second nature to the clan, whose members had a decided preference for consanguinity and affinity in their marriages.

22. Almada, *Gobernadores*, 452.

23. Beals, *Porfirio Díaz*, 427.

24. Silvestre published a small ad in *El Padre Padilla* on February 11, stating that he had been released under bond, and it remained to be seen whether he was to remain out. STP, Outgoing correspondence. Sandels, "Silvestre Terrazas, the Press," 209.

25. Almada, *Vida, proceso y muerte de Abraham González*, 75–76.

26. Sánchez Lamego, *Historia Militar*, 1:130; Sánchez Azcona, *Apuntes*, 192, 193; Carman, *United States Customs and the Madero Revolution*, 18. Sánchez Lamego said that of the three hundred men Benavides promised, he had only ten when he met Madero.

27. Beals, *Porfirio Díaz*, 423.

28. Vázquez Gómez, *Memorias Políticas*, 63, 65, 67; Kerig, *Luther T. Ellsworth*, 34.

Chapter 14

1. AHDN, Navarro to Guerra, January 7, 1911, exp. XI/481.5/61, folio 271.

2. "Young General Commands," *New York Times*, February 3, 1911. Pascual was not yet a general. At most, he was then a colonel, a rank Madero officially conferred on him two months later. Guzmán was the father of the well-known writer Martín Luis Guzmán.

3. Serrano, *Episodios*, 260.

4. John Sneed, "Day of Inactivity in Mexican Troubles, Reduction of Orozco," *Dallas Morning News*, February 11, 1911.

5. Garibaldi, *Toast to Rebellion*, 225–27; Siller Vázquez, *1911: La historia*, 1:73. In addition to Hay, the delegation included Raúl Madero, José Garibaldi, Rafael Aguilar, and Roque González Garza. Serrano, *Episodios*, 262.

6. Siller Vázquez, *1911: La historia*, 1:79.

7. Meyer, *Mexican Rebel*, 24–26.

8. Caraveo, *Crónica*, 47.

9. Almada, *Vida, proceso y muerte de Abraham González*, 39.

10. Almada, *Revolución*, 1:197.

11. Ibid., 1:200–201; Sánchez Lamego, *Historia Militar*, 1:98.

Chapter 15

1. "Reform in Mexico Needed—Limantour," *New York Times*, February 21, 1911.

2. "Expect Big Change in Mexican Cabinet," *New York Times*, March 17, 1911.

3. "Watch Crisis in Mexico Closely," *Phoenix Arizona Gazette*, March 25, 1911. U.S. consul Letcher reported that "Creel and the Terrazas family generally, as a result of oppressions and tyrannies practiced by them on the people of the state of Chihuahua were exceedingly unpopular. Creel himself was particularly distrusted." RDS, Letcher to State Dept., October 17, 1913, File No. 812.00/9484, 12.

4. Siller Vázquez, *1911: La historia*, 1:94; "De la Barra Tells of Diaz's Reforms," *New York Times*, March 27, 1911.

5. "Madero Will Fight Unless Diaz Retires," *New York Times*, April 3, 1911.

6. Jorge Vera Estañol noted that before leaving Europe, Limantour met with Bernardo Reyes, and the two agreed that Díaz would have to leave office. It was determined that they would both lead the nation, but left unsaid was whether it was to be a Limantour-Reyes ticket or the reverse. Limantour expected to have the Maderos' support should he make that move. Vera Estañol, *Revolución*, 129.

7. The Maderos had already attempted private negotiations with Díaz. In late February 1911, Madero's father, Francisco, and three of his brothers and Rafael Hernández, Madero's cousin, invited Francisco Vázquez Gómez to meet with them and a Díaz confidant in Corpus Christi, Texas. In another instance that added to the Madero family antipathy toward Vázquez Gómez, the Maderos alone met the Díaz envoy, because Vázquez Gómez would only meet with a credentialed Díaz delegate. Sánchez Azcona, *Apuntes*, 213–17.

8. Hopkins testimony, in U.S. Senate, Committee on Foreign Relations, *Revolutions in Mexico, Hearings*, 785.

9. In his *Memorias*, Vázquez had a different account of the meeting with some documents in support. He claimed that no one, including himself, demanded Díaz's resignation in New York and that his breach with Gustavo involved his reprimand of Gustavo over Gustavo's gushing about Limantour to the press, something Vázquez found inappropriate considering that Limantour had been the actual president for the previous five years, according to Vázquez, and was responsible for having named Corral vice president. The Maderos were also upset over Vázquez's tone of voice toward Limantour. In his memoir, Vázquez was

convinced that the Maderos had a deal with Limantour to name Limantour vice president so that he could become president when Díaz died or retired. Vázquez, *Memorias Políticas*, 97–98, 148; Vela González, *Diario de la Revolución*, 1:405–406.

10. Siller Vázquez, *1911: La historia*, 1:85.

11. Limantour, *Apuntes*.

12. Esquivel Obregón had Anti-Reelection Party credibility, as he had been at its convention heading the National Democratic Party faction and had his name placed into contention for the presidency and vice presidency, losing the presidential nomination to Madero by a vote of 159 to 23. Sánchez Azcona, *Apuntes*, 77. After the convention, Esquivel Obregón distanced himself from Madero and refused his call to revolt.

13. Vázquez Gómez's demand for credentials had a reasonable basis. Issuing credentials would give the rebels a better claim to belligerent status carrying the right to purchase arms and obtain international recognition.

14. Vera Estañol, *Revolución*, 158–59; Beals, *Porfirio Díaz*, 433–37.

Chapter 16

1. Meyer, *Mexican Rebel*, 28.

2. Taibo, *Pancho Villa*, 63. See also Katz, *Life and Times*, 75, 435.

3. Katz, *Life and Times*, 75, 435.

4. Caraveo, *Crónica*, 48.

5. Taibo, *Pancho Villa*, 69.

6. Serafina Orozco interview, in Martínez, *Fragments*, 42, 43.

7. Almada, *Revolución*, 1: 220–22.

8. *El Paso Herald*, April 18 and 19, 1911.

9. At that moment, Díaz was informally represented in Ciudad Juárez by Toribio Esquivel Obregón and Óscar Braniff. Madero had received clearance from Francisco Vázquez Gómez to issue the ultimatum as mentioned in a letter from Federico González Garza. BNM, González Garza to Madero, April 20, 1911, Fondo González Garza, Doc. 54686.

10. *El Paso Herald*, April 20 and 21, 1911.

11. Sánchez Lamego, *Historia Militar*, 1:103; *El Paso Herald*, April 22, 1911.

12. Katz, *Life and Times*, 109.

13. They extended the armistices of April 21, April 27, and May 2. BNM, Letters of Gen. Juan J. Navarro of April 27 and May 2, 1911, Docs. 43249, 43624, and 63750; BNM, Madero to Navarro, May 2, 1911, Doc. 63365.

14. The general assumption was that Francisco Madero Sr., his financier brother Ernesto, and their nephew Rafael L. Hernández were all pro-Díaz Científicos who were for leaving the general in the presidency. The record, however, was not that clear as shown by the impassioned letter sent by Ernesto Madero to Francisco Madero and his military leaders on May 2 in which Ernesto implored the rebels not to cede to Díaz's demand to remain in office. BNM, Ernesto Madero to Francisco Madero, May 2, 1910, Doc. 54161.

15. Vázquez Gómez, *Memorias Políticas*, 137.

16. Ibid.

17. These were confusing negotiations. There was Carvajal, Díaz's official, credentialed representative, but there were also Limantour's unofficial mediators, Esquivel Obregón and Braniff. On Madero's side, there was Madero himself and his official delegate Vázquez Gómez. Finally, there were several members of the Madero family communicating with both sides. There were private communications between most of these individuals. The only one maintaining formality in his communications was Carvajal, who took his instructions from Limantour. Madero appeared to have an official public position on Díaz's resignation but privately told Limantour's mediators that it was only a desire and not a requirement. Apparently, Madero was given a confidential letter from Díaz promising resignation at an undetermined time, which note Madero promised to keep secret. Vera Estañol, *Revolución*, 169, 172.

18. Vázquez Gómez, *Memorias Políticas*, 148, 151.

19. BNM, Carvajal note of May 6, 1911, Doc. 64675.

20. The number of conflicting accounts contributes to the confusion, including those of Juan Gualberto Amaya, Marcelo Caraveo, Máximo Castillo, Federico González Garza, Madero, Toribio Esquivel Obregón, Roque Estrada, Heliodoro Olea Arias, Juan Sánchez Azcona, Francisco Vázquez Gómez, and Francisco Villa.

21. The most explosive charges were leveled by Manuel Bonilla and by Federico González Garza, Madero's presidential secretary, who said that Limantour's delegates persuaded Orozco to pursue their plan and later to betray Madero, allegations Esquivel and others vehemently denied. González Garza, *La Revolución*, 275–76.

22. Carvajal confirmed that his role had ended. BNM, Carvajal to Madero, May 6, 1911, Doc. 64675, AMA Ms.M/228 c.2; "Madero Ends the Armistice," *New York Times*, May 7, 1911.

23. Villa thought that Madero erred in following the Boer general's counsel. Guzmán, *Memorias*, 85.

24. This is another example of the highly unorthodox activities surrounding the rebel camp, such as Díaz delegates being given the opportunity to meet with rebel military leaders to persuade them to call off the attack. This is more proof that Madero was not committed to the attack himself and was certainly open to Díaz continuing in office. It was also confirmation of criticisms leveled by some rebels, such as Villa, that Madero was too much under the influence of his family and his Boer advisor.

25. Esquivel Obregón, *Democracia y personalismo*, 54–58; Siller Vázquez, *1911: La historia*, 1:139.

26. The U.S. military commander in El Paso had that day warned both rebels and federal forces that stray rounds landing in El Paso would result in U.S. intervention. Sánchez Lamego, *Historia Militar*, 1:103.

27. In his memoir, Roque Estrada wrote that Madero himself had left Ciudad Juárez when he heard, incorrectly, that Díaz had resigned. Madero soon, however, returned to his adobe headquarters. Estrada, *Revolución*, 469.

28. "Vivid Story of Battle of Juarez by a Participant," *New York Times*, May 21, 1911. Much of the battle's chronology was taken from this lengthy article written by an unnamed American rebel officer serving under Boer general Ben Viljoen.

29. *New York Times*, May 8, 1911; *El Paso Herald*, May 9, 1911, 4.

30. *New York Times*, May 8, 1911.

31. BNM, Madero to Esquivel Obregón and Braniff, May 8, 1911, Doc. 64296, AMA Ms.M/243 c.3.

32. Esquivel Obregón, *Democracia y personalismo*, 60.

33. Guzmán, *Memorias*, 85–87.

34. Garibaldi's account differed as to details but agreed on the major points. He wrote that he, Orozco, and Villa met on the evening of the seventh and without Madero's approval planned to start the attack that night. Garibaldi, *Toast to Rebellion*, 287.

35. Sánchez Lamego, *Historia Militar*, 1:106; *El Paso Herald*, May 6, 1911.

36. Siller Vázquez, *1911: La historia*, 1:151. The same officer earlier called the rebels "cowards." "Tamborel Calls Rebels Cowards," *El Paso Herald*, front page, April 21, 1911. Esquivel Obregón mentioned another theory that rebels began to fire on federal troops after federal soldiers shot at a woman as she returned to the city after having taken food to rebels. Rebels, infuriated at federal forces, began shooting. Esquivel Obregón, *Democracia y personalismo*, 63. See also "Madero Lost Control of the Insurrectos, *Phoenix Arizona Republican*, May 9, 1911.

37. "Madero Holds Army Back," *New York Times*, May 9, 1911.

38. BNM, Madero to Orozco, May 8, 1911, Doc. 64576, AMA MsM/246 c.3; CEHM, Madero to Federico González Garza, May 8, 1911, Fondo González Garza, CMXV.17.1704.1 and CMXV.17.1706.1.

39. Sánchez Lamego, *Historia Militar*, 1:105–107; AGN, "La Insubordinación de Orozco," June 9, 1938, 34; AGN, Unnamed, undated publication, Colección INEHRM, exp. 430.

40. Siller Vázquez, *1911: La historia*, 1:156, 169. See also "Hard Fighting All Day," *New York Times*, May 10, 1911.

41. The Sheldon Hotel was the most important hotel of the Mexican Revolution. El Paso was the most important American center for the revolution, "and it was in the rooms and lobbies of its Sheldon Hotel that countless revolutionaries met, planned, plotted and prepared to fight one another or the federal government." Katz, *Life and Times*, 670.

42. Siller Vázquez, *1911: La historia*, 1:170. "Vivid Story of Battle of Juarez," *New York Times*, May 21, 1911; and *El Paso Herald*, May 9, 1911, 2, reported that Madero slept in his adobe headquarters or in a tent on the Mexican side, an account Vázquez agreed with in his *Memorias*, 172–73.

43. Almada, *Revolución*, 1:229–30. Authors Siller Vázquez and Berumen state that Italian Garibaldi wrote in his memoir that Orozco and Villa agreed on the night of the seventh, without consulting Madero, to start fighting on the eighth. Siller Vázquez, *1911: La historia*, 1:81. This is also the view of Friedrich Katz, who said that Orozco and Villa ordered rebel Reyes Robinson to have his troops fire at the federal soldiers. Katz, *Life and Times*, 109. Taibo also finds it more credible than not that Orozco and Villa conspired to start the shooting. Taibo wrote that to keep their hands clean after they issued the order, Orozco and Villa crossed into El Paso to eat or rest. Taibo, *Pancho Villa*, 94. Máximo Castillo said that the rebels started the firing because they disagreed with Madero's order to withdraw from Ciudad Juárez. Vargas Valdés, *Máximo Castillo*, 68. Orozco officer Marcelo Caraveo had a different view. He insisted that the shooting was not ordered but was instead provoked when some rebels approached federal trenches in search of water, setting off the gunfire. Caraveo, *Crónica*, 50. In his memoir, Vázquez Gómez agreed with Caraveo that the gunfire was accidental (*Memorias Políticas*, 171), and a credible El Paso observer also agreed. Joseph U. Sweeney statement, in Martínez, *Fragments*, 79. Sweeney was El Paso's mayor from 1907 to 1910.
44. Campobello, *Apuntes*, 18.
45. Beals, *Porfirio Díaz*, 438.
46. Estrada, *Revolución*, 471.

Chapter 17

1. "Hard Fighting All Day," *New York Times*, May 10, 1911; Siller Vázquez, *1911: La historia*, 1:169.
2. Siller Vázquez, *1911: La historia*, 1:169, 170.
3. Navarro, *Toma de Ciudad Juárez*, 7.
4. *El Paso Herald*, May 9, 1911, 3.
5. Caraveo, *Crónica*, 51.
6. "Hard Fighting All Day," *New York Times*, May 10, 1911.
7. *El Paso Herald*, May 8–10, 1911.
8. "Juarez Falls, General Navarro a Prisoner," *New York Times*, May 11, 1911. See also http://poweltonhistoryblog.blogspot.com/2009/11/another-innocent-swarthmore-student.html.
9. Siller Vázquez, *1911: La historia*, 1:174.
10. "Hard Fighting All Day," *New York Times*, May 10, 1911.
11. Testimony of Braulio Hernández, in U.S. Senate, Committee on Foreign Relations, *Revolutions in Mexico, Hearings*, 558. This also agrees with reports that after they secretly ordered the fighting to start on the morning of May 8, Orozco and Villa spent the day in El Paso to distance themselves from the unauthorized rebel attack.
12. Siller Vázquez, *1911: La historia*, 1:169, 174.
13. Navarro, *Toma de Ciudad Juárez*, 9.
14. Siller Vázquez, *1911: La historia*, 1:186–87.

15. Garibaldi said that Navarro surrendered to him. Garibaldi called Madero and told him that Orozco and Villa wanted to execute Navarro. Garibaldi, *Toast to Rebellion*, 294. Villa insisted that Navarro surrendered to his troops, and Navarro's sword was given to José Orozco. Guzmán, *Memorias*, 95.

16. *El Paso Herald*, May 10, 1911, 3.

17. "Juarez Falls, General Navarro a Prisoner," *New York Times*, May 11, 1911; "Madero Has Cabinet and Talks of Peace," *New York Times*, May 12, 1911.

18. Estrada, *Revolución*, 484.

19. There are some battle reports compiled by several observers, such as the one by Roque González Garza. CEHM, Roque González Garza, May 11, 1911, Fondo González Garza, CMXV.18.1739.1.

Chapter 18

1. "Orozco Arrests Madero in Row over Cabinet," *New York Times*, May 14, 1911.

2. *El Paso Herald*, May 10, 1911, 3.

3. Meyer, *Mexican Rebel*, 32, 34; Puente, *Pascual Orozco*, 32; "Madero Has Cabinet and Talks of Peace," *New York Times*, May 12, 1911.

4. Bonilla, *Diez años*, 207.

5. Siller Vázquez, *1911: La historia*, 1:203; Taibo, *Pancho Villa*, 104. Frías later sent Madero a handwritten note saying that it was never his intention to harm Navarro. BNM, Doc. 61718, May 18, 1911, AMA Ms.M/399 c.4.

6. Esquivel Obregón, *Democracia y personalismo*, 73–74.

7. The dates involved are in conflict. Some put the day of the altercation as May 12, but reliable news reports say it was May 13.

8. BNM, Circular, May 12, 1911, Doc. 66193, AMA Ms.M/279 c.3; BNM, Madero to Aguilar, May 12, 1911, Doc. 66188, AMA Ms.M/275 c.3. It was also possible that on May 12 Orozco attended the burial of Daniel Orozco, Pascual's cousin and a rebel soldier in Ciudad Juárez, who was killed when cleaning his pistol. *El Paso Herald*, May 12, 1911.

9. Caraveo, *Crónica*, 52

10. Esquivel Obregón, *Democracia y personalismo*, 74

11. Villa had lost several close friends in the group but not family members.

12. Guzmán, *Memorias*, 97–98.

13. Olea Arias, *Apuntes Históricos*, 102–103.

14. Esquivel Obregón, *Democracia y personalismo*, 74–75.

15. Ibid., 76.

16. Roque Estrada wrote in his memoir that Madero and Abraham González personally gave him their versions of the event. Estrada, *Revolución*, 476–77.

17. Vargas Valdés, *Máximo Castillo*, 149–52.

18. Marcelo Caraveo remembered that he and Orozco kept insisting on support and food for the troops. Caraveo wrote that Madero claimed to be busy whenever they tried to see him, seeing the press and attending banquets. Madero finally saw them and promised payment the next day. Caraveo, *Crónica*, 52.

19. Siller Vázquez, *1911: La historia*, 1:205.

20. Aguilar, *Madero sin máscara*, 84; "Orozco Arrests Madero in Row over Cabinet," *New York Times*, May 14, 1911.

21. Olea Arias, *Apuntes Históricos*, 104.

22. BNM, May 13, 1911, Doc. 62465, AMA Ms.M/301 c.3.

23. Meyer, *Mexican Rebel*, 33–36; "Orozco Arrests Madero in Row over Cabinet," *New York Times*, May 14, 1911; *El Diario*, May 14, 1911; *El Paso Herald*, May 13, 1911.

24. "Orozco Arrests Madero in Row over Cabinet," *New York Times*, May 14, 1911.

25. Bonilla, *Diez años*, 207, 209.

26. In addition to several detailed newspaper articles, among the accounts are those in several memoirs noted in the bibliography, including those of Aguilar, Amaya, Caraveo, Castillo in Vargas Valdés, Esquivel Obregón, Estrada, Garibaldi, González Garza, Madero, Olea Arias, Sánchez Azcona, Vázquez Gómez, and Villa in Guzmán. Historians have also written in detail about the event. Beezley, *Insurgent Governor*, 66; Katz, *Life and Times*, 111–14; Meyer, *Mexican Rebel*, 29–37; Ross, *Francisco Madero*, 167; Siller Vázquez, *1911: La historia*, 1:139, 203, 208; Taibo, *Pancho Villa*, 104–108, 112. News articles published on the day of the altercation recounted Madero's arrest and all of Orozco's complaints, that the troops were not fed or paid; that Navarro should be processed as a war criminal; and that the cabinet should resign. "Rebellion, Madero put under Arrest by the Chiefs of his Insurrecto Army," *Kansas City Star*, May 13, 1911.

27. Manuel Calero criticized Madero's forgiving Orozco and in "inflating Orozco's vanity" by exaggerating his value. To Calero, within Orozco's crude persona resided an ambitious man who wanted to be a general in the regular army or governor. Calero, *Decenio*, 94.

28. These included Sánchez Azcona, Roque Estrada and González Garza. Francisco Vázquez Gómez also believed that Esquivel Obregón and Braniff persuaded Orozco to betray Madero. Vázquez Gómez, *Memorias políticas*, 182–83.

29. Estrada, *Revolución*, 476, 477.

30. Garibaldi wrote a minimal account that Orozco and Villa demanded the execution of Navarro and other federal officers and that Orozco with pistol in hand threatened Madero. Garibaldi, *Toast to Rebellion*, 296.

31. Guzmán, *Memorias*, 99.

32. González Garza, *La Revolución*, 276.

33. Estrada, *Revolución*, 477.

34. Almada, *Revolución*, 1:232.

35. If Madero had a strong conviction about maintaining civilian control, he abandoned it, as the three war ministers after Carranza were all military men—Eugenio Rascón, José González Salas, and Manuel M. Plata.

36. Taibo, *Pancho Villa*, 107. "Orozco Arrests Madero in Row over Cabinet," *New York Times*, May 14, 1911; "Francisco I Madero y Pascual Orozco disputan por la vida del Gral. Navarro," *El Diario* (Mexico City), May 14, 1911.

37. Estrada, *Revolución*, 472. Some, including Madero, said that Orozco did not demand Navarro's head; rather, it was Orozco who suggested that the general should be freed. Madero, *Apuntes políticos*, 85–86. Madero's account contradicts several versions, including Villa in Guzmán's, *Memorias*, 97; Caraveo, *Crónica*, 52; Estrada, *Revolución*, 472, 473; and Olea Arias, *Apuntes Históricos*, 103. See also Almada, *Revolución*, 1:232.

38. "Madero Triumphs in Clash with General Orozco," *San Antonio Express*, May 14, 1911; BNM, Madero to Orozco, May 15, 1911, Doc. 48349, AMA Ms.M/344 bis c.3; BNM, May 15, 1911, Doc. 38944, AMA Ms.M/344 c c.3; CEHM, Madero and Orozco letters, May 15, 1911, Fondo González Garza, CMXV.18.1753.1.

39. Taracena, *Verdadera Revolución (1912–1914)*, 56.

40. Almada, *Revolución*, 1:240.

Chapter 19

1. BNM, Madero to Díaz, May 17, 1911, Doc. 66193, AMA Ms.M/258 c c.3.

2. "Peace Agreement Signed at Juarez," *New York Times*, May 22, 1911. José María Pino Suárez was also to sign but could not be located. Apparently, he had not been notified.

3. Ross, *Francisco Madero*, 165.

4. Katz, *Life and Times*, 119–20.

5. Almada, *Revolución*, 1:257–60; Beezley, *Insurgent Governor*, 72.

6. Stephen Bonsal, "Rioters Shot in Mexico City; Diaz Hold On," *New York Times*, May 25, 1911; "Diaz Resigns, De la Barra In," *New York Times*, May 26, 1911; Beals, *Porfirio Díaz*, 444; Vera Estañol, *Revolución*, 185–87. In fact, Díaz had been ill. He had an operation on his mouth, followed by a painful infection. Ibid., 179.

7. "Diaz Slips Away Bound for Spain," *New York Times*, May 27, 1911.

8. "Diaz Departs and Warns Mexico," *New York Times*, June 1, 1911; Beals, *Porfirio Díaz*, 448–49.

9. Shapleigh, "¡Viva Los Licenciados!" The article provides a comprehensive description of the event and the festivities surrounding Madero's victory.

10. "Madero Starts Today," *New York Times*, June 2, 1911.

11. "Mexico City Shaken, 63 Dead," *New York Times*, June 8, 1911.

12. Beezley, *Insurgent Governor*, 74, 75.

13. Meyer, *Mexican Rebel*, 38; Beezley, *Insurgent Governor*, 75.

14. *El Padre Padilla*, June 15, 1911.

15. Meyer, *Mexican Rebel*, 58. According to one observer, "All the world acclaimed him; they waited breathless to hear him speak, even a word." Starr, *Mexico and the United States*, 339.

16. Ibid.

17. Puente, *Pascual Orozco*, 34–37; Almada, *Revolución*, 1:244–45.

18. Puente, *Pascual Orozco*, 30–31. Braulio Hernández said that Orozco expected 100,000 pesos. Hernández testimony, in U.S. Senate, Committee on Foreign Relations, *Revolutions in Mexico, Hearings*, 559; "Trusted Chief Turns Traitor,"

El Paso Morning Times, March 6, 1912; Taracena, *Verdadera Revolución (1912–1914)*, 227; Meyer, *Mexican Rebel*, 54n4. Frederick Starr wrote that Madero paid Orozco 50,000 pesos for his services, but Orozco demanded an additional 50,000 pesos, and Madero refused, making Orozco unhappy. Starr, *Mexico and the United States*, 340.

19. Almada, *Revolución*, 1:240; *El Paso Morning Times*, March 12, 1912.
20. "American Millions in Mexico Hard Hit," *New York Times*, June 16, 1911.
21. Almada, *Gobernadores*, 456, 457.
22. Puente wrote, "Those who would year after year defraud the public treasury were upset over the presence of an honest man [González]." The elite knew that González was an unmovable obstacle, so they decided to make war to the death on González. Puente, *Pascual Orozco*, 71–72.
23. *El Paso Herald*, June 21, 1911; Beezley, *Insurgent Governor*, 75.

Chapter 20

1. Almada, *Revolución*, 1:245.
2. Ibid.
3. Beezley, *Insurgent Governor*, 40–41.
4. One observer wrote that Orozco was angry and was Madero's worst enemy, as were Francisco Vázquez Gómez and Roque Estrada. CEHM, Emeterio de la Garza to Limantour, October 18, 1911, Fondo Limantour, CDLIV.2a.1910.18.74.
5. In a Chihuahua poll, those responding favored Vázquez Gómez over Pino Suárez by a margin of 566 to 22. Almada, *Vida, proceso y muerte de Abraham González*, 66–67.
6. "This Indian will not be vice president." Vázquez Gómez, *Memorias Políticas*, 287. Another factor against Vázquez Gómez, in addition to the terrible relationship that he had with the Maderos, was that he was also seen as a former Reyista. Reyes had returned from Europe and declined a cabinet position. He was instead toying with a run against Madero, a fact that incensed Madero's partisans with Vázquez Gómez, and deteriorated the standing he once enjoyed in the party. Reyes decided not to run and instead urged his supporters to ignore the elections. He left Mexico for San Antonio. Sánchez Azcona, *Apuntes*, 306, 323.
7. Almada, *Revolución*, 1:246; Hernández testimony at the fall hearings in October 1912, in U.S. Senate, Committee on Foreign Relations, *Revolutions in Mexico, Hearings*, 549.
8. Sánchez Azcona, *Apuntes*, 304.
9. Beezley, *Insurgent Governor*, 86, 87.
10. Ibid., 81.
11. Katz, *Life and Times*, 134.
12. Meyer, *Mexican Rebel*, 43, 44.
13. CEHM, Electoral vote tabulation, October 20, 1911, Fondo González Garza, CMXV.22.2158.1.
14. Vargas Valdés, *Máximo Castillo*, 75.

15. Puente, *Pascual Orozco*, 71.

16. Almada, *Revolución*, 1:248, 249; Caraveo, *Crónica*, 60.

17. "Inaugurate Madero in Mexican Capital," *New York Times*, November 7, 1911.

18. Bonilla, *Diez años*, 294.

19. Vera Estañol, *Revolución*, 235. To Vera, Madero's first day in office was the start of his decline and the rise of another's star, as Orozco was the idol of the crowds that day.

20. "Madero's New Cabinet," *New York Times*, October 14, 1911; Ross, *Francisco Madero*, 218.

21. Katz, *Life and Times*, 132 and 852n11. Others thought that there were three cabinet Científicos, Ernesto Madero, Rafael Hernández, and Manuel Calero, all members of the Limantour group. Koth, "Madero, Dehesa y el cientificismo," 400n6.

22. Vázquez Gómez, *Memorias Políticas*, 249, 349.

23. García Moisés, *Madero*, 17–18.

24. "Alleged Orozco Letters Seized," *Dallas Morning News*, December 4, 1911.

25. Meyer, *Mexican Rebel*, 43; *El Paso Herald*, November 27, 1911, and December 2, 4, 5, and 11, 1911.

26. Vera Estañol, *Revolución*, 251–52; "Reyes, a prisoner says his revolt was a failure," *El Paso Herald*, December 26, 1911. The American ambassador wrote that the Reyes uprising "to the relief of all factions [came] to a most ignominious, undignified, and grotesque end." RDS, Wilson to Knox, January 23, 1912, File No. 812.00/2710.

27. Almada, *Revolución*, 1:271; "New Revolution Menaces Mexico," *New York Times*, August, 3, 1911.

28. Almada, *Revolución*, 1:272.

29. Ibid., 275, 276; Vera Estañol, *Revolución*, 253. Zapata named northerner Orozco chief even if he had never met him because no other name had the same prestige. Magaña, *Zapata*, 2:91–92.

30. RDS, State Dept. to Mexican Ambassador, January 4, 1912, File No. 812.00/2665. Mexicans also reminded the State Department of Emilio Vázquez Gómez's revolutionary activities in Texas. RDS, Wilson to State Dept., January 6, 1912, File No. 812.00/2692.

31. "El General Orozco Llegó anoche á la Capital," *El País*, January 19, 1912. Orozco denied that he had refused to fight Zapata and claimed that he did not know whether he would do so.

32. Almada, *Revolución*, 1:277, 284. See also Almada, *Vida, proceso y muerte de Abraham González*, 115, noting another version recounting that Orozco was asked to support approval for an unlimited leave for González with his replacement being Julio Luján, a former Porfirista. That account says that Orozco refused to go along with the plan. González agreed with the version but said that no replacement was suggested. Publicly, Madero said that Orozco was not asked to combat Zapata and was given duties in the North. Orozco said he was disposed to obey his orders. "Orozco Organizará los Cuerpos Rurales en el Norte," *El País*, January 20, 1912.

33. Almada, *Revolución*, 1:277–78.
34. Zapata quickly sent an emissary to Chihuahua to deliver the plan to Orozco and to explain why they would continue the revolution. Orozco was suspicious at first but soon promised in writing that he would support Zapata. Magaña, *Zapata*, 2:97–98; Meyer, *Mexican Rebel*, 47–50.
35. Almada, *Revolución*, 1:277.
36. Ibid., 1:279, 287. Hernández might have decided to split with González after Hernández was passed over and Aureliano González was appointed interim governor.
37. Almada, *Revolución*, 1:281–82; *New York Times*, February 26, 1912; *El Paso Herald*, February 2, 1912.
38. Vargas Valdés, *Máximo Castillo*, 78; Almada, *Vida, proceso y muerte de Abraham González*, 90.
39. González Ramírez, *Manifiestos Políticos*, 551–54.
40. "Orozco May Lead Revolt," *El Paso Herald*, February 6, 1912. Chihuahua consul Letcher was incorrectly reporting that the legislature had named Orozco governor and that the state was in rebellion against Madero. He had been offered the post but never accepted. RDS, Letcher to Knox, February 5 and 6, 1912, File Nos. 812.00/2742 and 2744. Chihuahua's outgoing interim governor was suggesting that, given the loss of Madero's control over the state, perhaps Orozco should be named its dictator. "May Make Orozco Military Dictator," *El Paso Herald*, February 6, 1912.
41. Sánchez Lamego, *Historia Militar*, 3:42–43, Almada, *Vida, proceso y muerte de Abraham González*, 90.
42. Almada, *Revolución*, 1:290, 291.
43. Ibid., 1:554–58; RDS, Wilson to Knox, February 7, 1912, File No. 812.00/2755; Almada, *Revolución*, 1:290. González returned with 300,000 pesos to distribute to the populace in hopes, it was assumed, that the sum would help calm the environment. *Periódico Oficial*, February 22, 1912, 2.

Chapter 21

1. Vera Estañol, *Revolución*, 257.
2. There were hints that Orozco was flirting with Díaz agents, including Toribio Esquivel Obregón, in Ciudad Juárez. Starr, *Mexico and the United States*, 339.
3. Márquez Terrazas, *Terrazas y Su Siglo*, 248.
4. Stephen Bonsal, "The Future of Mexico under the New Régime," *New York Times*, June 11, 1911.
5. RDS, Letcher to State Dept., March 4, 1912, 812.00/3192.
6. If Madero had his doubts about Orozco, he publicly insisted that Orozco was loyal. "Dice el Sr. Presidente que Orozco continúa leal" *El Tiempo*, February 25, 1912.
7. "Orozco Denies Disloyalty," *San Jose Mercury News*, February 7, 1912; "U.S. Watches Mexico Troops Ordered Ready," *Aberdeen (S.Dak.) Daily American*, February 7, 1912.

8. RDS, Letcher to State Dept., February 13, 1912, 812.00/2844 and March 20, 1912, 812.00/3424.

9. Knight, *Mexican Revolution*, 1:292.

10. Calero, *Decenio*, 94–95.

11. Ibid. Orozco wrote that there were a thousand reasons not to accept the governorship, including that others would see him as politically ambitious and that his current situation was very "delicate." AGN, Orozco to Piña, February 13, 1912, Fondo Madero, caja 36, exp. 953-2, folio 27,562.

12. Meyer, *Mexican Rebel*, 52; Almada, *Revolución*, 1:283.

13. The observant Chihuahua City U.S. consul Marion Letcher noted, "Suffice it to say that he has been assiduously cultivated since the last revolution, and all his passions played upon with great adroitness by those who were plotting against the Madero government." RDS, Letcher to State Dept., March 4, 1912, 812.00/3192. Letcher's term "assiduous" must have fit because others also characterized the oligarchy's courtship with that word. Knight wrote that the flattery and possible financial support "perhaps influenced Orozco's decision to join the rebels." Knight, *Mexican Revolution*, 1:297n304; Meyer, *Mexican Rebel*, 52.

14. Katz, *Life and Times*, 146; Knight, *Mexican Revolution*, 1:297. Enrile was a Díaz man through and through. He had certainly been a Díaz man of the Reyes stripe since 1902 and was a virulent anti-Maderista in May 1911 and during 1912. Even after he left Orozco, he went to Paris in 1913 in an unsuccessful effort to persuade Díaz to return to Mexico, *New York Tribune*, February 15, 1913, 3, and later attempted to court the general's nephew Félix Díaz.

15. RDS, Letcher to State Dept., May 29, 1912, 812.00/3930.

16. Thomas F. Logan, "Behind the Scenes at the Nation's Capital," *Philadelphia Inquirer*, May 20, 1912.

17. Such as the one from Juan Sarabia. CEHM, Juan Sarabia to Orozco, April 26, 1912, Fondo González Garza, CMXV. 25.2501.1.

18. "Consejos de guerra," *La Libertad*, July 17, 1884.

19. "Noticias de Paso del Norte," *El Siglo Diez y Nueve*, October 7, 1891.

20. "Fallo en un asunto sensacional," *El Popular*, February 27, 1903; "Un sentenciado por robo," *El País*, December 2, 1902.

21. *El Correo Español* (DF), November 20, 1898. See also "La acusación contra el Regidor de Zumpango," *La Patria*, January 31, 1900.

22. *El Correo Español* (DF), November 20, 1898; *La Patria*, August 12, 1899.

23. "Must Serve His Sentence," *Mexican Herald*, January 31, 1903. Perhaps Enrile became a committed Reyista and anti-Limantour after Limantour's Treasury Department accused Enrile of mishandling funds as a Treasury employee in Yucatán. CEHM, Rodolfo Reyes to Enrile, January 28, 1902, Fondo Bernardo Reyes, DLI-1.37.18039. Within months after he left his post, Enrile was employed at *La Protesta*.

24. Taracena, *Verdadera Revolución (1901–1911)*, 47; Raat, "Antipositivist Movement," 90. See also "Reyes hacia 'La Protesta,'" *Diario del Hogar*, July 11, 1911.

25. "Renuncia del Lic. Pallares," *El Popular*, March 12, 1903.

26. "Enrile y Fleury," *El Tiempo*, November 30, 1902.

27. "La prisión de Gonzalo Enrile," *El Popular*, December 21, 1903.

28. "Los Redactores de 'La Protesta' Libres," *El Tiempo*, March 22, 1903.

29. "Libertad de Don Gonzalo Enrile," *El País*, May 22, 1904.

30. His Chihuahua mail theft conviction and a claim against him for 1,850 pesos for refusing to pay for a load of barley delivered to him. Avisos Judiciales, *La Patria*, January 27, 1900.

31. "Una solicitud," *El País*, December 15, 1906.

32. Enrile and some of his codefendants were notorious in Mexico City courts and newspapers. Some of the reports follow.

    Avisos Judiciales, *La Patria*, January 27, 1900. The claim noted above for 1,850 pesos for refusing to pay for a load of barley delivered to him.

    "Notas de policía, por robo," *El País*, July 16, 1905. A server at Enrile's bar, Oro y Negro, accused him of stealing her tips. The article noted charges by others for purchasing merchandise but refusing to pay for it.

    "Un Juez calumniado," *El Popular*, July 1, 1906. This lengthy article reported Enrile in jail over two cases wherein he and his codefendants bought merchandise and refused payment. The article noted that the defendants were well known to *El Popular*'s readers.

    "Ecos de un proceso—Enrile gestiona su libertad," *El Imparcial*, December 15, 1906. Enrile was still in custody at least since July of that year. The defendants attempted to recuse the judge by falsely claiming their new lawyer was the judge's brother-in-law. Enrile also took the court file and refused to return it.

    "El Asunto Herrera y Socios," *El Popular*, July 21, 1906. The defendants were finally able to have the Judge recuse himself and get a new judge appointed.

    "El Asunto del Lic. José R. Del Castillo," *El Popular*, July 31, 1907. Defendants attempted to recuse the new judge claiming that he stole a client's file.

    Diario Oficial Estados Unidos Mexicanos, August 25, 1911. Suit for breach of contract. Enrile had rented some three thousand meters of film recording the 1910 centennial celebrations. He did not pay the rent or return the film.

    CEHM, Bernardo Reyes to Limantour, January 9, 1909, Fondo Bernardo Reyes, DLI. 39.7614.1. Bernardo Reyes said that Enrile had mishandled government funds while employed as a paymaster by the Treasury Department in Punta Allen, Yucatán. See CEHM, Rodolfo Reyes to Enrile, January 28, 1902, Fondo Bernardo Reyes, DLI-1.37.18039.

    An undated article in *El Norte* noted that Enrile had been in Mexico City's jail on six occasions. AGN, "Quien es Enrile," undated, Fondo Madero, caja 36, exp. 953-2, folio 27,593.

33. Given Díaz's age, he was not expected to complete the six-year term; the competition involved was in fact a fight for the presidency.

34. "2ª Junta Preparatoria del Partido Democrático," *Diario del Hogar*, December 20, 1908. Among those present were Rodolfo Reyes, Juan Sánchez Azcona, and Madero's cousin Rafael L. Hernández.

35. "Nuevos Cónsules," *El Diario*, December 23, 1908. In addition to Honduras, other reports mention postings in Brussels, Clifton, Arizona Territory, Philadelphia, and Eagle Pass, Texas, with only Honduras and Clifton confirmed by the author. "Incidente diplomático entre México y Estados Unidos," *El Tiempo*, August 29, 1910.

36. Within days of the Díaz government appointing Enrile to be a consul, Bernardo Reyes wrote to Limantour reminding him that Enrile had trouble when he was the paymaster in Punta Allen, Yucatán, implying that Enrile had mishandled funds there. Reyes did not mention that Enrile had worked for his newspaper, *La Protesta*, the cause of Reyes's loss of power. CEHM, Bernardo Reyes to Limantour, January 9, 1909, Fondo Bernardo Reyes, DLI. 39.7614.1.

37. "Enrile at Texarkana," *Dallas Morning News*, March 29, 1911.

38. "Fear Attack on Capital," *New York Times*, May 10, 1911.

39. "Vile Attack on Americans Prepared in Circular Form by a Mexican," *El Paso Herald*, February 26, 1912; SRE, Report, Mexican Consul in El Paso, L-E 745 R, Leg. 4, f 9.

40. "Rebel Threats to Take Juarez at Early Date," *Mexican Herald*, February 24, 1912.

41. González Ramírez, *Manifiestos Políticos*, 542.

42. "Revolt Making Progress in Mexico, Generals Trevino and Orozco Reported to Have Joined the Insurrectos," *Boise Idaho Statesman*, February 24, 1912.

43. RDS, Huntington Wilson to Wilson, February 25 and 26, 1912, File Nos. 812.00/2888a and 2912; RDS, Wilson to Knox, February 26, 1912, File No. 812.00/2906; Sánchez Lamego, *Historia Militar*, 3:43–44; Almada, *Vida, proceso y muerte de Abraham González*, 99; "Orozco Retira Las Fuerzas," *El Tiempo*, February, 28, 1912.

44. RDS, Edwards to State Dept., February 27, 1912, File No. 812.00/2930; Almada, *Revolución*, 1:291, 292; *Arizona Republican*, February 25, 1912.

45. RDS, Wilson to State Dept., February 27, 1912, File No. 812.00/2943. Ambassador Wilson suggested that Vázquez Gómez be expelled or prosecuted for his sedition.

46. "Cavalry Patrols the Border," *New York Times*, February 25, 1912; "Army Ready for Mexican Border, Situation in Mexico Critical," *Aberdeen (Wash.) Herald*, February 26, 1912.

47. "Enrile Arrested in Juarez," *Copper Era and Morenci (Ariz.) Leader*, March 8, 1912.

48. RDS, Letcher to State Dept., March 20, 1912, 812.00/3268.

49. "Manifiesto de Pascual Orozco para anunciar que se separa del mando de los Rurales y se lanza a la rebelión." González Ramírez, *Manifiestos Políticos*, 540–41.

50. Gimeno, *Canalla Roja*, 4, 5.

51. Almada, *Revolución*, 1:298–99. Joaquín Cortazar had served as interim governor of Chihuahua several times under Governors Ahumada and Creel. Almada cites Ramón Puente, who wrote that the demonstration was organized by the Terrazas-Creel clan and Pascual's friends, including his father. Puente, *Pascual Orozco*, 100–101. U.S. consul Letcher also agreed with those assessments: "The

movement, however, was so palpably staged by the antigovernment factions that it did not assume a serious aspect." He also felt that it was a farce led by the Cortazar. RDS, Letcher to State Dept., March 4 and 20, 1912, 812.00/3192 and 3424. A lengthy report by Consul Letcher on Villa raised questions about his loyalty to Madero. He may have been ready to join Orozco in his revolt. Letcher wrote that Abraham González told him that Villa's support was "anything but assured." RDS, Letcher to Secretary of State, August 25, 1914, File No. 812.00/13232.

52. Sánchez Lamego, *Historia Militar*, 3:44.

53. Knight, *Mexican Revolution*, 1:299, 300.

54. RDS, Taft Proclamation, March 2, 1912, File No. 812.00/3005c.

55. BOI Case Files, H. A. Thompson, February 24, 1912. It was well known before March 1 that Orozco had turned against Madero. Taracena, *Verdadera Revolución (1912–1914)*, 231.

56. *El Paso Herald*, February 27 and March 1, 1912.

Chapter 22

1. The *El Paso Morning Times* of March 6, 1912, reported that in their January meeting, Madero refused Orozco's request for an additional payment of 50,000 pesos to fulfill his demand for 100,000 pesos. Some attributed the rebellion to the denial of money.

2. Sánchez Lamego, *Historia Militar*, 3:44.

3. Puente, *Pascual Orozco*, 114.

4. Abraham González wrote that Villa withdrew from the engagement and suffered no casualties, whereas Orozco took some losses. CEHM, Abraham González to Federico González Garza, March 14, 1912, Fondo González Garza, CMXV.24.2352.1. In another rendition, Villa said that he withdrew and did not contest Orozco because he thought that it would endanger Abraham González, who, Villa thought, was in Orozco's custody. Ibid., 47. Conrado Gimeno wrote that Villa never attacked and withdrew instead, and Orozco forces falsely celebrated a victory in claiming that Villa suffered many casualties. Gimeno, *Canalla Roja*, 8. That is also the view of military historian Sánchez Lamego. Sánchez Lamego, *Historia Militar*, 3:47.

5. Almada, *Revolución*, 1:300.

6. Ibid., 1:297–300. See Puente, *Pascual Orozco*, 100–101; and Almada, *Vida, proceso y muerte de Abraham González*, 125–26. Governor González might also have called for Villa to defend the city from a threatened attack by Braulio Hernández forces. Mundt, "Revolution and Reaction," 31, citing RDS, Letcher to Knox, March 3, 1912, 812.00/3146 and 3112.5.

7. RDS, Letcher to State Dept., March 3, 1912, File No. 812.00/3027.

8. "Orozco to March to Mexico City," *New York Times*, March 5, 1912.

9. González said that he fled Chihuahua City to save his own life from the disorder orchestrated by Orozco. He hid out from March 2 until June 11, when he escaped from Chihuahua City and reached Huerta's federal command at Santa Rosalia on June 16. "Gov. Gonzalez to Legislature," *El Paso Morning Times*, August 9, 1912.

10. RDS, Letcher to State Dept., March 4, 1912, 812.00/3043.
11. RDS, Letcher to State Dept., March 7, 1912, 812.00/3188.
12. Almada, *Revolución*, 1:304–305; *El Paso Herald*, March 15, 1912.
13. The three *plans*, Nombre de Dios, Empacadora, and Orozquista, are occasionally confused. The principal plan was the Empacadora or Orozquista, a thirty-nine-clause manifesto issued on March 25.
14. RDS, Letcher to State Dept., March 5, 1912, File No. 812.00/3057.
15. Sánchez Lamego, *Historia Militar*, 3:44.
16. Almada, *Revolución*, 1:321; "Rebels Make Ready for a New Campaign," *Arizona Republican*, March 2, 1912; "Enrile Arrested in Juarez," *Copper Era and Morenci Leader*, March 8, 1912.
17. "Enrile to Face Gen. Orozco," *Copper Era and Morenci Leader*, March 15, 1912.
18. "Trusted Chief Turns Traitor," *El Paso Morning Times*, March 6, 1912.
19. It had nine of the body's fifteen votes.
20. Almada, *Revolución*, 1:303; *Periódico Oficial*, Estado de Chihuahua, March 7, 1912; Wasserman, *Persistent Oligarchs*, 17; RDS, Letcher to State Dept., March 7, 1912, File No. 812.00/30188.
21. AGN, Salazar, Hernández and Campa leaflet, March 8, 1912, Fondo Madero, box 60, exp. 345.
22. As soon as Orozco rose in rebellion, Mexico's U.S. ambassador requested that the United States not grant the rebellion belligerent status or allow the shipment of arms, positions that would prove critical to the revolt. RDS, Mexican ambassador to Acting Secretary of State, March 7, 1912, File No. 812.00/3059. The State Department, however, provided a full explanation of the law and concluded that under current law the United States could not prevent the exportation of arms, noting that "the Executive has no option but to allow them to pass into Mexican territory as the subject of legitimate commerce." RDS, Wilson to Mexican ambassador, March 8, 1912, File No. 812.113/221.
23. Meyer, *Mexican Rebel*, 57.
24. "No Cientifico Alliance," *El Paso Herald*, March 8, 9, 1912.
25. "Rebel Threats to Take Juarez at Early Date," *Mexican Herald*, February 24, 1912.
26. CEHM, Abraham González to Federico González Garza, March 14, 1912, Fondo González Garza, CMXV.24.2352.1.
27. RDS, Letcher to State Dept., March 12, 1912, 812.00/3268. Letcher added that Americans in Chihuahua were "generally disgusted over the treachery of Orozco."
28. "Davila Leaves Rebel Ranks, Orozco Stands with Cientificos," *El Paso Morning Times*, March 12, 1912, 1. The next day Juan Terrazas denied that his father had anything to do with Orozco, but he did not mention the remainder of the family. *El Paso Morning Times*, March 14, 1912, 7.
29. Márquez Terrazas, *Terrazas y Su Siglo*, 251. This is still another indication that Orozco was working with Enrile to betray Madero well before March 1. Another writer's unsourced claim was that Luis Terrazas gave Orozco 100,000 pesos at the time Enrile was brought into the rebellions. Aguirre Benavides, *Errores de Madero*, 152.

30. Katz, *Life and Times*, 143, 144.
31. Ibid., 143, citing BOI Case Reports, Case No. 232–1204, March 18, 1912; Almada, *Juárez y Terrazas*, 329–31. Zacarías Márquez Terrazas, supportive of Terrazas, also mentions the event at the Foreign Club, citing the archives of Ministry of Foreign Relations. Márquez Terrazas, *Terrazas y Su Siglo*, 251.
32. BOI Case Reports, Case No. 232–1204, March 18, 1912.
33. "Red Flag Leader Protects Terrazas Cattle," *El Paso Morning Times*, March 22, 1912.
34. Mormon Casas Grandes rancher George Look remembered that Orozco's Casas Grandes troops received and then defied Orozco's order protecting Terrazas cattle. Testimony of George Look, *Revolutions in Mexico, Hearings*, 24, 25. Ranchers also reported that, when presented with a protection letter signed by Orozco, they were still robbed. CEHM, Henry LNU to Hector Ramos, April 27, 1912, Fondo Federico González Garza, CMXV.26.2502.
35. *El Paso Herald*, March 12, 1912; "Red Flag Rebels Raid Terrazas Ranch," *El Paso Morning Times*, March 11, 1912, 1. It is possible that the order exempting Terrazas came later.
36. *El Correo de Chihuahua*, March 22, 1912. Taking 50,000 peso shares of the loan were the Banco Nacional, Banco Minero, and Banco de Sonora. The Banco Comercial Refaccionario took 20,000 pesos, Luis Terrazas Jr. took 10,000 pesos and clan ally Manuel Prieto took a 5,000 pesos share.
37. Almada, *Revolución*, 1:304–308.
38. As evidence that there were no forced loans, there was a Ciudad Juárez case. On March 9, Gen. Antonio Rojas, head of Orozco forces in Ciudad Juárez, imposed a forced loan on a local bank. The bank complained to Orozco, who then removed Rojas from his command and imprisoned him under a four-year sentence. Orozco then appointed his father to replace Rojas as head of his forces in Ciudad Juárez.
39. Testimony of Manuel Luján, in U.S. Senate, Committee on Foreign Relations, *Revolutions in Mexico, Hearings*, 300–301. Luján said that those funds were in addition to those the "leaders" personally contributed—that is, off the books. Luján, a member of the Terrazas clan, was married to the General's granddaughter.
40. U.S. senator Alden Smith estimated those monthly revenues at $100,000. Ibid., 767.
41. *El Paso Herald*, March 5, 1912. Taracena, *Verdadera Revolución (1912–1914)*, 77.
42. *Periódico Oficial*, Estado de Chihuahua, March 21 and 24, 1912. The bonds had a face amount of one thousand pesos, with a ten-year maturity and paid 5 percent interest. The governor's decree also authorized his withdrawal of recognition of the Madero government. See also Prendergast, "Orozco Rebellion."
43. "Uruachic, Chihuahua, Falls into Hands of Rebels without a Fight," *El Paso Herald*, March 21, 1912, 2.
44. Testimony of Felipe R. Gutiérrez, in U.S. Senate, Committee on Foreign Relations. *Revolutions in Mexico, Hearings*, 280. The few firms refusing were foreign-owned, including the gun dealer–hardware firm of Krakauer and Zork, but it suffered no consequences from its refusal. American firms, such as Krakauer's and Kettlesen

and Degetau, probably refused involvement as advised by Consul Letcher, who, following a directive from Taft, counseled Americans not to purchase bonds, pay levies, or become partisans. RDS, Letcher to State Dept., June 28, 1912, File No. 812.00/4357; CEHM, Abraham González to Federico González Garza, March 14, 1912, Fondo González Garza, CMXV.24.2352.1. Also see Knight, *Mexican Revolution*, 1:320.

45. Knight, *Mexican Revolution*, 1:298.

46. Ibid., 310–12; Prendergast, "Orozco Rebellion."

47. Witness Hopkins stated that Orozco spent over $2 million and that he received $1 million from the Chihuahua Chamber of Commerce and $100,000 monthly in customs revenue. Hopkins testimony in U.S. Senate, Committee on Foreign Relations, *Revolutions in Mexico, Hearings*, 767.

48. The figures vary, but estimates place the cost of Madero's revolution between 640,000 to 700,000 pesos. García Moisés, *Madero*, 28.

49. Katz wrote that the oligarchy overpaid soldiers as it wanted mercenaries interested only in money and not land reform. Katz, *Life and Times*, 146. That also seemed to be Consul Letcher's assessment. RDS, Letcher to State Dept., March 18, 1912, File No. 812.00/3297.

50. Meyer, *Mexican Rebel*, 69.

51. "Orozco to March on Mexico City." *New York Times*, March 5, 1912. In an assessment later proven correct, Consul Letcher wrote that Pascual's "forces are imperfectly armed and have an insufficiency of ammunition for the purpose of a general campaign." RDS, Letcher to State Dept., March 7, 1912, File No. 812.00/3188.

52. Meyer, *Mexican Rebel*, 69.

53. This, along with the allegation that Madero did not fulfill his promises, was one of several criticisms of Madero that the oligarchy began circulating even before Madero took power, "propaganda" the elites promoted to "loosen the hold of Madero upon the people." RDS, Letcher to State Dept., March 20, 1912, File No. 812.00/3424.

54. Almada, *Revolución*, 1:310–11.

55. Meyer, *Mexican Rebel*, 71.

56. Sánchez Lamego, *Historia Militar*, 3:53–54.

57. RDS, Public Resolution No. 22, SJ Res. 89, March 14, 1912, File No. 812.00/3226; RDS, the President's Proclamation, March 14, 1912, File No. 812.112R56/9.

58. Perhaps on Letcher's complaint, the United States made clear that food and other necessaries were not embargoed. RDS, Letcher to State Dept., March 22, 1912, File No. 812.00/3348; RDS, State Dept. to Letcher, March 24, 1912, File No. 812.113/249b; *El Paso Herald*, March 13, 14, 20, 21, and 23, 1912; *New York Times*, March 21, 1912.

59. Understandably often confused with the earlier Plan de la Empacadora.

60. Manifesto addressed to "Mexicanos" and signed by Pascual Orozco Jr., Gral. José Inés Salazar, Gral. Emilio P. Campa, Gral. J. J. Campos, Gral. Benjamín Argumedo, Gral. Francisco del Toro, Gonzalo C. Enrile, Corl. Demetrio Ponce, Corl. Félix Terrazas, R. Gómez Robelo, and José Córdova, Srio. AGN, Fondo Madero, caja 9, exp. 219-1, folio 6375; Meyer, *Mexican Rebel*, 60, 138.

61. Flores Magón had first adopted the slogan "Reforma, Libertad y Justicia" at least by June 1906. The PLM changed its slogan to "Tierra y Libertad," the same as Zapata's, on September 23, 1911, when it issued a new manifesto, supposedly leaving the old available to Orozco. Martínez Álvarez, *Práxedis Guerrero*, 50; Práxedis Guerrero, *Artículos Literarios*, 29.

62. Torres Parés and Villegas Moreno, *Diccionario de la Revolución*, 470.

63. Almada, *Revolución*, 1:312–13, 320–21. Magonista leader Juan Sarabia said he provided material for Orozco's manifesto but that Enrile replaced his own draft for Sarabia's. CEHM, Juan Sarabia to Orozco, April 26, 1912, Fondo González Garza, CMXV. 25.2501.1. The final draft was likely a mixture of Sarabia's and Enrile's writing.

64. "New Backers for Orozco Revolt," *El Paso Herald*, May 13, 1912.

65. Creel opted to use the practical dual strategy of stopping González in Chihuahua while supporting Madero in Mexico City, where he had forged business relations with Madero Científicos. "Creel Sees Anarchy Should Madero Fall," *New York Times*, March 6, 1912. See also "Creel is with Madero Party," *El Paso Herald*, March 29, 1912.

Chapter 23

1. As to enlistments, see "Orozco Disappointed over Indifference of People," *El Paso Morning Times*, March 31, 1912. As to desertions, see "Red Flag Officers Deserting," *El Paso Morning Times*, March 11, 1912, front page; "Villa's Forces Grow Larger," *El Paso Morning Times*, March 18, 1912, front page.

2. Magaña, *Zapata*, 2:120–21.

3. Ibid., 320–21.

4. The State Department refused to acknowledge the telegram because the United States had no relations with Orozco's rebellion. RDS, Orozco to Taft, April 5, 1912, File No. 812.00/3538; RDS, State Dept. to Letcher, April 11, 1912, 812.00/353; *El Paso Herald*, April 6, 1912. Apparently unaware of Orozco's telegram to Taft, Consul Letcher wired on April 7 that Orozco had not repudiated Enrile's manifesto. RDS, Letcher to Secretary of State, April 7, 1912, File No. 812.00/3533.

5. RDS, Orozco to Taft, April 5, 1912, File No. 812.00/3538; "Orozco Addresses Taft," *El Paso Herald*, April 6, 1912.

6. RDS, Letcher to Secretary of State, April 11, 1912, File No. 812.00/3576.

7. RDS, State Dept. to Edwards, April 10, 1912, File No. 812.00/3546; "Americans and Rebels Not on Good Terms," *Idaho Statesman*, April 14, 1912.

8. RDS, Acting Secretary of State Dept. to Letcher, April 14, 1912, File No. 812.00/3593c; RDS, Letcher to Secretary of State, April 17, 1912, File No. 812.00/2.

9. RDS, Orozco to Acting Secretary of State, April 18, 1912, File No. 812.00/3670.

10. *Unites States v. Alberto Echevarria*, et al., No. 1559, U.S. District Court, WD Texas.

11. Von Feilitzsch, *In Plain Sight*, 170–72, 179.

12. *El Paso Herald*, April 10, 1912. Not all U.S. officials, however, supported allowing Mexican agents to operate in the United States. The U.S. consul in Ciudad Porfirio

Díaz, Luther Ellsworth, objected to the practice. Kerig, *Luther T. Ellsworth*, 55.

13. "Neutrality Act Violation Charged," *El Paso Herald*, March 19, 1912.

14. *El Paso Herald*, July 19, 1912; Harris and Sadler, "'Underside' of the Mexican Revolution," 78; Harris and Sadler, *Secret War in El Paso*. Prominent hardware man and gun dealer Adolph Krakauer said that Madero agent Felix Sommerfeld alone had twenty-five to thirty spies watching his El Paso store during Orozco's rebellion. Testimony of Adolph Krakauer, in U.S. Senate, Committee on Foreign Relations, *Revolutions in Mexico, Hearings*, 123. See also Smith, "Mexican Secret Service," 65–85.

15. Under the law, diplomats, including Llorente, could request an arrest so that Mexico could demand extradition. The accused could be held for forty days in jail without bond until appropriate proof was produced. In that manner, Llorente had several Mexicans arrested who were later discharged when no proof was forthcoming. The practice left Llorente open to the charge that he was using the tactic to jail political refugees. "No Proof, the Prisoner Freed." *El Paso Herald*, October 2, 1912; *El Paso Morning Times*, October 8, 1912.

16. *El Paso Morning Times*, March 22, 1912, 4.

17. "Is Orozco to Remain Loyal?" *El Paso Morning Times*, February 7, 1912, front page.

18. Ibid.; *El Paso Morning Times*, February 9, 1912, 9.

19. Beezley, *Insurgent Governor*, 134–35.

20. *El Paso Morning Times*, March 13, 1912, front page.

21. Beezley, *Insurgent Governor*, 148n30.

22. "Enrile golpeados," *La Patria*, April 27, 1912; "Chihuahua Newspaper Suspends Publication," *El Paso Morning Times*, April 3, 1912, front page.

23. CEHM, Intelligence Report, May 21, 1911, Fondo González Garza, CMXV.24.2390.1.

24. Knight, *Mexican Revolution*, 1:320; "Enrile golpeados," *La Patria*, April 27, 1912.

25. *Periódico Oficial*, April 11, 14, and 18, 1912. The record is in conflict as to the number of deputies that were pro-oligarchy. Orozco's father was named a substitute deputy.

26. Meyer, *Mexican Rebel*, 80.

27. *Periódico Oficial*, May 10, 1912. De la Barra condemned Chihuahua's secession and called Orozco Rebellion "deplorable." *Financial America*, April 8, 1912.

28. RDS, Letcher to State Dept., May 29, 1912, 812.00/3930; *Periódico Oficial*, May 9, 1912. Postage was not the only problem. There was insufficient currency, so much so that Orozco approved as ersatz currency the use of letters of credit payable to the bearer. *Periódico Oficial*, March 28, 1912. Later banks required additional personal guarantees after the forgery of some instruments. *El Correo de Chihuahua*, May 11, 13, and 18, 1912.

29. Beezley, *Insurgent Governor*, 79. Senators Fall and Alden Smith met with Taft to have Taft rescind the embargo. The effort failed. AGN, Hopkins to Madero, December 29, 1912, caja 2, exp. 21, folios 33–37.

30. "Rebels Shout Viva Diaz at Banquet," *El Paso Herald*, April 15, 1912. Hernández felt duped by Orozco and tried to rejoin Madero, but Madero declined the offer.

RDS, Letcher to Knox, April 29, 1912, 812.3282; Mundt, "Revolution and Reaction," 65.

31. González Ramírez, *Manifiestos Políticos*, 548–49. The letter was in *El Padre Padilla*, May 7, 1912

32. The U.S. consul in Ciudad Juárez noted, "Special envoy of Pascual Orozco today formally appointed Vázquez Gómez Provisional President of Mexico at Ciudad Juárez, where the seat of government will for the present remain." RDS, Edwards to Secretary of State, May 4, 1912, File No. 812.00/3801; "El Lic. Don Emilio Vazquez Gomez Paso Ayer La Frontera Mejicana," *El País*, May 5, 1912; "Vazquez Gomez Becomes Provisional Mexican President," *El Paso Herald*, May 4, 1912.

33. RDS, Garrett to Secretary of State, May 7, 1912, File No. 812.00/3828; "Vazquez Gomez Quits Capital in Dark of Night, 'Beats It' for San Antonio by Train," *El Paso Herald* May 11, 1912; "Orozco Refuses to Recognize Gomez as New President," *Ft. Worth Star-Telegram*, May 7, 1912.

34. Letcher also sensed the influence of a behind-the-scenes power group: "Whatever Orozco's opinion of [Vázquez] Gómez might be there is a higher power behind the revolution which will not tolerate him as provisional president." RDS, Letcher to State Dept., May 29, 1912, 812.00/3930; *El Paso Herald*, April 24, 1912, May 3, 4, 5, 7, 10, 11, and 13, 1912; *New York Times*, May 10 and 11, 1912. See González Ramírez, *Manifiestos Políticos*, 550–51. The letter was published in *El Padre Padilla*, May 11 and 13, 1912.

35. González Ramírez, *Manifiestos Políticos*, 546–47. The letter was published in *El Padre Padilla*, April 8, 1912.

36. Almada, *Revolución*, 1:326; *El Paso Herald*, May 6, 1912.

37. "New Backers for Orozco Revolt," *El Paso Herald*, May 13, 1912.

38. CEHM, Intelligence Report, May 8, 1912, Fondo González Garza, CMXV.26.2544.1; CEHM, Intelligence Report, May 16, 1912, Fondo González Garza, CMXV.26.2586.1.2.

39. Editor's note in *Plan de Ayala*, 11–12, in RDS, J. E. Hernández to Bryan, October 17, 1913, File No. 812.00/9346.

40. CEHM, Intelligence Report, May 16, 1912, Fondo González Garza, CMXV.26.2586.1.2.

41. He was said to have four wounds from the stabbing and shooting. "Enrile Seriously Injured," *Idaho Statesman*, May 20, 1912.

42. Causa Número 80, Juzgado Primero de lo Penal, May 13, 1912, Archivo Histórico del Supremo Tribunal de Justicia del Estado de Chihuahua.

43. RDS, Letcher to State Dept., June 28, 1912, 812.00/4357. The editor of a Chihuahua City newspaper, however, said it was a dispute over a woman. *El Liberal*, May 17, 1912; Statement of José Reyes Estrada, Causa Número 80.

44. *El Paso Herald*, May 13, 1912; *Yakima (Wash.) Herald*, May 15, 1912.

45. CEHM, Intelligence Report, May 8, 1912, Fondo González Garza, CMXV.26 2544.1.

46. *El Paso Herald*, May 13, 14, 1912; RDS, Letcher to State Dept., June 28, 1912, 812.00/4357.

47. *El Paso Herald*, June 10, 1912. Llorente charged that Enrile had stolen movie films from a Mexico City firm. This was a charge Enrile had faced before, accused of renting three thousand meters of movie film of the 1910 centennial celebrations. He failed to pay the rental fee and refused to return the film. Enrile sat in jail for forty days as authorities waited for proof of his guilt. Ultimately, neither U.S. or Mexican agencies produced evidence, and Enrile was released on July 22, 1912. *San Francisco Call*, June, 12, 1912; *San Antonio Express*, July 7, 1912; *El Paso Morning Times*, July 23, 1912.

48. Mundt, "Revolution and Reaction," 79.

Chapter 24

1. Sánchez Lamego, *Historia Militar*, 3:58.

2. Ibid., 3:60–61.

3. Sánchez Lamego, *Historia Militar*, 3:68–73.

4. Knight, *Mexican Revolution*, 1:324.

5. Madero was frustrated with Huerta over Orozco's escape from Conejos. To Madero, Orozco had only one escape path, the rail line north. Madero told Huerta that he should have placed troops on the line and trapped Orozco. Despite losses, Orozco escaped to fight again. Madero knew that Huerta had the men, equipment, and ammunition. Orozco had fewer men, limited weapons and ammunition. Madero told Huerta to be more aggressive. He wanted Orozco finished off at Bachimba and told Huerta to send six hundred men to Cusihuiriáchi to cut off an escape. AGN, Madero to Huerta, June 6, 1912, Fondo Madero, box 18, exp. 441-1, folios 14,225–14,228; AGN, Madero to Huerta, May 20, 1912, Fondo Madero, caja 18, exp. 441-1, folios 14,236–14,239.

6. Sánchez Lamego, *Historia Militar*, 3:70–73.

7. Ibid., 73–75; Knight, *Mexican Revolution*, 1:327.

8. "Madero Army Wins; Rebels in Flight," *New York Times*, July 5, 1912. For Madero, Bachimba put an end to the Orozco threat. Knight, *Mexican Revolution*, 1:328.

9. Sánchez Lamego, *Historia Militar*, 3:76–81.

10. *Periódico Oficial*, June 6, 1912.

11. Almada, *Revolución*, 1:335. Consul Letcher reported, "Notwithstanding that the promoters of the revolution subscribed and otherwise provided a considerable sum for the beginning of the revolution, latterly these moneyed supporters of the revolution seem to have thrown the movement entirely upon the State of Chihuahua for its maintenance." RDS, Letcher to State Dept., June 28, 1912, File No. 812.00/4357.

12. Almada, *Revolución*, 1:355. This was of course contrary to what Enrile and Orozco promised the oligarchy in a time of hubris. Enrile assured the bondholders that Orozco would win and that the federal government would assume the bonds, make them a national debt, and pay them. Enrile told bondholders that the national government could not refuse to pay the bonds. "Uruachic, Chihuahua Falls," *El Paso Herald*, March 21, 1912.

13. Gutiérrez testimony, in U.S. Senate, Committee on Foreign Relations, *Revolutions in Mexico, Hearings*, 280.

14. Banco Nacional complained that it took 400,000 pesos in loans. Orozco also took the 150,000 pesos on deposit at the bank. Banks asked Ernesto Madero to help them with González, but the governor refused to honor the rebel administration's acts. Orozco also asked for the names of the bank depositors and the amount of funds they had on deposit. CEHM, Letters of Luis Elguero to Limantour, December 9, 1912, Fondo Limantour, CDLIV.2a.1910.11.12; CEHM, Hugo Scherer Jr. to Limantour, March 22 and May 10, 1912, Fondo Limantour, CDLIV.2a.1910.27.72 and 83.

15. CEHM, Abraham González to Federico González Garza, March 14, 1912, Fondo González Garza, CMXV.24.2352.1.

16. Almada, *Revolución*, 1:345; "Chihuahua Rejoices as Federals Enter," *New York Times*, July 8, 1912.

17. An anonymous but regular U.S. intelligence source noted, "Sentiment is turning very rapidly against Orozco, and he now has few friends even in the city of Chihuahua, where formerly he was the idol of the people." Troops were deserting and ammunition was scarce. CEHM, Intelligence Report, April 1, 1912, Fondo Gonzalez Garza, CMXV-25-2441. By then, Orozco was also seen as being against his own plan and movement. "Chihuahua's conservative classes had been able to exercise in their favor a strong influence that distanced him from Emilio Vázquez Gómez" who had fled from Mexico for his safety. Magaña, *Zapata*, 2:145.

18. "Orozco Leads Army West for New War," *New York Times*, July 7, 1912; Orozco to Fight in Guerrilla War," *New York Times*, July 11, 1912.

19. "Orozco Leads Army West for New War," *New York Times*, July 7, 1912.

20. "'Ahora Comienza la Revolución,' Dice Orozco," *El País*, July 5, 1912.

21. "Orozco Plans Flight, Ready to Quit Mexican Rebels since Disaffection Has Broken Out," *New York Times*, July 15, 1912; "Guerilla Warfare Is Expected in Mexico, General Orozco Admits Defeat in Rebellion, *Macon (Ga.) Telegraph*, July 13, 1912.

22. "Americans Flee from Chihuahua," *New York Times*, July 30, 1912; *New York Times*, August 1, 1912; Knight, *Mexican Revolution*, 1:328.

23. Among those leaving was the family of young George Romney, later governor of Michigan.

24. *El Paso Herald*, July 29 and 31, 1912.

25. Mundt, "Revolution and Reaction," 74, 110.

26. "With Gen. Venustiano Carranza's Army in Mexico," *New York Times*, November 9, 1913. See also Reséndez Fuentes, "Battleground Women," 525–53.

27. "Orozco in No Hurry to Leave," *Schulenburg (Tex.) Sticker*, August 9, 1912. Orozco was clearly bitter toward the United States and its embargo, which had sunk his rebellion. Consul Llorente wired that the American military commander received reports that a bitter Orozco might fire rounds into El Paso before leaving Ciudad Juárez. AGN, Llorente to Relaciones Exteriores, August 6, 1912, Fondo Madero, caja 25, exp. 667-2, folio 18,963.

28. "Mrs. Orozco Goes to Los Angeles," *El Paso Morning Times*, June 19, 1912.

29. RDS, Ciudad Juárez Consul to Secretary of State, August 16 and 20, 1912, File No. 812.00/4643. Once Orozco abandoned Ciudad Juárez, Huerta forwarded a

complete report to Madero. In closing the note, Huerta requested a transfer to Mexico City as his physicians were recommending that he undergo surgery for an unspecified ailment. AGN, Huerta to Madero, September 1, 1912, Fondo Madero, caja 18, exp. 441-1, folio 14,223; "Mexican Revolt Ending," *New York Times*, August 17, 1912; *El Paso Herald*, August 2, 16, and 20, 1912.

30. AGN, Llorente to Madero, August 27, 1912, Fondo Madero, caja 25, exp. 667-2, folio 18,984.

31. No relation to the author. Caballero was inspector of telegraphs in Mexico, and the government sought extradition on charges of defalcation of some 1,076 pesos that he was responsible for and were found missing. Authorities filed charges against Caballero in Chihuahua. SRE, Legajo 9-9-33, exp. 13.

32. Almada, *Revolución*, 1:356–57; *El Paso Herald*, September 2, 17, 19, and 23 and October 9, 1912. Pascual's father, Braulio Hernández, and Cástulo Herrera were later acquitted of the weapons charges. *El Paso Herald*, October 19, 1912.

33. Almada, *Revolución*, 1:353; Bonilla, *Régimen Maderista*, 45.

34. RDS, Edwards to State Dept., August 12, 1912, File No. 812.00/4614.

35. RDS, Laredo consul to Secretary of State, September 15, 1912, File No. 812.00/4933; RDS, Acting Secretary of State to American Ambassador, September 27, 1912, File No. 812.00/5131a. Rumors of a Huerta-Orozco anti-Madero collaboration went back at least to April 1912, around the time that Huerta arrived at Torreón to assume command over federal forces. Gen. Gildardo Magaña wrote, "It was learned that [Huerta] was going to rebel and that he didn't do so because he had begun negotiations with Orozco apparently conducted by Gonzalo Enrile in which Huerta would be president of the republic, but Orozco, perhaps under the influence of Mexico City politicians, was supporting general Jerónimo Treviño for president." Magaña, *Zapata*, 2:254. Taracena has a slightly different version in which Gen. Felipe Ángeles learned that Huerta and Blanquet would betray Madero but did not do so because in the negotiations they conducted through Enrile, Huerta and Blanquet wanted a Huerta presidency and Orozco wanted Treviño. Taracena, *Labor Social*, 63–64. Alan Knight suggests David de la Fuente as another possible intermediary between Huerta and Colorado rebels. Knight also mentions Huerta's rumored lifelong presidential ambitions. Knight, *Mexican Revolution*, 1:331–32.

36. *El Paso Herald*, September 14 and 16, 1912.

37. Almada, *Revolución*, 1:354–55.

38. Ibid., 352.

39. RDS, Vera Cruz Consul to State Dept., October 17, 1912, File No. 812.00/5258, 5271; RDS, Adee to Chargé d'Affaires, October 19, 1912, File No. 5272; RDS, Schuyler to State Dept., October 23, 1912, File No. 812.00/5333; *El Paso Herald*, September 28, October 16 and 23, 1912.

40. Knight, *Mexican Revolution*, 1:329. Leaders, Campa for one, fled into the United States and were arrested in Tucson. RDS, Wilson to State Dept., September 25, 1912, File No. 812.00/5063.

41. Madero floated a twenty-million-peso loan. Knight, *Mexican Revolution*, 1:330.
42. The Colorados were defeated at San Joaquín on September 20, 1912, leaving only tattered remnants. Knight, *Mexican Revolution*, 1:328–29.

Chapter 25

1. Trow, "Senator Albert B. Fall." Trow's dissertation gives a comprehensive view and analysis of Fall and his hearings on conditions in Mexico during the revolution as well as on U.S.-Mexico relations in that period.
2. Trow, "Albert B. Fall," 15–17.
3. When Orozco abandoned Ciudad Juárez in mid-August, many of his forces entered the United States, where they were promptly arrested on neutrality charges brought by Consul Llorente. The arrested included Emilio P. Campa, José Cordova, José Inés Salazar, and others. The State Department encouraged the detentions, but thought extradition to Mexico difficult given the lack of an extradition treaty. RDS, Acting Secretary of State to Secretary of War, File No. 812.00/5168b.
4. Bud-Frierman, Godley, and Wale, "Weetman Pearson in Mexico," 279–83.
5. Thus, the Dulles brothers, as managing partners of the law firm Sullivan & Cromwell, represented and defended the interests of United Fruit Company, petroleum companies, and other international firms precisely in the same manner when they became heads of the U.S. State Department and the Central Intelligence Agency (CIA). The difference was that when they led government agencies, the impact on their opponents was more consequential, such as it was for Iranian prime minister Muhammed Musaddiq, who was overthrown by the CIA in 1953 because of his oil policies, and for Guatemalan president Jacobo Arbenz, who was also overthrown by the CIA in 1954 when he sought to regulate United Fruit's Guatemalan operations.
6. Hopkins testimony, in U.S. Senate, Committee on Foreign Relations, *Revolutions in Mexico, Hearings*, 772.
7. Hopkins testified that Waters-Pierce hired him to expose graft in the Díaz administration. Ibid., 757.

Chapter 26

1. Villa repeatedly begged Madero for an audience and consideration and complained of prison conditions. AGN, Villa to Madero, July to December 1912, Fondo Madero, box 47, exp. 1292-1, folios 35,601–627.
2. Katz, *Life and Times*, 183–85.
3. The U.S. State and War Departments agreed on the policy to arrest and prosecute Orozco forces fleeing from Ojinaga. RDS, Acting Secretary of State to War Department, October 2, 1912, File No. 812.00/5168a. Specifically mentioning Orozco Sr. and Campa, they agreed, however, to deny extradition to Mexico. RDS, Acting Secretary of State to Attorney General, October 2, 1912, File No. 812.00/5168c. Also, SRE, Presidio and Marfa Consuls to Washington, D.C., embassy, September 16, 1912, legajo L-E 826 (3), folios 7, 11, and 20.
4. Meyer, *Mexican Rebel*, 88.

5. Orozco was said to have rheumatism. "General Orozco Disabled," *Oregonian* (Portland, Ore.), November 18, 1912; Meyer, *Mexican Rebel*, 87, 88.

6. "Orozco and Salazar Estranged," *Fort Worth Star-Telegram*, September 13, 1912.

7. Meyer, *Mexican Rebel*, 89, 90. Orozco once again proposed Porfirista Gen. Gerónimo Treviño as president. "Rebels Announce Terms," *Idaho Statesman*, January 28, 1913.

8. "Orozco Ready to Welcome an Invasion," *Herkimer (N.Y.) Evening Telegram*, December 28, 1912.

9. Meyer, *Mexican Rebel*, 93.

10. Krauze, *Mexico: Biography of Power*, 262.

11. Vela González, "Quincena." Citing Manuel Bonilla Jr., Francisco Vázquez Gómez said Madero named Huerta at the insistence of his father and his brother Gustavo. Vázquez Gómez, *Memorias*, 499–500. Even the Madero-hating U.S. ambassador noted the next day, "The President and Cabinet have abandoned the palace; whereabouts unknown. General Huerta, whose loyalty is questioned, is in charge of the palace." RDS, Wilson to State Dept., February 10, 1913, File No. 812.00/6075.

12. Maldonado, *Asesinatos*, 9.

13. "Wilson's Popularity Puzzles Officials, Ambassador's Close Relations with Huerta Not Understood in Washington," *New York Times*, February 21, 1913.

14. Katz, *Life and Times*, 195; Meyer, *Mexican Rebel*, 95.

15. Márquez Sterling, *Últimos días*, 464. In another version, Huerta and Gustavo ate at the Gambrinus Restaurant. Huerta asked Gustavo for half a million pesos to buy General Blanquet's loyalty, and Gustavo declined. At the end of the meal, Huerta got up to leave, saying that he had to visit an area outside the city. As he walked away, he felt under his coat and returned, asking for Gustavo to lend him his pistol as he had forgotten his own. Gustavo did so. Immediately after Huerta left, four Huerta staffers present arrested Gustavo. He was later taken to the Ciudadela, where Félix Díaz was in charge and where Gustavo was executed that night. "Diaz as a Murder Factor," *New York Times*, September 22, 1913.

16. Maldonado, *Asesinatos*, 6.

17. Ibid.

18. Márquez Sterling, *Últimos días*, 466–67.

19. "Madero Not to Die; Taft Gets a Pledge; Ambassador Wilson Had Unofficially Warned Huerta against a Resort to Barbarism," *New York Times*, February 22, 1913, sec. 3, 3. Wilson was unsympathetic to the pleas of Madero's wife that her husband's life be spared. Márquez Sterling, *Últimos días*, 546.

20. "Madero May Be Examined by a Lunacy Commission; Case before New Cabinet," *Miami Herald*, February 21, 1913.

21. Márquez Sterling, *Últimos días*; Maldonado, *Asesinatos*, 7.

22. Almada, *Vida, proceso y muerte de Abraham González*, 144. Francisco Vázquez Gómez wrote another rendition that his sources had related to him. He said that in a confrontation at Chapultepec, Félix Díaz slapped Madero, and then officer Francisco Cárdenas shot Madero in the forehead. Madero's body and the

arrested Pino Suárez were driven to Lecumberri, where Pino Suárez was shot after attempting to escape. Vázquez Gómez, *Memorias*, 542.

23. Maldonado, *Asesinatos*, 7.

24. "Huerta Promises to Satisfy Society on Killings," *New York Times*, February 24, 1913; "Official Accounts Differ, Public Doubts Statements that Murders Were Not Plotted," *New York Times*, February 24, 1913. The idea of an attack on the motorcade by Madero partisans was hatched by Huerta and Blanquet. Márquez Sterling, *Últimos días*, 480.

25. Márquez Sterling, *Últimos días*, 480

26. "Gonzalez on Trial for Plot," *New York Times*, February 26, 1913.

27. Beezley, *Insurgent Governor*, 155–58; Almada, *Vida, proceso y muerte de Abraham González*, 148, 149. Huerta, it was said, had hard feelings toward González, who had accused Huerta of disloyalty. RDS, Letcher to State Dept., October 17, 1913, File No. 812.00/9484, 26.

28. Katz, *Life and Times*, 196. In a different report, the train crew explained that the shackled González accidently fell between the moving cars as he was being taken from one coach to another. "Gonzalez Killed by Train on Way to His Trial," *Idaho Statesman*, March 31, 1913.

29. RDS, Henry Lane Wilson to State Dept., February 27, 1913, File No. 812.00/6412.

30. Almada, *Revolución*, 2:20–21.

31. Orozco to Díaz, "I congratulate you, Gen. Mondragon and the other distinguished chiefs, officials and troops for your heroic work and the happy ending obtained, which resulted in the fall of the Government of Madero." "Orozco Congratulates Díaz," *Dallas Morning News*, February 21, 1913.

32. "Confer with Northerners, Diaz Asks Orozco to Hasten to Capital to Meet Federals," *Idaho Statesman*, February 22, 1913.

33. "Conference Is Held; Reports Disagree," *Fort Worth Star-Telegram*, February 28, 1913; "Mexicans to Talk Peace in Texas," *El Paso Herald*, March 1, 1913; "Huerta Expects Peace within Thirty Days," *Idaho Statesman*, March 1, 1913.

34. The editor of a pamphlet on Zapata's Plan de Ayala had this scathing take on Orozco and his absence: "General Pascual Orozco, Jr., ceased being the Chief of the Revolution since the month of May of 1912, when, in disavowing Lic. Emilio Vázquez Gómez as Provisional President of the Republic, he betrayed the revolution in Chihuahua. Orozco sold out to the Científico Party under the influence of Ing. Alberto García Granados, Lic. Rafael Hernández Madero, General Jerónimo Treviño, General Luis Terrazas, Enrique C. Creel and others of the same group. Orozco has just confirmed his betrayal of the Plan de San Luis, reformed in Tacubaya, and abandoned his entire army at Ojinaga on September 14, 1912, and entered the United States where he remained in hiding, feigning illness. Upon the triumph of the 'Díaz-Huerta' coup in February of 1913, he emerged from his hideaway and returned to Mexican territory, putting himself under the command of the pseudo government of General Huerta in the capacity of a constable." RDS, J. E. Hernández to Bryan, October 17, 1913, File No. 812.00/9346, enclosing a copy

of Plan de Ayala; *Plan de Ayala*. Puebla, Puebla: Imprenta Comercial, 1913, 11–12.

35. Meyer, *Mexican Rebel*, 97, 98.

36. Márquez Terrazas, *Terrazas y Su Siglo*, 257.

37. The Orozquista group labeled "Peace Commission" returned to El Paso and included Orozco Sr., Crisóforo Caballero, José Córdova, Rafael R. Flores, Nicanor Valdez, Indalecio Vara, Juan Garza Galán and Adolfo Fuentes. RDS, Garrett to State Dept., March 1, 1913, in United States, *Foreign Relations of the United States, 1913*, 750, File No. 812.00/6443.

38. Almada, *Revolución*, 2:21–22.

39. Initially, Orozco joined Huerta, but the decision among Orozquistas was not unanimous. José Inés Salazar announced in favor of Vázquez Gómez and added that he would never support Huerta. Salazar and Orozco had apparently been at odds since the previous September and were differing again. Salazar was demanding land reform measures immediately, and Orozco responded that he would leave the matter up to Huerta. "Mexican Generals Disagree," *Dallas Morning News*, March 4, 1913; "Salazar Fights for Land Plan and Gomez," *Idaho Statesman*, March 11, 1913. Within two weeks, however, they were all with Huerta as Orozco, Salazar, and other Orozco staff were commissioned brigadier generals in the irregular auxiliary forces on March 17, 1913. AHDN, Pascual Orozco personal file, Archivo de Bóveda.

40. Enrique Creel soon reestablished relations with Huerta. In a letter, Creel relayed information regarding Carranza forces to Huerta. AHDN, Creel to Huerta, May 2, 1913, exp. XI/481.5/30, folio 1321–23.

41. "El Saludo Del Gral. Félix Díaz al Jefe Rebelde Pascual Orozco," and "Pascual Orozco, Cheche Campos, Caraveo y Argumedo Llegaron Anoche con los Sres. Comisionados de Paz," *El País*, March 13, 1913.

42. Order naming brigadier generals in irregular auxiliary forces, Pascual Orozco, Marcelo Caraveo, Benjamín Argumedo, José Inés Salazar, Emilio P. Campa, José de Jesus Campos, and David de la Fuente. Pascual Sr. made colonel in irregular auxiliary forces, which appointment was made permanent in August 1913. AHDN, Personnel file of Pascual Orozco Jr.

43. Meyer, *Mexican Rebel*, 99–102.

44. Ibid., 101.

45. "Washington's Hope Is Still Unshaken," *New York Times*, September 7, 1913; "Still Trust in Huerta," *New York Times*, September 9, 1913; "Huerta May Resign in Gamboa's Favor," *New York Times*, September 21, 1913; "Gamboa Nominated; Huerta Won't Run," *New York Times*, September 25, 1913; "Diaz Ticket Completed," *New York Times*, September 6, 1913; "Reyes Forsakes Huerta," *New York Times*, September 13, 1913.

46. In his prepared remarks to the Senate, Domínguez wrote, "The National Assembly has the duty of deposing Don Victoriano Huerta from the Presidency." RDS, O'Shaughnessy to State Dept., October 20, 1913, File No. 812.00/9529.

47. Vera Estañol, *Revolución*, 330–41; "President Dissolves Congress and Calls for New Elections," *Mexican Herald*, October 11, 1913; "Huerta Arrests 110 Legislators," *New York Times*, October 12, 1913. The United States refused to recognize the legality of any of Huerta's acts after October 11. RDS, September 21, 1914, and October 8, 1914, File No. 812.00/15.

48. Palavicini, *Diputados*, 398; Ramírez Rancaño, *Reacción*, 36; *El Diario*, October 16, 18, and 20, 1913; *El Pais*, October 18 and 21, 1913; *Mexican Herald*, November 5, 1913.

49. RDS, O'Shaughnessy to State Dept., October 23, 1913, File No. 812.00/9344.

50. Meyer, *Huerta*, 152.

51. Ibid., 153–54. Even after the election, the expectation was that Huerta would resign. On December 9, the congress declared the election null and called for a new election for July 1914. The congress, however, gave Huerta what he needed to remain in office when it resolved that Huerta would continue in the presidency until the next election. RDS, O'Shaughnessy to State Dept., December 10, 1913, File No. 812.00/10118; RDS, O'Shaughnessy to State Dept., December 9, 1913, File No. 812.00/10113.

52. Katz, *Life and Times*, 206.

53. Taibo, *Pancho Villa*, 181.

54. Ibid.

55. January 1, 1914, report by Fernando Serrano, consul, on the fall of Ojinaga. SRE, Legajo L-E 711, folios 86–92. It was not only the thought of Villa in control that drove many to seek refuge outside of Mexico, but also that in December 1913, Carranza let it be known that a death sentence awaited those who had collaborated with and recognized Huerta, and he issued a list of 366 individuals, including Orozco and Creel. Many if not most of those listed, fled from Mexico. Ramírez Rancaño, *Reacción*, 5, 8; Sax, *Mexicanos*.

56. Meyer, *Mexican Rebel*, 107–108.

57. Ibid., 109.

58. BOI Case Files, Report by E. M. Blanford, El Paso, February 23, 1914. The agent had information that Orozco was in Las Cruces, New Mexico, and mentioned that a copy of the indictment would be forwarded to allow agents to make an arrest. Orozco, however, was not found. The indictment was also mentioned in BOI Case Files, Report by El Paso agent E. M. Blanford, January 19, 1914. U.S. District Court records note two 1912 cases, *United States v. Pascual Orozco, Jr.*, Nos. 1628 and 1633.

59. BOI Case Files from January 3, 1914, and February 25, 1914. There was no way to tell whether the reports were accurate.

60. "La División del Norte Quedara Dividida en 3 Distritos Militares," *El Diario*, February 15, 1914; "Chihuahua State Is Divided into Three Districts," *Mexican Herald*, March 10, 1914; *Diario Oficial Estados Unidos Mexicanos*, April 17, June 11 and 17, and August 8, 1914; Almada, *Revolución*, 2:97; Almada, *Gobernadores*, 614.

61. AHDN, Personnel file of Pascual Orozco Jr., March 6 and 7, 1914. Orozco, Salazar, and García Hidalgo were all named division generals—Salazar over Juárez, Orozco over Chihuahua, and Carlos García Hidalgo over Parral, replacing Argumedo.

62. Meyer, *Mexican Rebel*, 112.

63. Ibid., 113.

64. Ibid., 109.

65. Katz, *Life and Times*, 355.

66. Ibid., 352.

67. Ibid., 353.

68. Ibid., 361, 362.

69. Carvajal confirmed the end of service for several Huertistas, including Orozco and Madero's assassin Francisco Cárdenas. AHDN, Order, July 28, 1914, Orozco personal file.

70. Meyer, *Mexican Rebel*, 116–17.

71. Three days after Huerta resigned, Orozco abandoned the barracks at San Luis Potosí, leading some four thousand soldiers who left with him. Whatever forces he may have had were soon dispersed and lost. "Orozco May Turn Guerrilla," *Kansas City Star*, July 18, 1914. The article noted that next to Huerta, Orozco was the man Constitutionalists hated most.

Chapter 27

1. Krauze, *Mexico: Biography of Power*, 340–41.

2. Katz, *Life and Times*, 383. Katz acknowledged two theories in explaining the Carranza-Villa split. One had Villa and Carranza as ideological foes. Alan Knight advanced another nonideological theory in which Villistas and Carrancistas saw the world differently. They returned to the old strong central government versus federation controversy, in which the federalists desired each area to be its own master. Villa was for relative independence of the North, and Carranza favored a united, strong central government. Katz, *Life and Times*, 390. This was also the continuation of the same fight Orozco had with Madero or between rural rebels and the urban middle-class reformers.

3. Meyer, *Huerta*, 214.

4. Meyer, *Mexican Rebel*, 115–16, or his actual assassin, according to Vázquez.

5. Ibid., 119n20.

6. "New Mexican War Begins in New York," *New York Times*, December 15, 1914; Meyer, "Mexican-German Conspiracy," 79–80.

7. CEHM, "Descubrese un complot para embrollarnos con México," Fondo Manuscritos del Primer Jefe del Ejército Constitucionalista, XXI.152.17350; CEHM, "Les conspirateurs Boches, Von Rintelen organisait la guerre entre le Mexique e les Etas-Unis," undated, unknown publication, ca. December 9, 1915, Fondo Manuscritos del Primer Jefe del Ejército Constitucionalista, XXI.63.6999.

8. Meyer, "Mexican-German Conspiracy," 80. Rintelen reportedly funded the San Antonio junta for the Germans, although this could be confusing the assembly with Labor's National Peace Council, a pro-German front group advocating U.S. neutrality. CEHM, Unnamed report, April 10, 1916, Fondo Manuscritos del Primer Jefe del Ejército Constitucionalista, XXI.73.8010.1.

9. Meyer, "Mexican-German Conspiracy," 81; CEHM, Jesús E. Luján to José Y. Limantour, April 7, 1915, Fondo José Y. Limantour, CDLIV.2a.1910.18.195. José Orozco was prosecuted for his part in the plot and said that the clerical party supported the effort and had promised $1 million in support. "Plot to Restore Huerta Revealed," *Morning Oregonian*, November 6, 1915.

10. Tuchman, *Zimmerman Telegram*, 40.

11. In the United States, antiwar sentiment included anti-British Irish, pro-Axis German Americans, Socialists and leftist reformers, suffragettes, and many others. Also, CEHM, Transcription of "Jugando el papel de Alemania," *New York City World*, January 15, 1916, Fondo Manuscritos del Primer Jefe del Ejército Constitucionalista, XXI.65.7237.1.

12. Tuchman, *Zimmermann Telegram*, 63.

13. *San Antonio Express*, February 7, 1915. In fact, many Mexican exiles found their names on lists Carranza supposedly made of those he intended to try for treason. Meyer, *Huerta*, 214–15.

14. Meyer, *Huerta*, 213. Unmentioned is whether this intrigue affected old El Aguila petroleum relationships with Weetman Pearson supplying the British navy on one side and his former colleague Creel helping the Germans on the other side.

15. "The Children of Cuauhtémoc, Hidalgo and Juárez in Texas." CEHM, Manifesto, "A los hijos de Cuauhtémoc, Hidalgo y Juárez en Texas," [Laredo], Texas, November 26, 1914, Fondo Manuscritos del Primer Jefe del Ejército Constitucionalista, XXI.39.4263.1–5.

16. Meyer, *Huerta*, 215, 216; Harris and Sadler, *Plan of San Diego*, 1–4. Meyer was one of many who believed that the Plan de San Diego later inspired the German 1917 Zimmermann Telegram. Meyer, "The Mexican-German Conspiracy," 80.

17. *New York Times*, April 13, 1915; Meyer, *Huerta*, 216; Meyer, "Mexican-German Conspiracy," 81. The State Department noted that Creel, Huerta, and other unnamed "prominent Mexicans" met in Seville on March 28 and left the next day for Cádiz. RDS, Gracey to Secretary of State, March 31, 1915, File No. 812.00/14751. Meyer wrote that Creel accompanied Huerta to New York, but while the passenger manifest for the vessel *Antonio López* notes the names of Huerta and his companions Abraham Ratner and José Delgado, Creel's name does not appear. The New York consulate's newspaper clipping service also has no report of Creel landing with or meeting Huerta in New York. SRE, Morning Papers, April 13, 1915, legajo 477-23. Sources reported Creel meeting in Los Angeles in early April 1915, with an oligarchy group, each member of which promised to donate $20,000 to Villa. They would do anything to remove Carranza even in donating to the man who was the oligarchy's recent scourge. AHDN, Telegram Villarreal to Carranza, April 7, 1915, exp. XI/481.5/15-1, folio 34.

18. Llorente warned the State Department before Huerta landed. RDS, Llorente to Secretary of State, April 10, 1915, File No. 812.0011187/11; Antonio, Villarreal, consul in Los Angeles, asked for Carranza's permission to file criminal charges against Huerta. AHDN, Villarreal to Carranza, April 18, 1915, exp. XI/481.5/15-1, folio 41. The State Department noted that state and the president had received many protests to the landing and requests that Huerta be extradited to Mexico for trial. United States, *Foreign Relations of the United States, 1915*, 828, File No. 812.001H87/13.

19. Germans deposited $800,000 for Huerta in Cuban and Mexican banks and promised delivery of munitions via U-boat. Katz, *Secret War*, 330. There is a question whether the near million dollars was ever deposited. The U.S. Department of Justice opened an investigation to determine the amount and source of funds received by Huerta. "May Show Germans in Huerta's Plot," *New York Times*, November 24, 1915.

20. Meyer, *Mexican Rebel*, 124–27; Meyer, "The Mexican-German Conspiracy," 85.

21. Meyer, *Huerta*, 218, 220.

22. BOI Case Reports, Case No. 232–14.

23. Tuchman, *Zimmermann Telegram*, 65, 66, 76; Rausche, "Exile and Death," 135–36.

24. AHDN, Andrés García to Carranza, June 28, 1915, exp. XI/481.5/97, folio 901.

25. AHDN, Juan N. Amador to Carranza, June 27, 1911, exp. XI/481.5/97, folios 764, 787, 882, and 883. Amador and others reported that several generals were on their way to El Paso, including Victor Huerta, José Delgado, artillery general Enrique González, José Alessio Robles, Alcocer, Victor Huerta Bravo, Vicente Calero, Ruiz Telles, Trías, Castro, and Landa.

26. Rausche, "Exile and Death," 138.

27. An AP reporter told Cobb that Huerta had left Kansas City on the Rock Island bound for El Paso with an expected arrival on June 27. Cobb to Secretary of State, June 26, 1915, United States, *Foreign Relations of the United States, 1915*, 828, File No. 812.001H87/20.

28. Tuchman, *Zimmermann Telegram*, 77–78.

29. Meyer, *Mexican Rebel*, 129.

30. Cobb's report to State Department stated, "Generals Huerta and Orozco are now in Federal Building. Agent Department of Justice, Beckham, has received instructions to detain them. Prior to the receipt of these instructions, by reason of your June 26 and urgency of situation, I insisted upon course pursued and assumed responsibility therefor. Late last night I learned through railroad of Huerta's plans to leave train at Newman Station, twenty miles north of El Paso. With Beckham, District Clerk, two deputy marshals, and Colonel G. H. Morgan accompanied by twenty-five soldiers that he carried to prevent disorder or any attempt at interference, we went to Newman Station this morning and found Orozco and Huerta's son-in-law awaiting train. We had prepared warrants to use if necessary, but found it unnecessary. Beckham invited Huerta and Orozco to accompany us to Federal building without arrest, which they did. Without display, we have treated them with consideration and every proper courtesy.

Huerta is suave though Orozco is not suave. I am sure they had revolutionary plans and that the action here has been both right and timely." Cobb to State Dept., June 27, 1915, in United States, *Foreign Relations of the United States, 1915*, 828, File No. 812.001H87/21.

31. AHDN, June 1915, exp. XI/481.5/97, folios 882–89; Carranza memorandum, June 28, 1915, and staff response. Carranza received notice of the arrests and updates from several sources. SRE, Legajo 13-30-25.

32. AHDN, Carranza staff Arredondo to Carranza, June 29, 1911, exp. XI/481.5/97, folio 913. Despite that report, in a lengthy memorandum, Llorente attempted to make a case for extradition to the State Department. Llorente to Secretary of State, July 1, 1915, in United States, *Foreign Relations of the United States, 1915*, 829–33, File No. 812.001H87/33.

33. It is surprising that the judge allowed a bond. The BOI previously reported that Orozco was indicted on April 15, 1912, for having violated U.S. neutrality laws, labeled him a fugitive, and hunted for him all during the latter half of 1914 and the first half of 1915. Yet, when he was arrested with Huerta, no one mentioned his fugitive status or the status of the 1912 indictment.

34. Serafina Orozco interview in Martínez, *Fragments*, 44, 45. Serafina's version conflicts with several other versions that had him escaping during the night by jumping out of a window. BOI Case Reports, Steve Pinckney, July 3, 1915.

35. "Orozco Escapes," *New York Times*, July 4, 1915; *El Paso Morning Times*, July 4, 1915.

36. The Havana Mexican Consulate filed detailed reports of their activities and mentioned involvement by Gonzalo Enrile. SRE, Legajo 477, exp. 11, folios 7–12.

37. SRE, New York Mexican Consulate, July 11, 1915, legajo 477, exp. 11, folio 38.

Chapter 28

1. *New York Times*, August 4, 1915; *Houston Post*, August 4, 1915.

2. *El Paso Morning Times*, August 27 and September 2, 1915; "Orozco Disappears Again," *Lexington (Ky.) Herald*, August 27, 1915.

3. "Orozco was Killed by American Posse," *New York Times*, September 1, 1915; "Gen. Orozco Is Slain in Fight with Posse," *Dallas Morning News*, September 1, 1915.

4. Serafina Orozco interview in Martínez, *Fragments*, 45.

5. Meyer, *Mexican Rebel*, 131–33.

6. "Great Funeral for Orozco Band," *New York Times*, September 4, 1915.

7. Inquest, Case No. 35, *State of Texas v. John A. Morine et al.*, 34th Judicial District Court, Culberson County, Texas, October term, 1915, 359–63. A copy of the inquest is attached as the appendix.

8. Wright, "Last Days of Pascual Orozco," 6.

9. Statement of W. H. Schrock, Inquest, 360.

10. One member of the posse said that the Mexicans paid thirty cents for the horseshoe work. RDS, Carnes report. Carnes to Cobb, September 1, 1915, 812.00/-16046.

11. Statement of John A. Morine, Inquest, 363.

12. The number in the posse differs in several accounts. *El Paso Morning Times* put the membership at twenty-four law officers and ranchers. "Death of Orozco Blocks Another Mexican Invasion Plot," *El Paso Morning Times*, September 1, 1915.

13. Morine Statement, Inquest, 363.

14. Ibid., 364–65; Schrock statement, Inquest, 361.

15. See Alexander, *Fearless Dave Allison*, 196. Being a member of the posse that had killed Orozco became a bragging point. To impress his prospective bride, one alleged posse member claimed to have been the one to have killed Pascual. He also claimed to have been wounded in the action, even after officials reported that the posse had no casualties. The groom's name does not appear among those indicted or even present at the event. "Man Claiming to Be One Who Shot Pascual. Folks Fighting over the Honor," *Clayton (N.Mex.) News*, December 4, 1915.

16. *El Paso Morning Times*, October 9, 1915.

17. Meyer, *Huerta*, 227.

18. "Gen. Huerta Dies at Home in Texas," *New York Times*, January 14, 1916; "To Bury Huerta in Mexico," *New York Times*, January 15, 1916; "Gen. Huerta, One Time Dictator of Mexico, Closes Book of Life," *El Paso Herald*, January 14, 1916; Meyer, *Mexican Rebel*, 134. Although Huerta's family wanted his remains repatriated to Mexico, that was never allowed, and his remains are interred in El Paso.

Chapter 29

1. Taracena, *Verdadera Revolución (1915–1917)*, 63. Orozco's sister Serafina also alleged that the bodies were dragged some distance. Taracena, *Verdadera Revolución (1915–1917)*, 147; Bolling, *Death Rides the River*, 156. The bodies were in a narrow canyon, and Judge Owen ordered the bodies taken by wagon to the Taylor Ranch. The wagon, they explained, could not enter the canyon, and the bodies had to be carried, or dragged according to some, for approximately three hundred yards.

2. CEHM, Cabrera to Carranza, September 25, 1915, Fondo Carranza, XXI.53.5841.1.

3. Immediately, the Mexican government in Washington asked for information regarding circumstances in the death of the five Mexicans, including Orozco. SRE, Arredondo to Lansing, September 1, 1915, legajo L-E 740, folio 6. The State Department responded on September 4 that the men were stealing horses. RDS, Arredondo to Sec. of State Robert Lansing, September 1, 1915, 812.00/16003; SRE, Adee to Arredondo, September 4, 1915, legajo L-E 740, folio 7. In El Paso, the Mexican Consulate also requested an investigation over the deaths to advise Carranza on the occurrence. *El Paso Morning Times*, September 5, 1915.

4. When the bodies arrived in El Paso, they were not met at the Union Depot as expected, where a large crowd was waiting, but were taken instead from the train at another station downtown. "Bodies of Slain Mexicans in City," *El Paso Morning Times*, September 2, 1915.

5. *El Paso Morning Times*, September 2, 1915. A Mexican San Antonio newspaper, *La Época*, carried an article headlined "Pascual Orozco y la Ley Fuga." See Meyer, *Mexican Rebel*, 132.

6. "Mexican Rising Feared; Border Is under Arms," *New York Tribune*, September 2, 1915.

7. "Pascual Orozco and the Fugitive Law," *La Época*, September 3, 1915, in Waldrep, *Lynching in America*, 178–79.

8. "Reprisals Feared for the Death of Pascual Orozco," *La Época*, September 3, 1915, in Waldrep, *Lynching in America*, 180–81.

9. RDS, Cobb to Sec. of State, September 3 and 4, 1915, 812.00/16015, 160016.

10. BOI Case Files, Letter to Bielaski, September 6, 1915.

11. "Mexican Rising Feared; Border Is under Arms," *New York Tribune*, September 2, 1915.

12. There is no question that Orozco, his people, and their conservative coalition had been busy for months raising money, buying weapons, and preparing for a significant revolt. There was a rumor that Orozco was carrying a large quantity of money when he was killed, perhaps 40,000 pesos. It would be reasonable to assume that he was carrying money to fund the revolution. After the trial, Judge Jackson ordered the return of "money" possessed by the deceased to the relatives, but the funds were never described or claimed. Wright, "Last Days of Pascual Orozco," 7. For years, rumors about the money persisted. Some even prospected for the cash along the chase trail, others were sure the sheriff or someone else had taken the funds. Taracena said the Loves killed Orozco when they learned he had money and then kept it. See also Bolling, *Death Rides the River*.

13. Bolling wrote that the posse might have changed the locations of the bodies to place them inside Culberson County. Talk of changing the location from El Paso to Culberson County and the erroneous photograph of Texas Rangers dragging bodies at the King Ranch a month later might be the sources of the "dragging" allegations. Judge Owen was clear in saying that the bodies were "carried" to the Taylor Ranch wagon. While they might have done so, there is little to substantiate the charge that they changed the site of the killings.

14. The Mexican Consulate and El Paso Spanish-language media assumed that U.S. authorities would undertake a thorough investigation, that a medical report would be issued, and federal investigators would interview witnesses. *El Paso Morning Times*, September 5, 1915. In fact, the record fails to reveal that any investigation ever took place.

15. "Ready for Orozco's Band, Ranchers under Arms to Meet any Attempted Reprisals," *New York Times*, September 2, 1915; "Mexican Rising Feared, Killing of Orozco Bitterly Resented," *New York Tribune*, September 2, 1915.

16. "Mexicans Cross Border," *Idaho Statesman*, September 2, 1915.

17. "Orozco Possemen Indicted," *El Paso Morning Times*, October 9, 1915; Case No. 35, *State of Texas v. John A. Morine et al.*, 354.

18. "Orozco Possemen Indicted," *El Paso Morning Times*, October 9, 1915.

19. Even stout posse defenders admit the plan, with one writing, "The [trial's] outcome was not a shocker. It did, however, put the matter to rest. Fifth Amendment protections against Double Jeopardy guaranteed burial of criminal charges—*as planned*" (emphasis added). Bell, "Hellfire and Hot Tamales," 63.

20. One reason why no witnesses were called was that the grand jury indicted anyone who could testify to the killing, yet another way to keep witnesses from being called. One writer, perplexed by the proceedings, noted that "evidently" there was no trial and the indictments were summarily dismissed. Voliva, "Guns of Green River Canyon," 14.

21. "Jury Verdict of Not Guilty Returned at Van Horn Following Trial," *Dallas Morning News*, October 9, 1915.

22. One writer noted that county attorney A. L. Green testified as a grand jury witness, asked the grand jury for the protective indictment, and served as the posse's defense lawyer. Normally county attorneys are state prosecutors handling misdemeanors. Green might have been playing many questionable roles in this instance. Bolling, *Death Rides the River*.

23. The file contains two verdict notations, one with J. E. Bean as the foreman and the other naming L. P. Wheat. See "Jury Verdict of Not Guilty Returned at Van Horn Following Trial," *Dallas Morning News*, October 9, 1915.

24. Case No. 35, *State of Texas v. John A. Morine et al.* It appears that families of the deceased did not claim the property, which was apparently later distributed to the posse as mementos. Voliva, "Guns of Green River Canyon," 14–15.

25. The Fifth Amendment provides, "Nor shall any person be subject for the same offence to be twice put in jeopardy of life or limb."

26. The biographer of the man in charge of the posse, Dave Allison, wrote, "Incontrovertibly, the indictment was a case of either CYA . . . or government scapegoating." Alexander, *Fearless Dave Allison*, 202. Given that the indictment was requested by and brought to immunize the posse, it clearly was not scapegoating. It was indeed a case of cover-up by the possemen, but even more so, a cover-up that would end the inquiry.

Chapter 30

1. Harris and Sadler make a strong case that Magonistas wrote the *plan* to incite a revolution on the border, but the revolt required a base in Mexico. For Carranza, it was the means to force U.S. recognition and allow weapon sales to that government. Carranza went along with the raids and then claimed Mexico was too weak and defenseless to police the border. They claim it worked, as Carranza obtained recognition on October 15, 1915. Harris and Sadler, *Plan de San Diego*, 26, 84–86.

2. Harris and Sadler, *Plan de San Diego*, 247–52; William D. Carrigan and Clive Webb, "When Americans Lynched Mexicans," *New York Times*, February 20, 1915. The Mexican government compiled a partial list of Mexicans killed by the Texas Rangers as of November 30, 1915. SRE, Legajo 477, exp. 10.

3. Carrigan, "When Americans Lynched Mexicans."

4. Despite numerous reports that Texas Rangers and U.S. Army units were part of the posse, that does not appear to be the case.

5. Webb, Walter Prescott, *The Texas Rangers*, Kindle edition. The Texas Joint Committee of the House and Senate instituted an investigation of the Texas State

Ranger Force in January 1919 during the Thirty-Sixth Texas Legislature to review the conduct of the Texas Ranger force during the period from 1914 to 1919. Records consist of a three-volume transcript of proceedings conducted by the committee during January and February 1919.

6. "Intervention Plot, Perhaps," *New York Times*, September 5, 1915. The *Times* was not alone in concluding that Orozco was connected to the Plan de San Diego. See Gerlach, "Conditions along the Border."

7. Alexander, *Fearless Dave Allison*. In the 1918 incident near the Orozco death scene, Texas Rangers killed fifteen Mexicans, whom the Rangers suspected were aiding cross-border raiders. The Rangers went to Porvenir and killed the males in that community. The incident is known as the Porvenir massacre, and the controversy it raised resulted in a legislative investigation of the Texas Rangers. See http://www.lib.utexas.edu/taro/tslac/50062/tsl-50062.html.

8. "Sierra Blanca Country Quiet," *El Paso Morning Times*, September 2, 1915.

9. Including Bolling, *Death Rides the River*; Voliva, "Guns of Green River Canyon"; Wright, "Last Days of Pascual Orozco"; Love interview; Alexander, *Fearless Dave Allison*; Bell, "Hellfire and Hot Tamales"; and Leftwich, "Death of General Pascual Orozco," 93–96.

10. RDS, Carnes to Cobb, September 1, 1915, 812.00/16046.

11. U.S. mounted customs inspector Joe Sitters and Texas Ranger Eugene Hulen were killed in Pilares Canyon in May, and Texas Ranger Robert Lee Burdett was killed near Fabens in El Paso County in June 1915. Alexander, *Fearless Dave Allison*, 184–85.

12. The Texas Department of State Health Services reports that a search of Texas death records fails to turn up anything for Pascual Orozco or Crisóforo Caballero.

13. Cobb sent a copy of the Carnes report to the State Department and added, "The undertaker has promised me a statement of just the condition of Orozco's body was in, and what wounds were found. This will be forwarded as soon as obtained." RDS, Cobb to Lansing, September 2, 1915, File No. 812.00/16046. If Kaster ever made a report, it has not turned up. A postmortem showing clean shots to the backs of the heads would have caused a tremendous uproar and scandal. Short of examining the remains today, it is impossible to know the cause of death.

14. Bolling included a photograph of men on horses dragging the bodies of four men. He identified the slain men as the Orozco group and the riders as named members of Allison's posse. The photograph, however, is a well-known image depicting an event that took place a month before at the Norias Ranch, one of the King ranches south of Kingsville, Texas, a location more than six hundred miles distant. Bolling, *Death Rides the River* (see also http://los-tejanos.com/border_war.html). The photograph has been mistakenly used several times. The photograph, correctly identifying the Norias Ranch, was published in an article dated two weeks before Orozco's killing. "How Texans Must Defend Homes against Mexican Bandits," *New York American*, August 14, 1915.

15. Caballero was arrested in December 1912, along with Orozco Sr., as they fled Ojinaga and crossed into the United States at Presidio.

that Orozco submitted a bill for 100,000 pesos and decided to rebel when only 50,000 pesos was paid. "Trusted Chief Turns Traitor," *El Paso Morning Times*, March 6, 1912. See also Almada, *Vida, proceso y muerte de Abraham González*, 54.

34. Puente, *Pascual Orozco*, 35–37.

35. Meyer, "Career of Pascual Orozco, Jr.," 272, 276. Meyer's opinion mirrored the assessment of Manuel Bonilla who said Orozco was, "one of the ignorant jefes lacking scruples and who were easily influenced by reactionaries led by the Terrazas." Bonilla, *Régimen Maderista*, 13.

36. Knight, *Mexican Revolution*, 1:290.

37. Ibid., 1:297–98. In an animated attack, Braulio Hernández said, "Orozco is an imbecile, dumb." Hernández testimony, in U.S. Senate, Committee on Foreign Relations, *Revolutions in Mexico, Hearings*, 557. Orozco was inclined to violence, was short on intelligence, and lacked loyalty, Márquez Sterling, *Últimos días*, 236–37. Others were equally as dismissive of Orozco. Even Científico Francisco Bulnes in *La Prensa* and others in an article in *La Época* wrote about Creel and the clan's seduction of Orozco. Orozco, they claimed, was necessary to their survival, and it was not hard work for them to bring Orozco to their side, as he was a *"simplón,"* a simpleton. *El Correo de Chihuahua*, August 14, 1912. Perhaps in Orozco's view that assessment may have been the typical city slicker's mistaken view of a slow-talking country rube, a charge frequently leveled at folks from the Northwest. It did, nevertheless, provide one explanation for Orozco's surprising betrayal. Orozco was not the only one insulted as an ignorant rural type. The Mexican press assailed and insulted Abraham González in the same manner. Bonilla, *Régimen Maderista*, 16. The virulent, anti-Madero Mexico City press called the college-educated, Ciudad Guerrero–born Abraham González "ignorant" and "a rancher" who had never lived in Mexico City, implying that he was an incompetent, country rube. Almada, *Vida, proceso y muerte de Abraham González*, 77.

38. Meyer, *Mexican Rebel*, 57, 61, 91–92, 98,

39. Ibid., 65–66.

40. Chihuahua U.S. consul Marion Letcher, who had the opportunity to observe Orozco closely and saw his interaction with the oligarchy, had this frank assessment: "Madero, doubtless realizing that Orozco was entirely unfitted either by education or experience for any post of great responsibility, did not offer him any post under the national government but left him rather as commander-in-chief of militia in the state of Chihuahua. This apparent slight offered a great opportunity to Madero's enemies to prey upon the vanity of Orozco, and it was not long before they had worked him up to a state of great indignation against his former companion in arms. The well-groomed gentlemen of the wealthy Chihuahua clubs, who would not have touched the hand of this person but little above the rank of peon a year previously, began to flatter him with all kinds of social attentions, and it required a bare two months of this subtle work for Orozco

to become their humble servant, body and soul. . . . Orozco was carefully tested, and it was found that he would do. He had no brains they knew; he was course, sensuous, and brutal, . . . but he had what they wanted at the time, a ready-made prestige and influence behind which they could mask their attack upon Madero." RDS, Letcher to State Dept., October 17, 1913, File No. 812.00/9484, 16.

41. Katz, *Life and Times*, 142.

42. Ibid., 142. Orozco may have been inspired by Ricardo Flores Magón to join the anti-Díaz revolt, but in 1913 Flores Magón associated Orozco with the Científicos. Flores Magón, Araujo, and Owen, *Land and Liberty*, 44.

43. Interview of Oscar Lesser Norwald, in Osorio, *Pancho Villa, Ese Desconocido*, 25. There might have been an even darker side to that part of Orozco's life. In late September of 1913, police officials initiated an investigation into a possible assault on two women and the near-fatal shooting of a Nombre de Dios police officer who had gone to their aid. The women were in a car and had been screaming for help. When the officer approached the car, a man, whose voice the officer identified as Orozco's, told him, "Don't you know who we are"? That man suddenly shot the officer just above the heart and drove off, leaving the wounded officer on the ground. Officials named Orozco and Ignacio Leyva Olea as the assailants. This was at a time when Orozco, under Huerta, oversaw Chihuahua. Other than filing a report with witness statements, officials took no other action against the pair until August 1915, when, Chihuahua authorities issued a citation in the official newspaper for the two women to appear and give testimony. Orozco was then on the run in the United States after he had escaped from custody in El Paso. The record does not reveal whether the women ever responded. Orozco was soon dead, leaving the cases unresolved. Criminal case against Pascual Orozco, September 25, 1913, and Causa Número 131, Juzgado Primero de lo Penal, September 18, 1915, ATJ; *Periódico Oficial*, August 8, 15, and 22, 1915.

44. González Ramírez, *Manifiestos Políticos*, 554–55.

45. Katz, *Life and Times*, 142.

46. "Mexican Generals Disagree," *Dallas Morning News*, March 4, 1913; "Salazar Fights for Land Plan and Gomez," *Idaho Statesman*, March 11, 1913.

47. Almada, *Vida, proceso y muerte de Abraham González*, 57–61, 63–64, 98.

48. Almada, *La Revolución*, 2:66.

49. Almada, *Vida, proceso y muerte de Abraham González*, 91.

50. Ibid., 77–79.

Epilogue

1. Luján testimony, in U.S. Senate, Committee on Foreign Relations, *Revolutions in Mexico, Hearings*, 297; Cockcroft, *Intellectual Precursors*, 62–63.

2. José Vasconcelos and Taibo say that no Madero profited from government service. Taibo, *Temporada de zopilotes*, 141.

3. Madero's naïveté in placing his trust in Huerta would cost thousands of Mexicans their lives, including his brother's and his own. Abraham González did not trust Huerta and thought that Madero had a "blind trust." González felt that

the federal army would never forgive the rebels for their defeat at Ciudad Juárez. "Mis memorias de la Revolución. Isidro Fabela. 12. Don Abraham y el General Victoriano Huerta," October 1977, 500 años de México en documentos, http:// www.biblioteca.tv/artman2/publish/1977_78/Mis_memorias_de_la_Revoluci_n_ Isidro_Fabela_12_Don_Abraham_y_el_General_Victoriano_Huerta.shtml.

4. Von Feilitzsch, *In Plain Sight*, 150.

5. Taibo, *Temporada de zopilotes*, 27.

6. Paul Garner, *Porfirio Díaz*.

7. Estevez, "Mexico among the World's Most Corrupt Nations." See also Randal C. Archibold, "In Mexico, a Growing Gap between Political Class and Calls for Change," *New York Times*, December 13, 2014, 4A.

8. The González reforms included increasing taxes for the wealthy to encourage development; providing tax relief for low and middle classes; stopping political *jefes* from taking state land so the land could instead be sold to working classes; eliminating political *jefes*; supporting unions and strikers; paying workers in currency rather than in scrip redeemable only at company stores; and abolishing company stores. Beezley, *Insurgent Governor*, 97, 101, 110.

9. RDS, Letcher to State Dept., March 20, 1912, File No. 812.00/3424.

10. Almada, *Revolución*, 2:18–20.

11. "Enrile, Sick, in El Paso Prison," *El Paso Herald*, June 10, 1912; "Gonzalo Enrile Fue Encarcelado Ayer en El Paso, Tex.," *El Diario*, June 10, 1912; "Embezzlement Charges," *San Francisco Call*, June 12, 1912.

12. "Porfirio Diaz Ready to Fight Americans," *New York Tribune*, February 15, 1913.

13. *El Pais*, February 24, 1913.

14. *El Diario*, October 18, 1913; *Mexican Herald*, November 5, 1913.

15. "Huerta's Message Awaited," *New York Times*, September 15, 1913.

16. Alessio Robles, *Perfiles de Saltillo*, 75–76. Enrile had one or more pending criminal cases in Coahuila that might be related to his incident. Perhaps, with this profile of Enrile, Alessio Robles had the final word in the earlier dispute they had. The pair almost engaged in a duel in Mexico City in 1920. "Mexico Returns to Man Killing," *Miami Herald*, November 5, 1920.

17. Enrile made claim to a shipment of arms in Havana that was being held by the Cuban government. CEHM, *San Antonio El Presente*, June 1, 1915, found in Fondo de la Barra, X-2.2.115.1; "Gonzalo Enrile Released from Custody," *El Paso Morning Times*, July 23, 1912.

18. Garciadiego and MacGregor, "Alemania," 441.

19. Fabela, *Documentos*, 17.

20. Von Feilitzsch, *Felix A. Sommerfeld and the Mexican Front*.

21. Boghardt, *Zimmermann Telegram*, 42–44, 58, 67–71. See also *Revolución y Régimen Constitucionalista*. Documento 739, in Fabela, *Documentos*, 17:19–20. Informe del Sr. Antonio Hernández Ferrer, Cónsul de México en La Habana, Cuba, sobre las actividades de Gonzalo Enrile. Habana, 24 enero 1916. Enrile was also in San Sebastian, Spain, visiting Porfirio Díaz Jr. to involve him in anti-Carranza efforts.

22. Garciadiego and MacGregor, "Alemania," 441; "Una Detención Llevada a Cabo en la Habana Pone en Claro el Complot del Gobierno Alemán," *El Nacional*, May 31, 1917; *San Antonio Light*, May 24, 1917; "Gonzalo C. Enrile Fue Arrestado en La Habana, Cuba," *El Paso Morning Times*, May 20, 1917.

23. This was a case involving a German investigation. BOI Case Files, State Dept. to BOI, May 19 and 24, 1917. "Maass" actually referred to Joaquin Maas, a general in Huerta's army and more than once governor of the state of Coahuila.

24. Federal Penal Case Numbers 88, 273 and 340, SCJN files.

25. "Mexico Returns to Man Killing," *Miami Herald*, November 5, 1920.

26. Casasola, *Seis Siglos*, 4:2262; Casasola, *Historia Gráfica*, 3:x, 1543. Sánchez Juárez followed his father in his affinity for Reyista figures, as Benito Juárez Maza was a Reyista in 1908.

27. "Una Conspiración fue descubierta en Oaxaca, *El Informador* (Guadalajara), June 5, 1921; "Mexico's Attitude on Property Rights," *New York Times Current History* 14 (April–Septeptember 1921): 711–13; "Mexican Plot Failed," *Washington Evening Star*, June 6, 1921; "Mexican Revolt Fails as Leaders Are Executed," *New York Tribune*, June 9, 1921; "Se Urdia en México, al Mismo Tiempo Que en Oaxaca, una Conspiración, Pero También se Logró Hacer Que Abortara," *El Informador*, June 6, 1921; "Anti-Obregón Plot was Widespread," *New York Times*, June 9, 1921.

28. Blanco Moheno, *Crónica*, 2:212.

29. Wasserman, "Enrique C. Creel," 659.

30. Grieb, "Standard Oil," 60; Bud-Frierman, Godley, and Wale, "Weetman Pearson in Mexico," 285.

31. Ibid., 287.

32. U.S. Senate, Committee on Foreign Relations, *Investigation of Mexican Affairs*, pt. 1, Senate Hearings, 278.

33. The National Action Party is the conservative party. Santiago Creel ran for the presidency under its banner and later served in the cabinet of President Vicente Fox.

34. Writer Francisco Martín Moreno alleges that Villa's killing was ordered by Plutarco Elías Calles and Álvaro Obregón. Moreno, *100 Mitos*, 97–98.

35. Death, March 15, 1955, at Hotel Dieu Hospital, El Paso, Texas, Texas Death Certificate; Almada, *Gobernadores*, 568–70.

36. Beelen, "Harding Administration and Mexico," 178–80.

37. Albro, *Always a Rebel*, 149–50; Lomnitz, *Ricardo Flores Magón*, 492. Lomnitz explained how rumors that he was murdered circulated. It appears that the prison physician and others at Leavenworth denied Magón medical treatment. Others said that Magón died from complications of diabetes. MacLachlan, *Anarchism*; Owen, "In the Manner of Preface."

38. Alexander, *Fearless Dave Allison*, 216, 245–47.

39. Texas Death Certificate.

40. The following is a review of relevant cases:

Case No. 1559. Charge of conspiracy to export arms from the United States to Mexico in violation of the March 1912 embargo. Defendants included Pascual Orozco Sr. and Cástulo Herrera. There were no charges against Orozco Jr. In October 1912, Orozco Sr. was arrested when he crossed into the United States from Ojinaga. He was tried and acquitted on the charges in October 1912. *El Paso Herald*, October 19, 1912.

Indictments Nos. 1628 and 1633. These were October 1912 charges of conspiracy to export and ship munitions from the United States to Mexico during the Orozco Rebellion. Named defendants included Pascual Orozco Jr. and Gonzalo Enrile. By the time of this indictment, Enrile had already been released of earlier charges and had left the jurisdiction. Other defendants were tried on the charges. Defendant Cabney was acquitted and defendant López had a hung jury. Orozco Jr. was never in custody on these charges, and the indictment was dismissed in 1914.

1915 law case on the forfeiture of Orozco's bond. The sureties were found liable except for Orozco's wife, Refugio, who was found not liable because she had never signed the bond.

41. Krauze, *Mexico: Biography of Power*, 359–65.
42. Ferris, "Land Title Difficulties," 16.
43. Nugent, *Spent Cartridges*, 94–95, 182.
44. Ibid.
45. Dobie, "Babicora."
46. In 1910 Hearst visited Díaz in Mexico City. He spoke glowingly about Díaz and even mused about starting a pro-Díaz Mexican newspaper. "Hearst May Start a Paper in Mexico," *El Paso Herald*, April 8, 1910, 1–2. See also Proctor, *William Randolph Hearst*, 8, 9.
47. Katz, "Pancho Villa and the Attack on Columbus," 105n8
48. Machado, "Mexican Revolution and the Destruction of the Mexican Cattle Industry," 12.
49. Machado, "Industry in Limbo," 619–21.
50. Dobie, "Babicora."
51. Mexican senator Jeffrey Max Jones from Nuevo Casas Grandes, Chihuahua.
52. Orozco, *Tierra de Libres*, 46.
53. Ibid., 41; Orozco, *Pascual Orozco (San Isidro)*; Nugent, *Spent Cartridges*, 94–95, 182.
54. Katz, *Life and Times*, 204.

Orozco, Pascual Jr. Head of a revolutionary group and army. Rose to rank of division general. Hero of the Battle of Ciudad Juárez and later head of the anti-Madero rebellion known as the Orozco or Colorado Rebellion of 1912.

Orozco, Pascual Sr. Father of Pascual Orozco Jr. Rose to rank of colonel under Díaz. Executed by Emiliano Zapata in 1913.

Orozquista. Follower of Pascual Orozco Jr.

Personalismo. An ideology with an attraction or opposition to an individual in contrast to an idea-based philosophy. It normally took the form of personal support for warring regional or local chieftains, caudillos, rather than for ideas.

Porfiriato. The Mexican era during the administration of President Porfirio Díaz.

Porfirista. Follower of Porfirio Díaz.

Reyes, Bernardo. Military and cabinet personality during the presidency of Porfirio Díaz and frequent aspirant to the presidency. He twice attempted rebellion against Francisco I. Madero, once resulting in imprisonment and, in 1913, in joining a larger coup against Madero, in which Reyes was killed.

Reyista. Follower of Bernardo Reyes.

Terrazas, General Luis. Longtime Chihuahua governor. Largest Mexican landowner and cattle rancher. Father-in-law of Enrique Creel.

Vázquez Gómez, Emilio. Brother of Francisco Vázquez Gómez, member of the provisional cabinet immediately after Díaz was deposed. He was forced out of the cabinet by Madero and attempted and failed on several occasions to form a revolutionary group to depose Madero, with Vázquez Gómez as the new president.

Vázquez Gómez, Francisco. A physician and vice presidential candidate of the Anti-Reelection Party on the ticket with Francisco I. Madero, whom Madero abandoned when he formed the new Progressive Constitutionalist Party and selected José María Pino Suárez as his new running mate.

Vazquista or Vasquista. Follower of Emilio Vázquez Gómez.

Zapata, Emiliano. Leader of southern revolt based in the state of Morelos. Fought to regain community lands and ejidos lost to sugar plantations. Rebelled against Madero and named Pascual Orozco Jr. head of his insurgency, then removed him when Orozco allied with Huerta. Executed Orozco's father, who had been sent to Morelos by Huerta to negotiate with Zapata.

Zapatista. Follower of Emiliano Zapata.

Bibliography

Archival Sources

Archivo General de la Nación. Revolución, Colecciones Madero y Revolución.

Archivo Histórico de Defensa Nacional, Expediente XI/481.5, numerous files.

Archivo Histórico de la Secretaría de Relaciones Exteriores. Colección Revolución Mexicana, Embajada Estados Unidos.

Archivo Histórico del Supremo Tribunal de Justicia del Estado de Chihuahua.

Bancroft Library, University of California at Berkeley. Silvestre Terrazas Papers.

Biblioteca Nacional de México. Various collections, including the Francisco I. Madero collection.

Centro de Estudios de Historia de México, México, DF. CEHM and CONDUMEX. Archives of Venustiano Carranza, Federico González Garza, José Yves Limantour, Francisco León de la Barra, Bernardo Reyes, and Félix Díaz.

Culberson County Texas District Clerk. Van Horn, Texas.

El Paso Public Library, Border Heritage Collection. El Paso, Texas.

Foreign Relations of the United States. Various annual reports issued by the U.S. State Department and published by the USGPO.

Library of Congress. Papers of George S. Patton, Manuscript Division.

National Archives and Records Administration, Fort Worth, Texas, records of the United States District Court for the Western District of Texas in El Paso.

Nuestra Señora de la Purísima Concepción, Parish Baptismal Records, Ciudad Guerrero, Chihuahua.

University of Texas, Center for American History. E. A. Dogie Wright Papers, "The Last Days of Pascual Orozco." Unpublished, undated manuscript.

University of Texas at El Paso, Special Collections.

Memoirs, Diaries, and Personal Accounts

Aguilar, Rafael. *Madero sin máscara.* México, DF: Imprenta Popular, 1911.

Amaya, Juan Gualberto. *Madero y los auténticos revolucionarios de 1910.* Chihuahua, Chih.: Estado d Chihuahua, 2010.

Bonilla, Manuel, Jr. *Diez años de guerra: sinopsis de la historia verdadera de la revolución mexicana, Primera Parte 1910–1913.* Mazatlán, Sinaloa: Impr. Avendaño, 1922.

———. *El Régimen Maderista.* México, DF: Editorial Arana, 1962.

Calero, Manuel. *Un Decenio de Política Mexicana.* New York: Manuel Calero, 1920.

Caraveo, Marcelo. *Crónica de la Revolución (1910–1929).* México, DF: Editorial Trillas, 1992.

Esquivel Obregón, Toribio. *Democracia y personalismo; relatos y comentarios sobre política actual.* México, DF: Imprenta A. Carranza, 1911.

Estrada, Roque. *La Revolución y Francisco I. Madero. Primero, segunda y tercera etapas.* Guadalajara, Jal.: Imprenta Americana, 1912.

Flipper, Henry O. *Black Frontiersman, the Memoirs of Henry O. Flipper.* Edited by Theodore D. Harris. Fort Worth: Texas Christian University Press, 1997.

Garibaldi, Giuseppe. *A Toast to Rebellion.* New York: Garden City Publishing, 1937.

González Garza, Federico. *La Revolución Mexicana, Mi Contribución Político-Literaria.* México, DF: A. Del Bosque, Impresor, 1936.

Grant, Ulysses. *Personal Memoirs.* Cleveland, Ohio: World, 1952.

Guzmán, Martín Luis. *Memorias de Pancho Villa.* México, DF: Compañía General de Ediciones, 1960.

Huerta, Victoriano. *Memorias de Victoriano Huerta.* México, DF: Ediciones "Vertice," 1957.

———. *Yo, Victoriano Huerta.* Edited by Ramos Malzárraga. México, DF: Editorial Contenido, 1975.

Limantour, José Yves. *Apuntes sobre mi vida pública (1892–1911).* México, DF: Editorial Porrúa, 1965.

Madero, Francisco I. *Apuntes políticos, 1905–1913.* México, DF: Clío, 2000.

Márquez Sterling, Manuel. *Los últimos días del presidente Madero (mi gestión diplomática en México).* Havana: Impr. El Siglo XX, 1917.

Navarro, Juan J. *La Toma de Ciudad Juárez (Parte de Guerra).* Ciudad Juárez, Chih.: UACJ, 1990.

Olea Arias, Heliodoro. *De Bachíniva a Ciudad Juárez: apuntes históricos de la Revolución de 1910–1911.* Chihuahua, Chih.: ALFFER Offset, 1961.

Sánchez Azcona, Juan. *Apuntes para la Historia de la Revolución Mexicana.* México, DF: INEHRM, 1961.

Terrazas, Joaquín. *Memorias, La Guerra contra los Apaches.* Chihuahua, Chih.: Centro de Libros la Prensa, 1994.

Vargas Valdés, Jesús. *Máximo Castillo y la Revolución en Chihuahua.* Chihuahua, Chih.: Nueva Vizcaya Editores, 2003.

Vázquez Gómez, Francisco. *Memorias Políticas, 1909–1913.* México, DF: Imprenta Mundial, 1933.

Von der Goltz, Horst. *My Adventures as a German Secret Agent.* New York: Robert M. McBride, 1917.

Books, Dissertations, and Theses

Aboites, Luis. *Breve Historia de Chihuahua.* México, DF: Fondo de Cultura Económica, 2006.

Aguirre Benavides, Adrián. *Errores de Madero.* México, DF: Editorial Jus, 1980.

Albro, Ward S. *Always a Rebel: Ricardo Flores Magón and the Mexican Revolution.* Fort Worth: Texas Christian University Press, 1992.

Alessio Robles, Miguel. *Perfiles del Saltillo.* México, DF: Editorial "Cvltvra," 1937.

Alexander, Bob. *Fearless Dave Allison, Border Lawman.* Silver City, N.Mex. High-Lonesome Books, 2003.

Almada, Francisco R. *Apuntes Históricos del Cantón Rayón.* Chihuahua, Chih.: Gobierno del Estado de Chihuahua, 1988.

———. *Geografía del Estado de Chihuahua.* Chihuahua, Chih.: Impresora Ruíz Sandoval, 1945.

———. *Gobernadores del Estado de Chihuahua.* Chihuahua, Chih.: Centro Librero La Prensa, 1980.

———. *Juárez y Terrazas.* México, DF: Libros Mexicanos, n.d.

———. *Resumen de Historia del Estado de Chihuahua.* Chihuahua, Chih.: Gobierno del Estado de Chihuahua, 1986.

———. *La Revolución en el Estado de Chihuahua.* Vol. 1. México, DF: Institución Nacional de Estudios Históricos de la Revolución Mexicana, 1964.

———. *La Revolución en el Estado de Chihuahua.* Vol. 2. México, DF: Institución Nacional de Estudios Históricos de la Revolución Mexicana, 1965.

———. *Vida, Proceso y Muerte de Abraham González.* México, DF: Institución Nacional de Estudios Históricos de la Revolución Mexicana, 1967.

Alonso, Ana María. *Thread of Blood: Colonialism, Revolution and Gender on Mexico's Northern Frontier.* Tucson: University Arizona Press, 1995. Also found at http://publishing.cdlib.org/ucpressebooks/view?docId=ft3q2nb28s&chunk.id=d0e29&toc.depth=1&toc.id=&brand=ucpress.

Álvarez, Salvador. *James Kirker, El Aventurero Irlandés.* Ciudad Juárez, Chih.: Meridiano Editores, 1991.

Beals, Carleton. *Porfirio Díaz, Dictator of Mexico.* Philadelphia: Lippincott, 1932.

Beezley, William H. *Insurgent Governor: Abraham González and the Mexican Revolution in Chihuahua.* Lincoln: University of Nebraska Press, 1973.

Beezley, William H., and Collin M. MacLachlan. *Mexicans in Revolution, 1910–1946: An Introduction.* Lincoln: University of Nebraska Press, 2009.

Black, Lowell D., and Sara H. Black. *An Officer and a Gentleman: The Military Career of Lieutenant Henry O. Flipper.* Dayton, Ohio: Lora, 1985.

Blanco Moheno, Roberto. *Crónica de la Revolución Mexicana.* Vol. 2. México, DF: Libro MEX Editores, 1959.

Boghardt, Thomas. *The Zimmermann Telegram.* Annapolis, Md.: Naval Institute Press, 2012.

Bolling, Robert S., Sr. *Death Rides the River.* Marshall, Mo.: Joe Kwon, 2011. Also found in Means, Joyce E. *Pancho Villa Days at Pilares.* Tucson: Joyce E. Means, 1994.

Bourke, John G. *An Apache Campaign in the Sierra Madre.* Lincoln: University of Nebraska Press, 1987.

Brondo Whitt, E. *Los Patriarcas del Papigochi.* Chihuahua, Chih.: Imprenta Comercial, 1952.

Brown, Jonathan C. *Oil and Revolution in Mexico.* Berkeley: University of California Press, 1992. http://ark.cdlib.org/ark:/13030/ft3q2nb28s/.

Campobello, Nellie. *Apuntes sobre la vida militar de Francisco Villa.* México, DF: EDIAP, 1940.

Carman, Michael Dennis. *United States Customs and the Madero Revolution.* El Paso: Texas Western Press, 1976.

Casasola, Gustavo. *Historia Gráfica de la Revolución, 1900–1960.* Vol. 3. México, DF: Editorial F. Trillas, 1960.

———. *Seis Siglos de historia gráfica de México, 1325–1925.* Vol. 4. México, DF: Ediciones Gustavo Casasola, 1967.

Chalkley, John F. *Zach Lamar Cobb.* El Paso: Texas Western Press, 1998.

Chávez Flores, José Carlos. *Peleando en Tomochi.* Chihuahua, Chih.: Gobierno del Estado de Chihuahua, 1955.

Chevalier, François. *Land and Society in Colonial Mexico: The Great Hacienda.* Berkeley: University of California Press, 1963.

Cockcroft, James D. *Intellectual Precursors of the Mexican Revolution, 1900–1913.* Austin: University of Texas Press, 1968.

Creel, Enrique. *Agricultura y Agrarismo.* México, DF: El Progreso, 1929.

Creelman, James. Diaz, *Master of Mexico.* New York: D. Appleton, 1911.

De la Helguera, Álvaro. *Enrique C. Creel, Apuntes Biográficos.* Madrid: Imprenta Ambrosio Pérez Asensio, 1910.

D'Este, Carlo. *Patton: A Genius for War.* New York: HarperCollins, 1995.

Didapp, Juan Pedro. *Los Estados Unidos y Nuestros Conflictos Internos.* México, DF: Tip. "El Republicano," 1913.

Diccionario Histórico y Biográfico de la Revolución Mexicana. Vol. 2. México, DF: Institución Nacional de Estudios Históricos de la Revolución Mexicana, 1994.

Eaton, James Demarest. *Life under Two Flags.* New York: A. S. Barnes, 1922.

Fabela, Isidro. *Documentos históricos de la Revolución Mexicana.* Vol. 17. México, DF: Editorial Jus, 1969.

Flores Hernández, Yvonne. *Cusihuiriáchi: Minería e Historia Regional.* Ciudad Juárez, Chih.: Universidad Autónoma de Ciudad Juárez, 1992.

Flores Magón, Ricardo, Antonio de P. Araujo, and William C. Owen. *Land and Liberty.* Los Angeles: Mexican Liberal Party, 1913.

Frías, Heriberto. *Tomochic.* México, DF: Editorial Porrúa, 2004.

Fuentes G., Adolfo, ed. *La Revolución de Chihuahua en las páginas del periódico "El Padre Padilla."* Vol. 1. Chihuahua, Chih.: Gobierno del Estado de Chihuahua, 2001.

Fuentes Mares, José. *Y México Se Refugió en el Desierto.* Chihuahua, Chih.: Centro Librero La Prensa, 1987.

Galaviz de Capdevielle, María Elena. *Rebeliones Indígenas en el Norte del Reino de la Nueva España.* México, DF: Editorial Campesina, 1967.

García Moisés, Enrique. *Madero, la Revolución sin Revolución: Política y Economía.* México, DF: UNAM, 2002.

Garner, Paul. *Porfirio Díaz.* New York: Routledge, 2014.

Gimeno, Conrado. *La Canalla Roja, Notas acerca del movimiento sedicioso*. El Paso, Tex., 1912.

Gobierno del Estado de Chihuahua. *Álbum Conmemorativo, Visita Á Chihuahua del Sr. Presidente, General Don Porfirio Díaz*. Chihuahua, Chih., 1909.

González Ramírez, Manuel. *Manifiestos Políticos, 1892–1912*. México, DF: Fondo de Cultura Económica, 1957.

Guerrero, Práxedis G. *Artículos Literarios y de combate, pensamientos: crónicas revolucionarias, etc.* México, DF: Grupo Cultural "Ricardo Flores Magón," 1924.

Guzmán, Martín Luis. *Memoirs of Pancho Villa*. Austin: University of Texas Press, 1965.

Hadley, Philip L. *Minería y sociedad en el centro minero de Santa Eulalia, Chihuahua*. México, DF: Fondo de Cultura Económica, 1975.

Hämäläinen, Pekka. *The Comanche Empire*. New Haven, Conn.: Yale University Press, 2008.

Harris, Charles H., III, and Louis R. Sadler. *The Plan de San Diego: Tejano Rebellion, Mexican Intrigue*. Lincoln: University of Nebraska Press, 2013.

———. *The Secret War in El Paso: Mexican Revolutionary Intrigue, 1906–1920*. Albuquerque: University of New Mexico Press, 2009.

———. *The Texas Rangers and the Mexican Revolution*. Albuquerque: University of New Mexico Press, 2004.

Hart, John Mason. *Revolutionary Mexico: The Coming and Process of the Mexican Revolution*. Berkeley: University California Press, 1989.

Instituto Nacional de Estudios Históricos de las Revoluciones de México. *Diccionario de Generales de la Revolución*. Vols. 1 and 2. México, DF: INEHRM, 2013.

Jones, John Price, and Paul Merrick Hollister. *The German Secret Service in America 1914–1918*. Boston: Small, Maynard, 1918.

Katz, Friedrich. *The Life and Times of Pancho Villa*. Stanford, Calif.: Stanford University Press, 1998.

———. *The Secret War in Mexico*. Chicago: University of Chicago Press, 1981.

Kerig, Dorothy Pierson. *Luther T. Ellsworth*. El Paso: Texas Western Press, 1975.

King, Frank M. *Longhorn Trail Drivers*. Los Angeles: Haynes, 1940.

Knight, Alan. *The Mexican Revolution*. 2 vols. Lincoln: University of Nebraska Press, 1986.

Krauze, Enrique. *Mexico: Biography of Power*. New York: Harper Perennial, 1998.

———. *Porfirio Díaz*. México, DF: Fondo de Cultura Económica, 1987.

Lister, Florence C., and Robert H. *Chihuahua: Storehouse of Storms*. Albuquerque: University of New Mexico Press, 1966.

Lloyd, Jane-Dale. *Cinco ensayos sobre la cultura material de rancheros y medieros del noroeste de Chihuahua, 1886–1910*. México, DF: Universidad Iberoamericana, 2001.

———. *El distrito Galeana en los albores de la revolución*. Chihuahua, Chih.: Biblioteca Chihuahuense, 2011.

———. *El Proceso de modernización capitalista en el noroeste de Chihuahua (1880–1910)*. México, DF: Universidad Iberoamericana, 1987.

Lomnitz, Claudio. *The Return of Comrade Ricardo Flores Magón*. New York: Zone Books, 2014.

Luna, Francisco Javier. *Miguel Hidalgo y Costilla*. México, DF: Editores Mexicanos Unidos, 2013.

Machado, Manuel A. *Centaur of the North*. Austin, Tex.: Eakin Press, 1988.

MacLachlan, Colin M. *Anarchism and the Mexican Revolution: The Political Trials of Ricardo Flores Magón in the United States*. Berkeley: University of California Press, 1991.

Madero, Francisco I. *La Sucesión Presidencial en 1910: El Partido Nacional Democrático*. San Pedro, Coah.: Francisco I. Madero, 1908.

Magaña, Gildardo. *Emiliano Zapata y el agrarismo en México*. 5 vols. México, DF: Editorial Ruta, 1951 (vols. 1–2) and 1952 (vols. 3–5).

Maldonado R., Calixto. *Los asesinatos de los Señores Madero y Pino Suárez, Como Ocurrieron*. México, DF, 1922.

Márquez Terrazas, Zacarías. *Memoria del Papigóchic, Siglos 17 y 18*. Chihuahua, Chih.: Gobierno del Estado de Chihuahua, 1993.

———. *Terrazas y Su Siglo*. Chihuahua, Chih.: Centro Librero la Prensa, 2003.

Martínez, Óscar J. *Fragments of the Mexican Revolution: Personal Accounts from the Border*. Albuquerque: University of New Mexico Press, 1983.

Martínez Álvarez, José Antonio. *Práxedis Guerrero. Pensamiento combatiente y otros documentos*. Digital edition, November 2015.

Mayo, C. M. *Metaphysical Odyssey into the Mexican Revolution*. México, DF: C. M. Mayo, 2013.

Means, Joyce E. *Pancho Villa Days at Pilares*. Tucson: Joyce E. Means, 1994.

Meyer, Michael C. "The Career of Pascual Orozco, Jr.: A Case Study of a Mexican Revolutionist." PhD diss., University of New Mexico, 1964.

———. *Huerta: A Political Portrait*. Lincoln: University of Nebraska Press, 1972.

———. *Mexican Rebel: Pascual Orozco and the Mexican Revolution, 1910–1915*. Lincoln: University of Nebraska Press, 1967.

Meyer, Michael C., and William L. Sherman. *The Course of Mexican History*. New York: Oxford University, 1995.

Moreno, Francisco Martín. *100 Mitos de la Historia de México*. México, DF: Aguilar, 2011.

Mort, Terry. *The Wrath of Cochise*. New York: Pegasus Books, 2013.

Mundt, Michael Norman. "Revolution and Reaction: The Mexico North Western Railway Company during the 1912 Pascual Orozco Rebellion." Master's thesis, New Mexico State University, 1991.

Neumann, José, S. J. *Historia de las Rebeliones en la Sierra Tarahumara (1626–1724)*. Chihuahua, Chih.: Editorial Camino, 1991.

Nugent, Daniel. *Spent Cartridges of Revolution: An Anthropological History of Namiquipa*. Chicago: University of Chicago Press, 1993.

Orozco, Victor. *El Estado de Chihuahua en el Parto de la Nación, 1810–1831*. Chihuahua, Chih.: Plaza y Valdés, 2007.

———. *Pascual Orozco (San Isidro) Pueblo Heroico*. Ciudad Juárez, Chih.: UACJ, 2013.

———. *Reflexiones sobre la historia nacional*. Ciudad Juárez, Chih.: UACJ, 2010.

———. *Tierra de Libres: los pueblos del distrito de Guerrero en el siglo XIX.* In Historia General de Chihuahua, vol. 3, pt. 1. Ciudad Juárez, Chih.: UACJ, 1995.

Osorio, Rubén. *Pancho Villa, Ese Desconocido.* Chihuahua, Chih.: Biblioteca Chihuahuense, 2004.

Owen, William C. "In the Manner of Preface: The Death of Ricardo Flores Magon" (1922). In Ricardo Flores Magón, *Sembrando Ideas.* México, DF: Grupo Cultural Ricardo Flores Magón, 1926. Available at Anarchy Archives. http://dwardmac. pitzer.edu/Anarchist_Archives/bright/magon/works/sembrando/prologoeng.html.

Palavicini, Félix Fulgencio. *Los diputados: lo que se ve y lo que no se ve de la Cámara.* México, DF: Tipografía El Faro, 1913.

Poniatowska, Elena. *Las Soldaderas.* México, DF: Ediciones Era, 1999.

Porras Muñoz, Guillermo. *Haciendas de Chihuahua.* Chihuahua, Chih.: Gobierno del Estado de Chihuahua, 1993.

Portilla, Santiago. *Una sociedad en armas: Insurrección antirreeleccionista en México, 1910–1911.* México, DF: El Colegio de México, 1995.

Proctor, Ben. *William Randolph Hearst: The Later Years, 1911–1951.* New York: Oxford University Press, 2007.

Puente, Ramón. *Pascual Orozco y la Revuelta de Chihuahua.* México, DF: Eusebio Gómez de la Puente, 1912.

Ramírez Rancaño, Mario. *La Reacción Mexicana y su Exilio Durante La Revolución de 1910.* México, DF: UNAM, 2002.

Ribot, Héctor. *Las últimas revoluciones.* México, DF: Imprenta 1a. de Humboldt, 1910.

Rivero, Gonzalo. *Hacia la Verdad, Episodios de la Revolución.* México, DF: Compañía Editora Nacional, 1911.

Ross, Stanley R. *Francisco Madero: Apostle of Mexican Revolution.* New York: Columbia University Press, 1955.

Salas, Elizabeth. *Soldaderas in the Mexican Military: Myth and History.* Austin: University of Texas Press, 1990.

Salmerón, Pedro. *Juárez, La rebelión interminable.* México, DF: Planeta, 2007.

Sánchez Lamego, Miguel A. *Historia Militar de la Revolución Mexicana en la Época Maderista.* Vols. 1–3. México, DF: INEHRM, 2011.

Sandels, Robert Lynn. "Silvestre Terrazas, the Press, and the Origins of the Mexican Revolution in Chihuahua." PhD diss., University of Oregon, 1967.

Sax, Antimaco. *Los mexicanos en el destierro.* San Antonio, Tex., 1916.

Scholes, France V., Marc Simmons, and José Antonio Esquibel, eds. *Juan Domínguez de Mendoza: Soldier and Frontiersman of the Spanish Southwest, 1627–1693.* Albuquerque: University of New Mexico Press, 2012.

Serrano, T. F. *Episodios de la revolución en México.* El Paso: Modern Printing, 1911.

Siller Vázquez, Pedro. *1911: La batalla de Ciudad Juárez.* Vol. 1, *La historia.* México, DF: Cuadro por Cuadro, 2006.

Taibo, Paco Ignacio, II. *El Cura Hidalgo y Sus Amigos.* México, DF: Planeta, 2014.

——— *Pancho Villa, Una biografía narrativa.* México, DF: Planeta, 2006.

———. *Temporada de zopilotes.* México, DF: Planeta, 2013.

Tamarón y Romeral, Pedro. *Demostración del Vastísimo Obispado de la Nueva Vizcaya—1765.* México, DF: Librería Porrúa, 1937.

Taracena, Alfonso. *La Labor Social del Presidente Madero.* Saltillo, Coah.: 1959

———. *La Verdadera Revolución Mexicana, (1901–1911).* México, DF: Editorial Porrúa, 2005.

———. *La Verdadera Revolución Mexicana, (1912–1914).* México, DF: Editorial Porrúa, 2008.

———. *La Verdadera Revolución Mexicana, (1915–1917).* México, DF: Editorial Porrúa, 1992.

———. *La Verdadera Revolución Mexicana.* Vol. 1. México, DF: Editorial Jus, 1960.

———. *La Verdadera Revolución Mexicana.* Vol. 1. Supplement. México, DF: Editorial Jus, 1965.

———. *La Verdadera Revolución Mexicana.* Vols. 7–9. México, DF: Editorial Jus, 1965.

Terrazas, Silvestre. *El Verdadero Pancho Villa.* México, DF: Ediciones Era, 1988.

Thord-Gray, Ivor. *Gringo Rebel: Mexico 1913–1914.* Coral Gables, Fla.: University of Miami Press, 1960.

Torres Parés, Javier, and Gloria Villegas Moreno, eds. *Diccionario de la Revolución Mexicana.* México, DF: UNAM, 2010.

Trow, Clifford Wayne. "Senator Albert B. Fall and Mexican Affairs: 1912–1920." PhD diss., University of Colorado, 1966.

Tuchman, Barbara W. *The Zimmermann Telegram.* New York: Ballantine Books, 1984.

Turner, John Kenneth. *Barbarous Mexico.* Chicago: Charles H. Kerr, 1910.

Ugalde, R. A. *Vida de Pascual Orozco, 1882–1915.* El Paso, 1915.

Ulloa, Berta. *Revolución Mexicana, 1910–1920.* Guías para la Historia Diplomática de México, no. 3. México, DF.: Secretaría de Relaciones Exteriores, 1963.

United States. *Foreign Relations of the United States, 1911.* Washington, D.C.:USGPO, 1918.

———. *Foreign Relations of the United States, 1912.* Washington, D.C.:USGPO, 1919.

———. *Foreign Relations of the United States, 1913.* Washington, D.C.:USGPO, 1920.

———. *Foreign Relations of the United States, 1914.* Washington, D.C.:USGPO, 1922.

———. *Foreign Relations of the United States, 1915.* Washington, D.C.:USGPO, 1924.

U.S. Congress. *Congressional Globe.* 46 vols. Washington, D.C., 1834–73.

U.S. Senate, Committee on Foreign Relations. *Investigation of Mexican Affairs: Hearing before a Subcommittee of the Committee on Foreign Relations.* Part 1. Washington, D.C.: USGPO, 1920.

———. *Investigation of Mexican Affairs. Preliminary Report and Hearings.* Washington, D.C.: USGPO, 1920.

———. *Revolutions in Mexico, Hearings.* Washington, D.C.: USGPO, 1913.

Valdés, José C. *El Porfirismo, Historia de un Régimen.* 2 vols. México, DF: UNAM, 1977.

Vanderwood, Paul J. *The Power of God against the Guns of Government: Religious Upheaval in Mexico at the Turn of the Nineteenth Century.* Stanford: Stanford University Press, 1998.

Vanderwood, Paul J., and Frank N. Samponaro. *Border Fury.* Albuquerque: University of New Mexico, 1988.

Vela González, Francisco. *Diario de la Revolución*. Vol. 1. Monterrey, N.L.: Universidad de Nuevo León, 1971.

Vera Estañol, Jorge. *La Revolución Mexicana, Orígenes y resultados*. México, DF: Editorial Porrúa, 1957.

Von Feilitzsch, Heribert. *Felix A. Sommerfeld and the Mexican Front in the Great War (Secret War Council)*. Amissville, Va.: Henselstone Verlag, 2014.

———. *In Plain Sight: Felix A. Sommerfeld Spymaster in Mexico, 1908 to 1914*. Amissville, Va.: Henselstone Verlag, 2012.

Waldrep, Christopher. *Lynching in America: A History in Documents*. New York: New York University Press, 2006.

Wasserman, Mark. *Capitalistas, Caciques y Revolución*. Chihuahua, Chih.: Centro Librero La Prensa, 1998.

———. *Persistent Oligarchs, Elites and Politics in Chihuahua, Mexico 1910–1940*. Durham, N.C.: Duke University Press, 1993.

———. *Pesos and Politics: Business, Elites, Foreigners, and Government in Mexico, 1854–1940*. Stanford, Calif.: Stanford University Press, 2015.

Webb, Walter Prescott. *The Texas Rangers*. Austin: University of Texas Press, 2008. Kindle edition.

Womack, John, Jr. *Zapata and the Mexican Revolution*. New York: Knopf, 1968.

Articles and Book Chapters

Alonso, Ana María. "U.S. Military Intervention, Revolutionary Mobilization, and Popular Ideology in the Chihuahua Sierra, 1916–1917." In *Rural Revolt in Mexico*, edited by Daniel Nugent, 207–38. Durham, N.C.: Duke University Press, 1998.

Aparecida de S. Lopes, María. "Revolución y ganadería en el norte de México." *Historia Mexicana* 57, no. 3 (January–March 2008): 863–910.

Arrizón, Alicia. "Soldaderas and the Staging of the Mexican Revolution." *TDR* 42, no. 1 (Spring 1998): 90–112.

Baldwin, Deborah. "Broken Traditions: Mexican Revolutionaries and Protestant Allegiances." *Americas* 40, no. 2 (October 1983): 229–58.

Bastian, Jean-Pierre. "Jacobinismo y ruptura revolucionaria durante el porfiriato." *Mexican Studies/Estudios Mexicanos* 7, no. 1 (Winter 1991): 29–46.

———. "Metodismo y clase obrera durante el Porfiriato." *Historia Mexicana* 33, no. 1, La sociedad capitalina en el Porfiriato (July–September 1983): 39–71.

———. "Los propagandistas del constitucionalismo en México (1910–1920)." *Revista Mexicana de Sociología* 45, no. 2 (April–June 1983): 321–51.

———. "Las sociedades protestantes y la oposición a Porfirio Díaz, 1877–1911." *Historia Mexicana* 37, no. 3 (January–March 1988): 469–512.

Beelen, George D. "The Harding Administration and Mexico: Diplomacy by Economic Persuasion." *Americas* 41, no. 2 (October 1984): 177–89.

Beezley, William H. "State Reform during the Provisional Presidency: Chihuahua, 1911." *Hispanic American Historical Review* 50, No. 3 (August 1970): 524–37.

Bell, Bob Boze. "Hellfire and Hot Tamales." *True West Magazine*, September 2010, 60–63. Also found at: http://www.truewestmagazine.com/hellfire-a-hot-tamales/.

Benedict, H. Bradley. "The Sale of the Hacienda of Tabaloapa: A Case-Study of Jesuit Property Redistribution in Mexico, 1771–1781." *Americas* 32, no. 2 (October 1975): 171–95.

———. "El saqueo de las misiones de Chihuahua, 1767–1777." *Historia Mexicana* 22, no. 1 (July–September 1972): 24–33.

Blanco, Mónica. "Toribio Esquivel Obregón, Encuentros y Desencuentros Con El Antirreeleccionismo." In "La revolución mexicana: distintas perspectivas." Special issue, *Historia Mexicana* 60, no. 2 (238, Octubre–Diciembre 2010): 791–831.

Blount, Bertha, and John G. Bourke. "An Apache Campaign: The Apache in the Southwest, 1846–1886." *Southwestern Historical Quarterly* 23, no. 1 (July 1919): 20–38.

Braddy, Haldeen. "The Loves of Pancho Villa." *Western Folklore* 21, no. 3 (July 1962): 175–182.

Brading, D. A. "La política nacional y la tradición populista." In *Caudillos y campesinos en la Revolución Mexicana*, edited by D. A. Brading, 13–31. México, DF: Fondo de Cultura Ecónomica, 1985.

Brand, Donald D. "The Early History of the Range Cattle Industry in Northern Mexico." *Agricultural History* 35, no. 3 (July 1961): 132–39.

Bud-Frierman, Lisa, Andrew Godley, and Judith Wale. "Weetman Pearson in Mexico and the Emergence of a British Oil Major, 1901–1919." Special Issue, *Business History Review* 844, no. 2 (May 2010): 275–300.

Butterfield, Dolores. "The Situation in Mexico." *North American Review* 196, no. 684 (November 1912): 649–64.

Cadenhead, Ivie E., Jr. "Flores Magón y el periódico 'The Appeal to Reason.'" *Historia Mexicana* 13, no. 1 (July–September 1963): 88–93.

Chavis, Ben. "All-Indian Rodeo: A Transformation of Western Apache Tribal Warfare and Culture." *Wicazo Sa Review* 9, no. 1 (Spring 1993): 4–11.

Christiansen, Paige W. "Pascual Orozco: Chihuahua Rebel." *New Mexico Historical Review* 36, no. 2 (April 1961): 97–120.

Creelman, James. "President Diaz, Hero of the Americas." *Pearson's Magazine*, March 1908, 231–77.

Cumberland, Charles C. "Precursors of the Mexican Revolution of 1910." *Hispanic American Historical Review* 22, no. 2 (May 1942): 344–56.

Davis, O. K. "Our 'Prisoners of War.'" *North American Review* 195, no. 676 (March 1912): 356–67.

Deeds, Susan M. "Jose Maria Maytorena and the Mexican Revolution in Sonora." Pts. 1 and 2. *Arizona and the West* 18, no. 1 (Spring 1976): 21–40; 18, no. 2 (Summer 1976): 125–48.

Dobie, J. Frank. "Babicora." *American Hereford Journal* 44, no. 17 (January 1, 1954): 56–58, 60, 174–75.

Estevez, Dolia. "Mexico among the World's Most Corrupt Nations in 2014, New Report Says." *Forbes*, December 11, 2014.

Ferris, William M. "Land Title Difficulties in Mexico." *Bulletin of the Business Historical Society* 24, no. 1 (March 1950): 13–22.

Fierro, Luis Carlos. "Historical Notes on the Vegetation of the Rangelands of Chihuahua." *Rangelands* 11, no. 4 (August 1989): 166–71.

Fisher, Louis. "The Law: When Wars Begin: Misleading Statements by Presidents." *Presidential Studies Quarterly* 40, no. 1 (March 2010): 171–84.

———. "The Mexican War and Lincoln's 'Spot Resolutions.'" Law Library of Congress, 2009. http://www.loc.gov/law/help/usconlaw/pdf/Mexican.war.pdf.

French, William E. "Business as Usual: Mexico North Western Railway Managers Confront the Mexican Revolution." *Mexican Studies/Estudios Mexicanos* 5, no. 2 (Summer 1989): 221–38.

Garciadiego, Javier, and Josefina MacGregor. "Alemania y la Revolución Mexicana." *Foro Internacional* 32, no. 4 (April–September 1992): 429–48.

Gerlach, Allen. "Conditions along the Border—1915: The Plan of San Diego." *New Mexico Historical Review* 43 (1968): 195–212.

Gill, Mario. "Teresa Urrea, la Santa de Cabora." *Historia Mexicana* 6, no. 4 (April–June 1957): 626–44.

González Navarro, Moisés. "Las ideas raciales de los científicos, 1890–1910." *Historia Mexicana* 37, no. 4 (April–June 1988): 565–83.

———. "La ideología de la Revolución Mexicana." *Historia Mexicana* 10, no. 4 (April–June 1961): 628–36.

Graebner, Norman A. "Lessons of the Mexican War." *Pacific Historical Review* 47, no. 3 (August 1978): 325–42.

Grieb, Kenneth J. "Standard Oil and the Financing of the Mexican Revolution." *California Historical Quarterly* 50, no. 1 (March 1971): 59–71.

Hackett, Charles Wilson. "The Mexican Revolution and the United States, 1910–1926." *World Peace Foundation Pamphlets* 9, no. 5 (1926): 338–446.

Hager, William M. "The Plan of San Diego Unrest on the Texas Border in 1915." *Arizona and the West* 5, no. 4 (Winter 1963): 327–36.

Hale, Charles A. "The Liberal Impulse: Daniel Cosío Villegas and the Historia Moderna de México." *Hispanic American Historical Review* 54, no. 3 (August 1974): 479–98.

Hall, Linda B., and Don M. Coerver. "Oil and the Mexican Revolution: The Southwestern Connection." *Americas* 41, no. 2 (October 1984): 229–44.

Hardy, B. Carmon. "The Trek South: How the Mormons Went to Mexico." *Southwestern Historical Quarterly* 73, no. 1 (July 1969): 1–16.

Harris, Charles H., III, and Louis R. Sadler. "The 1911 Reyes Conspiracy: The Texas Side." *Southwestern Historical Quarterly* 83, no. 4 (April 1980): 325–48.

———. "The Plan of San Diego and the Mexican–United States War Crisis of 1916: A Reexamination." *Hispanic American Historical Review* 58, no. 3 (August 1978): 381–408.

———. "The 'Underside' of the Mexican Revolution: El Paso, 1912." *Americas* 39, no. 1 (July 1982): 69–83.

Hart, John M. "Agrarian Precursors of the Mexican Revolution: The Development of an Ideology." *Americas* 29, no. 2 (October 1972): 131–50.

Hu-Dehart, Evelyn. "Development and Rural Rebellion: Pacification of the Yaquis in the Late Porfiriato." *Hispanic American Historical Review* 54, no. 1 (February 1974): 72–93.

Hutton, D. Graham. "The New-Old Crisis in Mexico." *Foreign Affairs* 16, no. 4 (July 1938): 626–39.

Iturribarria, Jorge Fernando. "Limantour y la caída de Porfirio Díaz." In "En el Cincuentenario de la Revolución." Special issue, *Historia Mexicana* 10, no. 2, (October–December 1960): 243–81.

Jastrzembski, Joseph C. "Treacherous Towns in Mexico: Chiricahua Apache Personal Narratives of Horrors." *Western Folklore* 54, no. 3 (July 1995): 169–96.

Katz, Friedrich. "Pancho Villa and the Attack on Columbus, New Mexico." *American Historical Review* 83, no. 1 (February 1978): 101–30.

Knight, Alan. "Caudillos y Campesinos en el México Revolucionario, 1910–1917." In *Caudillos y Campesinos en la Revolución Mexicana*, edited by D. A. Brading, 32–85. México, DF: Fondo de Cultura Económica, 1985.

Koth, Karl B., and Julieta Venegas. "Madero, Dehesa y el cientificismo: el problema de la sucesión gubernamental en Veracruz, 1911–1913." *Historia Mexicana* 46, no. 2 (October–December 1996): 397–424.

Landeros, Erik Del Ángel. "El intento de regreso de Huerta en 1915 y su relación con el conocimiento de Estados Unidos a Carranza." *Estudios de Historia Moderna y Contemporánea de México* 47 (January–June 2014): 121–53.

Lea, Henry Charles. "Hidalgo and Morelos." *American Historical Review* 4, no. 4 (July 1899): 636–51.

Leftwich, Bill. "Death of General Pascual Orozco." *Journal of Big Bend Studies* 2 (1990): 93–96.

Lloyd, Jane-Dale. "Modernización y corporatividad. Caracterización del ranchero fronterizo durante el Porfiriato: el caso del noroeste de Chihuahua, 1880–1912." In *Visiones del Porfiriato, Visiones de México*, edited by Jane-Dale Lloyd, Eduardo N. Mijangos Díaz, Marisa Pérez Domínguez, and María Eugenia Ponce Alcocer, 223–56. México, DF: Universidad Iberoamericana, 2004.

———. "Rancheros and Rebellion: The Case of Northwestern Chihuahua, 1905–1909." In *Rural Revolt in Mexico: U.S. Intervention and the Domain of Subaltern Politics*, edited by Daniel Nugent, 107–33. Durham, N.C.: Duke University Press, 1998.

Machado, Manuel A. "An Industry in Limbo: The Mexican Cattle Industry 1920–1924." *Agricultural History* 50, no. 4 (October 1976): 615–25.

———. "The Mexican Revolution and the Destruction of the Mexican Cattle Industry." *Southwestern Historical Quarterly* 79, no. 1 (July 1975): 1–20.

McCaa, Robert. "Missing Millions: The Demographic Costs of the Mexican Revolution." *Mexican Studies/Estudios Mexicanos* 19, no. 2 (Summer 2003): 367–400.

"Mexico's Attitude on Property Rights." *New York Times Current History* 14 (April–Septeptember 1921): 711–13.

Meyer, Michael. "The Arms of the Ypiranga." *Hispanic American Historical Review* 50, no. 3 (August 1970): 543–56.

———. "Felix Sommerfeld and the Columbus Raid of 1916." *Arizona and the West* 25, no. 3 (Autumn 1983): 213–28.

———. "The Mexican-German Conspiracy of 1915." *Americas* 23, no. 1 (July 1966): 76–89.

———. "The Militarization of Mexico, 1913–1914." *Americas* 27, no. 3 (January 1971): 293–306.

Prendergast, Simon. "Orozco Rebellion." In *Paper Money of Chihuahua*. http://papermoneyofchihuahua.com/the-history/orozcos-rebellion.html.

Peters, John G., and Susan Welch. "Political Corruption in America: A Search for Definitions and a Theory, or If Political Corruption Is in the Mainstream of American Politics Why is it not in the Mainstream of American Politics Research?" *American Political Science Review* 72, no. 3 (September 1978): 974–84.

Raat, William Dirk. "The Antipositivist Movement in Prerevolutionary Mexico, 1892–1911." *Journal of Interamerican Studies and World Affairs* 19, no. 1 (February 1977): 83–98.

———. "Ideas and Society in Don Porfirio's Mexico." *Americas* 30, no. 1 (July 1973): 32–53.

———. "U.S. Intelligence Operations and Covert Action in Mexico, 1900–47." In "Intelligence During the Second World War: Part 2." Special issue, *Journal of Contemporary History*, 22, no. 4 (Oct., 1987): 615–38.

Rausch, George J., Jr. "The Exile and Death of Victoriano Huerta." *Hispanic American Historical Review* 42, no. 2 (May 1962): 133–51.

Reséndez Fuentes, Andrés. "Battleground Women: Soldaderas and Female Soldiers in the Mexican Revolution." *Americas* 51, no. 4 (April 1995): 525–53.

Romero, Matías. "Philosophy of the Mexican Revolution." In *The Age of Porfirio Díaz*, edited by Carlos B. Gil, 13–14. Albuquerque: University of New Mexico Press, 1977.

Sandels, Robert. "Antecedentes de la revolución en Chihuahua." *Historia Mexicana* 24, no. 3 (January–March 1975): 390–402.

———. "Silvestre Terrazas and the Old Régime in Chihuahua." *Americas* 28, no. 2 (October 1971): 191–205.

Scholes, Walter V. "Church and State at the Mexican Constitutional Convention, 1856–1857." *Americas* 4, no. 2 (October 1947): 151–74.

Seymour, Deni J., and George Robertson. "A Pledge of Peace: Evidence of the Cochise-Howard Treaty Campsite." *Historical Archeology* 42, no. 4 (2008): 154–79.

Shapleigh, Ballard Coldwell. "¡Viva Los Licenciados¡" *El Paso Bar Journal* (June 2011): 13–18.

Sims, Harold D. "Espejo de Caciques: Los Terrazas de Chihuahua." *Historia Mexicana* 18, no. 3 (January–March, 1969): 379–99.

Skirius, John. "Railroad, Oil and Other Foreign Interests in the Mexican Revolution, 1911–1914." *Journal of Latin American Studies* 35, no. 1 (February 2003): 25–51.

Smith, Michael M. "The Mexican Secret Service in the United States, 1910–1920." *Americas* 59, no. 1 (July 2002): 65–85.

Smith, Ralph A. "The Scalp Hunter in the Borderlands 1835–1850." *Arizona and the West* 6, no. 1 (Spring 1964): 5–22.

Sonnichsen, C. L. "Colonel William C. Greene and the Strike at Cananea, Sonora, 1906." *Arizona and the West* 13, no. 4 (Winter 1971): 343–68.

Stark, Andrew. "Beyond Quid Pro Quo: What's Wrong with Private Gain from Public Office?" *American Political Science Review* 91, no. 1 (March 1997): 108–20.

U.S. State Department, Office of the Historian. "The Annexation of Texas, the Mexican-American War, and the Treaty of Guadalupe-Hidalgo, 1845–1848." http://history.state.gov/milestones/1830-1860/texas-annexation.

Vela González, Francisco. "La Quincena Trágica de 1913." *Historia Mexicana* 12, no. 3 (January–March 1963): 440–53.

Velasco Toro, José. "La rebelión yaqui en Sonora durante el siglo XIX." *Revista Mexicana de Sociología* 48, no. 1 (January–March 1986): 237–56.

Vigil, Ralph H. "Revolution and Confusion: The Peculiar Case of José Inés Salazar." *New Mexico Historical Review* 53, no. 2 (April 1978): 145–70.

Voliva, John D. "The Guns of Green River Canyon." *Arms Gazette*, October 1976, 12–15.

Wasserman, Mark. "Enrique C. Creel: Business and Politics in Mexico, 1880–1930." In "Business in Latin America." Special issue, *Business History Review* 59, no. 4 (Winter 1985): 645–62.

———. "Foreign Investment in Mexico, 1876–1910: A Case Study of the Role of Regional Elites." *Americas* 36, no. 1 (July 1979): 3–21.

———. "Oligarquía e intereses extranjeros en Chihuahua durante el porfiriato." *Historia Mexicana* 22, no. 3 (January–March 1973): 279–319.

———. "The Social Origins of the 1910 Revolution in Chihuahua." *Latin American Research Review* 15, no. 1 (1980): 15–38.

———. "Strategies for Survival of the Porfirian Elite in Revolutionary Mexico: Chihuahua during the1920s." *Hispanic American Historical Review* 67, no. 1 (February 1987): 87–107.

Weber, David J. "Mexico's Far Northern Frontier, 1821–1854: Historiography Askew." *Western Historical Quarterly* 7, no. 3 (July 1976): 279–93.

Interviews and Oral Histories

Bramblett, C. R. Kitt. Interview by Raymond Caballero, January 14, 2015, Sierra Blanca, Texas.

Cummings, Alice B. Interview No. 426 by Richard Estrada, March 1, 1978. UTEP Institute of Oral History, El Paso, Texas.

Love, Ed. Interview by Paul Patterson, June 6, 1971. Southwest Collection, Special Collections Library, Texas Tech University, Lubbock, Texas.

Wright, E. A. Interview No. 52 by John A. Cowan, July 16, 1968. UTEP Institute of Oral History, El Paso, Texas.

Online Resource

"La Adelita–Revolución Mexicana." YouTube video, posted by "culturamexicana." https://www.youtube.com/watch?v=K3w_x2r8fHo.

Berumen, Miguel Ángel. "1911 La Batalla por Ciudad Juárez." YouTube video. https://www.youtube.com/watch?v=uxZZW6lD3Lw.

"Documental: Revolución Mexicana 1910–1920." YouTube video, posted by "ultraaudiolight." https://www.youtube.com/watch?v=9UU5QsjtB6E.

Gral. Pascual Orozco Vázquez Facebook page. https://www.facebook.com/GralPascual OrozcoVazquez/photos_stream.

Hurtado, Jorge. "Las Efemérides de Jorge Hurtado, Agosto 30, Pascual Orozco Vázquez." YouTube video. https://www.youtube.com/watch?v=ol5O1wv8VtM.

Instituto Nacional de Estudios Históricos de las Revoluciones de México website. http://www.inehrm.gob.mx/.

Lopez, Alejandro. "The Storm that Swept Mexico." YouTube video. https://www.youtube.com/watch?v=pVWcgOcvgVo.

"México en 1910." YouTube video, posted by "ELTEJONSOLITARIO." https://www.youtube.com/watch?v=L8ymi3OWmTk.

Orozco Sánchez, Marco Antonio. *Pascual Orozco, el Rebelde del Norte* (blog). http://orozcoelrebeldedelnorte.blogspot.mx/.

"Pascual Orozco." YouTube video, posted by "CANAL13DEMICHOACAN." https://www.youtube.com/watch?v=hE-Il-axmlA.

"La rebelión de Pascual Orozco." YouTube video, posted by "Bicentenario México." https://www.youtube.com/watch?v=wq3Sr5ICB_s.

Acknowledgments

In writing this book, I have been the grateful beneficiary of histories, memoirs, and archival finding aids too numerous to detail beyond a bibliographical entry, but I will highlight a few. I relied heavily on the work of Chihuahua historian Francisco R. Almada, especially his two volumes on the revolution in Chihuahua and his biography of Abraham González. Michael C. Meyer took on the task of chronicling the controversial lives of Pascual Orozco and Victoriano Huerta; his works provided the platform for this book. The notes to this book reveal only a fraction of my reliance on the impressive research of Friedrich Katz, Paco Ignacio Taibo II, Alan Knight, Roberto Ramos, Miguel A. Sánchez Lamego, Charles H. Harris, Louis R. Sadler, William H. Beezley, Roberto Blanco Moheno, Pedro Vázquez Siller, William D. Raat, Zacarías Márquez Terrazas, and Victor Orozco. Mark Wasserman's detailed examination of Chihuahua's oligarchy and elites is essential in any study of the influential Terrazas-Creel family. Jane-Dale Lloyd's writings on the people of the Northwest was invaluable to understanding their history and culture and on why they joined the revolution and became its early leaders.

In researching Orozco and the revolution, I made extensive use of archival resources and generous staff assistance at the Bancroft Library at the University of California at Berkeley, as well as at various Mexican collections listed in the bibliography. Any book on the Mexican Revolution is enhanced by the memorable images documenting its personalities and events; thus, required stops are the El Paso Public Library and Special Collections at the University of Texas at El Paso.

I was fortunate to have a few friends read, critique, or edit the manuscript, and I appreciate their assistance and encouragement. They include Professors Oscar J. Martínez and Mark Cioc-Ortega, editor Melissa Finefrock, and friends Jane Earle and Steve Bender. Another reader was Joe Old, now deceased, who helped so much with his deep, detailed reading of the manuscript and his suggestions. My thanks also to Kent Calder and the staff of the Oklahoma University Press for undertaking this project and to the anonymous peer reviewers the Press selected, who made valuable, constructive suggestions that improved the manuscript.

Finally, a note of appreciation to several friends, who over the years had suggested that I write about the revolution. Most important among those is my wife, Mary Hull, who has been a constant and encouraging partner.

Index